100 READY-TO-RUN PROGRAMS & SUBROUTINES FOR THE IBM PC®

BY JEFF BRETZ & JOHN CLARK CRAIG

 TAB BOOKS Inc.

BLUE RIDGE SUMMIT, PA. 17214

FIRST EDITION

FIRST PRINTING

Library of Congress Cataloging in Publication Data

Bretz, Jeff.
100 ready-to-run programs and subroutines for the IBM PC.

Includes index.
1. IBM Personal Computer—Programming, I. Craig,
John Clark. II. Title. III. Title: One hundred
ready-to-run programs and subroutines for the IBM PC.
QA76.8.I2594B73   1983   001.64′2   82-19335
ISBN 0-8306-0540-1
ISBN 0-8306-1540-7 (pbk.)

Cover illustration by Keith Snow.

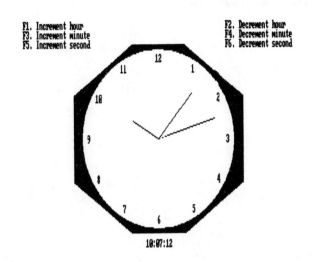

F1. Increment hour   F2. Decrement hour
F3. Increment minute   F4. Decrement minute
F5. Increment second   F6. Decrement second

10:07:12

Contents

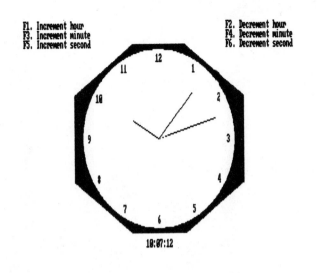

F1. Increment hour
F3. Increment minute
F5. Increment second

F2. Decrement hour
F4. Decrement minute
F6. Decrement second

10:07:12

Introduction

Most of the programs in this book are ready to load and run, but our main goal in writing this book was to provide a source of creative programming techniques. Every program demonstrates a technique, a trick, or a concept unique from the others in this book. For example, you'll find a wide variety of data input techniques in these programs. The INKEY$, input, line input, and other functions were used in several different ways to demonstrate the wide range of possible programming methods.

The programs were written in an open, easily read style, so that you can study the techniques presented. If your IBM Personal Computer has limited memory, you might consider deleting the remark lines, and restructuring the program lines by putting multiple statements on the same line. You'll find these programs easier to read and understand than many programs written in BASIC, partly because we were careful to open up the listings as described, and partly because of the excellent BASIC that IBM chose to use in their Personal Computer. This version of Microsoft BASIC has several outstanding features, but the feature most important in producing highly readable program listings is the ability to use long variable names. For example, a variable named "DATA.POINTER" is much more self documenting than "P2". Using longer variable names involves a little extra typing, but it's a habit worth developing. Your programs will be neater, easier to read, and by far easier to understand.

The programs in this book were developed using the color graphics board. Several of the programs use Screen 0 output exclusively. These programs will work with the IBM "green screen" monitor, probably with little or no modification. Many of the programs use the powerful graphics abilities of the IBM Personal Computer. These programs won't work with the IBM Monitor.

We had a lot of fun developing these programs. The IBM Personal Computer is truly an outstanding product and is a joy to work with. We hope that these programs will help you enjoy your computer as much as we have enjoyed ours.

Chapter 1

F1. Increment hour
F3. Increment minute
F5. Increment second

F2. Decrement hour
F4. Decrement minute
F6. Decrement second

10:07:12

Calendars, Clocks, and Time

The programs in this chapter use the graphic abilities of the IBM Personal Computer and its internal clock to create three useful programs dealing with the fourth dimension we call time.

CALENDAR

The Calendar program demonstrates the use of several calendar-related subroutines that you may find useful. At the heart of the program are subroutines for finding the astronomical Julian day number for a given date, and the date for a given astronomical Julian day number. Both of these subroutines also find the day of the week. These subroutines are described in more detail elsewhere in this book. The span of dates that may be used range from the year 1582 to the year 3999.

Three computations are available and are selected by pressing the appropriate special function key. Press F1 to generate a one-month calendar sheet. Press F2 to compute the day of the week and other facts about a given date. Press F3 to find the number of days between two dates. When you are finished, press F4 to quit.

You may type in the dates in just about any format you desire. A subroutine is provided that analyzes the entered date and figures out what month, day, and year it represents. Here are a few date entries that the subroutine can interpret correctly . . .

July 4, 1776	7/4/1776
4 JUL 1776	07041776

Note that an entry of "7/4/76" is interpreted as July 4, 1976. If the century is not indicated, it is assumed that you mean the twentieth century.

A useful feature of these subroutines is the ability to check a date to see if it is real. The date is first

1

```
         * * *   CALENDAR   * * *

   F1.    Sketch a one month calendar page

   F2.    Describe a given date

   F3.    Number of days between two dates

   F4.    Quit


        PRESS A SPECIAL FUNCTION KEY
```

Fig. 1-1. The options you may use in the *Calendar* program.

converted to its Julian number, and then back to a date. The date is valid if the result matches the original date.

Figures 1-1 through 1-4 show some of the displays that will appear on-screen when you run the calendar program.

```
                    JULY 1776

    SUN    MON    TUE    WED    THU    FRI    SAT

            1      2      3      4      5      6


     7      8      9     1Ø     11     12     13


    14     15     16     17     18     19     2Ø


    21     22     23     24     25     26     27


    28     29     3Ø     31
```

Fig. 1-2. The calendar display from the *Calendar* program.

```
12 / 25 / 1984 can also be written as DECEMBER 25, 1984.

The day of the week is TUESDAY.

It is day number 360 of 1984.

It is the 31040 day of the century.

And the astronomical julian day number is 2446060.
                        PRESS ANY KEY TO PROCEED
```

Fig. 1-3. Sample results of the *Calendar* program.

```
10 ' **********************
20 ' **     CALENDAR     **
30 ' **********************
40 '
50 CLEAR
60 SCREEN 0,0,0,0
70 CLS
80 KEY OFF
90 OPTION BASE 1
100 DIM MONTH.NAME$(12),WEEK.DAY$(7)
110 FOR I = 1 TO 12
120 READ MONTH.NAME$(I)
130 NEXT I
140 DATA JANUARY,FEBRUARY,MARCH,APRIL,MAY,JUNE,JULY
150 DATA AUGUST,SEPTEMBER,OCTOBER,NOVEMBER,DECEMBER
160 FOR I = 1 TO 7
170 READ WEEK.DAY$(I)
180 NEXT I
190 DATA SUNDAY,MONDAY,TUESDAY,WEDNESDAY,THURSDAY,FRIDAY,SATURDAY
200 LOCATE 1,29
210 PRINT "* * *   CALENDAR   * * *
220 LOCATE 7,1
230 PRINT TAB(20)"F1.   Sketch a one month calendar page
240 PRINT
250 PRINT TAB(20)"F2.   Describe a given date
```

```
Between 7 / 4 / 1776 and 7 / 4 / 1984 there are 75970 days.

            PRESS ANY KEY TO PROCEED
```

Fig. 1-4. Sample results of the option F3 in the *Calendar* program.

3

```
260 PRINT
270 PRINT TAB(20)"F3.    Number of days between two dates
280 PRINT
290 PRINT TAB(20)"F4.    Quit
300 LOCATE 25,25
310 PRINT "PRESS A SPECIAL FUNCTION KEY";
320 ON KEY(1) GOSUB 470
330 ON KEY(2) GOSUB 1220
340 ON KEY(3) GOSUB 1650
350 ON KEY(4) GOSUB 2010
360 KEY(1) ON
370 KEY(2) ON
380 KEY(3) ON
390 KEY(4) ON
400 '
410 WHILE QUIT = NOT.YET
420 KEY.BUFFER.CLEAR$ = INKEY$
430 WEND
440 CLS
450 END
460 '
470 ' F1 Subroutine, sketch a month
480 SCREEN 0,0,1,1
490 CLS
500 LOCATE 7,20
510 INPUT "What month ";Q$
520 IF Q$ = "" THEN 1190
530 GOSUB 2150
540 GOSUB 2220
550 MONTH = VAL(Q$)
560 IF MONTH THEN 600
570 FOR I = 1 TO 12
580 IF LEFT$(MONTH.NAME$(I),3) = LEFT$(Q$,3) THEN MONTH = I
590 NEXT I
600 IF MONTH THEN 650
610 LOCATE 8,12
620 PRINT "I don't recognize the month you entered ... try again
630 BEEP
640 GOTO 500
650 LOCATE 8,12
660 PRINT SPACE$(53);
670 LOCATE 9,20
680 INPUT "What year ";Q$
690 IF Q$ = "" THEN 1190
700 YEAR = VAL(Q$)
710 IF YEAR THEN 760
720 LOCATE 10.12
```

4

```
730 PRINT "I don't recognize the year you entered ... try again
740 BEEP
750 GOTO 670
760 IF YEAR < 100 THEN YEAR = YEAR + 1900
770 IF YEAR > 1581 AND YEAR < 4000 THEN 810
780 PRINT "The year must be in the range 1582 to 3999 ... try again
790 BEEP
800 GOTO 670
810 DAY = 1
820 GOSUB 2300
830 DAYOFWEEK = WEEKDAY
840 TITLE$ = MONTH.NAME$(MONTH)
850 JFIRST = JULIAN
860 MONTH = MONTH + 1
870 IF MONTH > 12 THEN MONTH = 1
880 IF MONTH = 1 THEN YEAR = YEAR + 1
890 GOSUB 2300
900 MONTHDAYS = JULIAN - JFIRST
910 CLS
920 LOCATE 1,37 - LEN(TITLE$) / 2
930 PRINT TITLE$ ; YEAR + (MONTH = 1)
940 DATE = 1
950 ROW = 6
960 COL = DAYOFWEEK * 7 + 10
970 LOCATE ROW,COL - (DATE < 10)
980 PRINT DATE
990 DATE = DATE + 1
1000 IF DATE > MONTHDAYS THEN 1040
1010 DAYOFWEEK = DAYOFWEEK MOD 7 + 1
1020 IF DAYOFWEEK = 1 THEN ROW = ROW + 3
1030 GOTO 960
1040 FOR ROWLINE = 4 TO ROW + 3 STEP 3
1050 LOCATE ROWLINE,15
1060 PRINT STRING$(50,"_");
1070 NEXT ROWLINE
1080 FOR ROW2 = 4 TO ROW + 1
1090 FOR COL2 = 15 TO 65 STEP 7
1100 LOCATE ROW2,COL2
1110 IF ROW2 = 4 THEN PRINT " "; ELSE PRINT "¦";
1120 NEXT COL2,ROW2
1130 FOR I = 1 TO 7
1140 LOCATE 3,7 * I + 10
1150 PRINT LEFT$(WEEK.DAY$(I),3);
1160 NEXT I
1170 BARMESS = 1
1180 GOSUB 2070
1190 SCREEN 0,0,0,0
```

```
1200 RETURN
1210 '
1220 ' F2 Subroutine, describe a date
1230 SCREEN 0,0,1,1
1240 CLS
1250 LOCATE 7,7
1260 LINE INPUT "Enter a date ... (any reasonable format) ";CAL$
1270 IF CAL$ = "" THEN 1620
1280 GOSUB 2600
1290 IF YEAR THEN 1340
1300 PRINT
1310 PRINT "Your date is unrecognizable, or isn't a valid date ...
     try again.
1320 BEEP
1330 GOTO 1250
1340 CLS
1350 LOCATE 5,6
1360 BS$ = CHR$(29)
1370 PRINT MONTH;"/";DAY;"/";YEAR;"can also be written as ";
1380 PRINT MONTH.NAME$(MONTH);DAY;BS$;",";YEAR;BS$;"."
1390 LOCATE 7,7
1400 PRINT "The day of the week is ";WEEK.DAY$(WEEKDAY);"."
1410 IF YEAR < 1600 THEN 1590
1420 JULIAN2 = JULIAN
1430 MONTH2 = MONTH
1440 DAY2 = DAY
1450 YEAR2 = YEAR
1460 MONTH = 12
1470 DAY = 31
1480 YEAR = YEAR - 1
1490 IF YEAR < 1582 THEN 1540
1500 GOSUB 2300
1510 YEARDAY = JULIAN2 - JULIAN
1520 LOCATE 9,7
1530 PRINT "It is day number"YEARDAY"of"YEAR2;BS$;"."
1540 YEAR = (INT(YEAR/100) - 1) * 100 + 99
1550 GOSUB 2300
1560 CENTDAY = JULIAN2 - JULIAN
1570 LOCATE 11,7
1580 PRINT "It is the"CENTDAY"day of the century.
1590 LOCATE 13,7
1600 PRINT "And the astronomical Julian day number is";JULIAN2;BS$;"."
1610 GOSUB 2070
1620 SCREEN 0,0,0,0
1630 RETURN
1640 '
1650 ' F3 Subroutine, days between dates
```

```
1660 SCREEN 0,0,1,1
1670 CLS
1680 LOCATE 7,7
1690 LINE INPUT "Enter one date ... (any reasonable format) ";CAL$
1700 IF CAL$ = "" THEN 1980
1710 GOSUB 2600
1720 IF YEAR THEN 1770
1730 LOCATE 9,1
1740 PRINT "Your date is unrecognizable, or isn't a valid date
     ... try again.
1750 BEEP
1760 GOTO 1680
1770 MONTH3 = MONTH
1780 DAY3 = DAY
1790 YEAR3 = YEAR
1800 JULIAN3 = JULIAN
1810 LOCATE 9,1
1820 PRINT SPACE$(79);
1830 LOCATE 9,7
1840 LINE INPUT "Enter second date ... ";CAL$
1850 IF CAL$ = "" THEN 1980
1860 GOSUB 2600
1870 IF YEAR THEN 1920
1880 LOCATE 11,1
1890 PRINT "Your date is unrecognizable, or isn't a valid date
     ... try again.
1900 BEEP
1910 GOTO 1830
1920 NUMDAYS = ABS(JULIAN3 - JULIAN)
1930 CLS
1940 LOCATE 7,7
1950 PRINT "Between";MONTH3;"/";DAY3;"/";YEAR3;"and";
1960 PRINT MONTH;"/";DAY;"/";YEAR;"there are";NUMDAYS;"days."
1970 GOSUB 2070
1980 SCREEN 0,0,0,0
1990 RETURN
2000 '
2010 ' F4 Subroutine, set quit flag
2020 QUIT = 1
2030 RETURN
2040 '
2050 '
2060 ' Subroutine, wait for user before proceeding
2070 LOCATE 25,28
2080 IF BARMESS = 0 THEN PRINT "PRESS ANY KEY TO PROCEED";
2090 K$ = INKEY$
2100 IF K$ = "" THEN 2090
```

```
2110 BARMESS = Ø
2120 RETURN
2130 '
2140 ' Subroutine, de-space Q$
2150 SP = INSTR(Q$," ")
2160 IF SP = Ø THEN 2220
2170 Q$ = LEFT$(Q$,SP-1) + MID$(Q$,SP+1)
2180 GOTO 2150
2190 RETURN
2200 '
2210 ' Subroutine, just capitalize Q$
2220 FOR QP = 1 TO LEN(Q$)
2230 CHAR$ = MID$(Q$,QP,1)
2240 IF CHAR$ < "a" OR CHAR$ > "z" THEN 2260
2250 MID$(Q$,QP,1) = CHR$(ASC(CHAR$)-32)
2260 NEXT QP
2270 RETURN
2280 '
2290 ' Subroutine, MONTH,DAY,YEAR to JULIAN,WEEKDAY
2300 JULIAN = INT(365.2422# * YEAR + 30.44 * (MONTH-1) + DAY + 1)
2310 T1 = MONTH - 2 - 12 * (MONTH < 3)
2320 T2 = YEAR + (MONTH < 3)
2330 T3 = INT(T2 / 100)
2340 T2 = T2 - 100 * T3
2350 WEEKDAY = INT(2.61 * T1 - .2) + DAY + T2 + INT(T2 / 4)
2360 WEEKDAY = (WEEKDAY + INT(T3 / 4) - T3 - T3 + 77) MOD 7 + 1
2370 T4 = JULIAN - 7 * INT(JULIAN / 7)
2380 JULIAN = JULIAN - T4 + WEEKDAY + 7 * (T4 < WEEKDAY - 1) + 1721060#
2390 RETURN
2400 '
2410 ' Subroutine, JULIAN to MONTH,DAY,YEAR,WEEKDAY
2420 T5 = JULIAN
2430 YEAR = INT((JULIAN - 1721061!) / 365.25 + 1)
2440 MONTH = 1
2450 DAY = 1
2460 GOSUB 2300
2470 IF JULIAN <= T5 THEN 2500
2480 YEAR = YEAR - 1
2490 GOTO 2460
2500 MONTH = INT((T5 - JULIAN) / 29 + 1)
2510 GOSUB 2300
2520 IF JULIAN <= T5 THEN 2550
2530 MONTH = MONTH - 1
2540 GOTO 2510
2550 DAY = T5 - JULIAN + 1
2560 GOSUB 2300
2570 RETURN
```

```
2580 '
2590 ' Subroutine, convert CAL$ to MONTH,DAY,YEAR
2600 Q$ = CAL$
2610 GOSUB 2220
2620 CAL$ = Q$
2630 MONTH = 0
2640 DAY = 0
2650 YEAR = 0
2660 FOR I = 1 TO 12
2670 IF INSTR(CAL$,LEFT$(MONTH.NAME$(I),3)) THEN MONTH = I
2680 NEXT I
2690 FOR I = 1 TO LEN(CAL$)
2700 CHAR$ = MID$(CAL$,I,1)
2710 IF CHAR$ < "0" OR CHAR$ > "9" THEN MID$(CAL$,I,1) = ":"
2720 NEXT I
2730 IF INSTR(CAL$,":") THEN 2790
2740 IF LEN(CAL$) <> 6 AND LEN(CAL$) <> 8 THEN 3040
2750 MONTH = VAL(LEFT$(CAL$,2))
2760 DAY = VAL(MID$(CAL$,3,2))
2770 YEAR = VAL(MID$(CAL$,5))
2780 GOTO 2930
2790 VFLAG = 0
2800 FOR I = 1 TO LEN(CAL$)
2810 CALVAL = VAL(MID$(CAL$,I))
2820 IF CALVAL = 0 THEN VFLAG = 0
2830 IF CALVAL = 0 OR VFLAG = 1 THEN 2920
2840 IF MONTH THEN 2870
2850 MONTH = CALVAL
2860 GOTO 2910
2870 IF DAY THEN 2900
2880 DAY = CALVAL
2890 GOTO 2910
2900 YEAR = CALVAL
2910 VFLAG = 1
2920 NEXT I
2930 IF YEAR < 100 AND YEAR > 0 THEN YEAR = YEAR + 1900
2940 IF YEAR < 1582 OR YEAR > 3999 THEN YEAR = 0
2950 IF YEAR = 0 THEN 3040
2960 MONTH2 = MONTH
2970 DAY2 = DAY
2980 YEAR2 = YEAR
2990 GOSUB 2300
3000 GOSUB 2420
3010 IF MONTH2 <> MONTH THEN YEAR = 0
3020 IF DAY2 <> DAY THEN YEAR = 0
3030 IF YEAR2 <> YEAR THEN YEAR = 0
3040 RETURN
```

CLOCK

Here's a creative way to set the clock hidden inside your IBM Personal Computer! The most straightforward method of setting the time is by typing in a value for the "variable" TIME\$. For example, to set your clock at 7 minutes past 10, you would type in and execute this: **TIME\$ = "10:07:00"**. A much more impressive method is demonstrated by this program!

Using a few of the powerful graphics commands available on the personal computer, the program draws the face of a clock. Once each second the hands of the clock are adjusted, the appropriate hands being erased and redrawn. Notice that the hands are not drawn with the line statement, but rather with a special form of the circle statement. By using negative values for the angles at which each circle is to start and

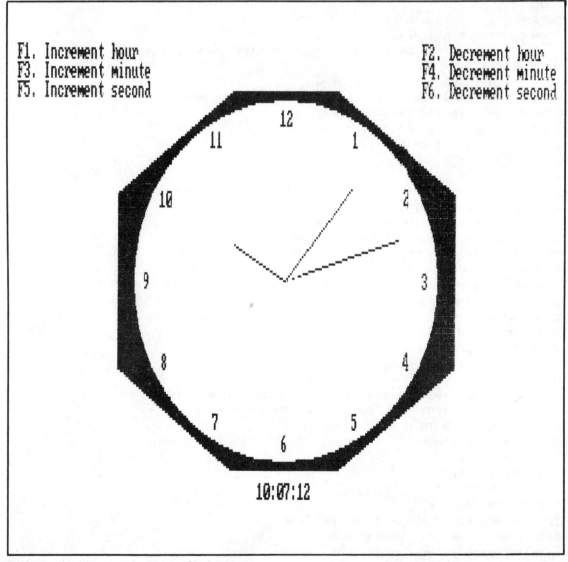

Fig. 1-5. The clockface created by the *Clock* program.

stop, the endpoints are connected to the center of the circle. And by choosing the start and stop points at the same point, the "circle" is drawn as a line radiating from the center. This technique avoids the tricky math involved in scaling and drawing the hands that would be necessary using the line statement.

Another useful technique was utilized to place the digits on the face of the clock. Each number is first printed in the upper left corner of the screen. The get and put commands are then used to pick up the digits and place them wherever desired. This trick can be used to label graphics or place words or numbers anywhere on the screen. Figure 1-5 shows the clock as it will be displayed on your video screen.

A couple of useful subroutines are found near the end of the *Clock* program. The first converts TIME$ into the variables H, M, and S. The second subroutine builds a string from the variables H, M, and S in the proper format for putting it into TIME$.

```
10 ' ********************
20 ' **      CLOCK      **
30 ' ********************
40 '
50 CLEAR
60 SCREEN 2
70 CLS
80 KEY OFF
90 DIM NUM(6)
100 XCENT = 319
110 YCENT = 99
120 PI = 3.141593
130 DEF FNANG(TIME) = PI / 2 - PI * TIME / 30 - 2 * PI * (TIME > 15)
140 LINE (120,20)-(519,178),1,BF        ' draw big white box
150 LINE (XCENT,0)-(0,YCENT),0          ' slice off four corners
160 LINE (XCENT,0)-(639,YCENT),0
170 LINE (XCENT,199)-(0,YCENT),0
180 LINE (XCENT,199)-(639,YCENT),0
190 PAINT (126,20),0                    ' paint out four corners
200 PAINT (512,175),0
210 PAINT (512,20),0
220 PAINT (126,175),0
230 RADIUS = 179
240 CIRCLE (XCENT,YCENT),RADIUS,0       ' draw dark circle inside
250 PAINT (XCENT,YCENT),0               ' darken entire circle
260 FOR D = 1 TO 12                     ' put numbers on clock face
270 GOSUB 800
280 XD = XCENT + 165 * COS(FNANG(D*5)) - 11 + 3 * (D > 9)
290 YD = YCENT - 68 * SIN(FNANG(D*5)) - 3
300 PUT (XD,YD),NUM
310 NEXT D
320 LOCATE 1,1
330 PRINT "F1. Increment hour";
340 LOCATE 2,1
350 PRINT "F3. Increment minute";
360 LOCATE 3,1
```

```
370 PRINT "F5. Increment second";
380 LOCATE 1,61
390 PRINT "F2. Decrement hour";
400 LOCATE 2,61
410 PRINT "F4. Decrement minute";
420 LOCATE 3,61
430 PRINT "F6. Decrement second";
440 ON KEY(1) GOSUB 860
450 ON KEY(2) GOSUB 920
460 ON KEY(3) GOSUB 980
470 ON KEY(4) GOSUB 1040
480 ON KEY(5) GOSUB 1100
490 ON KEY(6) GOSUB 1160
500 KEY(1) ON
510 KEY(2) ON
520 KEY(3) ON
530 KEY(4) ON
540 KEY(5) ON
550 KEY(6) ON
560 '
570 WHILE NOT.YET.TO.THE.END.OF.ALL.TIME....
580         WHILE T$ = TIME$
590         WEND
600     T$ = TIME$
610     SECOND2 = SECOND
620     MINUTE2 = MINUTE
630     HOUR2 = HOUR
640     SECOND = VAL(RIGHT$(T$,2))
650     MINUTE = VAL(MID$(T$,4))
660     HOUR = (VAL(LEFT$(T$,2)) MOD 12) * 5 + MINUTE / 12
670     LOCATE 24,37
680     PRINT T$;
690     CIRCLE (XCENT,YCENT),140,1,-FNANG(SECOND),-FNANG(SECOND)
700     CIRCLE (XCENT,YCENT),140,0,-FNANG(SECOND2),-FNANG(SECOND2)
710     IF MINUTE2 = MINUTE THEN 730
720     CIRCLE (XCENT,YCENT),120,0,-FNANG(MINUTE2),-FNANG(MINUTE2)
730     CIRCLE (XCENT,YCENT),120,1,-FNANG(MINUTE),-FNANG(MINUTE)
740     IF HOUR2 = HOUR THEN 760
750     CIRCLE (XCENT,YCENT),70,0,-FNANG(HOUR2),-FNANG(HOUR2)
760     CIRCLE (XCENT,YCENT),70,1,-FNANG(HOUR),-FNANG(HOUR)
770 WEND
780 '
790 ' Subroutine, get a number for putting anywhere
800 LOCATE 1,1
810 PRINT D;
820 GET (0,0)-(22,6),NUM
830 LINE (0,0)-(22,6),0,BF
```

```
840 RETURN
850 '
860 ' Key 1 subroutine
870 GOSUB 1230
880 H = (H + 1) MOD 24
890 GOSUB 1290
900 RETURN
910 '
920 ' Key 2 subroutine
930 GOSUB 1230
940 H = (H + 23) MOD 24
950 GOSUB 1290
960 RETURN
970 '
980 ' Key 3 subroutine
990 GOSUB 1230
1000 M = (M + 1) MOD 60
1010 GOSUB 1290
1020 RETURN
1030 '
1040 ' Key 4 subroutine
1050 TEMP$ = MID$(STR$((VAL(MID$(TIME$,4))+59)MOD 60),2)
1060 M = (M + 59) MOD 60
1070 GOSUB 1290
1080 RETURN
1090 '
1100 ' Key 5 subroutine
1110 GOSUB 1230
1120 S = (S + 1) MOD 60
1130 GOSUB 1290
1140 RETURN
1150 '
1160 ' Key 6 subroutine
1170 GOSUB 1230
1180 S = (S + 59) MOD 60
1190 GOSUB 1290
1200 RETURN
1210 '
1220 ' Subroutine, convert TIME$ into H,M,S
1230 H = VAL(LEFT$(TIME$,2))
1240 M = VAL(MID$(TIME$,4))
1250 S = VAL(RIGHT$(TIME$,2))
1260 RETURN
1270 '
1280 ' Subroutine, format H,M,S for input to TIME$
1290 CLOCK$ = MID$(STR$(S),2)
1300 IF S < 10 THEN CLOCK$ = "Ø" + CLOCK$
```

```
1310 CLOCK$ = MID$(STR$(M),2) + ":" + CLOCK$
1320 IF M < 10 THEN CLOCK$ = "0" + CLOCK$
1330 CLOCK$ = MID$(STR$(H),2) + ":" + CLOCK$
1340 IF H < 10 THEN CLOCK$ = "0" + CLOCK$
1350 TIME$ = CLOCK$
1360 RETURN
```

SIDEREAL CLOCK

Sidereal time is tied to the spinning of the earth in relation to the stars. At midnight sidereal time, the stars will be in the same location in the sky for any day of the year. Time, as we normally measure it, is relative to the sun. In one year the stars shift their midnight position in one complete circle. For this reason, your watch will disagree with a sidereal clock by 24 hours at the end of a year.

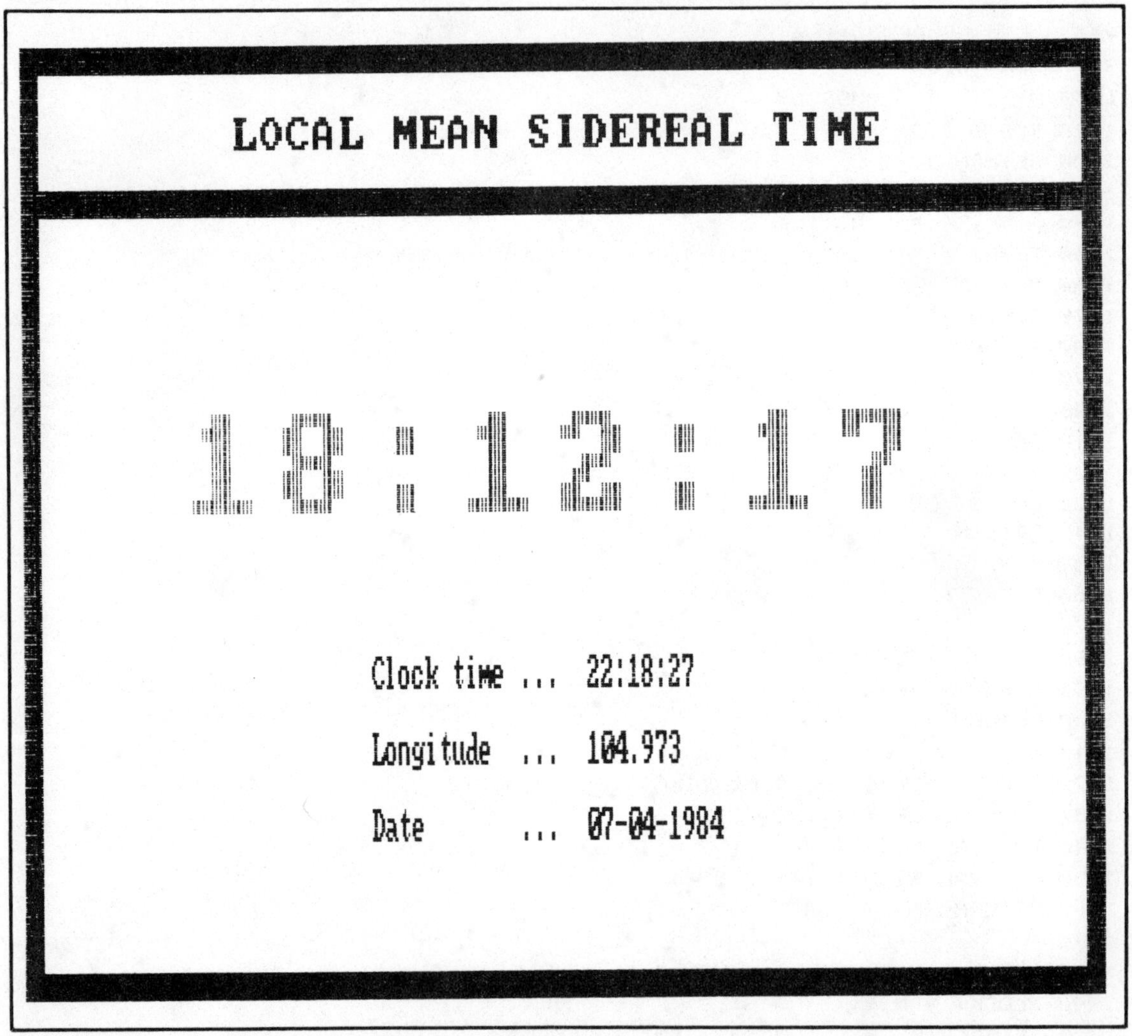

LOCAL MEAN SIDEREAL TIME

18:12:17

Clock time ... 22:18:27

Longitude ... 104.973

Date ... 07-04-1984

Fig. 1-6. The display produced by the *Sidereal Clock* program.

Sidereal time is useful for predicting the location of the stars and planets in the sky. This program generates a real-time graphic sidereal clock. You'll need to know your local longitude as sidereal time is a function of your exact east-west position on the earth. The TIME$ function provides the other data needed for computing local sidereal time.

Several of the graphics techniques used in this program are worth discussing. When the program first starts, you'll see small and large numerical digits being displayed in the upper left corner of the screen. Each digit is first printed in medium resolution (40 character wide mode) in the corner. The dot pattern is read from the screen, and an enlarged copy of the digit is drawn. The large digit is peeled off the screen and stored away in memory with the get statement. Later, these large characters are used in high resolution to display the sidereal time. In medium resolution the digits have color; when displayed in high resolution with the put statement, they appear gray.

Notice that there are three sizes of characters displayed even though the display is in high resolution. The title was first printed in the screen 1 mode; then retrieved from the screen with a get command. Later the put command placed it back on the screen 2 mode. This technique allows you to display larger white or gray characters in the screen 2 mode. Figure 1-6 shows the resulting display.

```
10 ' **********************
20 ' **      SIDEREAL     **
30 ' **********************
40 '
50 CLEAR
60 SCREEN 0,0,0
70 WIDTH 80
80 CLS
90 KEY OFF
100 PRINT "Current date is ";DATE$
110 INPUT "Enter a different date if desired ... ";Q$
120 IF Q$ <> "" THEN DATE$ = Q$
130 CLS
140 PRINT "Current time is approximately ";TIME$
150 INPUT "Enter a different time if desired ... ";Q$
160 IF Q$ <> "" THEN TIME$ = Q$
170 CLS
180 INPUT "What is your west longitude ";LONGITUDE
190 CLS
200 PRINT "Time zone offsets ...   (Standard) (Daylight savings)"
210 PRINT
220 PRINT "      Eastern          5          6"
230 PRINT "      Central          6          7"
240 PRINT "      Mountain         7          8"
250 PRINT "      Pacific          8          9"
260 PRINT
270 INPUT "What is your time zone difference from Greenwich ";TIMEZONE
280 SCREEN 1
290 SIZE = 32
300 DIM D0(SIZE),D1(SIZE),D2(SIZE),D3(SIZE),D4(SIZE)
310 DIM D5(SIZE),D6(SIZE),D7(SIZE),D8(SIZE),D9(SIZE),DC(SIZE)
```

```
320 DIM HEADING(555)
330 LOCATE 1,1
340 PRINT "LOCAL MEAN SIDEREAL TIME"
350 GET (0,0)-(192,6),HEADING
360 CLS
370 FOR I = 0 TO 10
380 LINE (20,20)-(41,47),0,BF
390 LOCATE 1,1
400 IF I < 10 THEN PRINT CHR$(48 + I); ELSE PRINT ":";
410 FOR ROW = 0 TO 8
420 FOR COL = 0 TO 6
430 IF POINT(COL,ROW) THEN LINE (COL*3+20,ROW*3+20)-(COL*3+22,ROW*3+22),1,BF
440 NEXT COL,ROW
450 IF I = 0 THEN GET (20,20)-(40,40),D0
460 IF I = 1 THEN GET (20,20)-(40,40),D1
470 IF I = 2 THEN GET (20,20)-(40,40),D2
480 IF I = 3 THEN GET (20,20)-(40,40),D3
490 IF I = 4 THEN GET (20,20)-(40,40),D4
500 IF I = 5 THEN GET (20,20)-(40,40),D5
510 IF I = 6 THEN GET (20,20)-(40,40),D6
520 IF I = 7 THEN GET (20,20)-(40,40),D7
530 IF I = 8 THEN GET (20,20)-(40,40),D8
540 IF I = 9 THEN GET (20,20)-(40,40),D9
550 IF I = 10 THEN GET (20,20)-(40,40),DC
560 NEXT I
570 CLS
580 SCREEN 2
590 'LINE (0,0)-(639,199),,B
600 LINE (10,5)-(629,194),,B
610 LINE (2,30)-(637,35),,B
620 LINE (0,32)-(639,32),0
630 PAINT (1,1)
640 PUT (127,15),HEADING
650 '
660 WHILE NOT THE.END.OF.THE.WORLD
670 WHILE T$ = TIME$
680 WEND
690 T$ = TIME$
700 GOSUB 1030
710 GOSUB 1090
720 GOSUB 1170
730 X = 100
740 Y = 77
750 GOSUB 850
760 LOCATE 17,27
770 PRINT "Clock time ...   ";T$;
780 LOCATE 19,27
```

```
790 PRINT USING "Longitude ...   ###.###";LONGITUDE;
800 LOCATE 21,27
810 PRINT "Date        ... ";DATE$;
820 WEND
830 '
840 ' Subroutine, SIDEREAL$ to screen at X,Y in large characters
850 FOR CHAR = 1 TO LEN(SIDEREAL$)
860 CHAR$ = MID$(SIDEREAL$,CHAR,1)
870 IF CHAR$ = "0" THEN PUT (X,Y),D0,PSET
880 IF CHAR$ = "1" THEN PUT (X,Y),D1,PSET
890 IF CHAR$ = "2" THEN PUT (X,Y),D2,PSET
900 IF CHAR$ = "3" THEN PUT (X,Y),D3,PSET
910 IF CHAR$ = "4" THEN PUT (X,Y),D4,PSET
920 IF CHAR$ = "5" THEN PUT (X,Y),D5,PSET
930 IF CHAR$ = "6" THEN PUT (X,Y),D6,PSET
940 IF CHAR$ = "7" THEN PUT (X,Y),D7,PSET
950 IF CHAR$ = "8" THEN PUT (X,Y),D8,PSET
960 IF CHAR$ = "9" THEN PUT (X,Y),D9,PSET
970 IF CHAR$ = ":" THEN PUT (X,Y),DC,PSET
980 X = X + 55
990 NEXT CHAR
1000 RETURN
1010 '
1020 ' Subroutine, TIME$ into HOUR,MINUTE,SECOND
1030 HOUR = VAL(LEFT$(TIME$,2))
1040 MINUTE = VAL(MID$(TIME$,4))
1050 SECOND = VAL(RIGHT$(TIME$,2))
1060 RETURN
1070 '
1080 ' Subroutine, DATE$ into MONTH,DAY,YEAR
1090 MONTH = VAL(LEFT$(DATE$,2))
1100 DAY = VAL(MID$(DATE$,4))
1110 YEAR = VAL(RIGHT$(DATE$,2))
1120 RETURN
1130 '
1140 ' Subroutine  HOUR,MINUTE,SECOND,
1150 '             MONTH,DAY,YEAR,
1160 '             TIMEZONE,LONGITUDE  converted to SIDEREAL$
1170 T1 = INT(DAY - 30 + 275 * MONTH / 9)
1180 IF MONTH < 3 THEN 1210
1190 T1 = T1 - 1
1200 IF YEAR MOD 4 THEN T1 = T1 - 1
1210 T2 = TIMEZONE + HOUR + MINUTE / 60 + SECOND / 3600
1220 T3 = (INT(T1 + 365.25 * YEAR - .25) - .5) / 36525!
1230 T4 = 23925.836# + 8640184.542# * T3 + 9.289999E-02 * T3 * T3
1240 SIDER = 360 * T4 / 86400! + 15.04106864# * T2 - LONGITUDE
1250 SIDER = (SIDER - 360 * INT(SIDER / 360)) * 24 / 360
```

```
1260 SHOUR = INT(SIDER)
1270 SMINUTE = INT(60 * (SIDER - SHOUR))
1280 SSECOND = INT(3600 * SIDER - 3600 * SHOUR - 60 * SMINUTE)
1290 SIDEREAL$ = MID$(STR$(SHOUR),1-(SHOUR>9)) + ":"
1300 SIDEREAL$ = SIDEREAL$ + MID$(STR$(SMINUTE),1-(SMINUTE>9)) + ":"
1310 SIDEREAL$ = SIDEREAL$ + MID$(STR$(SSECOND),1-(SSECOND>9))
1320 SP = INSTR(SIDEREAL$," ")
1330 IF SP = 0 THEN 1360
1340 MID$(SIDEREAL$,SP,1) = "0"
1350 GOTO 1320
1360 RETURN
```

Chapter 2

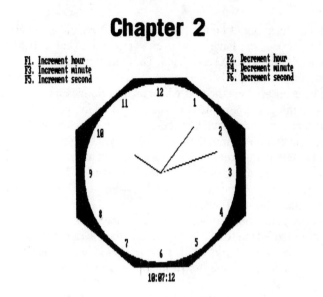

Educational and Informative

There is a wide variety of programs in this chapter: a code program that will assure you that your secret documents will remain undecipherable to the uninitiated, a spelling program that will drill you until you know the words, a program that will enable you to aim your satellite television antenna correctly and show you some useful graphic techniques at the same time, and three programs that enable you to solve common electronic problems.

CODE MASTER

This utility program provides you with the capabilities to create, encode, and decode messages. Included in the package is a text editor that could easily be expanded to perform general writing tasks. Two versions are listed: the first version is for a cassette based system and the other is for those systems with a minimum of 64K. This latter version can be used with cassette BASIC or either of the two disk BASICS.

The encryption system used in this program is very simple in concept, but very secure once used. Cryptography depends upon three items.

1. The plain text   This is the message.
2. The key   This is the pattern that is mixed with the plain text to encode it.
3. The cipher text   The cipher text is the encoded version of the message. If properly encoded, this version can be given to anyone who does not have the key, and they will not be able to understand it.

Item number two is the critical point in the process. The key should be easily generated and

19

nonrepeatable, so that a pattern cannot be found in the code. It should also have a very large number of variations so the same code does not have to be used every time. On the IBM Personal Computer, the command that fills this need is the RND(X) command. This command creates a string of random values and can be initialized to any preset point.

Once the text has been entered via the text editor as described below, you can direct the program to encode the message. Two things happen initially. You are asked for an input in the range of −32000 thru 32000. This value initializes the random number generator to a specific point. Then you are asked for key #2 which advances you a specified way into this particular key. Using these two values, you have a means of selecting one out of 64 million different codes. Once the key has been selected, the encoding starts.

The RND function generates a series of quasi-random values. This means that although they look random, the values are generated by means of a strict procedure. This has the advantage that it can be reproduced by someone else who has the key.

After the program has generated a random value, it examines the first character in the plain-text buffer where the text editor stored the text. Then the plain-text character's value and the random value are added using MOD 256 so no value is greater than 255. This value is placed in the encoded buffer in a position that corresponds to that in the plain-text buffer. The program later allows you to save the encoded message onto disk or cassette.

For decoding the message, the program works in just the opposite fashion. The program looks at the encoded message loaded into the encrypted-text buffer. In a one to one correspondence, the program subtracts the value of the key from the value of the cypher giving the original text. This text is then placed back in the plain-text buffer in its original place. It is then a simple matter to peek at the plain-text buffer and print the characters found there on the screen.

Security is assured because if either of the keys entered are not exactly correct, the random number generator will produce a different series of values and the decryption will fail. Try it yourself. If keys of 100 and 100 are used to encode the message and the message is decoded using 100 and 101, the only thing that will be printed is garbage.

Outside of the save and load portions of the program, which simply save and reload a binary memory file using the BLOAD and BSAVE commands, the only portion of the program that remains to be explained is the text editor. The text editor is unique in the fact that it works on the screen and also on a buffer in memory. Using the character keys, the four cursor controls, the backspace key, and the enter key, type your message as you want it on the screen. To change a line, type over it. As you enter your message, the program keeps track of where on the screen the cursor is and enters all ASCII characters typed on the screen into a buffer in memory. Since you are simply manipulating data in a buffer, any ASCII character may be entered. This will allow you to use the special character set for formulas or whatever you need. When you are finished typing, simply enter ALT-E and you will be returned to the menu.

```
1 CLS : KEY OFF : SCREEN Ø : WIDTH 8Ø
2 CLEAR ,15ØØØ
3 DEF SEG = Ø
4 GOTO 1Ø9Ø
100 PRINT "****************************************************************"
110 PRINT "**                       CODE-MASTER                        **"
120 PRINT "**                                                          **"
130 PRINT "**                                                          **"
140 PRINT "**   VERSION 1.Ø (32K version)            AUGUST 29, 1982   **"
150 PRINT "**                                                          **"
160 PRINT "**   ALLOWS YOU TO CREATE, ENCODE, AND DECODE MESSAGES      **"
```

```
170 PRINT "**    USING THE CASSETTE ON A 32K SYSTEM                    **"
180 PRINT "**                                                          **"
190 PRINT "************************************************************"
200 LOCATE 12,1
210 PRINT "ENTER YOUR SELECTION -
220 PRINT
230 PRINT "1. = CLEAR TEXT BUFFER
240 PRINT "2. = ENTER OR UPDATE TEXT FOR ENCRYPTION
250 PRINT "3. = ENCODE MESSAGE
260 PRINT "4. = DECODE MESSAGE AND PRINT IT
270 PRINT "5. = SAVE ENCODED MESSAGE TO CASSETTE
280 PRINT "6. = LOAD ENCODED MESSAGE FROM CASSETTE
290 LOCATE 12,30 : INPUT A
300 IF (A>6) OR (A<1) THEN CLS : GOTO 100
310 ON A GOTO 1000,2000,3000,4000,5000,6000
1000 CLS
1010 PRINT "************************************************************"
1020 PRINT "**                  CLEAR TEXT BUFFER                      **"
1030 PRINT "**    THE BUFFER FOR THE PLAIN TEXT MESSAGE IS (23 X 80) -1 **"
1040 PRINT "**    CHARACTERS IN LENGTH AND STARTS AT 20000 DECIMAL.    **"
1050 PRINT "**    IT WILL TAKE ABOUT 10 SEC TO CLEAR BUFFER TO ALL     **"
1060 PRINT "**    SPACES.                                              **"
1070 PRINT "************************************************************"
1080 LOCATE 10,1
1090 PRINT "PLEASE STAND BY FOR APPROX 10 SEC -
1100 FOR X = 20000 TO 21839
1110 POKE X,32
1120 NEXT
1130 LOCATE 25,1 : PRINT "PRESS ANY KEY TO CONTINUE - ";:INPUT A$
1140 CLS : GOTO 100
2000 CLS
2010 PRINT "************************************************************"
2020 PRINT "**              ENTER OR UPDATE TEXT FOR ENCRYPTION        **"
2030 PRINT "**                                                        **"
2040 PRINT "**    THE PRESENT MESSAGE BUFFER WILL BE DISPLAYED,  AND   **"
2050 PRINT "**    THE CURSOR WILL BE RETURNED TO HOME.                **"
2060 PRINT "**    ENTER YOUR TEXT USING -                             **"
2070 PRINT "**    THE 4 CURSOR CONTROL KEYS - UP, DOWN, LEFT, RIGHT   **"
2080 PRINT "**    THE ENTIRE ASCII CHARACTER SET -                    **"
2090 PRINT "**    THE BACKSPACE KEY AND THE ENTER KEY.                **"
2100 PRINT "**                                                        **"
2110 PRINT "**    FINALLY, WHEN YOU ARE FINISHED ENTERING THE TEXT -  **"
2120 PRINT "**    PRESS  ALT E  (FOR EXIT) TO RETURN TO THE MENU.     **"
2130 PRINT "**                                                        **"
2140 PRINT "************************************************************"
2150 '
2160 LOCATE 25,1 : PRINT "PRESS ENTER TO CONTINUE - " ;
```

```
2170 A$ = INKEY$ : IF A$ = "" THEN 2170 ELSE CLS : LOCATE ,,1
2180 FOR X = 20000 TO 21839
2190 PRINT CHR$(PEEK(X));
2200 NEXT
2210 LOCATE 25,1 : PRINT "USE    ALT E    TO EXIT. " : LOCATE 1,1,1
2220 A$ = INKEY$ : IF A$ = "" THEN 2220
2230 IF CSRLIN > 23 THEN LOCATE 23,POS(0)
2240 IF LEN(A$) = 2 THEN 2290
2250 IF (ASC(A$) = 8) AND (POS(0) > 1) THEN LOCATE CSRLIN,POS(0)-1 :
     PRINT " ";
     :LOCATE CSRLIN,POS(0)-1 : POKE 20000+(CSRLIN-1)*80+POS(0)-1,32:
     GOTO 2220
2260 IF (ASC(A$) = 13) AND (CSRLIN <23) THEN LOCATE CSRLIN+1,1 : GOTO 2220
2270 IF (ASC(A$) = 13) AND (CSRLIN = 23) THEN LOCATE 23,1 :GOTO 2220
2280 POKE 20000 + (CSRLIN-1)*80 + POS(0)-1,ASC(A$) : PRINT A$; : GOTO 2220
2290 B$ = MID$(A$,2,1) : B = ASC(B$)
2300 IF B = 71 THEN LOCATE 1,1
2310 IF (B = 72) AND (CSRLIN > 1) THEN LOCATE CSRLIN-1,POS(0)
2320 IF (B = 75) AND (POS(0) > 1) THEN LOCATE CSRLIN,POS(0)-1
2330 IF (B = 77) AND (POS(0) < 80) THEN LOCATE CSRLIN,POS(0)+1
2340 IF (B = 80) AND (CSRLIN < 23) THEN LOCATE CSRLIN+1,POS(0)
2350 IF (B = 18) THEN CLS : GOTO 100
2360 GOTO 2220
3000 CLS
3010 PRINT "***************************************************************"
3020 PRINT "**              ENCODE THE PLAIN TEXT MESSAGE                **"
3030 PRINT "**                                                          **"
3040 PRINT "**    ENTER KEY #1 TO INITIALIZE THE RANDOM GENERATOR.      **"
3050 PRINT "**    ENTER KEY #2 TO STEP YOU PART WAY INTO THE CODE.      **"
3060 PRINT "**                                                          **"
3070 PRINT "**    THE PROGRAM WILL TAKE THE PLAIN TEXT IN MEMORY AT     **"
3080 PRINT "**    20000 TO 21839 AND ENCRYPT IT, PLACING IT IN MEMORY   **"
3090 PRINT "**    AT 22000 TO 23839.                                    **"
3100 PRINT "**                                                          **"
3110 PRINT "**    FINALLY, THE PROGRAM WILL DISPLAY THE ENCRYPTED       **"
3120 PRINT "**    TEXT.                                                 **"
3130 PRINT "**                                                          **"
3140 PRINT "***************************************************************"
3150 '
3160 LOCATE 17,1 : CLEAR ,15000 : DEF SEG = 0
3170 PRINT "ENTER KEY #1 (FROM -32000 TO 32000) ";:INPUT A
3180 IF (A<-32000) OR (A>32000) THEN CLS : GOTO 3000
3190 RANDOMIZE A
3200 LOCATE 19,1
3210 PRINT "ENTER KEY #2 (FROM 1 TO 1000) ";: INPUT A
3220 IF (A<1) OR (A>1000) THEN LOCATE 19,30 : PRINT "          ":GOTO 3200
3230 FOR X = 1 TO A
```

```
3240 B = RND
3250 NEXT
3260 '
3270 LOCATE 25,1: PRINT "READY TO ENCODE - PRESS ENTER TO BEGIN ";:INPUT A$
3280 CLS : PRINT "PLEASE STAND BY - ENCODING REQUIRES APPROX 30 SEC - "
3290 FOR X = 20000 TO 21839
3300 CYPHER = INT(RND * 255)
3310 CODEDTEXT = CYPHER + PEEK(X)
3320 IF CODEDTEXT > 255 THEN CODEDTEXT = CODEDTEXT - 256
3330 POKE X+2000,CODEDTEXT
3340 NEXT
3350 LOCATE 25,1 : PRINT "CODING COMPLETE - PRESS ENTER TO VIEW ";: INPUT A$
3360 CLS
3370 FOR X = 22000 TO 23839
3380 PRINT CHR$(PEEK(X));
3390 NEXT
3400 LOCATE 25,1 : PRINT "PRESS ENTER TO RETURN TO MENU - ";: INPUT A$
3410 CLS : GOTO 100
4000 CLS
4010 PRINT "****************************************************************"
4020 PRINT "**              DECODE THE ENCRYPTED MESSAGE                  **"
4030 PRINT "**                                                           **"
4040 PRINT "**    ENTER KEY #1 TO INITIALIZE THE RANDOM GENERATOR.       **"
4050 PRINT "**    ENTER KEY #2 TO STEP YOU PART WAY INTO THE CODE.       **"
4060 PRINT "**                                                           **"
4070 PRINT "**    THE PROGRAM WILL TAKE THE ENCRYPTED TEXT IN MEMORY AT  **"
4080 PRINT "**    22000 TO 23839 AND DECODE IT, PLACING IT IN MEMORY     **"
4090 PRINT "**    AT 20000 TO 21839.                                     **"
4100 PRINT "**                                                           **"
4110 PRINT "**    FINALLY, THE PROGRAM WILL DISPLAY THE DECODED          **"
4120 PRINT "**    TEXT.                                                  **"
4130 PRINT "**                                                           **"
4140 PRINT "****************************************************************"
4150 '
4160 LOCATE 17,1 : CLEAR ,15000 : DEF SEG = 0
4170 PRINT "ENTER KEY #1 (FROM -32000 TO 32000) ";:INPUT A
4180 IF (A<-32000) OR (A>32000) THEN CLS : GOTO 4000
4190 RANDOMIZE A
4200 LOCATE 19,1
4210 PRINT "ENTER KEY #2 (FROM 1 TO 1000) ";: INPUT A
4220 IF (A<1) OR (A>1000) THEN LOCATE 19,30 : PRINT "        ":GOTO 3200
4230 FOR X = 1 TO A
4240 B = RND
4250 NEXT
4260 '
4270 LOCATE 25,1 : PRINT "READY TO DECODE - PRESS ENTER TO BEGIN ";:INPUT A$
4280 CLS : PRINT "PLEASE STAND BY - DECODING REQUIRES APPROX 30 SEC - "
```

```
4290 FOR X = 20000 TO 21839
4300 CYPHER = INT(RND * 255)
4310 CODEDTEXT = PEEK(X+2000) - CYPHER
4320 IF CODEDTEXT < 0 THEN CODEDTEXT = CODEDTEXT + 256
4330 POKE X,CODEDTEXT
4340 NEXT
4350 LOCATE 25,1 : PRINT "DECODING COMPLETE - PRESS ENTER TO VIEW ";:
     INPUT A$
4360 CLS
4370 FOR X = 20000 TO 21839
4380 PRINT CHR$(PEEK(X));
4390 NEXT
4400 LOCATE 25,1 : PRINT "PRESS ENTER TO RETURN TO MENU - ";: INPUT A$
4410 CLS : GOTO 100

5000 CLS
5010 PRINT "********************************************************"
5020 PRINT "**           SAVE ENCODED MESSAGE TO CASSETTE          **"
5030 PRINT "********************************************************"
5040 '
5050 LOCATE 5,1
5060 INPUT "ENTER THE FILENAME TO SAVE TO - (8 CHAR MAX) ";A$
5070 LOCATE 10,1
5080 PRINT "WARNING - MAKE SURE THE CASSETTE IS IN RECORD
5090 PRINT "THEN, PRESS ENTER -
5100 INPUT B$
5110 LOCATE 15,1
5120 PRINT "SAVING - ";A$
5130 BSAVE A$,22000,1840
5140 LOCATE 25,1 : PRINT "SAVE COMPLETE - PRESS ENTER TO RETURN TO MENU ";
5150 A$ = INKEY$ : IF A$ = "" THEN 5150 ELSE CLS : GOTO 100

6000 CLS
6010 PRINT "********************************************************"
6020 PRINT "**           LOAD ENCODED MESSAGE FROM CASSETTE        **"
6030 PRINT "********************************************************"
6040 '
6050 LOCATE 5,1
6060 INPUT "ENTER THE FILENAME TO READ FROM - (8 CHAR MAX) ";A$
6070 LOCATE 10,1
6080 PRINT "WARNING - MAKE SURE THE CASSETTE IS IN PLAY
6090 PRINT "THEN, PRESS ENTER -
6100 INPUT B$
6110 LOCATE 15,1
6120 PRINT "LOADING - ";A$
6130 BLOAD A$,22000
6140 LOCATE 25,1 : PRINT "LOAD COMPLETE - PRESS ENTER TO RETURN TO MENU ";
6150 A$ = INKEY$ : IF A$ = "" THEN 5150 ELSE CLS : GOTO 100
```

```
1 CLS : KEY OFF : SCREEN Ø : WIDTH 8Ø
2 CLEAR ,15ØØØ
3 DEF SEG = Ø : BUFFER = &HEA6Ø
4 GOTO 1Ø9Ø
100 PRINT "*****************************************************************"
110 PRINT "**                       CODE-MASTER                          **"
120 PRINT "**                                                            **"
130 PRINT "**                                                            **"
140 PRINT "**   VERSION 1.1 (64K)                    AUGUST 29, 1982     **"
150 PRINT "**                                                            **"
160 PRINT "**   ALLOWS YOU TO CREATE, ENCODE, AND DECODE MESSAGES        **"
170 PRINT "**   USING THE DISKETTE OR CASSETTE                           **"
180 PRINT "**   (DEFAULTS TO CURRENT DEVICE)                             **"
190 PRINT "*****************************************************************"
200 LOCATE 12,1
210 PRINT "ENTER YOUR SELECTION -
220 PRINT
230 PRINT "1. = CLEAR TEXT BUFFER
240 PRINT "2. = ENTER OR UPDATE TEXT FOR ENCRYPTION
250 PRINT "3. = ENCODE MESSAGE
260 PRINT "4. = DECODE MESSAGE AND PRINT IT
270 PRINT "5. = SAVE ENCODED MESSAGE TO DISKETTE OR CASSETTE
280 PRINT "6. = LOAD ENCODED MESSAGE FROM DISKETTE OR CASSETTE
290 LOCATE 12,30 : INPUT A
300 IF (A>6) OR (A<1) THEN CLS : GOTO 100
310 ON A GOTO 1000,2000,3000,4000,5000,6000
1000 CLS
1010 PRINT "*****************************************************************"
1020 PRINT "**                 CLEAR TEXT BUFFER                          **"
1030 PRINT "**   THE BUFFER FOR THE PLAIN TEXT MESSAGE IS (23 X 80) -1    **"
1040 PRINT "**   CHARACTERS IN LENGTH  AND STARTS AT 60000 DECIMAL.       **"
1050 PRINT "**   IT WILL TAKE ABOUT 10 SEC TO CLEAR BUFFER TO ALL         **"
1060 PRINT "**   SPACES.                                                  **"
1070 PRINT "*****************************************************************"
1080 LOCATE 10,1
1090 PRINT "PLEASE STAND BY FOR APPROX 10 SEC -
1100 FOR X = BUFFER TO BUFFER + &H72F
1110 POKE X,32
1120 NEXT
1130 LOCATE 25,1 : PRINT "PRESS ANY KEY TO CONTINUE - ";:INPUT A$
1140 CLS : GOTO 100
2000 CLS
2010 PRINT "*****************************************************************"
2020 PRINT "**             ENTER OR UPDATE TEXT FOR ENCRYPTION            **"
2030 PRINT "**                                                            **"
2040 PRINT "**   THE PRESENT MESSAGE BUFFER WILL BE DISPLAYED,   AND      **"
2050 PRINT "**   THE CURSOR WILL BE RETURNED TO HOME.                     **"
```

```
2060 PRINT "**    ENTER YOUR TEXT USING -                           **"
2070 PRINT "**    THE 4 CURSOR CONTROL KEYS - UP, DOWN, LEFT, RIGHT  **"
2080 PRINT "**    THE ENTIRE ASCII CHARACTER SET -                   **"
2090 PRINT "**    THE BACKSPACE KEY AND THE ENTER KEY.               **"
2100 PRINT "**                                                       **"
2110 PRINT "**    FINALLY, WHEN YOU ARE FINISHED ENTERING THE TEXT - **"
2120 PRINT "**    PRESS  ALT E  (FOR EXIT) TO RETURN TO THE MENU     **"
2130 PRINT "**                                                       **"
2140 PRINT "**********************************************************"
2150 '
2160 LOCATE 25,1 : PRINT "PRESS ENTER TO CONTINUE - " ;
2170 A$ = INKEY$ : IF A$ = "" THEN 2170 ELSE CLS : LOCATE ,,1
2180 FOR X = BUFFER TO BUFFER + &H72F
2190 PRINT CHR$(PEEK(X));
2200 NEXT
2210 LOCATE 25,1 : PRINT "USE    ALT E    TO EXIT. " : LOCATE 1,1,1
2220 A$ = INKEY$ : IF A$ = "" THEN 2220
2230 IF CSRLIN > 23 THEN LOCATE 23,POS(Ø)
2240 IF LEN(A$) = 2 THEN 2290
2250 IF (ASC(A$) = 8) AND (POS(Ø) > 1) THEN LOCATE CSRLIN,POS(Ø)-1 :
     PRINT " ";
     :LOCATE CSRLIN,POS(Ø)-1 : POKE BUFFER+(CSRLIN-1)*80+POS(Ø)-1,32:
     GOTO 2220
2260 IF (ASC(A$) = 13) AND (CSRLIN <23) THEN LOCATE CSRLIN+1,1 : GOTO 2220
2270 IF (ASC(A$) = 13) AND (CSRLIN = 23) THEN LOCATE 23,1 :GOTO 2220
2280 POKE BUFFER + (CSRLIN-1)*80 + POS(Ø)-1,ASC(A$) : PRINT A$; : GOTO 2220
2290 B$ = MID$(A$,2,1) : B = ASC(B$)
2300 IF B = 71 THEN LOCATE 1,1
2310 IF (B = 72) AND (CSRLIN > 1) THEN LOCATE CSRLIN-1,POS(Ø)
2320 IF (B = 75) AND (POS(Ø) > 1) THEN LOCATE CSRLIN,POS(Ø)-1
2330 IF (B = 77) AND (POS(Ø) < 80) THEN LOCATE CSRLIN,POS(Ø)+1
2340 IF (B = 80) AND (CSRLIN < 23) THEN LOCATE CSRLIN+1,POS(Ø)
2350 IF (B = 18) THEN CLS : GOTO 100
2360 GOTO 2220
3000 CLS
3010 PRINT "**********************************************************"
3020 PRINT "**               ENCODE THE PLAIN TEXT MESSAGE          **"
3030 PRINT "**                                                       **"
3040 PRINT "**    ENTER KEY #1 TO INITIALIZE THE RANDOM GENERATOR.   **"
3050 PRINT "**    ENTER KEY #2 TO STEP YOU FART WAY INTO THE CODE.   **"
3060 PRINT "**                                                       **"
3070 PRINT "**    THE PROGRAM WILL TAKE THE PLAIN TEXT IN MEMORY AT   **"
3080 PRINT "**    60000 TO 61839 AND ENCRYPT IT, PLACING IT IN MEMORY **"
3090 PRINT "**    AT 62000 TO 63839.                                 **"
3100 PRINT "**                                                       **"
3110 PRINT "**    FINALLY, THE PROGRAM WILL DISPLAY THE ENCRYPTED    **"
3120 PRINT "**    TEXT.                                              **"
```

```
3130 PRINT "**                                                            **"
3140 PRINT "*****************************************************************"
3150 '
3160 LOCATE 17,1 : CLEAR ,15000 : DEF SEG = 0 : BUFFER = &HEA60
3170 PRINT "ENTER KEY #1 (FROM -32000 TO 32000) ";:INPUT A
3180 IF (A<-32000) OR (A>32000) THEN CLS : GOTO 3000
3190 RANDOMIZE A
3200 LOCATE 19,1
3210 PRINT "ENTER KEY #2 (FROM 1 TO 1000) ";: INPUT A
3220 IF (A<1) OR (A>1000) THEN LOCATE 19,30 : PRINT "           ":GOTO 3200
3230 FOR X = 1 TO A
3240 B = RND
3250 NEXT
3260 '
3270 LOCATE 25,1 : PRINT "READY TO ENCODE - PRESS ENTER TO BEGIN ";:INPUT A$
3280 CLS : PRINT "PLEASE STAND BY - ENCODING REQUIRES APPROX 30 SEC - "
3290 FOR X = BUFFER TO BUFFER + &H72F
3300 CYPHER = INT(RND * 255)
3310 CODEDTEXT = CYPHER + PEEK(X)
3320 IF CODEDTEXT > 255 THEN CODEDTEXT = CODEDTEXT - 256
3330 POKE X+&H7D0,CODEDTEXT
3340 NEXT
3350 LOCATE 25,1 : PRINT "CODING COMPLETE - PRESS ENTER TO VIEW";: INPUT A$
3360 CLS
3370 FOR X = BUFFER + &H7D0 TO BUFFER + &HEFF
3380 PRINT CHR$(PEEK(X));
3390 NEXT
3400 LOCATE 25,1 : PRINT "PRESS ENTER TO RETURN TO MENU - ";: INPUT A$
3410 CLS : GOTO 100
4000 CLS
4010 PRINT "*****************************************************************"
4020 PRINT "**              DECODE THE ENCRYPTED MESSAGE                  **"
4030 PRINT "**                                                           **"
4040 PRINT "**    ENTER KEY #1 TO INITIALIZE THE RANDOM GENERATOR.       **"
4050 PRINT "**    ENTER KEY #2 TO STEP YOU PART WAY INTO THE CODE.       **"
4060 PRINT "**                                                           **"
4070 PRINT "**    THE PROGRAM WILL TAKE THE ENCRYPTED TEXT IN MEMORY AT  **"
4080 PRINT "**    62000 TO 63839 AND DECODE IT, PLACING IT IN MEMORY     **"
4090 PRINT "**    AT 60000 TO 61839.                                     **"
4100 PRINT "**                                                           **"
4110 PRINT "**    FINALLY, THE PROGRAM WILL DISPLAY THE DECODED          **"
4120 PRINT "**    TEXT.                                                  **"
4130 PRINT "**                                                           **"
4140 PRINT "*****************************************************************"
4150 '
4160 LOCATE 17,1 : CLEAR ,15000 : DEF SEG = 0 : BUFFER = &HEA60
4170 PRINT "ENTER KEY #1 (FROM -32000 TO 32000) ";:INPUT A
```

```
4180 IF (A<-32000) OR (A>32000) THEN CLS : GOTO 4000
4190 RANDOMIZE A
4200 LOCATE 19,1
4210 PRINT "ENTER KEY #2 (FROM 1 TO 1000) ";: INPUT A
4220 IF (A<1) OR (A>1000) THEN LOCATE 19,30 : PRINT "            ":GOTO 3200
4230 FOR X = 1 TO A
4240 B = RND
4250 NEXT
4260 '
4270 LOCATE 25,1 : PRINT "READY TO DECODE - PRESS ENTER TO BEGIN ";:INPUT A$
4280 CLS : PRINT "PLEASE STAND BY - DECODING REQUIRES APPROX 30 SEC - "
4290 FOR X = BUFFER TO BUFFER + &H72F
4300 CYPHER = INT(RND * 255)
4310 CODEDTEXT = PEEK(X+2000) - CYPHER
4320 IF CODEDTEXT < 0 THEN CODEDTEXT = CODEDTEXT + 256
4330 POKE X,CODEDTEXT
4340 NEXT
4350 LOCATE 25,1 : PRINT "DECODING COMPLETE - PRESS ENTER TO VIEW ";:
     INPUT A$
4360 CLS
4370 FOR X = BUFFER TO BUFFER + &H72F
4380 PRINT CHR$(PEEK(X));
4390 NEXT
4400 LOCATE 25,1 : PRINT "PRESS ENTER TO RETURN TO MENU - ";: INPUT A$
4410 CLS : GOTO 100
5000 CLS
5010 PRINT "**************************************************************"
5020 PRINT "**   SAVE ENCODED MESSAGE TO DISKETTE OR CASSETTE          **"
5030 PRINT "**************************************************************"
5040 '
5050 LOCATE 5,1
5060 INPUT "ENTER THE FILENAME TO SAVE TO - (8 CHAR MAX) ";A$
5070 LOCATE 10,1
5080 PRINT "WARNING - MAKE SURE THE CASSETTE IS IN RECORD OR
     DISKETTE INSERTED
5090 PRINT "THEN, PRESS ENTER -
5100 INPUT B$
5110 LOCATE 15,1
5120 PRINT "SAVING - ";A$
5130 BSAVE A$,(BUFFER + &H7D0),&H730
5140 LOCATE 25,1 : PRINT "SAVE COMPLETE - PRESS ENTER TO RETURN TO MENU ";
5150 A$ = INKEY$ : IF A$ = "" THEN 5150 ELSE CLS : GOTO 100
6000 CLS
6010 PRINT "**************************************************************"
6020 PRINT "**   LOAD ENCODED MESSAGE FROM DISKETTE OR CASSETTE        **"
6030 PRINT "**************************************************************"
6040 '
```

```
6050 LOCATE 5,1
6060 INPUT "ENTER THE FILENAME TO READ FROM - (8 CHAR MAX) ";A$
6070 LOCATE 10,1
6080 PRINT "WARNING - MAKE SURE THE CASSETTE IS IN PLAY OR DISK INSERTED
6090 PRINT "THEN, PRESS ENTER -
6100 INPUT B$
6110 LOCATE 15,1
6120 PRINT "LOADING - ";A$
6130 BLOAD A$
6140 LOCATE 25,1 : PRINT "LOAD COMPLETE - PRESS ENTER TO RETURN TO MENU ";
6150 A$ = INKEY$ : IF A$ = "" THEN 5150 ELSE CLS : GOTO 100
```

FREQUENCY

In electronics, there are two basic equations that relate frequency to reactance.

$$X(L) = 2 * PI * FREQUENCY * L$$

and

$$X(C) = 1 / (2 * PI * FREQUENCY * C)$$

X(L) and X(C) represent the inductive and capacitive reactance expressed in ohms; L equals the inductance in henrys; and C equals the capacitance expressed in farads. The frequency is expressed in Hz or cps.

When you enter two of the five values, the program will solve for the remaining three if possible. The program solves the problem based on the assumptions that X(L) = X(C) at resonance, and that the frequency given is the frequency at resonance. A sample problem is shown in Fig. 2-1.

```
**************************************
**    Resonant Frequency Calculator    **
**    Vers 1.1              Dec. 20,1982   **
**************************************


- Enter values or press enter to skip -
      (two values only please)


Frequency in hertz (resonate)      =   2000      hz
Capacitive reactance in ohms       =   450       ohms
Inductive reactance in ohms        =   450       ohms
Capacitance in pico-farads         =   176839    pf
inductance in micro-henries        =   35809.9   uh


           Press enter to continue -
```

Fig. 2-1. Sample results of the *Frequency* program.

```
100 CLS
110 SCREEN Ø
120 WIDTH 80
130 KEY OFF
140 '
150 PRINT "*****************************************
160 PRINT "**    Resonant Frequency Calculator    **
170 PRINT "**    Vers 1.1          Dec. 20,1982   **
180 PRINT "*****************************************
190 '
200 LOCATE  6,1
210 PRINT "- Enter values or press enter to skip -"
220 PRINT "        (two values only please)"
230 '
240 LOCATE 10,1
250 INPUT "Frequency in hertz (resonate)      = ",F
260 INPUT "Capacitive reactance in ohms       = ",XC
270 INPUT "Inductive reactance in ohms        = ",XL
280 INPUT "Capacitance in picofarads          = ",C
290 INPUT "inductance in microhenries         = ",L
300 '
310 PI = 6.28318                 '**   2 * pi
320 '
330 IF F = Ø THEN 400            '**   must calculate frequency
340 '
350 IF (XC <> Ø) THEN GOSUB 1000 : GOTO 800
360 IF (XL <> Ø) THEN GOSUB 1100 : GOTO 800
370 IF (C  <> Ø) THEN GOSUB 1200 : GOTO 800
380 IF (L  <> Ø) THEN GOSUB 1300 : GOTO 800
390 GOTO 900
400 '
410 IF (XC <> Ø) AND (C <> Ø) THEN GOSUB 1400 : GOTO 800
420 IF (XL <> Ø) AND (C <> Ø) THEN GOSUB 1430 : GOTO 800
430 IF (XL <> Ø) AND (L <> Ø) THEN GOSUB 1500 : GOTO 800
440 IF (XC <> Ø) AND (L <> Ø) THEN GOSUB 1530 : GOTO 800
450 IF (C <> Ø)  AND (L <> Ø) THEN GOSUB 1600 : GOTO 800
460 GOTO 900
470 '
800 '**  Routine to print values on screen
810 LOCATE 10,37 : PRINT F  : LOCATE 10,53 : PRINT "Hz"
820 LOCATE 11,37 : PRINT XC : LOCATE 11,53 : PRINT "ohms
830 LOCATE 12,37 : PRINT XL : LOCATE 12,53 : PRINT "ohms
840 LOCATE 13,37 : PRINT C  : LOCATE 13,53 : PRINT "pf
850 LOCATE 14,37 : PRINT L  : LOCATE 14,53 : PRINT "uh
860 LOCATE 20,1 : INPUT "Press enter to continue - ",A$
870 CLEAR : POKE 106,Ø : CLS : GOTO 150
880 '
```

30

```
900 '**  Error message routine - not enough data input
910 LOCATE 20,1
920 PRINT "Insufficient data to calculate values from
930 INPUT "Press enter to continue - ",A$
940 CLEAR : POKE 106,0 : CLS : GOTO 150
950 '
1000 '** Frequency and Xc are known
1010 C = 10^12 / ( PI * F * XC )
1020 XL = XC
1030 L = XL * 10^6 / ( PI * F )
1040 RETURN
1050 '
1100 '** Frequency and Xl are known
1110 L = XL * 10^6 / ( PI * F )
1120 XC = XL
1130 C = 10^12 / ( PI * F * XC )
1140 RETURN
1150 '
1200 '** Frequency and C are known
1210 XC = 10^12 / ( PI * F * C )
1220 XL = XC
1230 L = XL * 10^6 / ( PI * F )
1240 RETURN
1250 '
1300 '** Frequency and L are known
1310 XL = ( PI * F * L / 10^6 )
1320 XC = XL
1330 C = 10^12 / ( PI * F * XC )
1340 RETURN
1350 '
1400 '** XC and C are known
1410 XL = XC
1420 GOTO 1450
1430 '** XL and C are known
1440 XC = XL
1450 F = 10^12 / ( PI * C * XC )
1460 L = XL * 10^6 / ( PI * F )
1470 RETURN
1480 '
1500 '** XL and L are known
1510 XC = XL
1520 GOTO 1550
1530 '** XC and L are known
1540 XL = XC
1550 F = XL * 10^6 / ( PI * L )
1560 C = 10^12 / ( PI * XC * F )
1570 RETURN
```

```
1580 '
1600 '** C and L are known
1610 F = 10^9 / (PI * SQR( L * C ))
1620 XC = 10^12 / ( PI * F * C )
1630 XL = XC
1640 RETURN
```

GEOSYNCHRONOUS SATELLITE ANTENNA AIM

When you get your own satellite television antenna you'll already know where to aim it using this program. Even if you never have your own satellite antenna, this program demonstrates several unique techniques of information display that you might find useful in writing other programs.

Geosynchronous satellites appear to sit in the same spot in the heavens without falling to earth. Sounds a little fishy, but there's a logical explanation. Some satellites, such as the reconnaissance satellites in polar orbit, are very close to the upper edges of the atmosphere. In 24 hours, these low orbit objects travel around the earth several times. Objects in higher orbits, such as manned space stations, don't complete as many revolutions in each 24 hour period. The higher the orbit, the fewer the revolutions per day. In fact, if the orbit is moved from a minimum altitude of roughly 200 miles to an extreme of about 22,300 miles, it will then take 24 hours for the object to orbit the earth once. If a satellite is at an altitude of 22,300 miles directly above the equator and is orbiting towards the east, the earth will spin once while the satellite orbits once. This means that the satellite will stay above the same spot on the earth.

All "geosynchronous" satellites orbit at this altitude and are always above the equator. To pinpoint a given satellite's location, all we need to know is its earthly longitude, that is, what longitude line on the equator the satellite sits above. The equations in this program take the satellite's longitude and the location of your satellite antenna (the latitude and longitude of your backyard) and calculate the azimuth and elevation for aiming at the satellite.

The value calculated for the elevation is the number of degrees above the horizon you should aim the antenna. For example, 3 degrees is just barely above the horizon, and 90 degrees is straight up. The azimuth is an angular measurement made in a horizontal plane. The azimuth angles in this program are relative to the south, with positive angles being in a westward direction. For example, an azimuth of −45 degrees is southeast; 0 degrees is south; and 17 degrees is just a little west of south.

Let's work through an example before delving into some of the data display techniques. If you live in Richmond, Virginia, your antenna location is approximately at latitude 37.5 and longitude 77.4 degrees. Let's assume the satellite of concern is oribiting above the equator at longitude 117 degrees. Run the program and answer the questions with the known data as shown in Fig. 2-2. If you have a printer you may choose option "2" to generate a printed table of aiming data for all visible geosynchronous satellites as shown in Table 2-1. Otherwise, press "1" to use the screen graph part of the program.

After a few minutes the screen graph will be finished. Two keys control movement through the graph data. Press "—" to move the vertical-line cursor to the left, and "+" to move it to the right. Along the right side of the graph are all the values you entered, and the resulting values for the elevation and azimuth. As you move the vertical-line cursor, the satellite longitude is shifted. Move the line to the right a few degrees at a time until the satellite longitude reads 117 as in the illustration in Fig. 2-3. The vertical line intersects two curves, the elevation curve rises and falls. The azimuth curve rises from left to right across the graph. These two curves give you a visual feel for the antenna aim, but the numbers at the right specify the exact figures for a given satellite longitude. In this example you should aim the antenna dish at an azimuth of 53.65 degrees (a little west of southwest) and an elevation of 30.19 degrees.

```
******  GEOSYNCHRONOUS SATELLITE ANTENNA AIM  ******



Latitude (-90 to 90) is positive in the northern hemisphere ...

Enter the latitude of the antenna location ? 37.5


Longitude (-180 to 180) is positive in the western hemisphere ...

Enter the longitude of the antenna location ? 77.4



        1.  Screen chart only.
        2.  Printed table also. (Must have printer ready).



Press the appropriate number key, '1' or '2' ...
```

Fig. 2-2. The initial display created by the *Geosynchronous Satellite Antenna Aim* program.

If you've moved the vertical line left and right on the graph, you might have noticed an unusual fact. The curves of the chart are not erased. The vertical line is drawn and then erased as it is moved, but the points of the curve don't disappear. If the vertical line had been drawn with the line function, the points would have been erased, but this program is using the put function to place a tall narrow rectangle (one dot wide) on the screen using the XOR option. The XOR (exclusive or) variation of the put command has an amazing and very useful property. If an image is "put" twice in a row at the same point on the screen the original graphics is unaffected! The vertical line is "put" at the same location a second time to restore the data previously drawn there. The *Lem* game program (stands for lunar excursion module) demonstrates this technique even more vividly.

By using the vertical line as a graph cursor, we can scroll through a chart, choosing exact numbers for display. The data can be displayed with a higher resolution than pure graphics would provide, yet the overall graphics representation of the data is preserved.

Table 2-1. Sample Printed Results of the *Geosynchronous Satellite Antenna Aim* **Program.**

```
        * * *   GEOSYNCHRONOUS SATELLITE ANTENNA AIM  * * *

Antenna latitude   37.50
Antenna longitude  77.40
```

Satellite Longitude	Antenna Azimuth	Antenna Elevation	Satellite Longitude	Antenna Azimuth	Antenna Elevation
-1	-82.88	0.50	36	-55.37	28.93
0	-82.25	1.29	37	-54.42	29.63
1	-81.62	2.08	38	-53.46	30.33
2	-80.99	2.87	39	-52.47	31.01
3	-80.35	3.66	40	-51.47	31.69
4	-79.71	4.45	41	-50.45	32.36
5	-79.07	5.24	42	-49.42	33.02
6	-78.42	6.03	43	-48.36	33.68
7	-77.77	6.82	44	-47.29	34.32
8	-77.11	7.61	45	-46.19	34.95
9	-76.45	8.40	46	-45.08	35.57
10	-75.78	9.19	47	-43.94	36.18
11	-75.11	9.97	48	-42.79	36.78
12	-74.43	10.76	49	-41.61	37.37
13	-73.74	11.55	50	-40.41	37.94
14	-73.05	12.33	51	-39.19	38.50
15	-72.35	13.12	52	-37.95	39.05
16	-71.64	13.90	53	-36.69	39.58
17	-70.92	14.68	54	-35.41	40.10
18	-70.20	15.46	55	-34.10	40.60
19	-69.47	16.23	56	-32.77	41.09
20	-68.73	17.01	57	-31.42	41.56
21	-67.98	17.78	58	-30.05	42.01
22	-67.22	18.55	59	-28.65	42.44
23	-66.45	19.32	60	-27.24	42.85
24	-65.67	20.08	61	-25.80	43.25
25	-64.88	20.85	62	-24.35	43.63
26	-64.08	21.60	63	-22.87	43.98
27	-63.27	22.36	64	-21.37	44.31
28	-62.45	23.11	65	-19.86	44.63
29	-61.61	23.85	66	-18.33	44.92
30	-60.76	24.59	67	-16.78	45.19
31	-59.90	25.33	68	-15.21	45.43
32	-59.02	26.06	69	-13.63	45.65
33	-58.13	26.79	70	-12.04	45.85
34	-57.23	27.51	71	-10.44	46.02
35	-56.31	28.22	72	-8.83	46.17

```
10 ' ********************
20 ' **    GEOSYNCH    **
30 ' ********************
40 '
50 CLEAR
60 SCREEN 2
70 CLS
80 KEY OFF
90 OPTION BASE 1
```

Satellite Longitude	Antenna Azimuth	Antenna Elevation	Satellite Longitude	Antenna Azimuth	Antenna Elevation
73	-7.20	46.30	115	51.67	31.56
74	-5.57	46.40	116	52.67	30.88
75	-3.94	46.47	117	53.65	30.19
76	-2.30	46.52	118	54.62	29.49
77	-0.66	46.54	119	55.56	28.79
78	0.99	46.54	120	56.49	28.08
79	2.63	46.51	121	57.41	27.37
80	4.27	46.46	122	58.31	26.64
81	5.90	46.38	123	59.20	25.92
82	7.53	46.27	124	60.07	25.18
83	9.15	46.14	125	60.93	24.45
84	10.76	45.99	126	61.78	23.70
85	12.36	45.81	127	62.61	22.96
86	13.95	45.61	128	63.43	22.21
87	15.53	45.38	129	64.24	21.45
88	17.09	45.13	130	65.04	20.69
89	18.63	44.86	131	65.83	19.93
90	20.16	44.57	132	66.61	19.17
91	21.67	44.25	133	67.37	18.40
92	23.17	43.91	134	68.13	17.63
93	24.64	43.55	135	68.88	16.85
94	26.09	43.17	136	69.62	16.08
95	27.52	42.77	137	70.35	15.30
96	28.93	42.35	138	71.07	14.52
97	30.32	41.92	139	71.78	13.74
98	31.69	41.46	140	72.49	12.96
99	33.04	40.99	141	73.19	12.17
100	34.36	40.50	142	73.88	11.39
101	35.67	40.00	143	74.56	10.60
102	36.95	39.48	144	75.24	9.82
103	38.20	38.94	145	75.91	9.03
104	39.44	38.39	146	76.58	8.24
105	40.66	37.83	147	77.24	7.45
106	41.85	37.25	148	77.90	6.66
107	43.02	36.66	149	78.55	5.87
108	44.17	36.06	150	79.20	5.08
109	45.30	35.45	151	79.84	4.29
110	46.41	34.83	152	80.48	3.50
111	47.50	34.19	153	81.12	2.71
112	48.57	33.55	154	81.75	1.92
113	49.63	32.89	155	82.38	1.13
114	50.66	32.23	156	83.00	0.34

```
100 DIM AZIMUTH(360),ELEVATION(360)
110 DIM VLINE(39)
120 '
130 ' Create vertical line for use later
140 LINE (0,0)-(0,150)
150 GET (0,0)-(0,150),VLINE
160 '
170 ' Define radian and degree conversion functions
180 DEGREESPERRADIAN = 57.29578
```

```
190 DEF FNRAD(DEGREES) = DEGREES/DEGREESPERRADIAN
200 DEF FNDEG(RADIANS) = RADIANS*DEGREESPERRADIAN
210 '
220 ' Define ARC COS function
230 DEF FNACS(X) = 1.570796-ATN(X/SQR(1-X*X))
240 '
250 ' Get antenna latitude and longitude from user
260 ' Also ask for output guidance (printer or not)
270 CLS
280 LOCATE 3,15
290 PRINT "* * *  GEOSYNCHRONOUS SATELLITE ANTENNA AIM  * * *"
300 LOCATE 8,1
310 PRINT "Latitude (-90 to 90) is positive in the northern hemisphere ...
320 LOCATE 10,1
330 INPUT "Enter the latitude of the antenna location ";LATITUDE
340 LOCATE 13,1
350 PRINT "Longitude (-180 to 180) is positive in the western
    hemisphere ..."
360 LOCATE 15,1
370 INPUT "Enter the longitude of the antenna location ";LONGITUDE
380 LOCATE 18,9
390 PRINT "1.  Screen chart only.
400 LOCATE 19,9
410 PRINT "2.  Printed table also. (Must have printer ready).
420 LOCATE 22,1
430 PRINT "Press the appropriate number key, '1' or '2' ...
440 K$ = INKEY$
450 IF K$ <> "1" AND K$ <> "2" THEN 440
460 IF K$ = "2" THEN TABLEFLAG = 1 ELSE TABLEFLAG = 0
470 '
480 ' Build screen chart
490 CLS
500 LOCATE 1,15
510 PRINT "* * *  GEOSYNCHRONOUS SATELLITE ANTENNA AIM  * * *
520 LOCATE 6,60
530 PRINT "Antenna Location";
540 LOCATE 8,60
550 PRINT USING "Latitude  ###.##";LATITUDE;
560 LOCATE 9,60
570 PRINT USING "longitude ###.##";LONGITUDE;
580 LOCATE 13,60
590 PRINT "Satellite";
600 LOCATE 14,60
610 PRINT "longitude";
620 LOCATE 18,60
630 PRINT "Antenna aim";
640 LOCATE 20,60
```

```
650 PRINT "Azimuth";
660 LOCATE 21,60
670 PRINT "Elevation";
680 LINE (100,190)-(461,40),,B
690 LOCATE 25,14
700 PRINT "Satellite equatorial longitude (-180 to +180)";
710 '
720 ' Loop to put 12 words vertically on left
730 FOR I = 1 TO 12
740 LOCATE 5+I,1
750 READ A$
760 PRINT A$;
770 NEXT I
780 DATA Antenna,aiming,curves,"","","",""
790 DATA Azimuth,-90 to +90,""
800 DATA Elevation,0 to 90
810 '
820 ' Some of the math can be done just once to save time
830 EARTH = 6367
840 ORBIT = 42200!
850 EARTH2 = EARTH * EARTH
860 ORBIT2 = ORBIT * ORBIT
870 FACTOR = 2 * ORBIT * EARTH * COS(FNRAD(LATITUDE))
880 SINLAT = SIN(FNRAD(LATITUDE))
890 '
900 ' Compute antenna aim for 360 satellite locations
910 FOR SATLONG = 1 TO 360
920 PUT (SATLONG+101,40),VLINE,XOR
930 LONGDIFF = FNRAD(SATLONG - LONGITUDE - 180)
940 TERM1 = SQR(EARTH2 + ORBIT2 - FACTOR * COS(LONGDIFF))
950 TERM2 = TERM1 * TERM1
960 TERM3 = (TERM2 + EARTH2 - ORBIT2) / (2 * TERM1 * EARTH)
970 TERM4 = TAN(LONGDIFF) / SINLAT
980 AZIMUTH(SATLONG) = FNDEG(ATN(TAN(LONGDIFF)/SINLAT))
990 ELEVATION(SATLONG) = FNDEG(FNACS(TERM3)) - 90
1000 GOSUB 1590
1010 IF ELEVATION(SATLONG) < 0 THEN 1080
1020 '(Else plot the points on the chart)
1030 XP = SATLONG + 100
1040 YA = -15 * AZIMUTH(SATLONG) / 18 + 115
1050 YE = -15 * ELEVATION(SATLONG) / 9 + 190
1060 PSET (XP,YA)
1070 PSET (XP,YE)
1080 PUT (SATLONG+101,40),VLINE,XOR   'Erases line but not background
1090 NEXT SATLONG
1100 '
1110 ' Put line at peak elevation point on chart
```

```
1120 LOCATE 2,34
1130 PRINT SPACE$(11);
1140 SATLONG = CVI(MKI$(LONGITUDE + 180))
1150 GOSUB 1590
1160 PUT (SATLONG+100,40),VLINE,XOR
1170 IF TABLEFLAG = 0 THEN 1380
1180 '
1190 ' Output table to printer
1200 LPRINT TAB(15)"* * *  GEOSYNCHRONOUS SATELLITE ANTENNA AIM  * * *"
1210 LPRINT STRING$(2,10)
1220 LPRINT USING "Antenna latitude  ###.##";LATITUDE
1230 LPRINT USING "Antenna longitude ###.##";LONGITUDE
1240 LPRINT STRING$(3,10)
1250 LPRINT TAB(9)"Satellite"TAB(27)"Antenna"TAB(36)"Antenna"
1260 LPRINT TAB(9)"Longitude"TAB(27)"Azimuth"TAB(36)"Elevation"
1270 LPRINT STRING$(80,"-");
1280 FORMAT$ = SPACE$(10) + "######" + SPACE$(11)
1290 FORMAT$ = FORMAT$ + "###.##    ###.##"
1300 FOR LLONG = 1 TO 360
1310 IF ELEVATION(LLONG) <= 0 THEN 1330
1320 LPRINT USING FORMAT$;LLONG-180,AZIMUTH(LLONG),ELEVATION(LLONG)
1330 NEXT LLONG
1340 LPRINT CHR$(12);
1350 TABLEFLAG = 0
1360 '
1370 ' Manual scroll through screen chart
1380 LOCATE 4,17
1390 PRINT "Use '+' or '-' to scroll through chart"
1400 '
1410 K$ = INKEY$
1420 IF K$ <> "" THEN 1460 ELSE GOSUB 1590
1430 GOTO 1410
1440 '
1450 ' Move line left one notch
1460 IF K$ <> "-" THEN 1530
1470 PUT (SATLONG+100,40),VLINE,XOR
1480 SATLONG = SATLONG - 1
1490 IF SATLONG < 1 THEN SATLONG = 360
1500 GOTO 1160
1510 '
1520 ' Move line right one notch
1530 IF K$ <> "+" THEN 1410
1540 PUT (SATLONG+100,40),VLINE,XOR
1550 SATLONG = SATLONG MOD 360 + 1
1560 GOTO 1160
1570 '
1580 ' Subroutine to update numbers on screen
```

```
1590 LOCATE 14,72
1600 PRINT USING "####";SATLONG - 180
1610 LOCATE 20,70
1620 IF ELEVATION(SATLONG) >= 0 THEN PRINT USING "###.##";AZIMUTH(SATLONG);
1630 IF ELEVATION(SATLONG) < 0 THEN PRINT "------";
1640 LOCATE 21,70
1650 IF ELEVATION(SATLONG) >= 0 THEN PRINT USING "###.##";
     ELEVATION(SATLONG);
1660 IF ELEVATION(SATLONG) < 0 THEN PRINT "------";
1670 RETURN
```

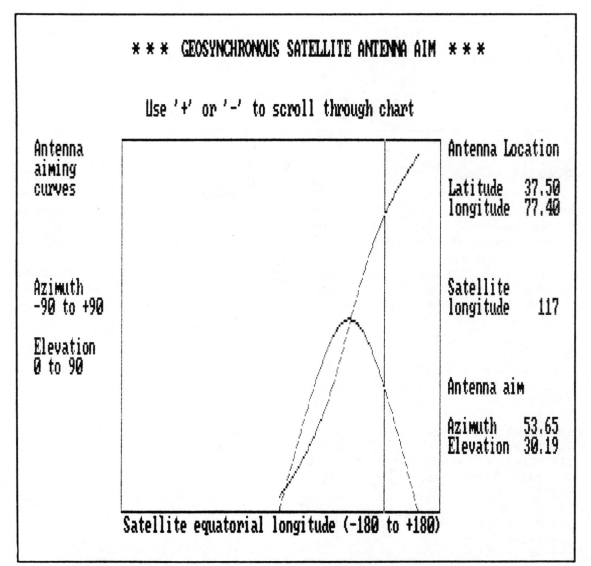

Fig. 2-3. The screen graph display produced by the *Geosynchronous Satellite Antenna Aim* program.

```
****************************************
**          OHMS LAW               **
**   VERS 1.1          DEC. 20,1982  **
****************************************


ENTER VALUES OR PRESS ENTER TO SKIP


VOLTAGE    = 5
CURRENT    = 1.06383E-03
RESISTANCE = 4700



PRESS ENTER TO CONTINUE -
```

Fig. 2-4. Sample results of the *Ohm's Law* program.

OHM'S LAW

One of the fundamental formulas in electronics is Ohm's law. This program is a simple way of solving the three relationships between voltage, current, and resistance dealt with in Ohm's law. The basic formula is usually expressed as $E = I \times R$, where E equals the voltage between two points in a circuit, I equals the current expressed in amps that is flowing through the element in question, and R is the element's resistance expressed in ohms.

To use the program, simply enter a value for two of the three variables, and the program will solve for the third. The program senses which of the values was not entered and solves for that value. Figure 2-4 shows the display after the third value has been calculated. Afterwards, the program loops back to the beginning for more data.

```
100 CLS
110 SCREEN 0
120 WIDTH 40
130 KEY OFF
140 '
150 PRINT "****************************************
160 PRINT "**          OHMS LAW               **
170 PRINT "**   VERS 1.1          DEC. 20,1982  **
180 PRINT "****************************************
190 '
200 LOCATE  7,1
210 PRINT "ENTER VALUES OR PRESS ENTER TO SKIP"
220 PRINT
230 PRINT
240 INPUT "VOLTAGE    = ",VOLTS
```

```
250 INPUT "CURRENT    = ",CURRENT
260 INPUT "RESISTANCE = ",RESISTANCE
270 IF VOLTS = Ø THEN LOCATE 10,14 : PRINT RESISTANCE * CURRENT
280 IF CURRENT = Ø THEN LOCATE 11,14 : PRINT VOLTS / RESISTANCE
290 IF RESISTANCE = Ø THEN LOCATE 12,14 : PRINT VOLTS / CURRENT
300 LOCATE 15,1
310 INPUT "PRESS ENTER TO CONTINUE - ",A$
320 CLEAR
330 POKE 106,0
340 CLS
350 GOTO 150
```

POWER CALCULATOR

In many electronic applications, there is a need to calculate the power consumed in a circuit or component. This calculation is based on the voltage and current that exist in the circuit in question according to the relationship of $P = E \times I$. Here, P equals the power consumed in the circuit in watts, E equals the voltage in the circuit in volts, and I equals the current through the circuit expressed in amps. If you take into account the fact that Ohm's law expresses a relationship between voltage, current, and resistance, you will find that if you want to solve for P, E, I, or R, all you need is two of the four values.

This program solves for the values using Ohm's law. If values are assigned to any two of the variables, the program will solve for the other two. The solution process breaks the problems into two groups: those that must be solved for power and those that do not. If power is not given, the program basically uses Ohm's Law to first solve for E, I, and R. Then a solution is easily found for the power used. If the power is given, one of the other two values is calculated, and then Ohm's law is used to find the last variable.

After you see the answers as shown in Fig. 2-5, simply press the enter key to restart the program.

```
      **********************************************
      **   POWER/VOLTAGE/CURRENT/RESISTANCE **
      **   VERS 1.1            DEC. 20,1982  **
      **********************************************


           - ENTER VALUES OR PRESS ENTER TO SKIP -
                 (TWO VALUES ONLY PLEASE)

           POWER       =  5.319149E-Ø3
           VOLTAGE     =  5
           CURRENT     =  1.Ø6383E-Ø3
           RESISTANCE  =  47ØØ




           PRESS ENTER TO CONTINUE -
```

Fig. 2-5. Sample results of the *Power Calculator* program.

```
100 CLS
110 SCREEN 0
120 WIDTH 40
130 KEY OFF
140 '
150 PRINT "****************************************
160 PRINT "**   POWER/VOLTAGE/CURRENT/RESISTANCE **
170 PRINT "**     VERS 1.1        DEC. 20,1982  **
180 PRINT "****************************************
190 '
200 LOCATE  7,1
210 PRINT "- ENTER VALUES OR PRESS ENTER TO SKIP -"
220 PRINT "         (TWO VALUES ONLY PLEASE)"
230 '
240 LOCATE 10,1
250 INPUT "POWER      = ",P
260 INPUT "VOLTAGE    = ",E
270 INPUT "CURRENT    = ",I
280 INPUT "RESISTANCE = ",R
290 '
300 IF (P = 0) THEN 350
310 IF (E <> 0) THEN I = P/E : R = E/I : GOTO 390
320 IF (I <> 0) THEN E = P/I : R = E/I : GOTO 390
330 IF (R <> 0) THEN I = SQR(P/R) : E = I*R : GOTO 390
340 '
350 IF (E <> 0) AND (I <> 0) THEN R = E/I : P = E*I : GOTO 390
360 IF (E <> 0) AND (R <> 0) THEN I = E/R : P = E*I : GOTO 390
370 IF (I <> 0) AND (R <> 0) THEN E = I*R : P = E*I : GOTO 390
380 '
390 LOCATE 10,14 : PRINT P
400 LOCATE 11,14 : PRINT E
410 LOCATE 12,14 : PRINT I
420 LOCATE 13,14 : PRINT R
430 '
440 CLEAR
450 LOCATE 17,1
460 INPUT "PRESS ENTER TO CONTINUE - ",A$
470 POKE 106,0
480 CLS
490 GOTO 150
```

SPELL

Remember those lists of words back in grade school that had to be memorized by Friday? Where was high technology when we needed it? Computers can help make learning fun. This program makes learning those lists of spelling words more enjoyable.

Any list of words can be entered; just be careful to spell correctly as you type them in. You, or your child, will be drilled on the list until each word is spelled correctly twice in a row. The words are picked from the list at random and displayed for a few seconds. The screen clears and you are asked to type the word in. The computer will tell you if your spelling is right or wrong. When a word is spelled correctly twice, it disappears from the list. After awhile only the words that have given you trouble will be chosen for display. When you finally spell each word correctly twice, a special congratulatory message is displayed.

```
10 ' ******************
20 ' **     SPELL     **
30 ' ******************
40 '
50 CLEAR
60 DEF SEG
70 SCREEN 1
80 COLOR 0,0
90 CLS
100 KEY OFF
110 RANDOMIZE VAL(MID$(TIME$,4,2) + RIGHT$(TIME$,2))
120 LOCATE 12,19
130 POKE &H4E,2
140 PRINT "SPELL
150 FOR DELTA = 3 TO 77 STEP 5
160 LINE (120-DELTA,87-DELTA)-(205+DELTA,97+DELTA),,B
170 NEXT DELTA
180 LOCATE 24,7
190 POKE &H4E,1
200 INPUT "How many words to learn";COUNT
210 DIM A$(COUNT),SCORE(COUNT)
220 FOR I = 1 TO COUNT
230 SCORE(I) = 2
240 NEXT I
250 CLS
260 COLOR 0,1
270 PRINT "Let's type in the words.
280 PRINT "Be careful to spell them correctly ...
290 PRINT
300 PRINT
310 FOR I = 1 TO COUNT
320 POKE &H4E,2
330 PRINT "Word number";I;" ";
340 POKE &H4E,3
350 INPUT CAP$
360 GOSUB 1210
370 A$(I) = CAP$
380 NEXT I
390 CLS
400 '
410 PTR = INT(RND * COUNT + 1)
420 J = 0
```

```
430 IF SCORE(PTR) THEN 490
440 PTR = PTR MOD COUNT + 1
450 J = J + 1
460 IF J > COUNT THEN 980
470 GOTO 430
480 '
490 CLS
500 COLOR 0,1
510 LOCATE 13,20 - LEN(A$(PTR)) / 2
520 POKE &H4E,3
530 PRINT A$(PTR);
540 FOR I = 9 TO 99 STEP 3
550 LINE (0,99-I)-(319,99-I),2
560 LINE (0,99+I)-(319,99+I),2
570 NEXT I
580 IF SCORE(PTR) = 2 THEN GOSUB 1160
590 CLS
600 COLOR 0,1
610 LOCATE 9,7
620 POKE &H4E,1
630 PRINT "Now try to spell it ..."
640 POKE &H4E,3
650 LOCATE 14,17 - LEN(A$(PTR)) / 2
660 IF LEN(INKEY$) THEN 660
670 INPUT CAP$
680 GOSUB 1210
690 IF CAP$ = A$(PTR) THEN 800
700 '
710 ' Whoops, better luck next time
720 CLS
730 LOCATE 14,9
740 PRINT "Sorry ......    ";A$(PTR);
750 GOSUB 1160
760 SCORE(PTR) = 2
770 GOTO 410
780 '
790 ' Wow, sit back and enjoy sucess for a spell
800 CLS
810 COLOR 0,0
820 POKE &H4E,1
830 LOCATE 13,16
840 PRINT "Very good !"
850 FOR I = 23 TO 123 STEP 5
860 X1 = 160 - 3 * I
870 X2 = 160 + 3 * I
880 Y1 = 99 - I
890 Y2 = 99 + I
```

```
900 LINE (X1,99)-(160,Y1)
910 LINE -(X2,99)
920 LINE -(160,Y2)
930 LINE -(X1,99)
940 NEXT I
950 SCORE(PTR) = SCORE(PTR) - 1
960 GOTO 410
970 '
980 CLS
990 POKE &H4E,3
1000 LOCATE 1,1
1010 PRINT "You did it!  Now you know how to spell
1020 PRINT "all these words...",,,,,
1030 POKE &H4E,1
1040 FOR I = 1 TO COUNT
1050 PRINT A$(I),
1060 NEXT I
1070 POKE &H4E,2
1080 PRINT
1090 PRINT
1100 PRINT TAB(11)"CONGRATULATIONS !
1110 PRINT TAB(11)STRING$(17,"_");
1120 LOCATE 22
1130 END
1140 '
1150 ' Subroutine, delay for awhile
1160 FOR DELAY = 1 TO 777
1170 NEXT DELAY
1180 RETURN
1190 '
1200 ' Subroutine, capitalization
1210 FOR CHAR = 1 TO LEN(CAP$)
1220 CHAR$ = MID$(CAP$,CHAR,1)
1230 IF CHAR$ < "a" OR CHAR$ > "z" THEN 1250
1240 MID$(CAP$,CHAR,1) = CHR$(ASC(CHAR$)-32)
1250 NEXT CHAR
1260 RETURN
```

Chapter 3

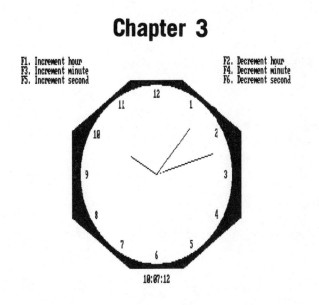

F1. Increment hour   F2. Decrement hour
F3. Increment minute   F4. Decrement minute
F5. Increment second   F6. Decrement second

Games and Other Fun

The programs in this chapter utilize the graphics capabilities of the IBM Personal Computer to create a variety of attention-getting programs—from action games to biorhythm charts.

AMAZE

This program generates random mazes. The method used here is original and appears to generate mazes several times faster than other maze-generating programs. The mazes may be drawn with just a few paths or with many. The maximum size maze is 159 paths wide and 99 high. Note that the time required to generate the maximum size maze is considerable (maybe half an hour or so). Try something like 20 high by 20 wide for your first maze.

If you have a printer with graphics capability you can produce a printed copy of the maze by pressing the p key after the maze is finished. If you press any other key, the maze is erased and another one is drawn.

Next time you're getting ready for a long trip in the ol' family car, generate a dozen or so mazes to help keep the little ones happy—and maybe one or two really tough ones for the grownups. Figures 3-1 and 3-2 show mazes produced by this program.

```
10 ' ***************************
20 ' **        AMAZE         **
30 ' ***************************
40 '
50 CLEAR
60 SCREEN 1
70 CLS
80 KEY OFF
```

```
90 COLOR Ø,1
100 LOCATE 12,12
110 PRINT "***  AMAZE  ***"
120 GOSUB 760
130 CLS
140 LOCATE 7,1
150 INPUT "How many paths wide ";WIDE
160 IF WIDE > Ø AND WIDE < 160 THEN 200
170 PRINT "Valid range is 1 to 159
180 BEEP
190 GOTO 150
200 INPUT "How many paths high ";HIGH
210 IF HIGH > Ø AND HIGH < 100 THEN 260
220 PRINT "Valid range is 1 to 99
230 BEEP
240 GOTO 200
250 '
260 WINC = 320\(WIDE+1)
270 HINC = 200\(HIGH+1)
280 CLS
290 LINE (Ø,Ø)-(WIDE*WINC,HIGH*HINC),,B
300 COUNT = WIDE * HIGH
310 FOR I = Ø TO COUNT
320 PTR = (PTR+997) MOD COUNT
330 X = INT(PTR/HIGH)
340 Y = PTR - X * HIGH
350 X = X * WINC
360 Y = Y * HINC
370 IF POINT(X,Y) THEN 600
380 DIR = INT(4*RND+1)
390 DIR2 = DIR
400 DIR = DIR MOD 4 + 1
410 XN = ((DIR=1)-(DIR=3)) * WINC + X
420 YN = ((DIR=2)-(DIR=4)) * HINC + Y
430 IF POINT(XN,YN) = Ø THEN 550
440 LINE (X,Y)-(XN,YN)
450 DIR = INT(4*RND+1)
460 FOR K = 1 TO 4
470 DIR = DIR MOD 4 + 1
480 XN = ((DIR=1)-(DIR=3)) * WINC + X
490 YN = ((DIR=2)-(DIR=4)) * HINC + Y
500 IF POINT(XN,YN) THEN 590
510 LINE (X,Y)-(XN,YN)
520 X = XN
530 Y = YN
540 GOTO 450
550 IF DIR <> DIR2 THEN 580
```

```
560 X = XN
570 Y = YN
580 GOTO 400
590 NEXT K
600 NEXT I
610 '
620 ' Open the doors on each side
630 Y = (HIGH \ 2) * HINC
640 LINE (0,Y)-(0,Y+HINC),0
650 LINE (WIDE*WINC,Y)-(WIDE*WINC,Y+HINC),0
660 '
670 ' Done ...
680 ' If user presses "p" then dump graphics to printer,
690 ' Else draw another maze whenever any key is pressed.
700 K$ = INKEY$
710 IF K$ = "" THEN 700
720 IF K$ = "p" OR K$ = "P" THEN GOSUB 870
730 GOTO 130
740 '
750 ' Wait for user and be randomizing the generator
760 LOCATE 25,9
770 PRINT "Press any key to begin";
780 RNDM = RND
790 K$ = INKEY$
800 IF K$ = "" THEN 780
810 RANDOMIZE 64000! * RND - 32000
820 LOCATE 25,1
830 PRINT SPACE$(39);
840 RETURN
850 '
860 ' Subroutine to dump graphic maze to printer
870 DEF SEG = &HB800
880 E$ = CHR$(27)
890 WIDTH "LPT1:",255
900 LPRINT E$+"1";
910 LPRINT E$+"W" + CHR$(1);
920 FOR ROW = 0 TO 79
930 A$ = ""
940 FOR COL = 99 TO 0 STEP -1
950 LOCA$ = CHR$(PEEK(COL * 80 + ROW))
960 LOCB$ = CHR$(PEEK(COL * 80 + ROW + &H2000))
970 A$ = A$ + LOCB$ + LOCB$
980 A$ = A$ + LOCA$ + LOCA$
990 IF COL <> 49 THEN 1020
1000 LPRINT E$+"K"+CHR$(144)+CHR$(1)+A$;
1010 A$ = ""
1020 NEXT COL
```

```
1030 LPRINT A$
1040 NEXT ROW
1050 RETURN
```

Fig. 3-1. A simple maze produced by the *Amaze* program.

Fig. 3-2. A difficult maze produced by the *Amaze* program.

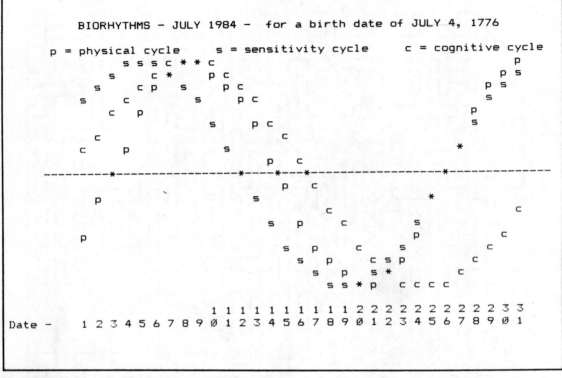

Fig. 3-3. The screen chart produced by the *Biorhythms* program.

BIORHYTHMS

Biorhythms have been a controversial subject for several years now. People definitely do have cycles in their metabolic functions. One obvious example is our 24 hour sleep-wake cycle. Hormones increase and decrease in our bodies in rough cycles of daily, monthly, and even yearly time spans.

The biorhythm chart shows how your "cognitive", "sensitive", and "physical" bodily functions vary over their respective 33, 28, and 23 day cycles. It is assumed that these three cycles start at birth and stay exactly synchronized throughout your life. Various studies have failed to either prove or disprove the validity of these cycles. Some people plan their lives around their biorhythm charts; others laugh at the idea. It is fun to compare your chart with how you've been feeling recently.

Each of the three cycles is a mathematical curve called a sine wave. Your best days are when the curves peak at the top or bottom of the chart. The "critical" days occur when the curves cross the center line of the chart. Watch out when two or three cycles coincide and cross the center line on the same day. These double or triple critical days are supposed to be your worst. A sample chart is shown in Fig. 3-3.

Even if you don't find biorhythms intriguing, this program demonstrates several useful techniques and subroutines. Because the chart is generated entirely in text (screen 0) mode, this program will work with any monitor. The cycles are produced using several colors, so if you have a color monitor, you'll get best results.

Several calendar related subroutines were used in this program. Notice that the range of valid dates covers several centuries. (Has anyone ever checked General Custer's chart?)

```
10 ' ************************
20 ' **        BIORHYTHM      **
30 ' ************************
40 '
50 CLEAR
60 SCREEN 0,0,0,0
70 COLOR 7,0,0
80 CLS
90 KEY OFF
100 OPTION BASE 1
110 PI = 3.141593
120 DEF FNDOWN(AMT) = INT(13.5-9*SIN(2*PI*(JULIAN-JULIANB)/AMT))
130 DEF FNACROSS = 9+DAY+DAY
140 DEF FNSCR$ = CHR$(SCREEN(CSRLIN,POS(0)))
150 DIM MONTH.NAME$(12)
160 FOR I = 1 TO 12
170 READ MONTH.NAME$(I)
180 NEXT I
190 DATA JANUARY,FEBRUARY,MARCH,APRIL,MAY,JUNE,JULY
200 DATA AUGUST,SEPTEMBER,OCTOBER,NOVEMBER,DECEMBER
210 '
220 CLS
230 LOCATE 7,7
240 LINE INPUT "Enter birth date ... (any reasonable format) ";CAL$
250 IF CAL$ = "" THEN 280
260 GOSUB 1510
270 IF YEAR THEN 320
280 LOCATE 9,1
290 PRINT "The date is unrecognizable, or isn't a valid date ... try again.
300 BEEP
310 GOTO 230
320 MONTHB = MONTH
330 DAYB = DAY
340 YEARB = YEAR
350 JULIANB = JULIAN
360 LOCATE 9,1
370 PRINT SPACE$(79);
380 LOCATE 9,7
390 LINE INPUT "Enter today's date ... ";CAL$
400 IF CAL$ = "" THEN 430
410 GOSUB 1510
420 IF YEAR THEN 470
430 LOCATE 11,1
440 PRINT "Your date is unrecognizable, or isn't a valid date ... try again.
450 BEEP
460 GOTO 380
470 DAY = 1
```

```
480 GOSUB 1210
490 JULIAN1 = JULIAN
500 MONTH = MONTH MOD 12 + 1
510 IF MONTH = 1 THEN YEAR = YEAR + 1
520 GOSUB 1210
530 JULIAN2 = JULIAN - 1
540 JULIAN = JULIAN1
550 GOSUB 1330
560 '
570 WIDTH 80
580 COLOR 7,0,1
590 CLS
600 LABEL$ = "BIORYTHMS - "+MONTH.NAME$(MONTH)+STR$(YEAR)
610 LABEL$ = LABEL$ + " -  for a birth date of "
620 LABEL$ = LABEL$ + MONTH.NAME$(MONTHB) + STR$(DAYB)
630 LABEL$ = LABEL$ + "," + STR$(YEARB)
640 LOCATE 1,40 - LEN(LABEL$)/2
650 PRINT LABEL$;
660 LOCATE 25,1
670 COLOR 14,0
680 PRINT "Date -";
690 LOCATE 3,7
700 COLOR 10,0
710 PRINT "p = physical cycle";
720 LOCATE 3,30
730 COLOR 11,0
740 PRINT "s = sensitivity cycle";
750 LOCATE 3,56
760 COLOR 13,0
770 PRINT "c = cognitive cycle";
780 DAY = 0
790 COLOR 9,0
800 LOCATE 13,6
810 PRINT STRING$(70,"-");
820 FOR JULIAN = JULIAN1 TO JULIAN2
830 COLOR 14,0
840 DAY = DAY + 1
850 LOCATE 24,9 + DAY + DAY
860 IF DAY > 9 THEN PRINT CHR$(48+INT(DAY/10));
870 LOCATE 25,9 + DAY + DAY
880 PRINT CHR$(48+DAY MOD 10);
890 COLOR 10,0
900 LOCATE FNDOWN(23) , FNACROSS
910 IF FNSCR$ = " " THEN PRINT "p"; ELSE COLOR 12,0 : PRINT "*";
920 IF FNDOWN(23) <> 14 THEN 960
930 LOCATE 13,FNACROSS - 1
940 COLOR 12,0
```

54

```
950 PRINT "*";
960 COLOR 11,0
970 LOCATE FNDOWN(28) , FNACROSS
980 IF FNSCR$ = " " THEN PRINT "s"; ELSE COLOR 12,0 : PRINT "*";
990 COLOR 13,0
1000 LOCATE FNDOWN(33) , FNACROSS
1010 IF FNSCR$ = " " THEN PRINT "c"; ELSE COLOR 12,0 : PRINT "*";
1020 IF FNDOWN(33) <> 14 THEN 1060
1030 LOCATE 13,FNACROSS - 1
1040 COLOR 12,0
1050 PRINT "*";
1060 NEXT JULIAN
1070 LOCATE 9,1
1080 K$ = INKEY$
1090 IF K$ = "" THEN 1080
1100 END
1110 '
1120 ' Subroutine, capitalize cal$
1130 FOR CP = 1 TO LEN(CAL$)
1140 CHAR$ = MID$(CAL$,CP,1)
1150 IF CHAR$ < "a" OR CHAR$ > "z" THEN 1170
1160 MID$(CAL$,CP,1) = CHR$(ASC(CHAR$)-32)
1170 NEXT CP
1180 RETURN
1190 '
1200 ' Subroutine, MONTH,DAY,YEAR to JULIAN,WEEKDAY
1210 JULIAN = INT(365.2422# * YEAR + 30.44 * (MONTH-1) + DAY + 1)
1220 T1 = MONTH - 2 - 12 * (MONTH < 3)
1230 T2 = YEAR + (MONTH < 3)
1240 T3 = INT(T2 / 100)
1250 T2 = T2 - 100 * T3
1260 WEEKDAY = INT(2.61 * T1 - .2) + DAY + T2 + INT(T2 / 4)
1270 WEEKDAY = (WEEKDAY + INT(T3 / 4) - T3 - T3 + 77) MOD 7 + 1
1280 T4 = JULIAN - 7 * INT(JULIAN / 7)
1290 JULIAN = JULIAN - T4 + WEEKDAY + 7 * (T4 < WEEKDAY - 1) + 1721060#
1300 RETURN
1310 '
1320 ' Subroutine, JULIAN to MONTH,DAY,YEAR,WEEKDAY
1330 T5 = JULIAN
1340 YEAR = INT((JULIAN - 1721061!) / 365.25 + 1)
1350 MONTH = 1
1360 DAY = 1
1370 GOSUB 1210
1380 IF JULIAN <= T5 THEN 1410
1390 YEAR = YEAR - 1
1400 GOTO 1370
1410 MONTH = INT((T5 - JULIAN) / 29 + 1)
```

```
1420 GOSUB 1210
1430 IF JULIAN <= T5 THEN 1460
1440 MONTH = MONTH - 1
1450 GOTO 1420
1460 DAY = T5 - JULIAN + 1
1470 GOSUB 1210
1480 RETURN
1490 '
1500 ' Subroutine, convert CAL$ to MONTH,DAY,YEAR
1510 GOSUB 1130
1520 MONTH = 0
1530 DAY = 0
1540 YEAR = 0
1550 FOR I = 1 TO 12
1560 IF INSTR(CAL$,LEFT$(MONTH.NAME$(I),3)) THEN MONTH = I
1570 NEXT I
1580 FOR I = 1 TO LEN(CAL$)
1590 CHAR$ = MID$(CAL$,I,1)
1600 IF CHAR$ < "0" OR CHAR$ > "9" THEN MID$(CAL$,I,1) = ":"
1610 NEXT I
1620 IF INSTR(CAL$,":") THEN 1680
1630 IF LEN(CAL$) <> 6 AND LEN(CAL$) <> 8 THEN 1930
1640 MONTH = VAL(LEFT$(CAL$,2))
1650 DAY = VAL(MID$(CAL$,3,2))
1660 YEAR = VAL(MID$(CAL$,5))
1670 GOTO 1820
1680 VFLAG = 0
1690 FOR I = 1 TO LEN(CAL$)
1700 CALVAL = VAL(MID$(CAL$,I))
1710 IF CALVAL = 0 THEN VFLAG = 0
1720 IF CALVAL = 0 OR VFLAG = 1 THEN 1810
1730 IF MONTH THEN 1760
1740 MONTH = CALVAL
1750 GOTO 1800
1760 IF DAY THEN 1790
1770 DAY = CALVAL
1780 GOTO 1800
1790 YEAR = CALVAL
1800 VFLAG = 1
1810 NEXT I
1820 IF YEAR < 100 AND YEAR > 0 THEN YEAR = YEAR + 1900
1830 IF YEAR < 1582 OR YEAR > 3999 THEN YEAR = 0
1840 IF YEAR = 0 THEN 1930
1850 MONTH2 = MONTH
1860 DAY2 = DAY
1870 YEAR2 = YEAR
1880 GOSUB 1210
```

```
1890 GOSUB 1330
1900 IF MONTH2 <> MONTH THEN YEAR = Ø
1910 IF DAY2 <> DAY THEN YEAR = Ø
1920 IF YEAR2 <> YEAR THEN YEAR = Ø
1930 RETURN
```

CHOMPER, THE LITTLE DOT EATER

This program demonstrates how to create and move graphics of your choice around the screen. Although you may recognize the little Chomper as a frivolous arcade character, the purpose behind this program is instructional. Being able to create shapes and patterns and move them is a prime requisite for programming any of the video arcade type games. Chomper is created from eight different patterns that are sorted in memory and then printed on the screen as needed. The patterns needed and their values are given below and on page 58.

These patterns work together in sets of two. If you examine the top two patterns on the left you will see that they form the left hemisphere of a circle. The top two on the right form the right side of the circle in a closed state, and the bottom two sets form the right side of a circle with slices removed which represent the different mouths of Chomper. Like movies, if these images are flashed on the screen in the proper sequence fast enough, they will produce the sensation of motion through the persistance of vision.

&HØ7	. . . . . * * *	&HEØ	* * * . . . . .
&H1F	. . . * * * * *	&HF8	* * * * * . . .
&H3F	. . * * * * * *	&HFC	* * * * * * . .
&H7F	. * * * * * * *	&HFE	* * * * * * * .
&H7F	. * * * * * * *	&HFE	* * * * * * * .
&HFF	* * * * * * * *	&HFF	* * * * * * * *
&HFF	* * * * * * * *	&HFF	* * * * * * * *
&HFF	* * * * * * * *	&HFF	* * * * * * * *

&HFF	* * * * * * * *	&HFF	* * * * * * * *
&HFF	* * * * * * * *	&HFF	* * * * * * * *
&HFF	* * * * * * * *	&HFF	* * * * * * * *
&H7F	. * * * * * * *	&HFE	* * * * * * * .
&H7F	. * * * * * * *	&HFE	* * * * * * * .
&H3F	. . * * * * * *	&HFC	* * * * * * . .
&H1F	. . . * * * * *	&HF8	* * * * * . . .
&HØ7	. . . . . * * *	&HEØ	* * * . . . . .

57

```
&HEØ    * * * . . . . .        &HEØ    * * * . . . . .
&HF8    * * * * * . . .        &HF8    * * * * * . . .
&HFC    * * * * * * . .        &HFC    * * * * * * . .
&HF8    * * * * * . . .        &HFE    * * * * * * * .
&HFØ    * * * * . . . .        &HFE    * * * * * * * .
&HEØ    * * * . . . . .        &HFE    * * * * * * * .
&HCØ    * * . . . . . .        &HF8    * * * * * . . .
&H8Ø    * . . . . . . .        &HCØ    * * . . . . . .


&H8Ø    * . . . . . . .        &HCØ    * * . . . . . .
&HCØ    * * . . . . . .        &HF8    * * * * * . . .
&HEØ    * * * . . . . .        &HFE    * * * * * * * .
&HFØ    * * * * . . . .        &HFE    * * * * * * * .
&HF8    * * * * * . . .        &HFE    * * * * * * * .
&HFC    * * * * * * . .        &HFC    * * * * * * . .
&HF8    * * * * * . . .        &HF8    * * * * * . . .
&HEØ    * * * . . . . .        &HEØ    * * * . . . . .
```

Although this program was written for a 16K cassette-based system, you can run it on any IBM Personal Computer system you own by changing a few values.

The key is in a 1K buffer area you reserve in memory to hold the patterns. Using the identical method used in the *New-Font* program in Chapter 7 to produce new characters, we will generate eight characters with the eight shapes we have developed. With each character residing in an 8×8 pixel square on the screen, we can define any character with eight bytes. These bytes are poked into the buffer starting at the lowest address and proceding to the top of the buffer. After you have set the pointer to the bottom of the buffer, all that is necessary to get the pattern is to **PRINT CHR$ (128 through 135)** for the eight patterns.

To configure the program for different amounts of memory, lines 180 through 220 must be customized for your own computer.

```
18Ø FOR X = &H3CØØ TO &H3FFF     = 16K SYSTEM

18Ø FOR X = &H7CØØ TO &H7FFF     = 32K SYSTEM

18Ø FOR X = &HBCØØ TO &HBFFF     = 48K SYSTEM

18Ø FOR X = &HFCØØ TO &HFFFF     = 64K SYSTEM
```

```
190 POKE X,Ø

200 NEXT


210 POKE &H7D,&H3C              = 16K SYSTEM

210 POKE &H7D,&H7C              = 32K SYSTEM

210 POKE &H7D,&HBC              = 48K SYSTEM

210 POKE &H7D,&HFC              = 64K SYSTEM


220 DEF SEG = &H3CØ             = 16K SYSTEM

220 DEF SEG = &H7CØ             = 32K SYSTEM

220 DEF SEG = &HBCØ             = 48K SYSTEM

220 DEF SEG = &HFCØ             = 64K SYSTEM
```

The rest of the program is simply a means of printing the characters in the correct order and in the correct locations on the screen.

```
100 '**********************************************
110 '**                 CHOMPER                 **
120 '**                                         **
130 '**  JULY 13, 1982          VERSION 1.1  **
140 '**********************************************
150 SCREEN 2:KEY OFF
160 CLEAR ,10000
170 DEF SEG = Ø
180 FOR X = &HFCØØ TO &HFFFF
190 POKE X,Ø
200 NEXT
210 POKE &H7D,&HFC
220 DEF SEG = &HFCØ
230 FOR X = Ø TO 63
240 READ Y
250 POKE X,Y
260 NEXT
270 DATA &HØ7 ,&H1F ,&H3F ,&H7F ,&H7F ,&HFF ,&HFF ,&HFF
280 DATA &HEØ ,&HF8 ,&HFC ,&HFE ,&HFE ,&HFF ,&HFF ,&HFF
290 DATA &HFF ,&HFF ,&HFF ,&H7F ,&H7F ,&H3F ,&H1F ,&HØ7
300 DATA &HFF ,&HFF ,&HFF ,&HFE ,&HFE ,&HFC ,&HF8 ,&HEØ
310 DATA &HEØ ,&HF8 ,&HFC ,&HF8 ,&HFØ ,&HEØ ,&HCØ ,&H8Ø
320 DATA &H8Ø ,&HCØ ,&HEØ ,&HFØ ,&HF8 ,&HFC ,&HF8 ,&HEØ
330 DATA &HEØ ,&HF8 ,&HFC ,&HFE ,&HFE ,&HFE ,&HF8 ,&HCØ
```

```
340 DATA &HC0 ,&HF8 ,&HFE ,&HFE ,&HFE ,&HFC ,&HF8 ,&HE0
350 CLS
360 FOR X = 2 TO 24 STEP 3
370 FOR Y = 1 TO 70 STEP 4
380 LOCATE X,Y+3
390 PRINT ".";
400 NEXT Y,X
410 FOR X = 2 TO 24 STEP 3
420 FOR Y = 1 TO 70 STEP 4
430 LOCATE X,Y
440 PRINT CHR$(32);CHR$(128);CHR$(129);CHR$(32);
450 LOCATE X+1,Y
460 PRINT CHR$(32);CHR$(130);CHR$(131);CHR$(32);
470 FOR Z = 1 TO 50:NEXT
480 LOCATE X,Y+1
490 PRINT CHR$(32);CHR$(128);CHR$(134);CHR$(32);
500 LOCATE X+1,Y+1
510 PRINT CHR$(32);CHR$(130);CHR$(134);CHR$(32);
520 FOR Z = 1 TO 50:NEXT
530 LOCATE X,Y+2
540 PRINT CHR$(32);CHR$(128);CHR$(132);CHR$(32);
550 LOCATE X+1,Y+2
560 PRINT CHR$(32);CHR$(130);CHR$(133);CHR$(32);
570 FOR Z = 1 TO 50:NEXT
580 LOCATE X,Y+3
590 PRINT CHR$(32);CHR$(128);CHR$(134);CHR$(32);
600 LOCATE X+1,Y+3
610 PRINT CHR$(32);CHR$(130);CHR$(135);CHR$(32);
620 FOR Z = 1 TO 50:NEXT
630 LOCATE X,Y+4
640 PRINT CHR$(32);CHR$(128);CHR$(129);CHR$(32);
650 LOCATE X+1,Y+4
660 PRINT CHR$(32);CHR$(130);CHR$(131);CHR$(32);
670 NEXT Y
680 LOCATE X,65
690 PRINT "                "
700 LOCATE X+1,65
710 PRINT "                "
720 NEXT X
```

FLY

This program is a state-of-the-art version of the old "pea shuffle" game. Follow the shuffling fly closely now . . . SCHWAAPF! Is it under swatter number one, number two, or number three? If you guess correctly the next fly buzzes around a little faster. If you miss, the next fly is a little slower. In effect, this game is self-adjusting for your current skill level.

This program demonstrates the use of several of the powerful graphics and sound techniques available in your IBM Personal Computer. The flies and swatters are created using the draw statement,

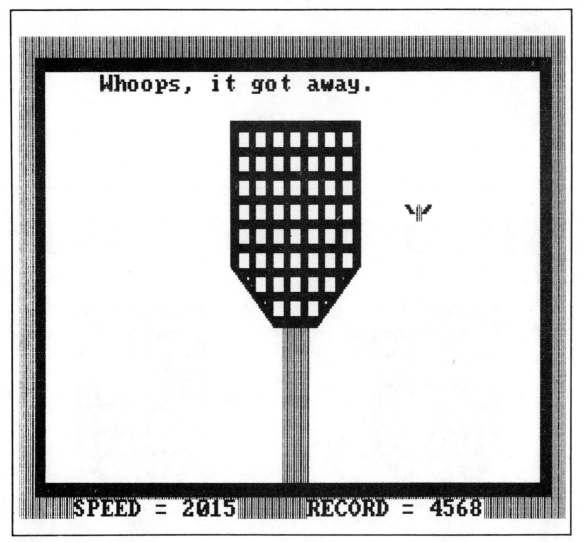

Fig. 3-4. Display created by the *Fly* program.

and then manipulated quickly as complete images using the get and put commands. The various sound effects are generated with the sound and play statements.

The instructions are simple. Load the *Fly* program and run it. Now look closely at the fly as it buzzes randomly between positions 1, 2, and 3, (left, center, and right side of the screen). Suddenly three fly swatters appear, one of which covers the fly at its current position. You are to guess where the fly is. Press "1", "2", or "3" in response to the question at the top of the screen. Each correct guess results in a slightly faster fly and a higher score. The highest score you've earned so far and your current score are displayed at the bottom of the screen. The highest score possible is 9999. You'll get a special message when you get to this score. Figures 3-4 and 3-5 show two possible outcomes of attempts to "swat" the fly.

Now you can show your friends a program that requires debugging every time it is run! (Sorry, I just couldn't resist it.)

```
10 '****************
20 '**     FLY     **
30 '****************
40 '
50 CLEAR
60 GOSUB 1730
70 SCREEN 1
80 KEY OFF
90 CLS
100 COLOR 0,0
110 OPTION BASE 1
```

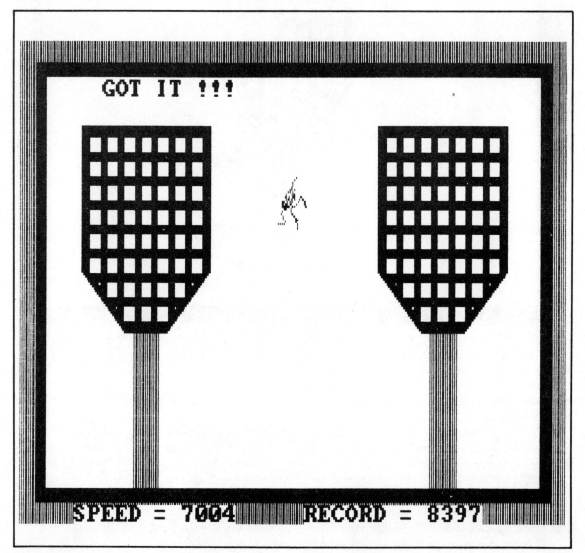

Fig. 3-5. Display created by the *Fly* program.

```
120 DEFINT X,Y
130 DIM FLY0(21),FLY1(21),FLY2(21)
140 DIM SWAT(714)
150 DIM X(3),Y(3)
160 DELAY=3000
170 '
180 ' Build the fly images
190 BODY$="c1u5be1d6r1u6bf1d5"
200 URWING$="c3bu3br1e3r1g3r1e3"
210 ULWING$="bg3bl7h3l1f3l1h3"
220 DRWING$="c3br6h3l1f3l1h3"
230 DLWING$="bl5g3l1e3l1g3"
240 DRAW BODY$+URWING$+ULWING$
250 DRAW "bd20br6"
260 DRAW BODY$+DRWING$+DLWING$
270 GET (131,91)-(152,103),FLY0
280 GET (151,91)-(172,103),FLY1
290 GET (151,105)-(172,117),FLY2
300 '
310 ' Build the swatter image
320 CLS
330 LINE (0,50)-(75,135),3,BF
340 FOR X = 5 TO 65 STEP 10
350 FOR Y = 55 TO 125 STEP 10
360 LINE (X,Y)-(X+5,Y+5),0,BF
370 NEXT Y,X
380 FOR Y = 106 TO 135
390 IF Y < 111 THEN CLR=3 ELSE CLR=0
400 DRAW "c=clr; bm0,=y; m+25,25 m+25,0 m+25,-25"
410 NEXT Y
420 LINE (30,136)-(45,199),1,BF
430 GET (0,50)-(75,199),SWAT
440 '
450 ' Draw the screen border
460 CLS
470 LINE(0,0)-(319,199),2,BF
480 LINE(9,9)-(310,190),3,BF
490 '
500 ' Next fly appears
510 LINE(15,15)-(304,184),0,BF
520 FOR I = 1 TO 7+5*RND
530 FLY=INT(3*RND+1)
540 BUZZ=0
550 SOUND 47,0
560 SOUND 63+7*RND,999
570 WHILE BUZZ < DELAY
580 PUT(74*FLY,67),FLY1,PSET
```

```
590 PUT(74*FLY,67),FLY2,PSET
600 BUZZ=BUZZ+99
610 WEND
620 SOUND 47,0
630 PUT(74*FLY,67),FLY0,PSET
640 NEXT I
650 '
660 ' Swatters schwaapf onto screen
670 FOR SWIPE = 1 TO 3
680 SOUND 999,1
690 PUT (87*SWIPE-51,35),SWAT
700 NEXT SWIPE
710 '
720 ' How well did you follow the fly?
730 K$ = INKEY$
740 IF K$ <> "" THEN 730
750 LOCATE 3,7
760 PRINT "Check which swatter (1,2,3) ?
770 K$=INKEY$
780 IF K$ = "" THEN 770
790 IF K$<>"1" AND K$<>"2" AND K$<>"3" THEN 770
800 GUESS=VAL(K$)
810 LINE (87*GUESS-51,35)-(87*GUESS+24,184),0,BF
820 IF GUESS <> FLY THEN 1260
830 '
840 ' Another one bytes the dust
850 DELAY=.7370001*DELAY
860 GOSUB 1490
870 LOCATE 3,7
880 PRINT "GOT IT !!!";TAB(37);
890 SPOT=74*GUESS+9
900 FOR I = 0 TO 40
910 FREQ=99*SIN(2.1-I/17)^3+678
920 SOUND 99,0
930 SOUND FREQ,2
940 IF I MOD 3 = 0 THEN DRAW "bm=spot;,67"
950 CLR=INT(3*RND+1)
960 DX=INT(9*RND-4)
970 DY=INT(9*RND-4)
980 DRAW "c=clr; m+=dx;,=dy;"
990 NEXT I
1000 LINE (15,15)-(304,184),0,BF
1010 IF RANK=99 THEN 1620
1020 IF RANK <> 11 THEN 1100
1030 '
1040 ' You made it past the first level of proficiency
1050 RANK=1
```

```
1060 LINE (15,15)-(304,184),0,BF
1070 LOCATE 12,4
1080 PRINT "YOU JUST MADE 'SENIOR DE-BUGGER'!!!"
1090 PLAY"MF O3 T200 L5 MS cde.cffcd.cde.cffcd..."
1100 IF RANK <> 12 THEN 1180
1110 '
1120 ' You made it past the second level of proficiency
1130 RANK=2
1140 LINE (15,15)-(304,184),0,BF
1150 LOCATE 12,4
1160 PRINT "WOW! What a professional! Buzz on!";
1170 PLAY"MF O3 T200 L5 MS ccg.ccg.efgedccffcd..."
1180 LINE (15,15)-(304,184),0,BF
1190 LOCATE 12,4
1200 PRINT "Oh oh! Here comes a faster fly ...";
1210 FOR I = 1 TO 999
1220 NEXT I
1230 GOTO 510
1240 '
1250 ' missed it
1260 DELAY=1.47*DELAY
1270 IF DELAY > 3000 THEN DELAY=3000
1280 GOSUB 1490
1290 LINE (87*FLY-51,35)-(87*FLY+24,184),0,BF
1300 LOCATE 3,7
1310 PRINT "Whoops, it got away.";TAB(37);
1320 SOUND 57,47
1330 FOR I = 1 TO 100
1340 PUT (74*FLY,67),FLY1,PSET
1350 PUT (74*FLY,67),FLY2,PSET
1360 NEXT I
1370 LINE (15,15)-(304,184),0,BF
1380 LOCATE 12,7
1390 IF DELAY = 3000 THEN MISS$="Here comes another one ..."
1400 IF DELAY < 3000 THEN MISS$="Here comes a slower fly ..."
1410 PRINT MISS$;
1420 IF SPEED < 9000 THEN RANK=1
1430 IF SPEED < 8000 THEN RANK=0
1440 FOR I = 1 TO 999
1450 NEXT I
1460 GOTO 510
1470 '
1480 ' Compute score and rank
1490 SPEED=(3000-DELAY)*10/3
1500 IF SPEED < 0 THEN SPEED=0
1510 LOCATE 25,5
1520 PRINT USING "SPEED = ####";SPEED;
```

```
1530 IF SPEED > RECORD THEN RECORD=SPEED
1540 LOCATE 25,22
1550 PRINT USING "RECORD = ####";RECORD;
1560 IF SPEED > 8000 AND RANK < 1 THEN RANK=11
1570 IF SPEED > 9000 AND RANK < 2 THEN RANK=12
1580 IF SPEED > 9999 THEN RANK=99
1590 RETURN
1600 '
1610 ' best score possible!
1620 LOCATE 10,5
1630 PRINT "YOU DID IT!!! NO BUGS LEFT!!!"
1640 LOCATE 12,5
1650 PRINT "Welcome to the S.W.A.T. team !"
1660 PLAY "T169 L9 MS abcdefgacegecacgfedfdfdgdccedabbcaegfc"
1670 BGD = INT(RND * 6)
1680 PLT = INT(RND * 2)
1690 COLOR BGD,PLT
1700 GOTO 1660
1710 '
1720 ' Subroutine, reset random number sequence
1730 RANDOMIZE VAL(MID$(TIME$,4,2) + RIGHT$(TIME$,2))
1740 RETURN
```

DE-JUMBLE

This program is dedicated to those people who have been stumped trying to unscramble the letters in newspaper game sections. For any word that is 3 characters in length, there are 6 possible combinations of those letters. For a word that is 4 characters in length, the number of possible combinations increases to 24. Similarly, a word that is 5 characters in length has 120 possible combinations, and for a word of 6 characters you will find that there is over 700 possible combinations of those letters !!! Of course, most of these combinations are not valid words in the English language!

This program will take any word of up to 6 characters in length and scramble them in every possible way as shown in Fig. 3-6. All of the possible combinations are then printed on the screen. If the word is 6 characters long, it will take a while to cycle through all 46,656 computations the computer needs to perform to display those 720 possible combinations of the letters in the word, so—please be patient!

Once the words are displayed, all you need to do is to visually scan them for a valid English word. Of course, if more than one of the combinations of letters should happen to form a valid word in the English language, you're on your own!

```
100 '***************************************************************
110 '**                 DE-JUMBLE THE NEWSPAPER GAME             **
120 '**                      DE-SCRAMBLER                        **
130 '**                                                          **
140 '**        VERS 1.1                        SEPT 11, 1982     **
150 '***************************************************************
160 '
170 SCREEN 2:KEY OFF:CLS:DEFINT A-Z
180 '
```

```
        FOR THE JUMBLE OF CRMHA
        THERE ARE 120 ANSWERS -

        CRMHA     CRMAH     CRHMA     CRHAM     CRAMH
        CRAHM     CMRHA     CMRAH     CMHRA     CMHAR
        CMARH     CMAHR     CHRMA     CHRAM     CHMRA
        CHMAR     CHARM     CHAMR     CARMH     CARHM
        CAMRH     CAMHR     CAHRM     CAHMR

        RCMHA     RCMAH     RCHMA     RCHAM     RCAMH
        RCAHM     RMCHA     RMCAH     RMHCA     RMHAC
        RMACH     RMAHC     RHCMA     RHCAM     RHMCA
        RHMAC     RHACM     RHAMC     RACMH     RACHM
        RAMCH     RAMHC     RAHCM     RAHMC

        MCRHA     MCRAH     MCHRA     MCHAR     MCARH
        MCAHR     MRCHA     MRCAH     MRHCA     MRHAC
        MRACH     MRAHC     MHCRA     MHCAR     MHRCA
        MHRAC     MHACR     MHARC     MACRH     MACHR
        MARCH     MARHC     MAHCR     MAHRC

        HCRMA     HCRAM     HCMRA     HCMAR     HCARM
        HCAMR     HRCMA     HRCAM     HRMCA     HRMAC
        HRACM     HRAMC     HMCRA     HMCAR     HMRCA
        HMRAC     HMACR     HMARC     HACRM     HACMR
        HARCM     HARMC     HAMCR     HAMRC

        ACRMH     ACRHM     ACMRH     ACMHR     ACHRM
        ACHMR     ARCMH     ARCHM     ARMCH     ARMHC
        ARHCM     ARHMC     AMCRH     AMCHR     AMRCH
        AMRHC     AMHCR     AMHRC     AHCRM     AHCMR
        AHRCM     AHRMC     AHMCR     AHMRC
```

Fig. 3-6. Sample results of the *De-Jumble* program.

```
190 LOCATE 1,10:PRINT "DE-JUMBLE - THE NEWSPAPER PAPER GAME DE-SCRAMBLER"
200 LOCATE 4,8:PRINT "THIS PROGRAM WILL PRINT OUT ALL POSSIBLE COMBINATIONS"
210 LOCATE 5,14:PRINT "OF WORDS FROM UP TO A 6 LETTER 'JUMBLE'"
220 LOCATE 9,14:INPUT "PLEASE ENTER THE 'JUMBLED' WORD HERE -";A$:CLS
230 L=LEN(A$) : ON L GOTO 350,400,460,550,640,730
240 PRINT "I AM SORRY BUT I CAN ONLY HANDLE UP TO A 6 CHARACTER 'JUMBLE'"
250 GOTO 220
260 '
270 '****************************************************************************
280 '
```

```
290 ' THIS PROGRAM CALCULATES ALL OF THE POSSIBLE COMBINATIONS OF THE INPUT
300 ' LETTERS. FROM THESE IT PRINTS ALL COMBINATIONS THAT ARE NOT REPEATS -
310 ' IE. KAS OR SAK FROM ASK, BUT NOT AAS OR SKK ETC.
320 '
330 '*******************************************************************
340 '
350 SCREEN 1
360 PRINT "FOR THE JUMBLE OF ";A$;" THERE IS ONLY ONE ANSWER - "
370 LOCATE 4,1:FOR Z = 1 TO 1000:NEXT Z:PRINT A$:PRINT
380 LOCATE 7,1:INPUT "PRESS ENTER TO CONTINUE";Z$:CLS:GOTO 170
390 '
400 SCREEN 1
410 PRINT "FOR THE JUMBLE OF ";A$:PRINT " THERE ARE 2 ANSWERS - "
420 Y$(1) = MID$(A$,1,1) : Y$(2) = MID$(A$,2,1)
430 LOCATE 4,1:FOR Z = 1 TO 1000:NEXT Z:PRINT Y$(1);Y$(2);"   ";Y$(2);Y$(1)
440 LOCATE 7,1:INPUT "PRESS ENTER TO CONTINUE";Z$:CLS:GOTO 170
450 '
460 SCREEN 1
470 FOR X = 1 TO 3 : A$(X) = MID$(A$,X,1) : NEXT X
480 PRINT "FOR THE JUMBLE OF ";A$:PRINT "THERE ARE 6 ANSWERS - "
490 LOCATE 4,1:FOR L = 1 TO 3 : FOR M = 1 TO 3 : FOR N = 1 TO 3
500 IF (L=M) OR (L=N) OR (M=N) THEN 520
510 PRINT A$(L);A$(M);A$(N);"   ";
520 NEXT N,M,L
530 LOCATE 7,1:INPUT "PRESS ENTER TO CONTINUE";Z$:CLS:GOTO 170
540 '
550 SCREEN 1
560 FOR X = 1 TO 4 : A$(X) = MID$(A$,X,1) : NEXT X
570 PRINT "FOR THE JUMBLE OF ";A$:PRINT "THERE ARE 24 ANSWERS - "
580 LOCATE 4,1:FOR L=1 TO 4:FOR M=1 TO 4:FOR N=1 TO 4:FOR O=1 TO 4
590 IF (L=M) OR (L=N) OR (L=O) OR (M=N) OR (M=O) OR (N=O) THEN 610
600 PRINT A$(L);A$(M);A$(N);A$(O);"     ";
610 NEXT O,N,M,L
620 LOCATE 11,1:INPUT "PRESS ENTER TO CONTINUE";Z$:CLS:GOTO 170
630 '
640 SCREEN 1
650 FOR X = 1 TO 5 : A$(X) = MID$(A$,X,1) : NEXT X
660 PRINT "FOR THE JUMBLE OF ";A$:PRINT "THERE ARE 120 ANSWERS - "
670 LOCATE 4,1:FOR L=1 TO 5:FOR M=1 TO 5:FOR N=1 TO 5:FOR O=1 TO 5:
    FOR P=1 TO 5
680 IF (L=M) OR (L=N) OR (L=O) OR (L=P) OR (M=N) OR (M=O) OR (M=P) OR
    (N=O) OR (N=P) OR (O=P) THEN 700
690 PRINT A$(L);A$(M);A$(N);A$(O);A$(P);"     ";
700 NEXT P,O,N,M :PRINT:PRINT:NEXT L
710 PRINT : INPUT "PRESS ENTER TO CONTINUE";Z$:CLS:GOTO 170
720 '
730 SCREEN 1
```

```
740 FOR X = 1 TO 6 : A$(X) = MID$(A$,X,1) : NEXT X
750 PRINT "FOR THE JUMBLE OF ";A$:PRINT "THERE ARE 720 ANSWERS - "
760 LOCATE 4,1:FOR L = 1 TO 6 : FOR M = 1 TO 6 : PRINT :PRINT :
    FOR N = 1 TO 6 :FOR O = 1 TO 6 : FOR P = 1 TO 6 : FOR Q = 1 TO 6
770 IF L=M OR L=N OR L=O OR L=P OR L=Q OR M=N OR M=O OR M=P OR M=Q OR
       N=O OR N=P OR N=Q OR O=P OR O=Q OR P=Q THEN 790
780 PRINT A$(L);A$(M);A$(N);A$(O);A$(P);A$(Q);"   ";
790 NEXT Q,P,O,N,M,L
800 INPUT "PRESS ENTER TO CONTINUE - ";Z$:CLS:GOTO 170
810 '
```

OUT ON A LEM

One advantageous feature of computers is the ability to simulate dangerous, expensive, or time-consuming events. A new bridge design can be mathematically simulated to test for strength in high winds. If it "crumbles" inside the computer a lot of time, money, and maybe even lives will have been saved.

This program lets you safely practice your space pilot skills. There's no big loss if you "crumble" and dig a crater with your lunar excursion module. To correct the situation, all you have to do is run the

```
* * *  OUT ON A LEM  * * *


A challenging game of skill ...

Use the special function keys F1
through F3 to run your left, right,
and vertical thrusters.  You are to
land the lunar excursion module (LEM)
as gently and accurately as possible.

Turn a given thruster off by pressing
the same key a second time.

Watch your fuel supply!

If you have fuel left, the onboard
computer will -attempt- to return
you to earth ...



             Press any key to begin
```

Fig. 3-7. The instructions for the LEM program.

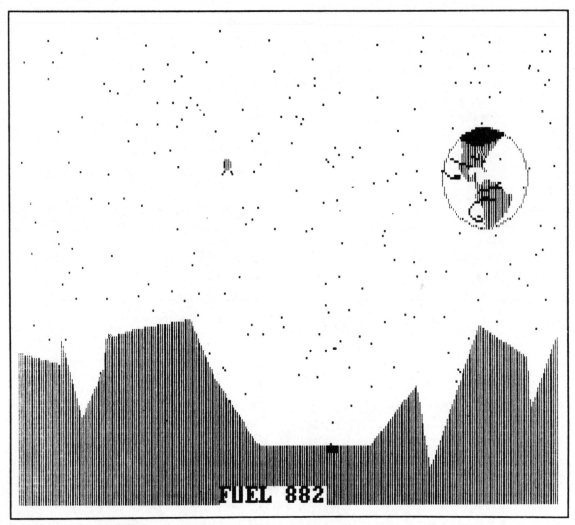

Fig. 3-8. Display produced by the *LEM* program.

program again! The landing is "real time", which means you must react at the proper time to turn your engines off and on. The landing skills are easy to learn, but difficult to master. Figure 3-7 through 3-10 show you what might happen to you when you play. Have fun!

Graphics programmers should take a close look at the LEM image (the lunar excursion module) as it drifts across the screen. Notice that as the image passes over the stars, they are unaffected. In fact, if you fly over the face of the earth, you'll notice that the image of the earth is unaffected. The reason for this effect is that the LEM image is "put" onto the screen using the XOR option. To erase the image, just before redrawing it in a new position, the image is "put" a second time at the same location, again using the XOR option. An interesting thing happens when an image is "put" to the screen twice using the XOR option . . . nothing; that is, the original background graphics returns undisturbed. This same technique is used to draw and erase the engine exhaust lines around the LEM. This technique opens lots of doors for many action graphics programs.

70

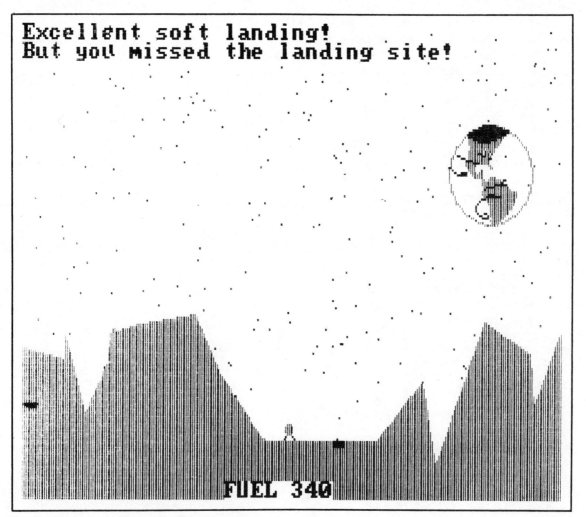

Fig. 3-9. Display produced by the *LEM* program.

```
10 ' ****************
20 ' **    LEM    **
30 ' ****************
40 '
50 SCREEN 1
60 CLS
70 KEY OFF
80 LOCATE 2,7
90 PRINT "* * *  OUT ON A LEM  * * *
100 LOCATE 5,1
110 PRINT "A challenging game of skill ...
120 LOCATE 7,1
130 PRINT "Use the special function keys F1
```

```
140 PRINT "through F3 to run your left, right,
150 PRINT "and vertical thrusters.  You are to
160 PRINT "land the lunar excursion module (LEM)
170 PRINT "as gently and accurately as possible.
180 PRINT
190 PRINT "Turn a given thruster off by pressing
200 PRINT "the same key a second time.
210 PRINT
220 PRINT "Watch your fuel supply!
230 PRINT
240 PRINT "If you have fuel left, the onboard
250 PRINT "computer will -attempt- to return
260 PRINT "you to earth ...
270 '
280 LOCATE 25,9
290 PRINT "Press any key to begin";
300 '
310 ' Starting point for each landing attempt
320 IF LEN(INKEY$) THEN 320
330 K$ = INKEY$
340 IF K$ = "" THEN 330
350 '
360 COLOR 0,1
370 CLS
380 '
390 ' Activate engine keys
400 ON KEY(1) GOSUB 1990
410 ON KEY(2) GOSUB 2030
420 ON KEY(3) GOSUB 2070
430 KEY (1) ON
440 KEY (2) ON
450 KEY (3) ON
460 '
470 ' A different game each second of the hour
480 T$ = MID$(TIME$,4,2) + MID$(TIME$,7)
490 RANDOMIZE VAL(T$)
500 '
510 ' Build the space ship image
520 LINE (3,1)-(5,5),2,BF
530 LINE (2,2)-(6,4),2,BF
540 LINE (1,7)-(2,6),3
550 LINE (6,6)-(7,7),3
560 DIM SHIP(7)
570 GET (0,0)-(8,8),SHIP
580 '
590 ' Build vertical exhaust image
600 LINE (9,1)-(11,1)
```

```
610 DIM EXHAUSTX(1)
620 GET (9,1)-(11,1),EXHAUSTX
630 '
640 ' Build horizontal exhaust image
650 LINE (1,9)-(1,12)
660 DIM EXHAUSTY(1)
670 GET (1,9)-(1,12),EXHAUSTY
680 '
690 ' Sprinkle a few stars around
700 CLS
710 FOR I = 1 TO 300
720 PSET (320*RND,200*RND)
730 NEXT I
740 '
750 ' Draw the earth
760 CIRCLE (277,63),25,1
770 PAINT (277,63),1
780 DRAW "c3bm272,42r7d1r4l13d1l4r22d1l24g1r2313d1l20"
790 DRAW "r3d1r14l4d1l8c2l3u1l1d2r18e3l1g1l12f1l15d2r4"
800 DRAW "l16d1r14d1l15d1r14g1l13d1r13g1l13"
810 DRAW "d1r13f2l1h3l3g1l18d1r6g1l14f1r3f1l13f1r6u2l1d1l1"
820 DRAW "d2l3r5d1r1g1r1l312u1l17e1r3d3r7l15f1r15f1l16"
830 DRAW "g1r21d1l21f1r20g1l18f1r17g1l15"
840 DRAW "f1r13d1l13d1r11d1l11d1r9g1l17g1r6g1l14d1r2l15"
850 DRAW "bm273,54c1u1e1r1f2"
860 DRAW "c3bd2l2b12bu1l2h1l1bd4l3h1l3h1l2h1l1"
870 DRAW "bg5r1f2r1f1r5u1l13"
880 DRAW "bm273,79r1f1d1l13h1l1h2u2e3r2e1r9l3h1l14"
890 DRAW "bh2e1r4e1r7l3e2r1"
900 '
910 ' Choose site for landing pad
920 XL = 140 + 50 * RND
930 YL = 180 - 10 * RND
940 '
950 ' Create topographical features of moon
960 M1 = M2
970 M2 = M1 + 37 * RND
980 IF M2 > 319 THEN M2 = 319
990 H1 = H2
1000 H2 = 190 - 70 * RND
1010 IF H1 = 0 THEN 990
1020 IF M2 < XL - 39 THEN 1050
1030 IF M2 > XL + 39 THEN 1050
1040 H2 = YL
1050 LINE (M1,H1)-(M2,H2),1
1060 IF M2 < 319 THEN 960
1070 PAINT (0,199),1
```

```
1080 '
1090 ' Draw the landing pad
1100 LINE (XL-3,YL)-(XL+3,YL+2),,BF
1110 '
1120 ' Slightly random starting location for ship
1130 SHIPX = 50 * RND
1140 SHIPY = 20 * RND
1150 '
1160 ' Slightly random starting velocity for ship
1170 VELX = 7 + RND * 3
1180 VELY = 1 + RND
1190 '
1200 ' Starting conditions
1210 PUT (SHIPX,SHIPY),SHIP,XOR
1220 FACTOR = .1
1230 FUEL = 999
1240 THRUSTUP = 3
1250 '
1260 ' Main flight loop starts here
1270 PULSE = PULSE MOD 7 + 1
1280 IF PULSE = 1 THEN SOUND 1200-FUEL/5,1
1290 IF THRUSTUP < 0 THEN FUEL = FUEL - 9.7
1300 IF THRUSTSIDE THEN FUEL = FUEL - 5.3
1310 IF FUEL < 0 THEN FUEL = 0
1320 IF FUEL > 99 THEN 1460
1330 SOUND 99,0
1340 IF FUEL > 0 THEN SOUND 400,1
1350 IF FUEL > 0 THEN 1460
1360 '
1370 ' No more fuel left, disengage engines
1380 SOUND 2000,1
1390 KEY (1) OFF
1400 KEY (2) OFF
1410 KEY (3) OFF
1420 THRUSTUP = 3
1430 THRUSTSIDE = 0
1440 '
1450 ' Compute new velocities and positions
1460 VELX = VELX + FACTOR * THRUSTSIDE * 3
1470 OLDX = SHIPX
1480 SHIPX = SHIPX + FACTOR * VELX * 3
1490 VELY = VELY + FACTOR * THRUSTUP
1500 OLDY = SHIPY
1510 SHIPY = SHIPY + FACTOR * VELY
1520 '
1530 ' Put exhaust images in view if necessary
1540 IF THRUSTSIDE < 0 THEN PUT (SHIPX+7,SHIPY+3),EXHAUSTX,XOR : FLGL = 1
```

```
1550 IF THRUSTSIDE > Ø THEN PUT (SHIPX-2,SHIPY+3),EXHAUSTX,XOR : FLGR = 1
1560 IF THRUSTUP < Ø THEN PUT (SHIPX+4,SHIPY+7),EXHAUSTY,XOR : FLGU = 1
1570 '
1580 ' Have we drifted off screen?
1590 IF SHIPY < Ø THEN 1910
1600 IF SHIPX < 2 THEN 1910
1610 IF SHIPX > 308 THEN 1910
1620 '
1630 ' Erase old ship image via XOR to preserve background
1640 PUT (OLDX,OLDY),SHIP,XOR
1650 '
1660 ' Draw new ship image, XOR onto background
1670 PUT (SHIPX,SHIPY),SHIP,XOR
1680 '
1690 ' Erase the exhaust images if necessary
1700 IF FLGL THEN PUT (SHIPX+7,SHIPY+3),EXHAUSTX,XOR : FLGL = Ø
1710 IF FLGR THEN PUT (SHIPX-2,SHIPY+3),EXHAUSTX,XOR : FLGR = Ø
1720 IF FLGU THEN PUT (SHIPX+4,SHIPY+7),EXHAUSTY,XOR : FLGU = Ø
1730 '
1740 ' Skip landing check for awhile if returning to earth
1750 IF LAND <= Ø THEN 1800
1760 LAND = LAND - .Ø7
1770 GOTO 1840
1780 '
1790 ' Are landing pads touching the moon (and not the earth)?
1800 IF POINT (SHIPX,SHIPY+8) = 1  AND SHIPY > 85 THEN 2110
1810 IF POINT (SHIPX+8,SHIPY+8) = 1 AND SHIPY > 85 THEN 2110
1820 '
1830 ' Update the fuel supply
1840 LOCATE 25,16
1850 PRINT USING "FUEL ###";FUEL;
1860 '
1870 ' Keep on flying
1880 GOTO 1270
1890 '
1900 ' We just drifted off screen
1910 CLS
1920 LOCATE 12,4
1930 IF LAND = Ø THEN PRINT "MISSION ABORTED, RETURN TO EARTH"
1940 IF LAND <> Ø THEN PRINT "        WELCOME HOME HERO!        "
1950 IF LAND <> Ø THEN PLAY "L4 DEEEDEF L1 E"
1960 RUN 320
1970 '
1980 ' Subroutine F1 ... left engine control
1990 THRUSTSIDE = -(THRUSTSIDE <> 1)
2000 RETURN
2010 '
```

```
2020 ' Subroutine F2 ... right engine control
2030 THRUSTSIDE = (THRUSTSIDE <> -1)
2040 RETURN
2050 '
2060 ' Subroutine F3 ... vertical engine control
2070 THRUSTUP = 7 * (THRUSTUP = 3) - 3 * (THRUSTUP = -7)
2080 RETURN
2090 '
2100 ' We landed! But how did we fare?
2110 LOCATE 1,1
2120 VEL = ABS(VELX) + ABS(VELY)
2130 IF VEL < 4 THEN 2350
2140 '
2150 ' Disintegrating ship, parts streaking out from crater
2160 PRESET (SHIPX+4,SHIPY+8)
2170 FOR I = 1 TO VEL * .7
2180 DELX = 9 * VEL * (RND-.5)
2190 DELY = 7 * VEL * (-RND)
2200 DRAW "C2 NM+=DELX;,=DELY;"
2210 NEXT I
2220 '
2230 ' Fast enough to dig new crater?
2240 IF VEL < 8 THEN 2300
2250 PRT$ = "New crater is #### meters wide ...          "
2260 PRINT USING PRT$ ; VEL * VEL / 7
2270 GOTO 2780
2280 '
2290 ' Landing was too rough, sorry
2300 PRINT "Damaged beyond repair ...            "
2310 PRINT "Enjoy your stay !          ";
2320 GOTO 2780
2330 '
2340 ' Landed ok, just how well did you do?
2350 IF VEL < 3 THEN 2390
2360 PRINT "Fairly soft landing            "
2370 GOTO 2570
2380 '
2390 IF VEL < 2 THEN 2430
2400 PRINT "Nice job! ";
2410 GOTO 2570
2420 '
2430 IF VEL < 1 THEN 2470
2440 PRINT "Excellent soft landing!";
2450 GOTO 2570
2460 '
2470 IF SHIPX-XL+4 < 3 THEN 2510
2480 PRINT "Superior landing job!";
```

```
2490 GOTO 2570
2500 '
2510 PRINT "The President calls with his";
2520 LOCATE 2,1
2530 PRINT "congratulations on a superb landing!";
2540 GOTO 2740
2550 '
2560 ' Ok, so how close to the landing pad are you?
2570 DIS = ABS(SHIPX-XL+4) + ABS(SHIPY-YL+8)
2580 LOCATE 2,1
2590 IF DIS < 50 THEN 2630
2600 PRINT "But you're way out in the boonies!";
2610 GOTO 2740
2620 '
2630 IF DIS < 10 THEN 2670
2640 PRINT "But you missed the landing site!";
2650 GOTO 2740
2660 '
2670 IF DIS < 3 THEN 2710
2680 PRINT USING "But you missed the spot by ## meters.";DIS
2690 GOTO 2740
2700 '
2710 PRINT "And you landed right on target!";
2720 '
2730 ' Music for good landings ...
2740 PLAY "o4t128ml16cmsc#e-.mlc mse-c#c.mlcmsffl1f"
2750 GOTO 2810
2760 '
2770 ' Music for disastrous landings ...
2780 PLAY "mst6416n3n7n3n713n2"
2790 '
2800 ' Shall we try a return to earth?
2810 IF (FUEL <> 0) AND (VEL < 4 ) THEN 2820 ELSE RUN 320
2820 LOCATE 1,1
2830 PRINT "Earth calling - return home              ";
2840 LOCATE 2,1
2850 PRINT "                                         ";
2860 VELX = 0
2870 VELY = -1
2880 LAND = 1
2890 THRUSTUP = -7
2900 THRUSTSIDE = 0
2910 FOR Z = 1 TO 2000
2920 NEXT Z
2930 LOCATE 1,1
2940 PRINT "LEM computer engaged - returning home    ";
2950 KEY (1) OFF
```

```
2960 KEY (2) OFF
2970 KEY (3) OFF
2980 IF LEN(INKEY$) THEN 2980
2990 GOTO 1270
```

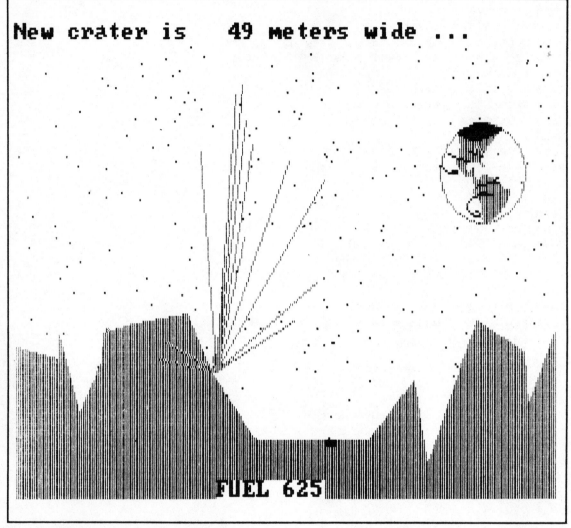

Fig. 3-10. Display produced by the *LEM* program.

TELETYPE

Whether you use this program as an eye-catcher or as a fun way to send messages, *Teletype* is an interesting way to get your point across. This program simulates the sight and sound of a mechanical teletype or impact printer. The information that you want to display is sorted in data strings located at the end of the program, but this could be easily changed to enable the program to read the message from a disk or cassette and print it out to the screen.

```
100 '*****************************************************
110 '**                     TELETYPE                   **
120 '**   NOVEMBER 5, 1982              VERSION 1.1   **
130 '*****************************************************
140 '
150 CLS : SCREEN Ø : WIDTH 80 : KEY OFF
160 ON ERROR GOTO 300
170 FOR X = 1 TO 23
180 READ A$
190 FOR Y = 1 TO LEN(A$)
200 B$ = MID$(A$,Y,1)
210 PRINT B$;
220 IF B$ <> " " THEN SOUND 800,1
230 FOR Z = 1 TO 85 : NEXT Z
240 NEXT Y
250 FOR Z = 1 TO 500 : NEXT Z
260 IF X = 23 THEN LOCATE 25,1 : INPUT "PRESS ENTER TO CONTINUE - ";C$:CLS
270 PRINT
280 NEXT X
290 GOTO 170
300 LOCATE 25,1 : INPUT "PRESS ENTER TO CONTINUE - ";C$ : CLS : END
310 DATA "NOW IS THE TIME FOR ALL GOOD MEN TO COME TO THE AID OF THEIR PARTY."
320 DATA " "
330 DATA "WE THE PEOPLE OF THE UNITED STATES IN ORDER TO FORM A MORE PERFECT"
340 DATA "UNION, ESTABLISH JUSTICE, INSURE DOMESTIC TRANQUILITY, PROVIDE FOR"
350 DATA "THE COMMON DEFENSE, PROMOTE THE GENERAL WELFARE, AND SECURE THE "
360 DATA "BLESSINGS OF LIBERTY TO OURSELVES AND OUR POSTERITY, DO ORDAIN AND"
370 DATA "ESTABLISH THIS CONSTITUTION FOR THE UNITED STATES OF AMERICA."
```

TONE GAME

This program plays a musical game in which you attempt to repeat a sequence of tones output by the computer. If you are successful at repeating the sequence, the computer will add a new tone to the list and have you repeat it. As you progress in the game, the sequence of tones runs faster and faster. By the time you have achieved the final and 32nd level, you can count yourself a master of memory.

But, if you miss a tone, you have to start over . . . Good Luck!

```
100 '*****************************************************
110 '**                    TONE MATCH                  **
120 '**   NOVEMBER 24, 1982            VERSION 2.Ø    **
130 '*****************************************************
140 '
150 RANDOMIZE : CLS : SCREEN 1
160 LOCATE 10,15 : PRINT "TONE MATCH"
170 DIM A(100)
180 COUNTER = 1
190 A(COUNTER) = INT(RND*4+1)
```

```
200 TEMPO = 5-COUNTER/4 : IF TEMPO < 2 THEN TEMPO = 2
210 GOSUB 410  '*********  PRINT LIST OF SOUNDS AND NUMBERS
220 '
230 '*******************  ROUTINE TO ACCEPT GUESS
240 FOR X = 1 TO COUNTER
250 B$ = INKEY$ : IF B$ = "" THEN 250 ELSE B = VAL(B$)
260 IF A(X) <> B THEN SOUND 50,30 : GOTO 350
270 SOUND 250+250*A(X),TEMPO
280 NEXT
290 COUNTER = COUNTER + 1
300 SOUND 25000,25
310 IF COUNTER > 32 THEN FOR X = 40 TO 2000 STEP 10:SOUND X,1:NEXT:GOTO 180
320 GOTO 190  '*********  GOOD SEQUENCE, CONTINUE ON
330 '
340 '*******************  INCORRECT INPUT HANDLING SECTION
350 SOUND 25000,25      '**
360 GOSUB 410           '**  PRINT LIST OF SOUNDS AND NUMBERS
370 SOUND 25000,25      '**
380 GOTO 180            '**  START OVER
390 '
400 '*******************  ROUTINE TO PRINT NUMBERS AND CREATE SOUNDS
410 FOR X = 1 TO COUNTER
420 SOUND 250+250*A(X),TEMPO
430 LOCATE 12,A(X)*2+14 : PRINT A(X);
440 SOUND 25000,TEMPO
450 LOCATE 12,14 : PRINT "                    "
460 NEXT
470 RETURN
```

TRAX

This is a game which requires skill and a good memory. The object of the game is to find the Trax Monsters hidden on a 10 × 10 grid playing surface. The monsters will be randomly placed around the board, and the only clue to where they are hiding will be in the form of a distance given from their hiding place to where you guessed. If you guess one of their hiding places, the word **FOUND** will appear beside the appropriate monster's number and a face will appear on the board to signify a hit. If you miss, an asterisk will be placed in the correct location on the board.

For example, if one of the monsters was hiding at 7,4 on the board and you guessed 3,2, the game would give you a distance missed of the square root of $((7-3)^2+(4-2)^2)$ or 4.47 units. This is simply the distance between the two points according to the formula for the length of the hypotenuse of a triangle, $C^2 = A^2 + B^2$. The on-screen display is shown in Fig. 3-11.

The program demonstrates the use of two routines explained elsewhere in the book. First, the label **TRAX** is printed in large 8 × 8 sized letters by using the *Message* program; and second, the data is formatted for input with the *Data-in* program listed and explained later in the book.

The program is composed of five subroutines and a final major section that plays the game. The five subroutines set the screen for the game and create the playing field and necessary labels. The last section accepts input, updates the screen as necessary, and restarts the game after a win if requested to.

```
TTTTT   RRRRRR     AA       XX      XX
T TT T    RR  RR   AAAA       XX    XX
   TT     RR   RR  AA  AA      XX  XX
   TT     RRRRR    AA  AA       XXX
   TT     RR  RR   AAAAAA       XXX
   TT     RR   RR  AA   AA     XX  XX
  TTTT    RRR  RR  AA   AA    XX    XX


  \~~~~~/        #1 =   5.39        0 XXXXXXXXXX
   \   /                            1 XXXXXXXXXX
    \ /          #2 =  FOUND        2 XXXXXXXXXX
  /     \                           3 XXXXXXX*XX
 / [] [] \       #3 =   1.00        4 XXXXXXXXXX
 =   *   =                          5 XX*XXXXXXX
 =       =       #4 =   5.00        6 XXXXXXXXXX
 = ***** =                          7 XXXXXXXXXX
  \     /        #5 =   8.06        8 XXXXXXX?XX
   \   /                            9 XXXXXXXXXX


     LAST GUESS = 8,7              0123456789

     ENTER YOUR SHOT   (↓,►)  7,7
```

Fig. 3-11. Display produced by the *Trax* program.

```
1 '**********************************************
2 '**                    TRAX                **
3 '**                                        **
4 '**   VERSION 1.1              JULY 7, 1982 **
5 '**********************************************
10 KEY OFF : CLS : SCREEN 2
20 RANDOMIZE : CLS : SCREEN 1
30 GOSUB 1000  ' SCAN AND PRINT THE LETTERS 'TRAX' IN 8X8 FORMAT
40 GOSUB 2000  ' DRAW A BOX AROUND THE SCREEN
50 GOSUB 3000  ' DRAW THE 'TRAX' FACE
60 GOSUB 4000  ' DRAW THE PLAYING FIELD
70 GOSUB 5000  ' PRINT THE LABLES FOR THE SCREEN
80 GOTO  6000  ' PLAY THE GAME
90 '
```

```
1000 '*************************************************
1010 '**   THIS SECTION SCANS FOR THE PATTERN FOR   **
1020 '**   THE LETTERS OF 'TRAX'                    **
1030 '*************************************************
1040 A$ = "TRAX"
1050 B$ = ""
1060 FOR S = 1 TO 4 : B$ = B$ + MID$(A$,S,1) : NEXT
1070 A$ = B$
1080 FOR S = LEN(A$) + 1 TO 4
1090 A$ = A$ + " "
1100 NEXT
1110 DEF SEG = &HF000      ' LAST 64K OF MEMORY MAP
1120 TABLE = &HFA6E        ' LOCATION OF FIRST CHARACTER
1130 X = 2 : Y = 5 : LOCATE X,Y
1140 FOR CHARACTER = 1 TO 4              ' FOR EACH CHARACTER
1150 A = ASC(MID$(A$,CHARACTER,1))     ' GET THE ASCII VALUE
1160 CODE = TABLE + A * 8               ' POINT INTO THE TABLE
1170 FOR BYTE = 0 TO 7                  ' FOR EACH BYTE
1180 PATTERN = PEEK (CODE + BYTE)
1190 LOCATE X,Y
1200 IF PATTERN < 128 THEN PRINT " ";:GOTO 1230
1210 PRINT CHR$(A);
1220 PATTERN = PATTERN - 128
1230 IF PATTERN < 64 THEN PRINT " ";:GOTO 1260
1240 PRINT CHR$(A);
1250 PATTERN = PATTERN - 64
1260 IF PATTERN < 32 THEN PRINT " ";:GOTO 1290
1270 PRINT CHR$(A);
1280 PATTERN = PATTERN - 32
1290 IF PATTERN < 16 THEN PRINT " ";:GOTO 1320
1300 PRINT CHR$(A);
1310 PATTERN = PATTERN - 16
1320 IF PATTERN < 8 THEN PRINT " ";:GOTO 1350
1330 PRINT CHR$(A);
1340 PATTERN = PATTERN - 8
1350 IF PATTERN < 4 THEN PRINT " ";:GOTO 1380
1360 PRINT CHR$(A);
1370 PATTERN = PATTERN - 4
1380 IF PATTERN < 2 THEN PRINT " ";:GOTO 1410
1390 PRINT CHR$(A);
1400 PATTERN = PATTERN - 2
1410 IF PATTERN < 1 THEN PRINT " ";:GOTO 1430
1420 PRINT CHR$(A);
1430 PATTERN = PATTERN - 1
1440 X = X + 1
1450 NEXT BYTE
1460 X = X - 8 : Y = Y + 8 : IF Y > 35 THEN X = X + 8 : Y = 1
```

```
1470 NEXT CHARACTER
1480 RETURN
2000 '************************************************
2010 '**    THIS SECTION DRAWS A BOX AROUND THE      **
2020 '**    SCREEN                                   **
2030 '************************************************
2040 LINE (0,0)-(319,0)
2050 LINE -(319,199)
2060 LINE -(0,199)
2070 LINE -(0,0)
2080 RETURN
3000 '************************************************
3010 '**    THIS SECTION DRAWS THE TRAX MONSTER      **
3020 '************************************************
3030 A1$ = " \~~~~~/ " : LOCATE 12,4 : PRINT A1$;
3040 A2$ = "  \    /  " : LOCATE 13,4 : PRINT A2$;
3050 A3$ = "   _\_/_  " : LOCATE 14,4 : PRINT A3$;
3060 A4$ = " /      \ " : LOCATE 15,4 : PRINT A4$;
3070 A5$ = "= [] [] =" : LOCATE 16,4 : PRINT A5$;
3080 A6$ = "=    *   =" : LOCATE 17,4 : PRINT A6$;
3090 A7$ = "= ***** =" : LOCATE 18,4 : PRINT A7$;
3100 A8$ = "= ***** =" : LOCATE 19,4 : PRINT A8$;
3110 A9$ = " \_____/ " : LOCATE 20,4 : PRINT A9$;
3120 RETURN
4000 '************************************************
4010 '**    THIS SECTION DRAWS THE PLAYING FIELD     **
4020 '************************************************
4030 A10$ = "XXXXXXXXXX"
4040 LOCATE 11,30 : PRINT A10$;
4050 LOCATE 12,30 : PRINT A10$;
4060 LOCATE 13,30 : PRINT A10$;
4070 LOCATE 14,30 : PRINT A10$;
4080 LOCATE 15,30 : PRINT A10$;
4090 LOCATE 16,30 : PRINT A10$;
4100 LOCATE 17,30 : PRINT A10$;
4110 LOCATE 18,30 : PRINT A10$;
4120 LOCATE 19,30 : PRINT A10$;
4130 LOCATE 20,30 : PRINT A10$;
4140 LOCATE 22,30 : PRINT "0123456789";
4150 FOR X = 0 TO 9 : LOCATE X+11,28 : PRINT CHR$(X+48) : NEXT
4160 RETURN
5000 '************************************************
5010 '**    THIS SECTION PRINTS THE LABLES           **
5020 '************************************************
5030 LOCATE 12,15 : PRINT "#1 =";
5040 LOCATE 14,15 : PRINT "#2 =";
5050 LOCATE 16,15 : PRINT "#3 =";
```

```
5060 LOCATE 18,15 : PRINT "#4 =";
5070 LOCATE 20,15 : PRINT "#5 =";
5080 RETURN
6000 '*********************************************
6010 '**   THIS SECTION PLAYS THE GAME            **
6020 '*********************************************
6030 FOR A = 1 TO 15
6040 B = RND * 9 + 1
6050 C = RND * 9 + 1
6060 LOCATE 10+B,29+C : PRINT CHR$(2);
6070 A5$ = "= -- -- =" : LOCATE 16,4 : PRINT A5$;
6080 FOR X = 1 TO 100 : NEXT X
6090 LOCATE 10+B,29+C : PRINT CHR$(88);
6100 A5$ = "= [] [] =" : LOCATE 16,4 : PRINT A5$;
6110 FOR X = 1 TO 100 : NEXT X
6120 NEXT A
6130 A7$ = "=        =" : LOCATE 18,4 : PRINT A7$;
6140 A8$ = "= ***** =" : LOCATE 19,4 : PRINT A8$;
6150 LOCATE 24,5 : PRINT "ENTER YOUR SHOT   (";CHR$(25);",";CHR$(16);")";
6160 FOR X = 1 TO 10 : A(X) = INT (RND * 9 + 1) : NEXT
6170 FOR X = 1 TO 5 : FOUND(X) = 1 : NEXT
6180 ROW = 24 : COLUMN = 29 : LENGTH = 3
6190 GOSUB 7000
6200 IF LEN(B$) <> 3 THEN GOTO 6190
6210 IF (ASC(MID$(B$,1,1)) < 48) OR (ASC(MID$(B$,1,1)) > 57) THEN GOTO 6190
6220 IF (ASC(MID$(B$,3,1)) < 48) OR (ASC(MID$(B$,3,1)) > 57) THEN GOTO 6190
6230 IF (ASC(MID$(B$,2,1)) <> 44) THEN GOTO 6190
6240 XPOS = ASC(MID$(B$,1,1))-48
6250 YPOS = ASC(MID$(B$,3,1))-48 : LOCATE 22,7 : PRINT "LAST GUESS = " ;B$;
6260 FOR X = 1 TO 5
6270 IF FOUND (X) = 0 THEN 6360
6280 DISTANCE = SQR ( (XPOS-A(X))^2 + (YPOS-A(X+5))^2 )
6290 IF DISTANCE <> 0 THEN 6340
6300 FOUND(X) = 0
6310 LOCATE 10+2*X,20 : PRINT "FOUND";
6320 LOCATE 11+XPOS,30+YPOS : PRINT CHR$(1); : X = 5
6330 GOTO 6360
6340 LOCATE 10+2*X,20 : PRINT USING "##.##";DISTANCE
6350 LOCATE 11+XPOS,30+YPOS : PRINT "*";
6360 NEXT X
6370 FOUND = 0
6380 FOR X = 1 TO 5 : FOUND = FOUND + FOUND(X) : NEXT
6390 IF FOUND <> 0 THEN 6180
6400 FOR X = 1 TO 10 : FOR Y = 1 TO 10
6410 LOCATE X+10,Y+29 : PRINT " ";
6420 FOR Z = 1 TO 50 : NEXT Z
6430 NEXT Y : NEXT X
```

```
6440 LOCATE 24,5 : PRINT "ANOTHER GAME (Y/N) ?                    ";
6450 ROW = 24 : COLUMN = 26 : LENGTH = 1
6460 GOSUB 7000
6470 IF B$ = "Y" OR B$ ="y" THEN GOTO 50 ELSE CLS : END
7000 '***********************************************
7010 '**   THIS SECTION GETS THE INPUT COORDINATES **
7020 '***********************************************
7030 B$ = ""
7040 FOR X = 1 TO LENGTH
7050 B$ = B$ + "-"
7060 NEXT X
7070 LOCATE ROW,COLUMN
7080 PRINT B$;
7090 POINTER = 1 : A$ = " "
7100 WHILE (ASC(A$) <> 13)
7110 A$ = INPUT$(1)
7120 IF (POINTER > LENGTH) AND (ASC(A$) = 13) THEN 7240
7130 IF (POINTER > LENGTH) AND (ASC(A$) = 8) THEN 7190
7140 IF (POINTER > LENGTH) THEN 7240
7150 IF (ASC(A$) >= 32) THEN MID$(B$,POINTER,1) = A$ :
     POINTER = POINTER + 1 :  GOTO 7220
7160 IF (POINTER = 1) AND (ASC(A$) = 8) GOTO 7220
7170 IF (ASC(A$) <> 8) THEN 7210
7180    MID$(B$,POINTER,1) = "-"
7190    MID$(B$,POINTER-1,1) = "-"
7200    POINTER = POINTER -1
7210 IF (ASC(A$) = 13) THEN B$ = MID$(B$,1,POINTER-1) : POINTER = LENGTH + 1
7220 LOCATE ROW,COLUMN
7230 PRINT B$;
7240 WEND
7250 RETURN
```

WATCHOUT

This program is an arcade type game set up with several options of play. You may choose to play against the computer or against another human player, with or without border lines, obstacles, and sound effects. There are eight combinations of these options. The program will have you select one combination before the game starts.

There are two players on the screen, one red and one green. (If you have a black and white monitor, delete the color statements in lines 80 and 490. The game still plays well in black and white.) There's just one rule to remember . . . Don't run into anything! As the players advance, they leave a red or green path. Don't run into either of these paths, the border, or obstacles if present. You can't stop your player, the only control you have is turning left or right relative to the direction of travel. So, try to surround your opponent while preserving any free space you can. Eventually, someone will run into something. Pieces will fly; crashing sounds will be heard; and the opponent will rack up some points. The points scored increase with the lengths of the paths, so hang in there as long as possible. Figures 3-12 and 3-13 show the final displays in two games.

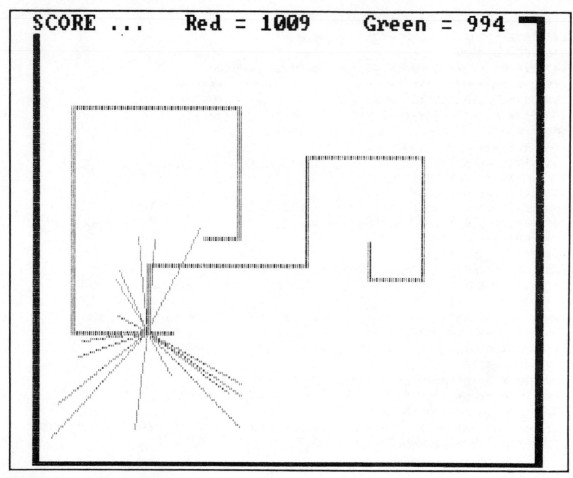

Fig. 3-12. Sample *Watchout* game.

```
10 ' ***********************
20 ' **     WATCHOUT      **
30 ' ***********************
40 '
50 CLEAR
60 DEFINT A-Z
70 SCREEN 1
80 COLOR 0,1
90 KEY OFF
100 CLS
110 LOCATE 3,17
120 PRINT "Z A P P"
130 PRINT
140 PRINT
150 PRINT "Select the game ...
```

```
160 PRINT
170 PRINT "GAME        1    2    3    4    5    6    7    8
180 PRINT
190 PRINT "Players   one  one  one  one  two  two  two  two";
200 PRINT "Border     no   no  yes  yes   no   no  yes  yes";
210 PRINT "Blocks     no  yes   no  yes   no  yes   no  yes";
220 K$ = INKEY$
230 IF K$ = "" THEN 220
240 IF K$ < "1" OR K$ > "8" THEN 220
250 IF K$ < "5" THEN PLAYERS = 1 ELSE PLAYERS = 2
260 IF K$ < "3" OR (K$ > "4" AND K$ < "7") THEN BORDER = Ø ELSE BORDER = 1
270 IF VAL(K$) / 2 - INT(VAL(K$)/2) THEN BLOCKS = Ø ELSE BLOCKS = 1
280 PRINT
290 PRINT "Game selected ... ";K$
300 PRINT
310 PRINT "Do you want sound effects ?   ";
320 K$ = INKEY$
330 IF K$ = "" THEN 320
340 IF INSTR("NnYy",K$) = Ø THEN 320
350 NOISE = -(INSTR("NnYy",K$) > 2)
360 IF NOISE THEN PRINT "YES" ELSE PRINT "NO"
370 PRINT
380 IF PLAYERS = 1 THEN 400
390 PRINT "Red    plays the '\' and 'z' keys.
400 PRINT "Green plays the '.' and '/' keys.
410 PRINT "(for left and right turns).
420 PRINT
430 PRINT "PRESS THE SPACE BAR TO BEGIN !";
440 K$ = INKEY$
450 IF K$ <> " " THEN 440
460 '
470 WHILE NOT TIME.TO.QUIT
480 CLS
490 COLOR 1,Ø
500 RANDOMIZE VAL(MID$(TIME$,4,2) + RIGHT$(TIME$,2))
510 RESTORE
520 READ COUNT,XINC,YINC,XA,YA,XB,YB,CRASHFLAG
530 DATA Ø,3,2,210,98,105,98,Ø
540 IF BLOCKS = Ø THEN 670
550 FOR I = 1 TO 3 + RND * 7
560 X1 = (INT(318 * RND) * XINC) MOD 318
570 X2 = (INT(318 * RND) * XINC) MOD 318
580 Y1 = (INT(200 * RND) * YINC) MOD 200
590 Y2 = (INT(200 * RND) * YINC) MOD 200
600 IF X1 > X2 THEN SWAP X1,X2
610 IF Y1 > Y2 THEN SWAP Y1,Y2
620 IF Y1 > 98 OR Y2 < 98 THEN 650
```

```
630 IF X1 <= 105 AND X2 >= 105 THEN 560
640 IF X1 <= 210 AND X2 >= 210 THEN 560
650 LINE (X1,Y1)-(X2,Y2),,BF
660 NEXT I
670 IF BORDER THEN LINE (XINC,YINC)-(318-XINC,200-YINC),,B
680 IF BORDER THEN PAINT (0,0)
690 DXA = INT(RND * 3 - 1)
700 DYA = INT(RND * 3 - 1)
710 IF ABS(DXA) = ABS(DYA) THEN 690
720 DXB = INT(RND * 3 - 1)
730 DYB = INT(RND * 3 - 1)
740 IF ABS(DXB) = ABS(DYB) THEN 720
750 K$ = INKEY$
760 IF K$ <> "" THEN 750
770 '
780 WHILE CRASHFLAG = 0
790 IF NOISE THEN SOUND 37,0
800 K$ = INKEY$
810 TURNS = 0
820 IF K$ = "." THEN SWAP DXA,DYA : DYA = -DYA
830 IF K$ = "/" THEN SWAP DXA,DYA : DXA = -DXA
840 IF PLAYERS = 1 THEN 880
850 IF K$ = "\" THEN SWAP DXB,DYB : DYB = -DYB
860 IF K$ = "z" THEN SWAP DXB,DYB : DXB = -DXB
870 GOTO 980
880 IF K$ <> "." AND K$ <> "/" THEN 910
890 SWAP DXB,DYB
900 IF RND < .5 THEN DYB = -DYB ELSE DXB = - DXB
910 XT = (XB + DXB * XINC + 318) MOD 318
920 YT = (YB + DYB * YINC + 200) MOD 200
930 IF POINT (XT,YT) = 0 THEN 980
940 DXB = -DXB
950 DYB = -DYB
960 TURNS = TURNS + 1
970 IF TURNS < 4 THEN 890
980 XA = (XA + DXA * XINC + 318) MOD 318
990 YA = (YA + DYA * YINC + 200) MOD 200
1000 XB = (XB + DXB * XINC + 318) MOD 318
1010 YB = (YB + DYB * YINC + 200) MOD 200
1020 IF NOISE THEN SOUND 37 + COUNT + COUNT,99
1030 IF POINT (XA,YA) THEN CRASHFLAG = 1
1040 LINE (XA,YA)-(XA+XINC-1,YA+YINC-1),1,BF
1050 IF POINT (XB,YB) THEN CRASHFLAG = 2
1060 LINE (XB,YB)-(XB+XINC-1,YB+YINC-1),2,BF
1070 COUNT = COUNT + 1
1080 WEND
1090 '
```

```
1100 IF NOISE THEN SOUND 37,0
1110 IF CRASHFLAG = 1 THEN PSET (XA,YA)
1120 IF CRASHFLAG = 2 THEN PSET (XB,YB)
1130 FOR I = 1 TO 17
1140 XR = RND * 130 - 65
1150 YR = RND * 100 - 50
1160 DRAW "C=CRASHFLAG;NM+=xr;,=yr;"
1170 IF NOISE THEN SOUND RND * 777 + 2222,1
1180 NEXT I
1190 IF CRASHFLAG = 1 THEN RED = RED + COUNT
1200 IF CRASHFLAG = 2 THEN GRE = GRE + COUNT
1210 LOCATE 1,1
1220 PRINT "SCORE ...   Red =";RED;"   Green =";GRE
1230 FOR DELAY = 1 TO 1111 STEP 5 + 17 * NOISE
1240 IF NOISE AND CRASHFLAG = 1 THEN SOUND 1148 - DELAY,1
1250 IF NOISE AND CRASHFLAG = 2 THEN SOUND 37 + DELAY,1
1260 NEXT DELAY
1270 WEND
```

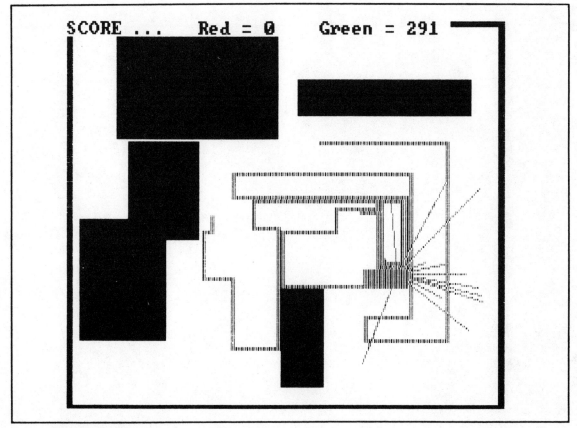

Fig. 3-13. Sample *Watchout* game.

Chapter 4

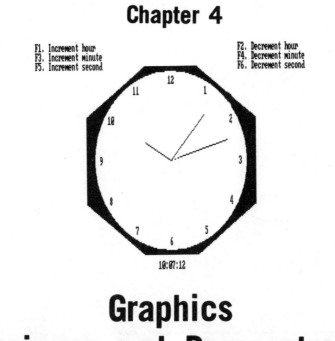

Graphics
Techniques and Demonstrations

The programs in this chapter demonstrate the wealth of graphic abilities the IBM Personal Computer offers you. Different techniques of creating abstract and animated art, graphs, and plots are illustrated.

HIGH-RESOLUTION GRAPHICS

This package of four abstract art programs illustrates a possible solution to the problem of creating very high resolution graphics. The first three programs create different versions of the same graphic. The versions differ in the total number of points computed and graphed, but not in their overall size or shape. The last creates a symmetric view of the figure without the use of the sine function.

The first version plots every fifth horizontal line, producing a graphic that looks as if you cut it with an egg slicer. See Fig. 4-1. This version is great to use while you are trying to create new graphics using this system because it only takes thirty minutes to an hour to create, rather than the usual three hours or so.

The second version of the graphic creates an image that has the appearance of a topographical map as shown in Fig. 4-2. This version is similar to the first except that on every fifth line plotted, the program plots the entire horizontal line.

The third version computes and plots every point in the plot area as defined by the program for a total of 136 × 401 or 54,536 graphic points! Because of the way the program sets the dots on the screen, a sense of shading and realism results as shown in Fig. 4-3.

After the three versions complete their plotting, they save a memory image of the screen to cassette or diskette.

Theory of Operation

The program cycles through two loops. The first loop is a counter for the 136 rows of dots the program

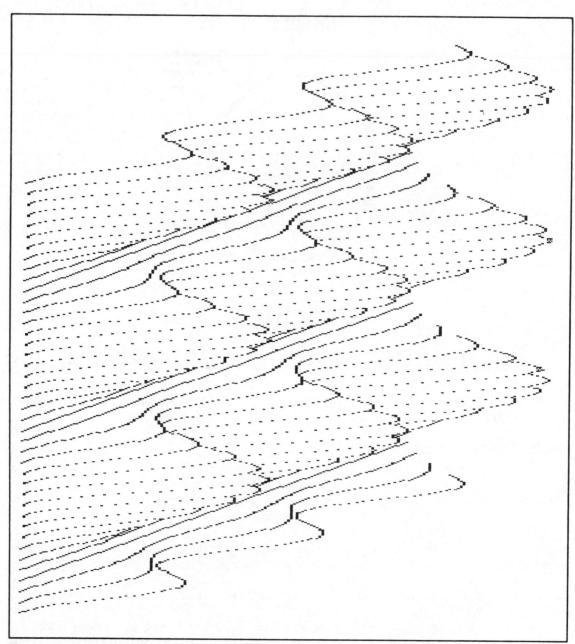

Fig. 4-1. Display produced by the *High-Resolution Graphics* program.

will plot, and the second loop is a counter for the 400 dots in each line. A scale factor is generated for both the x and y directions to be used to make the data fit within the assigned area.

For each position, an x value and a y value are computed. These values are multiplied to give the height of the point. Then the point is plotted with a horizontal position that depends on the row number and the horizontal position of the dot, plus a constant to center the graph. The vertical position is dependent upon the computed height and the row position. Making the horizontal position dependent on the value of the row creates a graph that slopes down and to the right on the screen.

The last function is a simple BSAVE of the video memory. This way the picture can be recreated easily by entering the following:

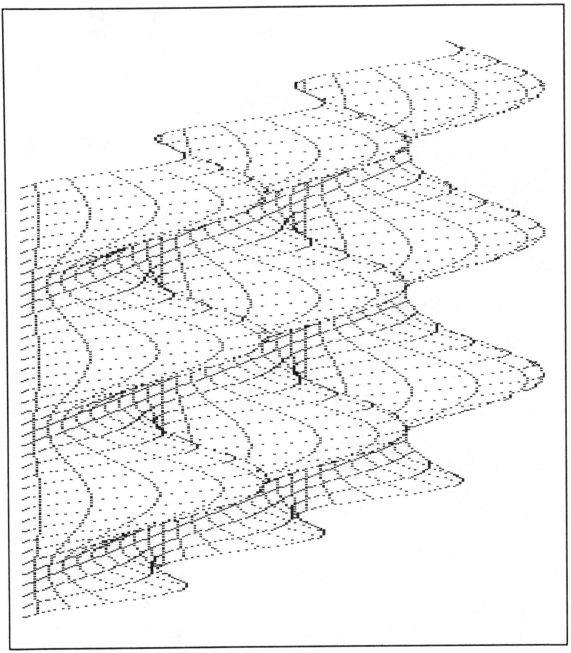

Fig. 4-2. Display produced by the *High-Resolution Graphics* program.

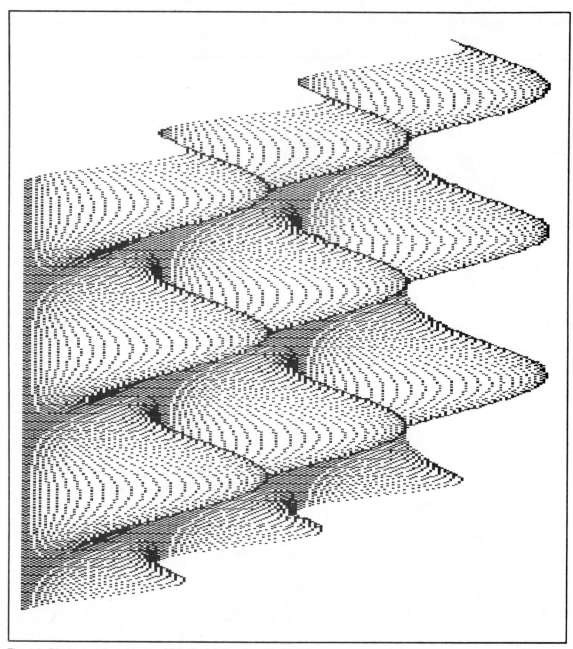

Fig. 4-3. Display produced by the *High-Resolution Graphics* program.

```
10   CLS : SCREEN 2 : KEY OFF
20   DEF SEG = &HB800
30   BLOAD "PIC#1"
40   GOTO 40 (OR THE PRINT DUMP ROUTINE CAN GO HERE)
```

```
50  ’ WARNING : THIS PROGRAM CREATES A 3-D
60  ’ IMAGE BUT REQUIRES 1 HOUR TO DO SO.
70  ’ IT WILL OVERWRITE ANY FILE CALLED
80  ’PIC#1.BAS  ON THE DISK WITH A 16K
90  ’ MEMORY FILE OF THE IMAGE
100 ’**********************************
110 ’**   3-D #01    HI-RES SLICED   **
120 ’**********************************
130 ’**   CREATE + SAVE A PICTURE    **
140 ’**********************************
150 SCREEN 2:KEY OFF:CLS
160 INPUT "Enter the number of humps in the Y direction - " ; A
170 XHUMPS = ABS(A * 6.28318) / 145
180 INPUT "Enter the number of humps in the X direction - " ; A
190 YHUMPS = ABS(A * 6.28318) / 400
200 INPUT "Enter the scale factor for the height - " ; SCALER
210 CLS
220 ’
230 FOR XDIR = 0 TO 135
240 FOR YDIR = 0 TO 400 STEP 5
250 XHEIGHT = SIN(XDIR * XHUMPS) + 1
260 YHEIGHT = SIN(YDIR * YHUMPS) + 1
270 DOT = XDIR + 50
280 HEIGHT = XHEIGHT * YHEIGHT * SCALER
290 LINE (DOT + YDIR,DOT )-(DOT + YDIR,DOT - HEIGHT),0
300 IF YDIR/2 = INT(YDIR/2) THEN PSET(DOT + YDIR,DOT - HEIGHT)
310 NEXT
320 NEXT
330 ’
340 DEF SEG = &HB800
350 BSAVE "PIC#1",0,&H4000
360 GOTO 360
* * * * * * * * * * * * * * * * * * * * * * * * * * * * * * * * * * * * * * * * * * * *
50  ’ WARNING : THIS PROGRAM CREATES A 3-D
60  ’ IMAGE BUT REQUIRES 1 HOUR TO DO SO.
70  ’ IT WILL OVERWRITE ANY FILE CALLED
80  ’PIC#2.BAS  ON THE DISK WITH A 16K
90  ’ MEMORY FILE OF THE IMAGE
100 ’**********************************
110 ’**   3-D #02    TOPOGRAPHICAL   **
120 ’**********************************
130 ’**   CREATE + SAVE A PICTURE    **
140 ’**********************************
150 SCREEN 2:KEY OFF:CLS
160 INPUT "Enter the number of humps in the Y direction - " ; A
170 XHUMPS = ABS(A * 6.28318) / 145
180 INPUT "Enter the number of humps in the X direction - " ; A
```

```
190 YHUMPS = ABS(A * 6.28318) / 400
200 INPUT "Enter the scale factor for the height - " ; SCALER
210 CLS
220 '
230 FOR XDIR = 0 TO 135 : IF XDIR MOD 5 = 0 THEN A = 1 ELSE A = 5
240 FOR YDIR = 0 TO 400 STEP A
250 XHEIGHT = SIN(XDIR * XHUMPS) + 1
260 YHEIGHT = SIN(YDIR * YHUMPS) + 1
270 DOT = XDIR + 50
280 HEIGHT = XHEIGHT * YHEIGHT * SCALER
290 LINE (DOT + YDIR,DOT )-(DOT + YDIR,DOT - HEIGHT),0
300 IF YDIR/2 = INT(YDIR/2) THEN PSET(DOT + YDIR,DOT - HEIGHT)
310 NEXT
320 NEXT
330 '
340 DEF SEG = &HB800
350 BSAVE "PIC#2",0,&H4000
360 GOTO 360
* * * * * * * * * * * * * * * * * * * * * * * * * * * * * * * * * * * * * * * * * * * * * *
50 'WARNING : THIS PROGRAM CREATES A 3-D
60 'IMAGE BUT REQUIRES 3 HOURS TO DO SO.
70 'IT WILL OVERWRITE ANY FILE CALLED
80 'PIC#3.BAS  ON THE DISK WITH A 16K
90 'MEMORY FILE OF THE IMAGE
100 '********************************
110 '**    3-D #03  HIGH RESOLUTION    **
120 '********************************
130 '**    CREATE + SAVE A PICTURE    **
140 '********************************
150 SCREEN 2:KEY OFF:CLS
160 INPUT "Enter the number of humps in the Y direction - " ; A
170 XHUMPS = ABS(A * 6.28318) / 145
180 INPUT "Enter the number of humps in the X direction - " ; A
190 YHUMPS = ABS(A * 6.28318) / 400
200 INPUT "Enter the scale factor for the height - " ; SCALER
210 CLS
220 '
230 FOR XDIR = 0 TO 135
240 FOR YDIR = 0 TO 400
250 XHEIGHT = SIN(XDIR * XHUMPS) + 1
260 YHEIGHT = SIN(YDIR * YHUMPS) + 1
270 DOT = XDIR + 50
280 HEIGHT = XHEIGHT * YHEIGHT * SCALER
290 LINE (DOT + YDIR,DOT )-(DOT + YDIR,DOT - HEIGHT),0
300 IF YDIR/2 = INT(YDIR/2) THEN PSET(DOT + YDIR,DOT - HEIGHT)
310 NEXT
320 NEXT
```

```
330 '
340 DEF SEG = &HB800
350 BSAVE "PIC#3",0,&H4000
360 GOTO 360
*************************************************************
50  ' WARNING : THIS PROGRAM CREATES A 3-D
60  ' IMAGE BUT REQUIRES 1 HOUR TO DO SO.
70  ' IT WILL OVERWRITE ANY FILE CALLED
80  ' PIC#4.BAS  ON THE DISK WITH A 16K
90  ' MEMORY FILE OF THE IMAGE
100 '******************************
110 '**   3-D #04    TOPO-SYMETRIC   **
120 '******************************
130 '**    CREATE + SAVE A PICTURE    **
140 '******************************
150 SCREEN 2:KEY OFF:CLS
160 INPUT "Enter the number of humps in the Y direction - " ; A
170 XHUMPS = ABS(A * 6.28318) / 145
180 INPUT "Enter the number of humps in the X direction - " ; A
190 YHUMPS = ABS(A * 6.28318) / 400
200 INPUT "Enter the scale factor for the height - " ; SCALER
210 CLS
220 '
230 FOR XDIR = 0 TO 135 : IF XDIR MOD 5 = 0 THEN A = 1 ELSE A = 5
240 FOR YDIR = 0 TO 400 STEP A
250 XHEIGHT = ((XDIR-67) * XHUMPS)^2 + 1
260 YHEIGHT = ((YDIR-200) * YHUMPS)^2 + 1
270 DOT = XDIR + 50
280 HEIGHT = SIN(SQR(XHEIGHT + YHEIGHT)) * SCALER + SCALER
290 LINE (DOT + YDIR,DOT )-(DOT + YDIR,DOT - HEIGHT),0
300 IF YDIR/2 = INT(YDIR/2) THEN PSET(DOT + YDIR,DOT - HEIGHT)
310 NEXT
320 NEXT
330 '
340 DEF SEG = &HB800
350 BSAVE "PIC#4",0,&H4000
360 GOTO 360
```

IMAGINARY RODS

This program is just for fun. Using some of the graphics commands and a circle routine that can be used in Cassette BASIC, this program creates an optical illusion that will surprise you even as you watch it form.

```
10  '**********************************************************
20  '**                    IMAGINARY RODS                  **
30  '**                                                    **
40  '**  VERSION 1.1                     28 JULY 1982      **
```

```
50 '***********************************************************************
60 SCREEN 2 : KEY OFF : CLS
70 GOSUB 150              ' DRAW THE RODS EXCEPT FOR THE ENDS
80 N = 1 : GOSUB 280
90 LOCATE 24,1 : PRINT " LET THE  I.B.M. P.C. TURN THE ORDINARY - ";
95 LINE (38,192)-(168,192)
100 FOR X = 1 TO 3000 : NEXT
110 N = 0 : GOSUB 280
115 FOR X = 1 TO 3000 : NEXT
120 LOCATE 24,43 : PRINT "INTO THE EXTRA-ORDINARY        ";
130 GOSUB 400
140 LOCATE 1,1 : END
150 '******************************************* DRAW THE RODS
160 LINE (600,100)-(300,0)
170 LINE (300,0)-(100,48)
180 LINE (100,48)-(400,148)
190 LINE (100,48)-(100,77)
200 LINE (100,77)-(350,160)
210 LINE (550,112)-(300,29)
220 LINE (450,136)-(200,53)
230 LINE (300,28)-(200,53)
240 LINE (500,124)-(300,57)
250 LINE (300,57)-(300,28)
260 LINE (300,57)-(250,69)
270 RETURN
280 '******************************************* DRAW OR ERASE THE ENDS
290 LINE (600,100)-(550,112),N
300 LINE -(550,140),N
310 LINE -(600,128),N
320 LINE -(600,100),N
330 LINE (550,140)-(500,124),N
340 LINE (450,136)-(400,148),N
350 LINE -(400,176),N
360 LINE -(450,164),N
370 LINE -(450,136),N
380 LINE (400,176)-(350,160),N
390 RETURN
400 '******************************************* DRAW CIRCLES ON RODS
410 A = 375 : B = 154 : GOSUB 450
420 A = 475 : B = 130 : GOSUB 450
430 A = 575 : B = 106 : GOSUB 450
440 RETURN
450 FOR X = -28 TO 28
460 Y = SQR( 784 - (X*X) ) /2.4
470 PSET (A+X,B+Y) : PSET (A+X,B-Y)
480 NEXT
490 RETURN
```

98

DESIGNS

These programs are simple exercises using the put and get commands. In the first program, a circle is created with the circle and paint commands. Then, using the get command, the entire area around the circle is placed into an array called x. Then the array is "put" back onto the screen with the XOR operation. This causes all the points under the circle to be reversed; that is, all white points are set black, and all black points are set white. See Fig. 4-4. The second program works in the same manner, but uses a sine function to plot the points. See Fig. 4-5. The extra program, *Easy Come – Easy Go* illustrates that if you perform a "put" twice to the same location, the area will be left as it was before the first "put" XOR'd the area. See Fig. 4-6.

```
100 '***************************************************
110 '**   design1 : a simple exercise for put and get   **
120 '***************************************************
130 SCREEN 2 : KEY OFF : CLS : DIM X(3000) : A = 10
140 CIRCLE (300,100),90
150 PAINT (300,100),1
160 GET (200,50)-(400,150),X
170 CLS
180 FOR Y = 1 TO 439 STEP 5
190 A = A + 1
200 PUT (Y,A),X,XOR
210 NEXT
220 GOTO 220


100 '***************************************************
110 '**   design2 : a simple exercise for put and get   **
120 '***************************************************
130 SCREEN 2 : KEY OFF : CLS : DIM X(3000) : A = 10
140 CIRCLE (300,100),90
150 PAINT (300,100),1
160 GET (200,50)-(400,150),X
170 CLS
180 FOR Y = 1 TO 439 STEP 5
190 A = SIN(Y*.015) * 45 + 50
200 PUT (Y,A),X,XOR
210 NEXT
220 GOTO 220


100 '***************************************************
110 '**                EASY COME - EASY GO                **
120 '***************************************************
130 DIM ARRAY(100) : M = 1 : Z = 0
140 SCREEN 2 : KEY OFF : CLS : DIM X(3000) : A = 10
150 CIRCLE (300,100),90
160 PAINT (300,100),1
170 GET (200,50)-(400,150),X
```

```
180 CLS
190 FOR Z = 1 TO 100
200 Y = RND * 439
210 ARRAY (Z) = Y
220 NEXT Z
230 LOCATE 5,1 : PRINT "easy come - ";
240 FOR Z = 1 TO 100
250 Y = ARRAY(Z)
260 A = SIN(Y*.015) * 45 + 50
270 PUT (Y,A),X,XOR
280 NEXT Z
290 LOCATE 5,1 : PRINT "easy come - easy go";
300 FOR Z = 100 TO 1 STEP -1
310 Y = ARRAY(Z)
320 A = SIN(Y*.015) * 45 + 50
330 PUT (Y,A),X,XOR
340 NEXT Z
```

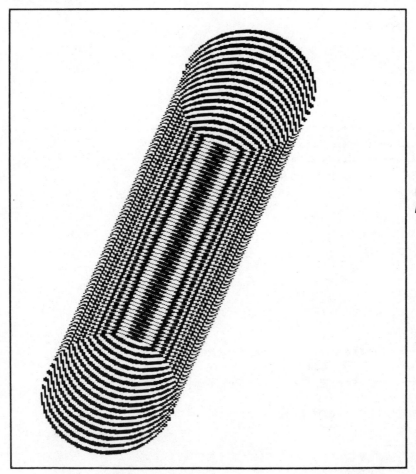

Fig. 4-4. Display produced by the *Designs* program.

Fig. 4-5. Display produced by the *Designs* program.

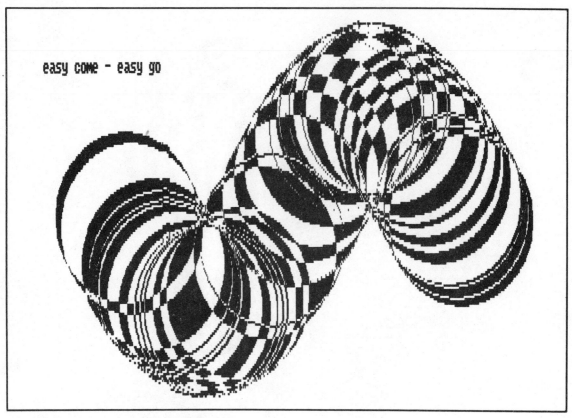

Fig. 4-6. Display produced by the *Designs* program.

GRAPHICS DEMONSTRATIONS

This chapter illustrates some of the patterns and figures that are possible on the IBM P.C. The graphic commands combined with the all-points-addressable 16K screen provide you with a means to create images of concepts that would have been virtually impossible to represent graphically just a few years ago.

If you have the Color/Graphics Monitor Adapter Board, you have a means of generating pictures with a resolution of 200 × 640 pixels!!! that means there are 128 thousand addressable locations on the screen. Depending on the screen selected and the commands used, you may draw lines, circles, and complex shapes; superimpose one shape upon another; and do any number of graph and scientific investigations. All this is possible without the use of a plotter. Movement is easily achieved so you can create arcade-style games. Finally, if you really like the patterns developed on the screen, there is a program to dump the pattern to a printer.

Graph 1 and Graph 2

It is just as intriguing to watch these graphs being plotted as it is to view them in their final forms. Consisting entirely of straight line segments, they quickly build from a one-dimensional line to their final pictured form. The total time to completion is just a few seconds. One of the resulting images is shown in Fig. 4-7.

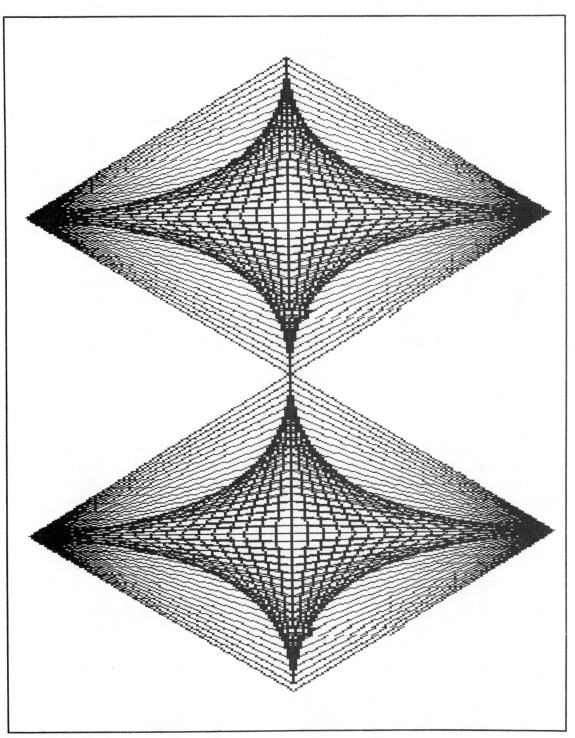

Fig. 4-7. Display produced by the *Graph 1* program.

```
10 '*********************************
20 '**            GRAPH01           **
30 '*********************************
40 SCREEN 2:KEY OFF:CLS
50 A=0:B=100:C=319:D=100:E=320:F=100:G=619:H=100
60 LINE (A,100)-(160,B):LINE (E,100)-(480,F)
70 LINE (160,B)-(C,100):LINE (480,F)-(G,100)
80 LINE (C,100)-(160,D):LINE (G,100)-(480,H)
90 LINE (160,D)-(A,100):LINE (480,H)-(E,100)
100 A=A+8:B=B-6:C=C-8:D=D+6:E=A+320:G=C+320:H=D:F=B
110 IF G > 315 THEN 60
```

```
10 '*********************************
20 '**            GRAPH02           **
30 '*********************************
40 SCREEN 1:KEY OFF:CLS
50 A=1:B=100:C=319:D=100
60 LINE (A,100)-(160,B)
70 LINE -(C,100)
80 LINE -(160,D)
90 LINE -(A,100)
100 A=A+8:B=B+5:C=C-8:D=D-5
110 IF C<0 THEN 120 ELSE 60
120 GOTO 120
```

Graph 3

Here is a short program that demonstrates the power and speed of the line command when it is used with the box argument. The program creates a series of nine flowing displays as shown in Fig. 4-8. All of the displays are created using the same algorithm except for a counter that is incremented after each box is drawn on the screen. Even though they all derive from the same procedure, it is interesting how different they all are.

```
10 '*********************************
20 '**            GRAPH03           **
30 '*********************************
40 A=1:B=1
50 SCREEN 1:KEY OFF:CLS
60 X1=0:X2=319:Y1=0:Y2=199
70 LINE (X1+A,Y1+A)-(X2-A,Y2-A),B,B
80 X1=X1+9:X2=X2-9:Y1=Y1+1.2:Y2=Y2-1.2
90 A=A+.5
100 IF X2-A>0 THEN 70
110 B=B+1
120 IF B<10 THEN FOR Z = 1 TO 1000          : NEXT : GOTO 50
```

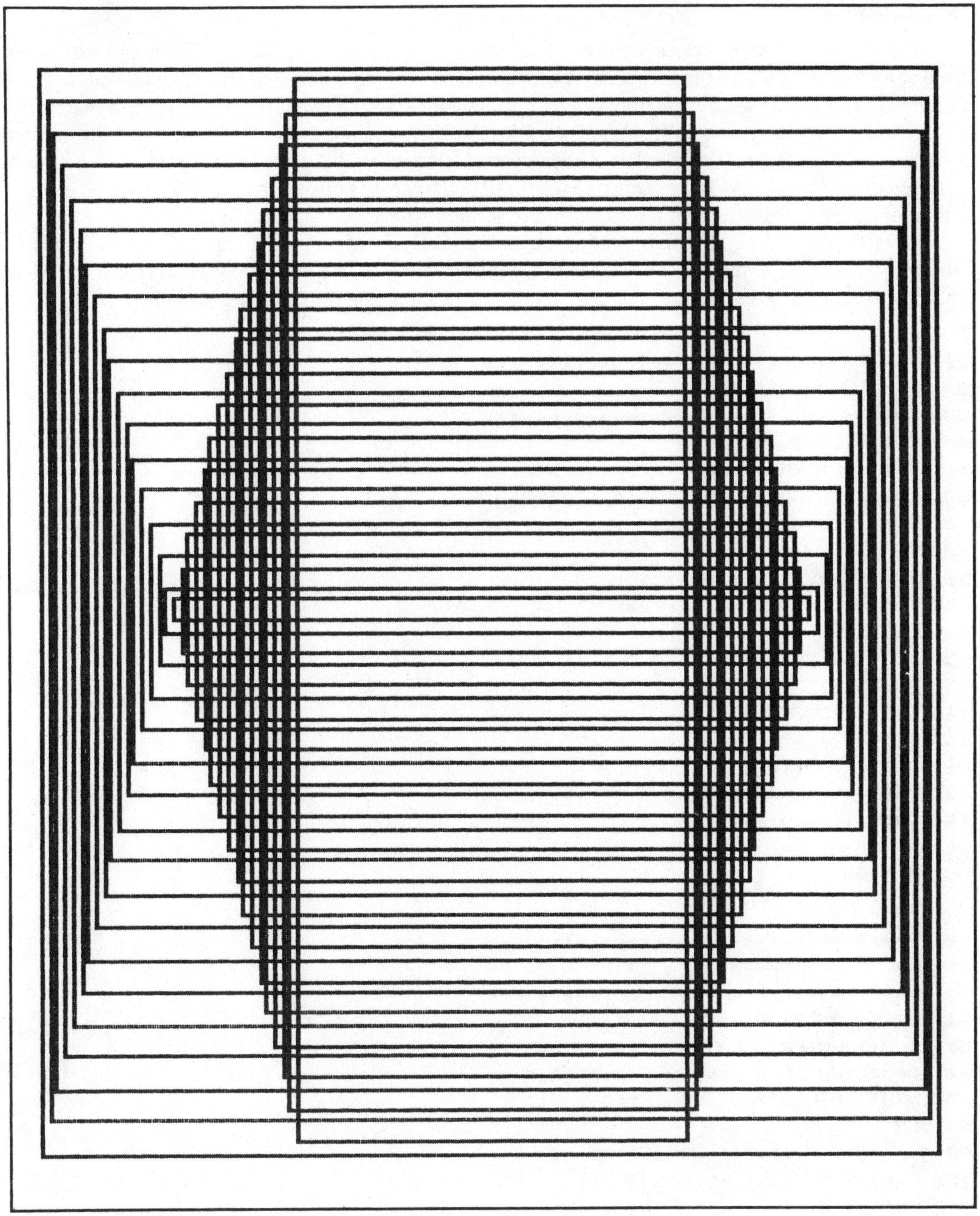

Fig. 4-8. Display produced by the *Graph 3* program.

Graphs 4 and 4A

These programs will produce patterns by using the interference method. A series of rays extend out from any point selected on the screen with the maximum spacing depending on the value you input for density. The larger the value input, the wider the maximum spacing between the lines. A value that seems to give good density results is 16. A series of rays is then extended out from a second point located anywhere on the screen. The overlay of these patterns creates what is called an interference pattern between these two points. The effect is similar to the effect that is created by throwing two rocks into a still pond or lake. The points of interference are located where the waves cross.

From these two programs, many very pretty and unusual designs can be created in a very short time. One program overlays white lines on white lines, and the other overlays black lines on white lines, in effect erasing parts of the lines. Figures 4-9 and 4-10 show designs created by these programs.

```
10 '********************************
20 '**          GRAPH04          **
30 '********************************
40 SCREEN 2:KEY OFF:CLS
50 INPUT "ENTER X1 AND Y1";A(1),B(1)
60 INPUT "ENTER X2 AND Y2";A(2),B(2)
70 INPUT "DENSITY OF LINES";D
80 CLS
90 A=A(1):B=B(1):GOSUB 120
100 A=A(2):B=B(2):GOSUB 120
110 GOTO 110
120 FOR X = 0 TO 199 STEP D/4
130 LINE (0,X)-(A,B)
140 LINE (639,X)-(A,B)
150 NEXT X
160 FOR Y = 0 TO 639 STEP D/2
170 LINE (Y,0)-(A,B)
180 LINE (Y,199)-(A,B)
190 NEXT Y
200 RETURN


10 '*********************************
20 '**          GRAPH04A          **
30 '*********************************
40 SCREEN 2:KEY OFF:CLS
50 INPUT "ENTER X1 AND Y1";A(1),B(1)
60 INPUT "ENTER X2 AND Y2";A(2),B(2)
70 INPUT "DENSITY OF LINES";D
80 CLS
90 A=A(1):B=B(1):C=1:GOSUB 120
100 A=A(2):B=B(2):C=0:GOSUB 120
110 GOTO 110
120 FOR X = 0 TO 199 STEP D/4
130 LINE (0,X)-(A,B),C
```

```
140 LINE (639,X)-(A,B),C
150 NEXT X
160 FOR Y = 0 TO 639 STEP D/2
170 LINE (Y,0)-(A,B),C
180 LINE (Y,199)-(A,B),C
190 NEXT Y
200 RETURN
```

Fig. 4-9. Display produced by the *Graph 4* program.

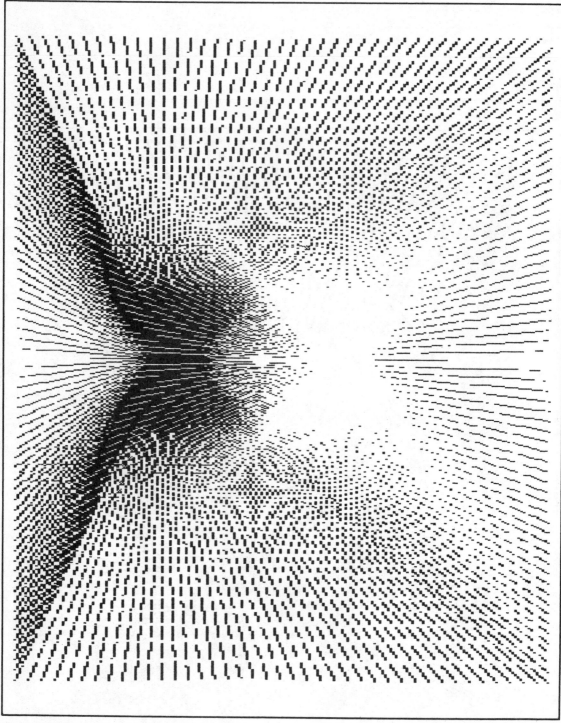

Fig. 4-10. Display produced by the *Graph 4A* program.

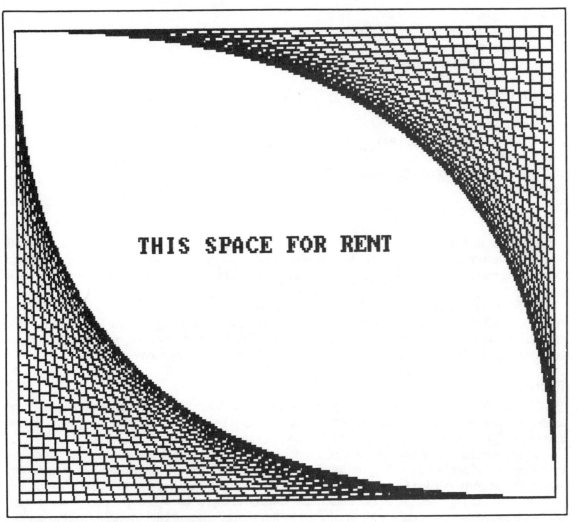

Fig. 4-11. Display produced by the *Graph 5* program.

Graph 5

The program that drew Fig. 4-11 uses a very simple concept that creates the illustration in a matter of about two seconds. From point 0,0 on the screen, a line is drawn across the screen to the right-hand border. Then the first point is moved over 8 dots; the second point is moved down 5 points; and a line is drawn between them. As this process is repeated across the screen, a similar set of lines is drawn down the left hand side and across the bottom. The message is simply centered on the screen and could be modified to anything you desire.

```
10 '*********************************
20 '**         GRAPH05           **
30 '*********************************
40 SCREEN 1:KEY OFF:CLS
```

```
50 N=8 : O=5
60 LINE (0,0)-(0,0)
70 A=0:B=0:C=0:D=0
80 IF D > 320 THEN 130
90 LINE (A,0)-(320,B)
100 LINE (0,C)-(D,320)
110 A=A+N:B=B+O:C=B:D=A
120 GOTO 80
130 LINE (319,0)-(319,199)
140 LOCATE 12,10
150 PRINT"THIS SPACE FOR RENT";
160 GOTO 160
```

Graph 6

Many people have trouble with mathematics. One of the difficulties is in how the different concepts have been illustrated. For example, the trignometric functions, which are functions describing movement (such as the movement of a point as it travels around a circle), have usually been illustrated with a static graph.

But thanks to the development of computers, this does not have to be the case any longer. With the computer's ability to generate graphs and to create sound, a whole new approach has been added to the realm of education. This program simply illustrates how effective the combination of sight and sound can be in reinforcing the concepts involved in a complex subject such as trigonometry.

Theory of Operation

The program starts out by generating an axis on which to draw the functions. Since the trig functions are *periodic* and repeat after 360 degrees or 2 pi radians, which is another way to measure angles, I selected a length of 628 for the axis, because it is very close in value to 2 pi multiplied by 100.

Then selecting one of the functions at a time, I started generating a graph of that function. The functions were generated by scaling the graphs to a size that fit neatly on the screen and drawing line segments that corresponded to the height of the function. As each line segment was drawn, a tone was generated that was proportional to the value of the function at that point. What this created was a graph which reinforced the concept of a rising or falling waveform with a rising or falling tone. As a last point, the graph was labeled to show the relationships between the graphs and the angles of a circle. See Fig. 4-12.

```
10 '*********************************
20 '**          GRAPH06          **
30 '*********************************
40 SCREEN 2:KEY OFF:CLS:N=5
50 LOCATE 3,25 :PRINT"STANDARD TRIG FUNCTIONS";
60 LOCATE 5,25:PRINT"                ";
70 FOR Y = 1 TO 2000 : NEXT Y
80 LOCATE 5,25:PRINT"                ";
90 'DRAW CENTER LINE ON GRAPH
100 LINE (628,99)-(0,99)
110 LOCATE 14,1:PRINT 0:LOCATE 14,19:PRINT 90
120 LOCATE 14,38:PRINT 180:LOCATE 14,58:PRINT 270:LOCATE 14,76:PRINT 360
```

```
130 FOR Y = 1 TO 500:NEXT Y
140 LOCATE 4,4:PRINT "= TAN (X)"
150 LINE (0,99)-(0,99)
160 FOR X = 0 TO 628 STEP N
170 IF ABS(TAN(X/100)) > 6 THEN LINE (X,199)-(X,199),0 : GOTO 210
180 IF ABS(COS(X/100)) > .2 THEN LINE -(X,100-20*(TAN(X/100)))
190 IF ABS(1000 * (TAN(X/100)) + 1000) < 37 THEN 210
200 SOUND (200 * (TAN(X/100)) + 1200),1
210 NEXT X
220 FOR Y = 1 TO 500:NEXT Y
230 LOCATE 5,4:PRINT "= SIN (X) "
```

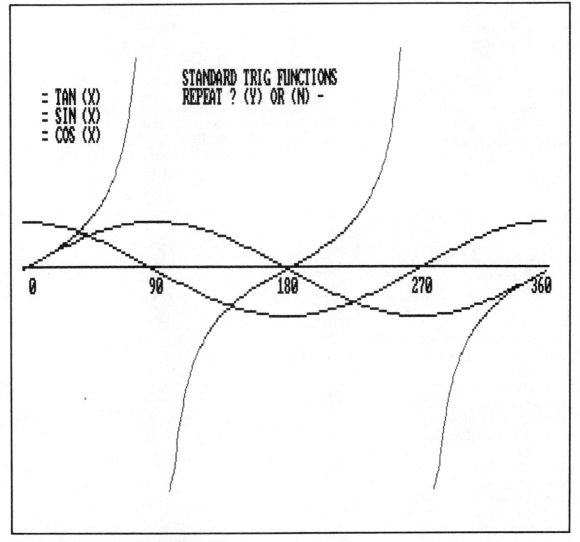

Fig. 4-12. Display produced by the *Graph 6* program.

```
240 LINE (Ø,99)-(Ø,99)
250 FOR X = Ø TO 628 STEP N
260 LINE -(X,100-20*SIN(X/100))
270 SOUND (1000 * SIN(X/100) + 1037),1
280 NEXT X
290 FOR Y = 1 TO 500:NEXT Y
300 LOCATE 6,4:PRINT "= COS (X)"
310 LINE (Ø,80)-(Ø,80)
320 FOR X = Ø TO 628 STEP N
330 LINE -(X,100-20*COS(X/100))
340 SOUND (1000 * COS(X/100) + 1037),1
350 NEXT X
360 LOCATE 4,25:PRINT "REPEAT ? (Y) OR (N) - ";
370 A$ = INKEY$ : IF A$ = "" THEN 370
380 IF A$ = "Y" THEN 10
390 CLS
```

Graph 7

This program illustrates the method of generating your own character set. Using the concept that will be expanded upon in the *Font-80* and *New-Font* programs, this program first turns on all 64 dots that make up each of the characters in the top 128 characters in the ASCII set. Then after displaying all the characters, it places random patterns in each of the top 128 characters and again displays the entire character set as shown in Fig. 4-13. Although this program is mainly for illustration, it demonstrates a very useful concept.

```
10 '*********************************
20 '**           GRAPHØ7            **
30 '*********************************
40 SCREEN 2:KEY OFF:CLS
50 CLEAR ,10000
60 DEF SEG = Ø
70 POKE &H7D,&HBC
80 SCREEN 2
90 FOR X = 48128! TO 49151!
100 POKE X , 255
110 NEXT
120 GOSUB 190
130 SCREEN 2
140 FOR X = 48128! TO 49151!
150 POKE X,RND * 255
160 NEXT
170 GOSUB 190
180 END
190 FOR X = 14 TO 255
200 PRINT CHR$(X);" ";
210 NEXT
220 RETURN
```

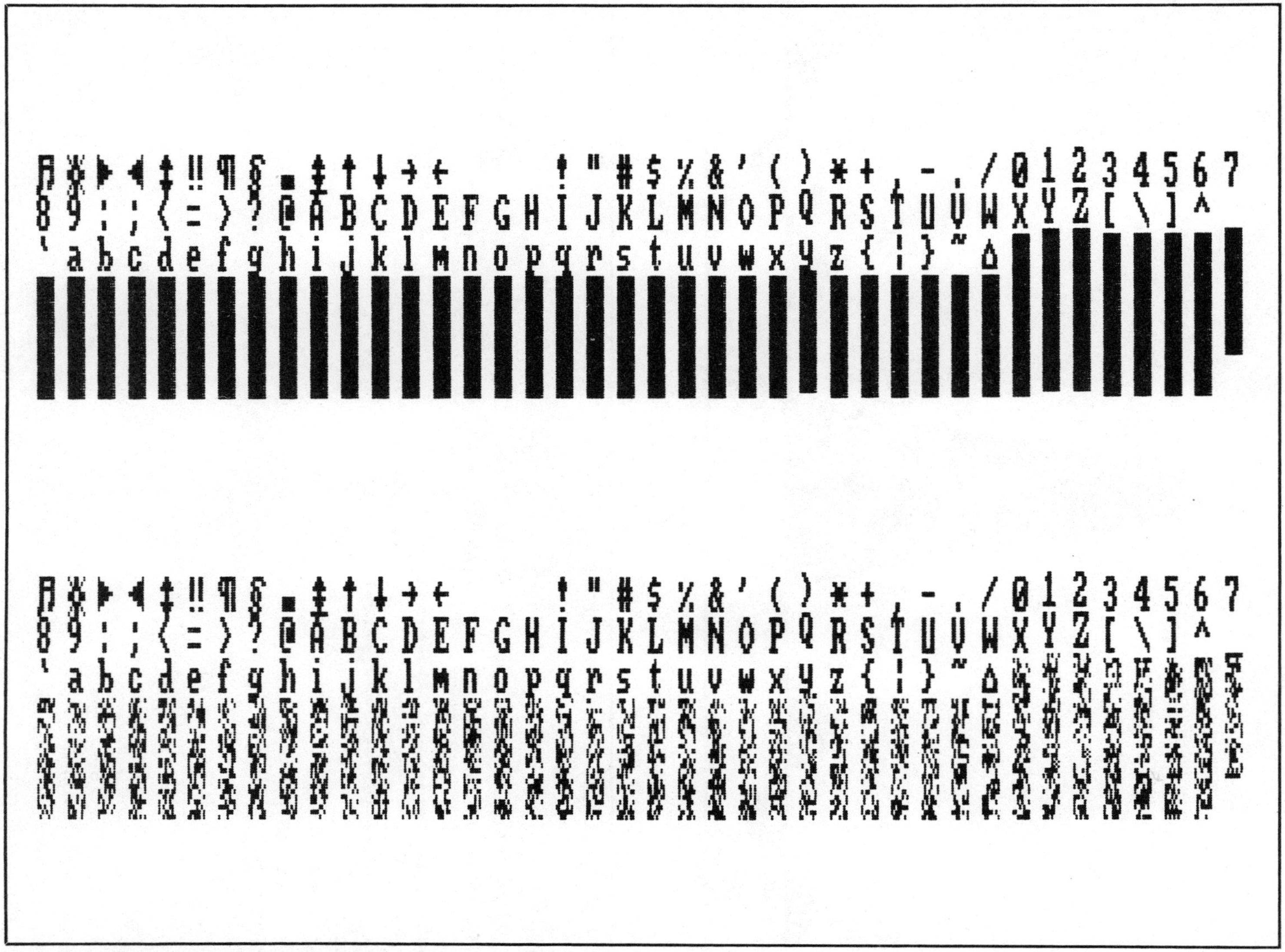

Fig. 4-13. Patterns produced by the *Graph 7* program.

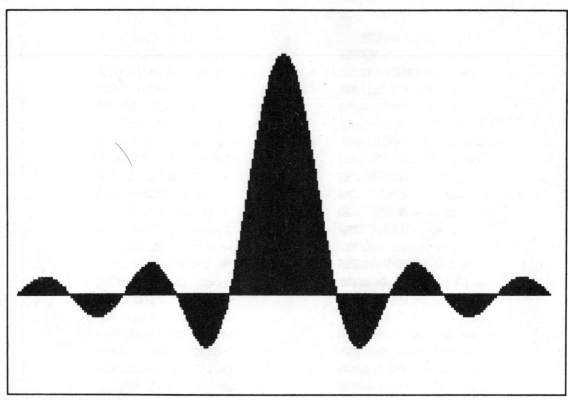

Fig. 4-14. Display produced by the *Graph 8* program.

Graph 8

SIN(x)/x is one of the mathematical functions that creates an unusual and pretty design. This program draws a graph of this function, but with a twist . . . . . See Fig. 4-14.

```
100 '*****************************
110 '**         GRAPH08         **
120 '*****************************
130 '
140 SCREEN 1:CLS
150 LINE (317,150)-(3,150)
160 FOR A = 3 TO 317
170 X = ( A - 160 ) * .1
180 IF X = 0 THEN X = .1
190 LINE -(A,150 - 100 * SIN(X)/X)
200 NEXT
210 FOR A = 3 TO 317
220 X = ( A - 160 ) * .1
230 IF X = 0 THEN X = .1
240 LINE (A,150)-(A,150 - 100 * SIN(X)/X)
250 NEXT
```

Graphs 9 and 9A

By setting dots on the screen, these programs generate what are commonly referred to as a family of graphs. In these cases the graphs are of the absolute value of the sin(x) function. The only difference between the two programs is that the maximum value of the first graph is dependent on the value of a constant, and the values for the second graph are dependent on the sine function. This dependency gives the graph its three dimensional curved appearance. See Fig. 4-15.

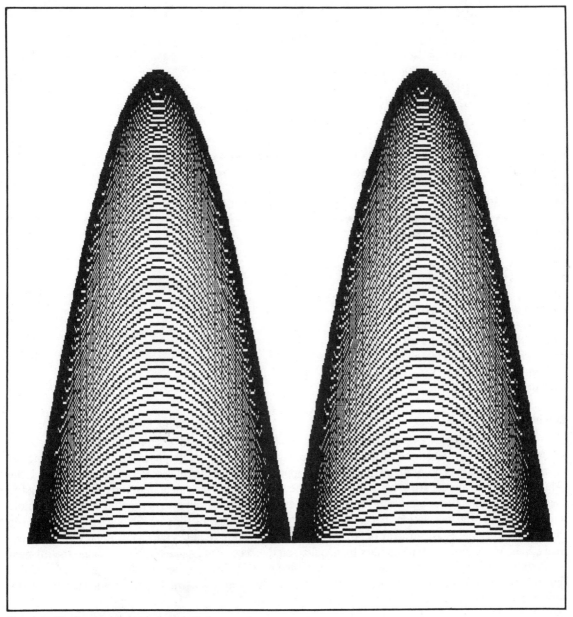

Fig. 4-15. Display produced by the *Graph 9* program.

```
10 '************************************************
20 '**        GRAPH09      -      FAMILY OF SINES        **
30 '**                                                  **
40 '**    VERSION 1.1                 14 JULY 1982  **
50 '************************************************
60 CLS : SCREEN 2 : KEY OFF
70 LINE (628,199)-(1,199)
80 FOR X = 5 TO 198 STEP 5
90 LINE (1,199)-(1,199)
100 FOR XAXIS = 1 TO 628 STEP 1
110 NEWAXIS = XAXIS * .01
120 SINVAL = ABS(SIN(NEWAXIS)) * -X + 199
130 PSET (XAXIS,SINVAL)
140 NEXT XAXIS,X
150 GOTO 150


10 '************************************************
20 '**        GRAPH09A     -      FAMILY OF SINES        **
30 '**                                                  **
40 '**    VERSION 1.1                 14 JULY 1982  **
50 '************************************************
60 CLS : SCREEN 2 : KEY OFF
70 LINE (628,199)-(1,199)
80 FOR X = .04 TO 3.14159 STEP .04
85 Z = SIN(X) * 199
90 LINE (1,199)-(1,199)
100 FOR XAXIS = 1 TO 628 STEP 1
110 NEWAXIS = XAXIS * .01
120 SINVAL = ABS(SIN(NEWAXIS)) * -Z + 199
130 PSET (XAXIS,SINVAL)
140 NEXT XAXIS,X
150 GOTO 150
```

Graphs 10A-G

These programs create graphs that appear three-dimensional. The programs run very fast in basic and produce clear images. Most graphic programs create three-dimensional graphs actively while the function is being analyzed. This program takes a different approach. The program creates an array into which the values that are calculated are stored. After all of the points have been calculated, the program, using the line command, plots the points for the array. This method has the advantages of creating a graph that plots very rapidly once the calculations have been performed and of allowing for easy scaling of the graph. Even though these examples use an array of 961 elements, the program requires only a few minutes to run. As a final bonus, if a function is too complex to visualize on the screen, it is an easy job to change the for-next loops so they only calculate the values for one quadrant of the graph and then run the program again. All of the points excluded from the calculations will assume a value of zero and will be drawn as a flat plane on the screen allowing you to see the sector easily.

For example, change:

60 FOR Y = −15 TO 15
70 FOR X = −15 TO 15

To . . .

60 FOR Y = 0 TO 15
70 FOR X = 0 TO 15

Or . . .

60 FOR Y = −15 TO 0
70 FOR X = 0 TO 15

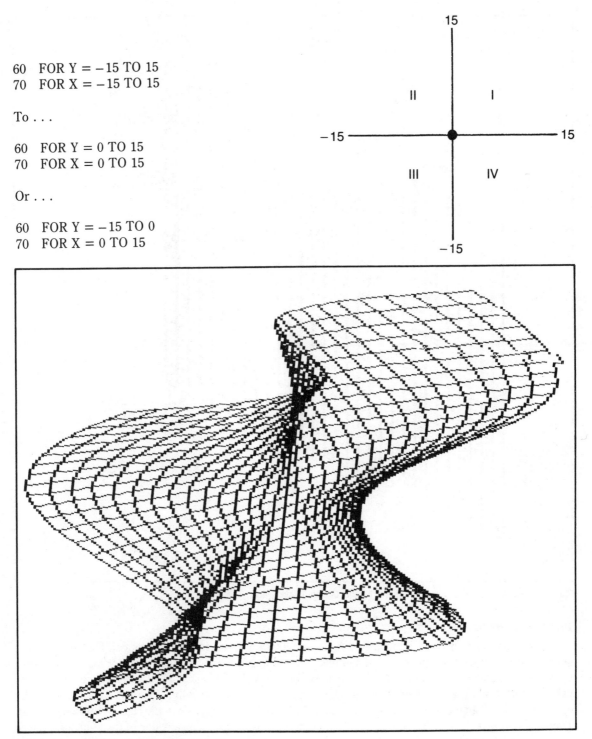

Fig. 4-16. Display produced by the *Graph 10* program.

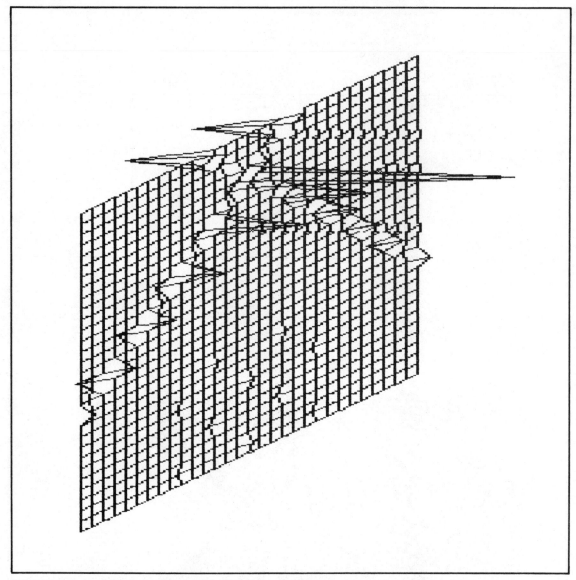

Fig. 4-17. Sample of the displays produced by the *Graph 10* program.

Theory of Operation

The program is divided into three simple sections enclosed in for-next loops. The first section generates the values from the function and places them into the array in their correct locations. These values correspond to the height of each point above or below the XY plane. The last two sections take the values from the array, and connect them first horizontally and then vertically. The rows and columns of the graph are plotted out on the screen as horizontal lines with each line shifted to the right of the one above it. Then the value that has been calculated for that point is added to the vertical value of the point and shifted accordingly. This procedure gives the graph it's three-dimensional effect. See Figs. 4-16 through 4-20.

```
10 '*********************************
20 '**         GRAPH10A          **
30 '*********************************
40 SCREEN 2:KEY OFF:CLS:DIM A(31,31)
50 DEFINT X,Y,Q
60 FOR Y = -15 TO 15
70 FOR X = -15 TO 15
80 IF X + Y = Ø THEN F = Ø : GOTO 100
90 F = X*Y*(X^2-Y^2)/(X^2+Y^2)
100 A(X+16,Y+16)=F
110 NEXT X
120 NEXT Y
130 FOR X = 1 TO 31 : FOR Y = 1 TO 31
140 VALUE = A(X,Y)
```

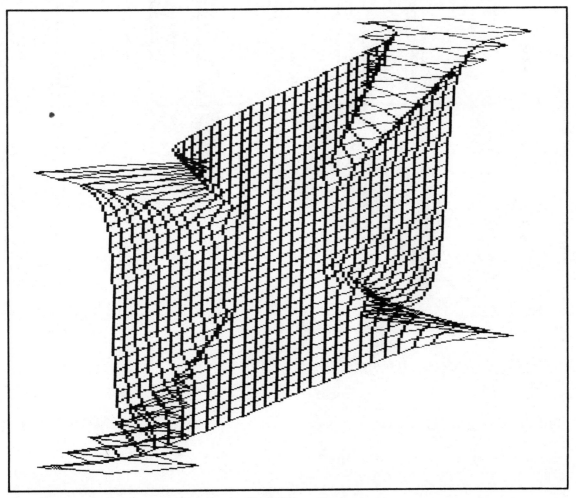

Fig. 4-18. Sample of the displays produced by the *Graph 10* program.

119

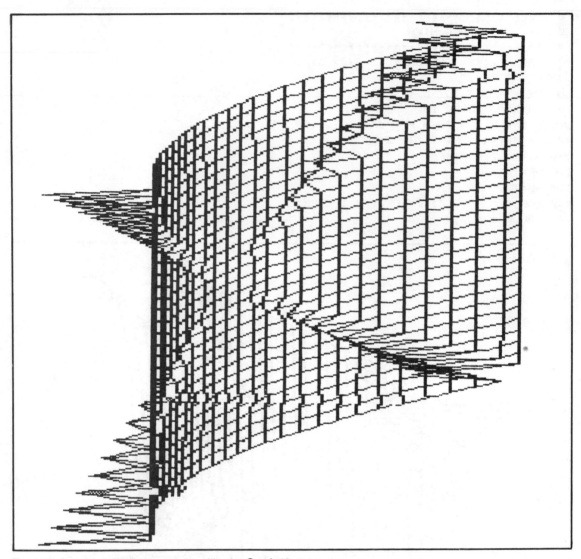

Fig. 4-19. Sample of the displays produced by the *Graph 10* program.

```
150 XPOS = (X*10) + 50 + (Y*5)
160 YPOS = (Y*4) + 30 + VALUE/2
170 IF Y = 1 THEN LINE (XPOS,YPOS)-(XPOS,YPOS) ELSE LINE -(XPOS,YPOS)
180 NEXT Y,X
230 FOR Y = 1 TO 31 : FOR X = 1 TO 31
240 VALUE = A(X,Y)
250 XPOS = (X*10) + 50 + (Y*5)
260 YPOS = (Y*4) + 30 + VALUE/2
270 IF X = 1 THEN LINE (XPOS,YPOS)-(XPOS,YPOS) ELSE LINE -(XPOS,YPOS)
280 NEXT X,Y
```

120

```
10 '*********************************
20 '**         GRAPH10B           **
30 '*********************************
40 SCREEN 2:KEY OFF:CLS:DIM A(31,31)
50 DEFINT X,Y,Q
60 FOR Y = -15 TO 15
70 FOR X = -15 TO 15
80 IF ABS(X) = ABS(Y) THEN 110
90 F = (SIN(X)+COS(Y))/(SIN(X)-COS(Y))
100 A(X+16,Y+16)=F
110 NEXT X
120 NEXT Y
```

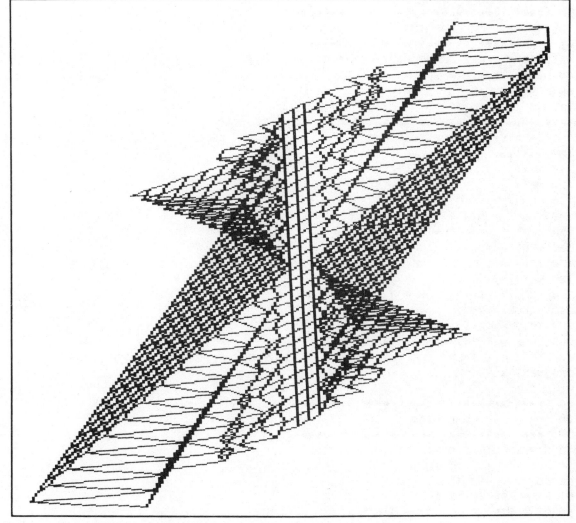

Fig. 4-20. Sample of the displays produced by the *Graph 10* program.

```
130 FOR X = 1 TO 31 : FOR Y = 1 TO 31
140 VALUE = A(X,Y)
150 XPOS = (X*10) + 50 + (Y*5)
160 YPOS = (Y*4) + 30 + VALUE/100
170 IF Y = 1 THEN LINE (XPOS,YPOS)-(XPOS,YPOS) ELSE LINE -(XPOS,YPOS)
180 NEXT Y,X
230 FOR Y = 1 TO 31 : FOR X = 1 TO 31
240 VALUE = A(X,Y)
250 XPOS = (X*10) + 50 + (Y*5)
260 YPOS = (Y*4) + 30 + VALUE/100
270 IF X = 1 THEN LINE (XPOS,YPOS)-(XPOS,YPOS) ELSE LINE -(XPOS,YPOS)
280 NEXT X,Y


10 '**********************************
20 '**          GRAPH10C             **
30 '**********************************
40 SCREEN 2:KEY OFF:CLS:DIM A(31,31)
50 DEFINT X,Y,Q
60 FOR Y = -15 TO 15
70 FOR X = -15 TO 15
80 IF ABS(X) = ABS(Y) THEN 110
90 F = X*Y*(X^2+Y^2)/(X^2-Y^2)
100 A(X+16,Y+16)=F
110 NEXT X
120 NEXT Y
130 FOR X = 1 TO 31 : FOR Y = 1 TO 31
140 VALUE = A(X,Y)
150 XPOS = (X*10) + 50 + (Y*5)
160 YPOS = (Y*4) + 30 + VALUE/100
170 IF Y = 1 THEN LINE (XPOS,YPOS)-(XPOS,YPOS) ELSE LINE -(XPOS,YPOS)
180 NEXT Y,X
230 FOR Y = 1 TO 31 : FOR X = 1 TO 31
240 VALUE = A(X,Y)
250 XPOS = (X*10) + 50 + (Y*5)
260 YPOS = (Y*4) + 30 + VALUE/100
270 IF X = 1 THEN LINE (XPOS,YPOS)-(XPOS,YPOS) ELSE LINE -(XPOS,YPOS)
280 NEXT X,Y


10 '**********************************
20 '**          GRAPH10D             **
30 '**********************************
40 SCREEN 2:KEY OFF:CLS:DIM A(31,31)
60 FOR Y = -15 TO 15
70 FOR X = -15 TO 15
87 A1 = X*6.28/35 : B1 = Y*6.28/35
90 A2 = SIN (A1) : B2 = SIN(B1) : F = A2*B2
100 A(X+16,Y+16)=F
```

```
110 NEXT X
120 NEXT Y
130 FOR X = 1 TO 31 : FOR Y = 1 TO 31
140 VALUE = A(X,Y)
150 XPOS = (X*10) + 50 + (Y*5)
160 YPOS = (Y*4) + 30 + VALUE*45
170 IF Y = 1 THEN LINE (XPOS,YPOS)-(XPOS,YPOS) ELSE LINE -(XPOS,YPOS)
180 NEXT Y,X
230 FOR Y = 1 TO 31 : FOR X = 1 TO 31
240 VALUE = A(X,Y)
250 XPOS = (X*10) + 50 + (Y*5)
260 YPOS = (Y*4) + 30 + VALUE*45
270 IF X = 1 THEN LINE (XPOS,YPOS)-(XPOS,YPOS) ELSE LINE -(XPOS,YPOS)
280 NEXT X,Y


10 '********************************
20 '**          GRAPH10E          **
30 '********************************
40 SCREEN 2:KEY OFF:CLS:DIM A(31,31)
50 DEFINT X,Y,Q
60 FOR Y = -15 TO 15
70 FOR X = -15 TO 15
80 IF ABS(X) = ABS(Y) THEN 110
90 F = X*X/8-Y*Y/12 * 200
100 A(X+16,Y+16)=F
110 NEXT X
120 NEXT Y
130 FOR X = 1 TO 31 : FOR Y = 1 TO 31
140 VALUE = A(X,Y)
150 XPOS = (X*10) + 50 + (Y*5)
160 YPOS = (Y*4) + 30 + VALUE/100
170 IF Y = 1 THEN LINE (XPOS,YPOS)-(XPOS,YPOS) ELSE LINE -(XPOS,YPOS)
180 NEXT Y,X
230 FOR Y = 1 TO 31 : FOR X = 1 TO 31
240 VALUE = A(X,Y)
250 XPOS = (X*10) + 50 + (Y*5)
260 YPOS = (Y*4) + 30 + VALUE/100
270 IF X = 1 THEN LINE (XPOS,YPOS)-(XPOS,YPOS) ELSE LINE -(XPOS,YPOS)
280 NEXT X,Y


10 '********************************
20 '**          GRAPH10F          **
30 '********************************
40 SCREEN 2:KEY OFF:CLS:DIM A(31,31)
50 DEFINT Q
60 FOR Y = -1 TO 1 STEP .1
70 FOR X = -1 TO 1 STEP .1
```

```
80 IF ABS(X) = ABS(Y) THEN 110
90 F = SIN(SQR(X*X+Y*Y))*9000
100 A(X*10+16,Y*10+16)=F
110 NEXT X
120 NEXT Y
130 FOR X = 1 TO 31 : FOR Y = 1 TO 31
140 VALUE = A(X,Y)
150 XPOS = (X*10) + 50 + (Y*5)
160 YPOS = (Y*4) + 30 + VALUE/100
170 IF Y = 1 THEN LINE (XPOS,YPOS)-(XPOS,YPOS) ELSE LINE -(XPOS,YPOS)
180 NEXT Y,X
230 FOR Y = 1 TO 31 : FOR X = 1 TO 31
240 VALUE = A(X,Y)
250 XPOS = (X*10) + 50 + (Y*5)
260 YPOS = (Y*4) + 30 + VALUE/100
270 IF X = 1 THEN LINE (XPOS,YPOS)-(XPOS,YPOS) ELSE LINE -(XPOS,YPOS)
280 NEXT X,Y


10 '********************************
20 '**          GRAPH10G          **
30 '********************************
40 SCREEN 2:KEY OFF:CLS:DIM A(31,31)
60 FOR Y = -15 TO 15
70 FOR X = -15 TO 15
80 IF Y = 0 THEN 110
90 F = (X MOD Y) / 15
100 A(X+16,Y+16)=F
110 NEXT X
120 NEXT Y
130 FOR X = 1 TO 31 : FOR Y = 1 TO 31
140 VALUE = A(X,Y)
150 XPOS = (X*10) + 50 + (Y*5)
160 YPOS = (Y*4) + 30 + VALUE*45
170 IF Y = 1 THEN LINE (XPOS,YPOS)-(XPOS,YPOS) ELSE LINE -(XPOS,YPOS)
180 NEXT Y,X
230 FOR Y = 1 TO 31 : FOR X = 1 TO 31
240 VALUE = A(X,Y)
250 XPOS = (X*10) + 50 + (Y*5)
260 YPOS = (Y*4) + 30 + VALUE*45
270 IF X = 1 THEN LINE (XPOS,YPOS)-(XPOS,YPOS) ELSE LINE -(XPOS,YPOS)
280 NEXT X,Y
```

BEAMS

Here is another optical illusion of the same type as the *Imaginary Rods* program. This program is short enough to enter in a matter of minutes. Many of the two-dimensional illusions can be created in exactly this way.

```
10 '*********************************************************************
20 '**                    BEAMS                                       **
30 '**                                                                **
40 '**  VERSION 1.1                        28 JULY 1982               **
50 '*********************************************************************
60 SCREEN 2 : KEY OFF : CLS
70 LINE (Ø,100)-(225,199) : LINE -(450,100) : LINE -(225,0) : LINE -(Ø,100)
80 LINE (54,100)-(225,175) : LINE -(396,100) : LINE -(225,24) :
   LINE -(54,100)
90 LINE (108,100)-(225,151) : LINE-(342,100) : LINE -(225,48) :
   LINE -(108,100)
100 LINE (225,Ø)-(225,24) : LINE (225,199)-(225,175)
110 LINE (108,100)-(54,100) : LINE (396,100)-(342,100)
200 LINE (54,100)-(26,88)
210 LINE (396,100)-(422,112)
220 LINE (225,48)-(251,36)
230 LINE (225,151)-(199,163)
240 LINE (251,36)-(251,12)
250 LINE (199,163)-(199,187)
300 LOCATE 22,50 : PRINT "I.B.M.   SOFTWARE";
310 LINE (392,177)-(520,177)
320 LOCATE 13,28 : PRINT "*";: FOR X = 1 TO 50 : NEXT
330 LOCATE 13,28 : PRINT " ";: FOR X = 1 TO 50 : NEXT
340 GOTO 320
```

KALEIDOS

The *Kaleidos* program is a gentle, hypnotizing, colorful graphics program that will fascinate your friends. Medium resolution color squares are placed on the screen in four symmetrical locations. Random numbers are used to select colors, locations, and directions for the migration of the squares. The net effect is a colorful, changing pattern with symmetry on your IBM Personal Computer color graphics screen.

One subroutine is presented that is quite useful. At line 400 is a subroutine that initializes the random number generator at the start of the program. The time of the day is used to provide the randomizing speed. A different random number sequence is generated for every second of the hour. For game programs, this subroutine will help guarantee a different random sequence each time the game is run.

```
10 ' **********************
20 ' **     KALEIDOS     **
30 ' **********************
40 '
50 CLEAR
60 SCREEN Ø,Ø,Ø,Ø
70 WIDTH 40
80 KEY OFF
90 CLS
100 GOSUB 400
```

```
110 FGD = INT(RND * 16)
120 CHAR$ = CHR$(219)
130 LOCATE 1,1,0
140 '
150 ' Main loop starts here
160 IF RND < .1 THEN FGD = INT(RND * 16)
170 COLOR FGD
180 X = INT(40 * RND + 1)
190 Y = INT(23 * RND + 1)
200 DX = INT(3 * RND - 1)
210 DY = INT(3 * RND - 1)
220 IF DX = 0 THEN 200
230 IF DY = 0 THEN 200
240 IF X < 1 OR X > 40 THEN 160
250 IF Y < 1 OR Y > 23 THEN 160
260 GOSUB 330
270 X = X + DX
280 Y = Y + DY
290 GOTO 240
300 '
310 ' Subroutine, put color squares in four
320 ' symmetrical places on screen
330 LOCATE Y,X : PRINT CHAR$;
340 LOCATE Y,41-X : PRINT CHAR$;
350 LOCATE 24-Y,X : PRINT CHAR$;
360 LOCATE 24-Y,41-X : PRINT CHAR$;
370 RETURN
380 '
390 ' Subroutine, reset random number sequence
400 RANDOMIZE VAL(MID$(TIME$,4,2) + RIGHT$(TIME$,2))
410 RETURN
```

PAINTING

This short program demonstrates the fascinating artistic talents of the paint command. The program is relatively simple, but the contortions that the paint command puts your IBM Personal Computer through would lead you to believe that a very complicated set of graphics computations are under way.

Another purpose of this program is to demonstrate a subroutine that thoroughly shuffles the random number generator. Program line 260 initializes the random number sequence with a different starting point for each second of an hour. For most purposes this provides plenty of random sequences. To get the same sequence a second time you would need to start a program exactly one hour later, to the second. Line 270 to 300 provide an even higher degree of randomizing. The WHILE—WEND loop will execute an unknown number of times, depending on the exact time that the program is started. During this unknown fraction of a second the randomize statement in line 290 will continue to reset the random number sequence. This subroutine guarantees a random starting point for your sequence of random numbers. This program probably doesn't need this degree of randomness, but if you are writing a game and want to guarantee a fresh sequence each time the program is run, this subroutine will do the trick.

```
10 ' **********************
20 ' **     PAINTING     **
30 ' **********************
40 '
50 ' We need lots of stack bytes
60 CLEAR ,,3000
70 '
80 ' Start with a clean slate
90 SCREEN 2
100 KEY OFF
110 GOSUB 260
120 CLS
130 '
140 ' Fill screen with lots of vertical lines
150 FOR X = 1 TO 640 STEP 2
160 LINE (X,200*RND)-(X,200*RND)
170 NEXT X
180 '
190 ' Get the paint brush out
200 PAINT (320,100)
210 '
220 ' One more time
230 RUN
240 '
250 ' Subroutine, thoroughly randomize the random numbers
260 RANDOMIZE VAL(MID$(TIME$,4,2) + RIGHT$(TIME$,2))
270 TEMP$ = TIME$
280 WHILE TEMP$ = TIME$
290 RANDOMIZE 65000! * RND - 32500
300 WEND
310 RETURN
```

SPHERE

This program draws a striped sphere rotated in space as you desire as shown in Fig. 4-21. You are asked for rotation angles for each of the three axes. The positive x axis is to the right on the screen, the positive y axis goes up the screen, and the positive z axis comes out of the screen towards you.

Rotation follows the "right hand rule." Extend your thumb and loosely curl your fingers on your right hand. Imagine that your thumb follows an axis in a positive direction. Your fingers then curve around your thumb in the direction of rotation of a positive angle. By visualizing this correctly, you can control the pivoting of the sphere into any desired orientation.

The sphere is striped with as many stripes as you wish. If you don't rotate the sphere around any of the three axes the stripes will appear as concentric circles.

The function FNDTR converts degrees to radians. The trigonometric functions in BASIC operate on angles measured in radians, so FNDTR helps prepare degree measurements for further calculations.

The function FNATN2 is an improved version of the "built in" ATN function. A common problem in analytic geometry is to find the angle from the origin of a point (X,Y) in a plane. If the point is in the first quadrant (X and Y are both positive values), the angle is found as $ATN(Y/X)$. Complications arise when the

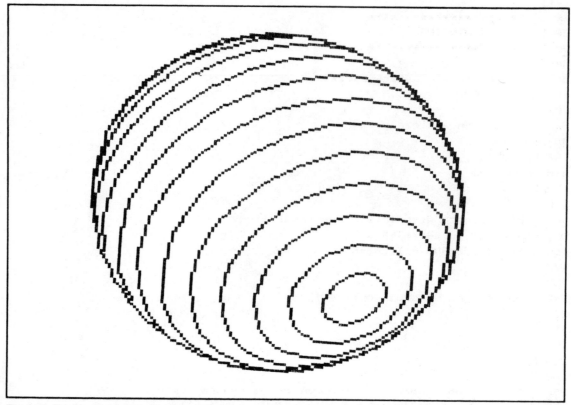

Fig. 4-21. Display produced by the *Sphere* program.

point is in one of the other three quadrants, or on one of the axes. For example, the point 0,7 is at 90 degrees from the positive x axis, but trying to compute ATN(7/0) will result in an error condition. FNATN2 will find the ATN function for points anywhere in the X,Y plane.

```
10 ' ****************************
20 ' **        SPHERE        **
30 ' ****************************
40 '
50 CLEAR
60 SCREEN 1
70 KEY OFF
80 CLS
90 LOCATE 7,1
100 PRINT "(degrees) ...
110 PRINT
120 INPUT "Rotation around the Y axis ";H
130 INPUT "Rotation around the X axis ";P
140 INPUT "Rotation around the Z axis ";B
150 INPUT "And how many stripes ";STRIPES
160 '
```

```
170 'initialize things
180 DEF FNDTR(DEGREES)=3.141593*DEGREES/180
190 DEF FNATN2(Y,X) = -ATN(Y/(X-(X=0)))*(X<>0)-1.570796*SGN(Y)
                      *(X=0)+3.141593*(X<0)*((Y>=0)-(Y<0))
200 OPTION BASE 1
210 DIM MROT(3,3)
220 CLS
230 '
240 'build the rotation matrix
250 SH=SIN(FNDTR(-H))
260 CH=COS(FNDTR(-H))
270 SP=SIN(FNDTR(P))
280 CP=COS(FNDTR(P))
290 SB=SIN(FNDTR(B))
300 CB=COS(FNDTR(B))
310 MROT(1,1)=CH*CB+SH*SP*SB
320 MROT(1,2)=CH*SB-SH*SP*CB
330 MROT(1,3)=SH*CP
340 MROT(2,1)=-CP*SB
350 MROT(2,2)=CP*CB
360 MROT(2,3)=SP
370 MROT(3,1)=CH*SP*SB-SH*CB
380 MROT(3,2)=-SH*SB-CH*SP*CB
390 MROT(3,3)=CH*CP
400 '
410 'stripe lines
420 FOR PHI = 0 TO 180 STEP 180/STRIPES
430 CPHI=COS(FNDTR(PHI))
440 SPHI=SIN(FNDTR(PHI))
450 XL=0
460 YL=0
470 FOR THETA = 0 TO 360 STEP 15
480 CTHETA=COS(FNDTR(THETA))
490 STHETA=SIN(FNDTR(THETA))
500 XS=CTHETA*SPHI
510 YS=STHETA*SPHI
520 ZS=CPHI
530 XR=MROT(1,1)*XS+MROT(2,1)*YS+MROT(3,1)*ZS
540 YR=MROT(1,2)*XS+MROT(2,2)*YS+MROT(3,2)*ZS
550 ZR=MROT(1,3)*XS+MROT(2,3)*YS+MROT(3,3)*ZS
560 XSL=88
570 XSR=232
580 YSL=160
590 YSR=40
600 XSC=(XR+1)*(XSR-XSL)/2+XSL
610 YSC=(YR+1)*(YSR-YSL)/2+YSL
620 IF PHI <> 0 THEN 670
```

```
630 THETA = 360
640 XPA = XSC
650 YPA = YSC
660 ZSGN = SGN(ZR)
670 IF ZR >= 0 THEN 700
680 XL = 0
690 YL = 0
700 IF XL OR YL THEN LINE(XL,YL)-(XSC,YSC)
710 XL=XSC
720 YL=YSC
730 NEXT THETA,PHI
740 CIRCLE (160,100),72
750 IF ZSGN <> -1 THEN 780
760 XPA = 320 - XPA
770 YPA = 200 - YPA
780 ANG=FNATN2(100-YPA,160-XPA)
790 FOR DIST = 1 TO 199
800 XPA=XPA+COS(ANG)
810 YPA=YPA+SIN(ANG)
820 IF POINT (XPA,YPA) <> 0 THEN 850
830 CLR = CLR MOD 3 + 1
840 PAINT (XPA,YPA),CLR,3
850 NEXT DIST
860 PAINT(1,1),0,3
870 BGD=(BGD+1)MOD 16
880 PLT=(PLT+1)MOD 2
890 IF BGD=0 AND PLT=0 THEN BGD=1
900 COLOR BGD,PLT
910 '
920 ' One second delay
930 TM$ = TIME$
940 WHILE TIME$ = TM$
950 WEND
960 GOTO 870
```

SPOKES

This program allows you to draw spheres, but with a difference. When run, this program asks you for the number of points to be used in creating the sphere. Then the program systematically connects all of the points on the edge of the sphere with all of the others. See Fig. 4-22.

Interesting variations include using the ",,B" qualifier for boxes in the program line that prints the lines and ",X MOD 2" to print one white line and then one black line, etc.

```
10 '**********************************************
20 '**              SPOKES                    **
30 '**                                        **
40 '**  19 NOV. 1982           VERSION 1.1    **
50 '**********************************************
```

```
60 '
70 SCREEN 2 : CLS : KEY OFF
80 INPUT "Number of spokes on wheel - ";N
90 ANGLE = 360 / N
100 RADIANS = ANGLE /57.29578
110 CLS
120 FOR X = 1 TO N
130 FOR Y = X TO N
140 SX = SIN(X * RADIANS) * 225 + 320
150 SY = SIN(Y * RADIANS) * 225 + 320
160 CX = COS(X * RADIANS) * 95 + 100
170 CY = COS(Y * RADIANS) * 95 + 100
180 LINE (SY,CY)-(SX,CX)
190 NEXT Y,X
```

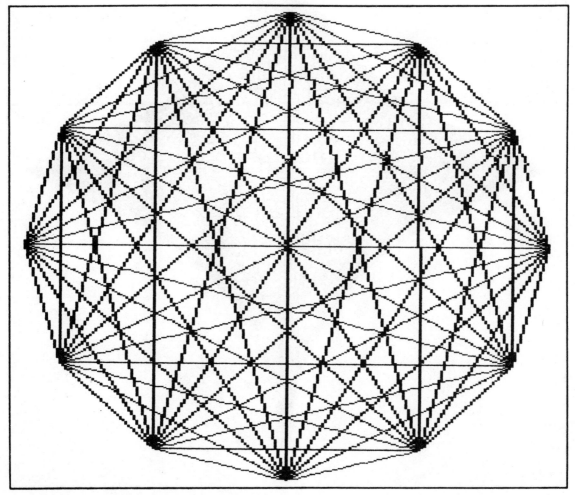

Fig. 4-22. Display produced by the *Spokes* program.

STAR

This program draws a four pointed star using multiple straight lines as shown in Fig. 4-23. The background and foreground colors are chosen at random, making this a good demonstration of the many possible color combinations available on your IBM Personal Computer.

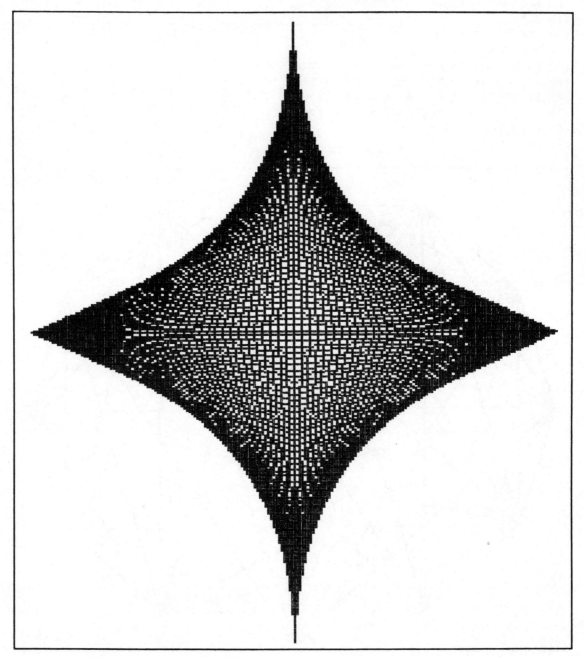

Fig. 4-23. Display produced by the *Star* program.

```
10 ' ******************
20 ' **      STAR       **
30 ' ******************
40 '
50 CLEAR
60 SCREEN 1
70 KEY OFF
80 RANDOMIZE VAL(RIGHT$(TIME$,2))
90 '
100 WHILE NOT YET.BORING OR YUKKY
110 CLS
120 INC = INT(9*RND+3)
130 X1 = 320
140 X2 = 0
150 Y1 = 99
160 Y2 = 99
170 BACKGROUND = INT(16*RND)
180 PALETTE = INT(2*RND)
190 COLOR BACKGROUND,PALETTE
200 STRIPES = INT(4*RND)
210 LINE (X1,99)-(160,Y1),STRIPES
220 LINE -(X2,99),STRIPES
230 LINE -(160,Y2),STRIPES
240 LINE -(X1,99),STRIPES
250 X1 = X1 - INC
260 X2 = X2 + INC
270 Y1 = Y1 - INC
280 Y2 = Y2 + INC
290 IF X1 >= X2 THEN 210
300 FOR I = 1 TO 999
310 NEXT I
320 WEND
```

TUNNEL

Using the line command with the "B" extension, this graphic program creates an illusion of traveling down an endless tunnel.

```
100 '*******************************
110 '**          TUNNEL          **
120 '*******************************
130 SCREEN 2 : CLS
140 FOR X = 20 TO 0 STEP -.4
150 LINE (X*16,X*5)-(639-(X*16),199-(X*5)),1,B
160 NEXT X
170 FOR X = 19.8 TO 0 STEP -.4
180 LINE (X*16,X*5)-(639-(X*16),199-(X*5)),0,B
```

```
190 NEXT X
200 FOR X = 19.8 TO Ø STEP -.4
210 LINE (X*16,X*5)-(639-(X*16),199-(X*5)),1,B
220 NEXT X
230 GOTO 170
```

WAND

One of the arcade games uses a wand as the opponent in a battle in which you attempt to build a series of blocks to secure a portion of the screen. The wand moves around the screen randomly, and if it crosses one of the lines on an uncompleted block, you lose. This program uses BASIC in order to simulate the action of the Wand.

The Wand is created very simply. Through a loop in the program, six different sets of lines are kept in memory. These six sets are drawn one at a time with limits on how much they may vary from their immediate predecessor. The values that make up the ends of the lines are stored in an array. After the fifth line has been drawn, the program searches back and rewrites the first line in black, in effect erasing it. This continues: a line is written and the sixth one back is erased. This creates a sensation of motion. The sound is created by measuring the horizontal length of the line and creating a tone that corresponds with this value.

```
100 '*********************************************
110 '**                 WAND                   **
120 '**                                         **
130 '**   VERSION 1.1           JULY 13,1982    **
140 '*********************************************
150 A = 320:B = 100:C = 320:D = 150:L = 1
160 SCREEN 2:CLS:KEY OFF
170 OPTION BASE 1
180 DIM A1 (6,4)
190 A1 (L,1) = A
200 A1 (L,2) = B
210 A1 (L,3) = C
220 A1 (L,4) = D
230 LINE (A,B)-(C,D),1
240 N1 = L
250 L = (L + 1) MOD 7:IF L = Ø THEN L = 1
260 N2 = L
270 LINE (A1 (L,1),A1 (L,2))-(A1 (L,3),A1 (L,4)),Ø
280 A = A + RND * 100 - 51
290 IF A >= 639 THEN A = 639
300 IF A <= Ø THEN A = Ø
310 B = B + RND * 30 - 15.5
320 IF B >= 199 THEN B = 199
330 IF B <= Ø THEN B = Ø
340 C = C + RND * 30 - 15
350 IF A > C AND A - C > 100 THEN C = A - 100
360 IF C > A AND C - A > 100 THEN C = A + 100
370 IF C >= 639 THEN C = 639
```

```
380 IF C <= Ø THEN C = Ø
390 D = D + RND * 3Ø - 15
4ØØ IF B > D AND B - D > 75 THEN D = B - 75
41Ø IF D > B AND D - B > 75 THEN D = B + 75
42Ø IF D >= 199 THEN D = 199
43Ø IF D <= Ø THEN D = Ø
44Ø SOUND ABS(LOG(ABS(A-C)))*1ØØ+37,1
45Ø GOTO 19Ø
```

Chapter 5

Mathematics

The eight programs in this chapter offer important tools to the serious mathematician. Complex number problems may be solved; sine and cosine values may be figured in double precision; and three-dimensional vectors may be analyzed. Students and casual mathematicians will especially appreciate programs like the ones on simultaneous equations and fractions.

COMPLEX NUMBERS

Complex numbers play an important role in many branches of engineering. This program turns your IBM Personal Computer into a complex number calculator. Several of the most common calculations and functions of complex numbers are provided. These include addition, subtraction, multiplication, division, square root, exponential, natural logarithmic, and inverse functions.

At the start of the program are several notes to remind you of the features and functions available. Then, after you press the space bar, the screen clears; short reminders are displayed at the top of the screen; and you begin to type the complex number calculations near the bottom of the screen. Type your calculations in the same way that you would write them on paper. There are just a few rules and guidelines to keep in mind.

A complex number is comprised of two normal looking numbers grouped as a pair. The first number is the "real" part, and the second number is the "imaginary" part. A common way to write a complex number is to enclose both numbers in a pair of parenthesis, with the second number (the "imaginary" part) preceded by either the letter "i" or "j". Here are a few examples of this notation:

(3+i4)	(17.3−j32.1)	(−.5+j9)
(−i7)	(3.14+j0)	(3.14)

The last two examples are equivalent. Real or imaginary parts of zero value don't have to be written.

To type in complex calculations for this program, remember to use parenthesis for every complex number. You may use either "i" or "j" for the complex part, and zero quantities need not be shown. For example, to calculate the produce of (3+i4) and (0−i6) you may type in

(3+j4) * (−i6) and press the enter key.

The complex answer to each computation is displayed and stored in variables A and B. The solution can be plugged into the next computation by typing in (A+iB). For example, to compute (2+i3) * (4−i5) / (i7) you can first type in

(2+i3) * (4−i5) and press the enter key.

The temporary result is displayed on the right and the prompt symbol reappears on the left. Now type in

(A+iB) / (i7) and press the enter key.

The solution appears on the right. To make it even easier to chain your computations, you may even drop the "A+iB" part and just type in a pair of parenthesis, like this:

() / (i7) and press the enter key.

The addition, subtraction, multiplication, and division functions always require two complex numbers—no more and no less. The rest of the functions all require exactly one complex number. For example, to compute the square root of (3−j4), type in

SQR (3−j4) and press the enter key.

The computations scroll off the screen at the top so the last few computations remain visible. A list of the available functions is always displayed at the top of the screen.

A copy of the first screen is provided in Fig. 5-1 for reference. Also, a copy of a screen with several typical computations is shown in Fig. 5-2.

```
10 ' ********************
20 ' **     COMPLEX     **
30 ' ********************
40 '
50 CLEAR
60 SCREEN 0,0,0,0
70 CLS
80 KEY OFF
90 LOCATE 2,21
100 PRINT "* * *   COMPLEX NUMBER CALCULATOR   * * *
110 LOCATE 4,1
120 PRINT "Functions for one complex number   ...   SQR(), EXP(), LOG(), 1/()
130 PRINT "Functions for two complex numbers ...   + - * /
140 PRINT
```

```
150 PRINT "Results are returned in variables A and B, and may be used in
160 PRINT "further calculations.  Use of (A+iB) or () inputs previous
    results
170 PRINT
180 PRINT "Examples of legal input ...
190 PRINT TAB(20)"(3+i4)+(2-i2)
200 PRINT TAB(20)"(3+i4)*(2)
210 PRINT TAB(20)"(a+ib)*(2)
220 PRINT TAB(20)"*(2-i3)          ...same as  (A+iB)*(2-i3)
230 PRINT TAB(20)"(2-i3)*()        ...same as  (2-i3)*(A-iB)
240 PRINT TAB(20)"+(j4)
250 PRINT
260 PRINT "Spaces may be used anywhere.
270 PRINT "You may use either 'i' or 'j' for the imaginary part.
280 PRINT "All values should be enclosed in parenthesis.
290 PRINT "Simply type in your problems and press the enter key.
300 PRINT
310 PRINT TAB(20)"PRESS THE SPACE BAR TO BEGIN"
320 K$ = INKEY$
330 IF K$ <> " " THEN 320
340 CLS
350 GOTO 1450
360 '
370 LOCATE 24,5
380 PRINT "} ";
390 LINE INPUT FUN$
400 GOSUB 1740
410 GOSUB 1820
420 PP = INSTR(FUN$,"()")
430 IF PP = 0 THEN 460
440 FUN$ = LEFT$(FUN$,PP-1) + "(A+IB)" + MID$(FUN$,PP+2)
450 GOTO 420
460 C$ = FUN$
470 LP = INSTR(C$,"(")
480 RP = INSTR(C$,")")
490 IF LP = 0 OR RP - LP < 2 THEN 2010
500 D$ = MID$(C$,LP+1,RP-LP-1)
510 GOSUB 1520
520 R1 = R : R2 = 0
530 I1 = I : I2 = 0
540 C$ = LEFT$(C$,LP-1) + MID$(C$,RP+1)
550 LP = INSTR(C$,"(")
560 RP = INSTR(C$,")")
570 IF C$ <> "" THEN 610
580 A = R1
590 B = I1
600 GOTO 920
610 IF LP AND (RP - LP > 1) THEN 670
```

```
620 R2 = R1
630 I2 = I1
640 R1 = A
650 I1 = B
660 GOTO 740
670 D$ = MID$(C$,LP+1,RP-LP-1)
680 C$ = LEFT$(C$,LP-1) + MID$(C$,RP+1)
690 GOSUB 1520
700 R2 = R
710 I2 = I
720 '
730 ' Addition
740 IF INSTR(C$,"+") = Ø THEN 800
750 A = R1 + R2
760 B = I1 + I2
770 GOTO 1370
780 '
790 ' Subtraction
800 IF INSTR(C$,"-") = Ø THEN 860
810 A = R1 - R2
820 B = I1 - I2
830 GOTO 1370
840 '
850 ' Multiplication
860 IF INSTR(C$,"*") = Ø THEN 920
870 A = R1 * R2 - I1 * I2
880 B = R1 * I2 + I1 * R2
890 GOTO 1370
900 '
910 ' Division
920 IF INSTR(C$,"/") = Ø THEN 1010
930 IF INSTR(C$,"1/") THEN 1010
940 NUM = R1 * R2 + I1 * I2
950 DEN = R2 * R2 + I2 * I2
960 A = NUM / DEN
970 B = (I1 * R2 - R1 * I2) / DEN
980 GOTO 1370
990 '
1000 ' Exponential
1010 IF INSTR(C$,"EXP") = Ø THEN 1070
1020 A = EXP(R2) * COS(I2)
1030 B = EXP(R2) * SIN(I2)
1040 GOTO 1370
1050 '
1060 ' Natural Logarithm
1070 IF INSTR(C$,"LOG") = Ø THEN 1210
1080 X = R2
```

```
1090 Y = I2
1100 GOSUB 1890
1110 IF MAG > 0 THEN 1160
1120 LOCATE 24,40
1130 PRINT "Illegal value for LOG function"
1140 A = 0
1150 GOTO 1170
1160 A = LOG(MAG)
1170 B = ANG
1180 GOTO 1370
1190 '
1200 ' Square Root
1210 IF INSTR(C$,"SQR") = 0 THEN 1270
1220 A = SQR((R2 + SQR(R2 * R2 + I2 * I2)) / 2)
1230 B = I2 / A / 2
1240 GOTO 1370
1250 '
1260 ' Inverse
1270 IF INSTR(C$,"1/") = 0 THEN 1330
1280 R1 = 1
1290 I1 = 0
1300 GOTO 940
1310 '
1320 ' Function not recognized
1330 LOCATE 24,40
1340 IF LEN(C$) THEN PRINT "Unknown function
1350 '
1360 ' output of result
1370 LOCATE 24,40
1380 PRINT "=   ";
1390 FUN$ = "(" + STR$(A) + "+i" + STR$(B) + ")"
1400 GOSUB 1820
1410 PTR = INSTR(FUN$,"+i-")
1420 IF PTR THEN MID$(FUN$,PTR,3) = " -i"
1430 GOSUB 1820
1440 PRINT FUN$
1450 LOCATE 1,1
1460 PRINT TAB(9)"Functions ...   +   -   *   /   SQR()   EXP()   LOG()   1/()
1470 PRINT TAB(9)"Returned   ...   (A+iB)   'A' and/or 'B' may be used
     for input
1480 PRINT SPACE$(160)
1490 GOTO 370
1500 '
1510 ' subroutine for separating out R and I from D$
1520 FUN$ = D$
1530 GOSUB 1820
1540 DA = INSTR(FUN$,"A")
```

```
1550 IF DA = Ø THEN 1580
1560 D$ = LEFT$(FUN$,DA-1) + STR$(A) + MID$(FUN$,DA+1)
1570 GOTO 1520
1580 DB = INSTR(FUN$,"B")
1590 IF DB = Ø THEN 1620
1600 D$ = LEFT$(FUN$,DB-1) + STR$(B) + MID$(FUN$,DB+1)
1610 GOTO 1520
1620 JP = INSTR(FUN$,"I")
1630 IF JP = Ø THEN JP = INSTR(FUN$,"J")
1640 I = Ø
1650 R = VAL(D$)
1660 IF JP = Ø THEN 1710
1670 I = VAL(MID$(FUN$,JP+1))
1680 IF JP = LEN(FUN$) THEN I = 1
1690 IF JP < 2 THEN 1710
1700 IF MID$(FUN$,JP-1,1) = "-" THEN I = -I
1710 RETURN
1720 '
1730 ' subroutine for capitalization
1740 FOR CHAR = 1 TO LEN(FUN$)
1750 IF MID$(FUN$,CHAR,1) < "a" THEN 1780
1760 IF MID$(FUN$,CHAR,1) > "z" THEN 1780
1770 MID$(FUN$,CHAR,1) = CHR$(ASC(MID$(FUN$,CHAR,1))-32)
1780 NEXT CHAR
1790 RETURN
1800 '
1810 ' subroutine to remove spaces
1820 SP = INSTR(FUN$," ")
1830 IF SP = Ø THEN 1860
1840 FUN$ = LEFT$(FUN$,SP-1) + MID$(FUN$,SP+1)
1850 GOTO 1820
1860 RETURN
1870 '
1880 ' subroutine ... rectangular to polar ... X,Y to MAG,ANG
1890 MAG = SQR(X*X + Y*Y)
1900 NINETY = 2 * ATN(1)
1910 IF X THEN ANG = ATN(Y/X) ELSE ANG = NINETY * ((Y<Ø) - (Y>Ø))
1920 IF X < Ø THEN ANG = ANG + 2 * NINETY * ((ANG>Ø) - (ANG<=Ø))
1930 RETURN
1940 '
1950 ' subroutine ... polar to rectangular ... MAG,ANG to X,Y
1960 X = MAG * COS(ANG)
1970 Y = MAG * SIN(ANG)
1980 RETURN
1990 '
2000 ' no comprehendo
2010 LOCATE 24,40
```

```
2020 PRINT "Syntax problem ... try again"
2030 GOTO 1370
```

```
 * * *   COMPLEX NUMBER CALCULATOR   * * *

Functions for one complex number  ...   SQR(), EXP(), LOG(), 1/()
Functions for two complex numbers ...   + - * /

Results are returned in variables A and B, and may be used in
further calculations.  Use of (A+iB) or () inputs previous results

Examples of legal input ...
                    (3+i4)+(2-i2)
                    (3+i4)*(2)
                    (a+ib)*(2)
                    *(2-i3)          ...same as (A+iB)*(2-i3)
                    (2-i3)*()        ...same as (2-i3)*(A-iB)
                    +(j4)

Spaces may be used anywhere.
You may use either 'i' or 'j' for the imaginary part.
All values should be enclosed in parenthesis.
Simply type in your problems and press the enter key.

               PRESS THE SPACE BAR TO BEGIN
```

Fig. 5-1. The instructions for the *Complex Number* program.

```
    Functions ...    + - * /  SQR()  EXP()  LOG()  1/()
    Returned  ...    (A+iB)  'A' and/or 'B' may be used for input

} sqr(3+i4)
                                =  (2+i1)

} () * ()
                                =  (3+i4)

} asdfgh
                             Syntax problem ... try again
                                =  (3+i4)

} (a+ib) / (i7)
                                =  (.5714285-i.4285715)

} (A+jB) * (j7)
                                =  (3.000001+i3.999999)

} log(27-i39)
                                =  (3.859343-i.9652517)

} EXP  ()
                                =  (27-i39.00001)

}
```

Fig. 5-2. Sample results of the *Complex Number* program.

FRACTIONS

This program solves problems involving fractions. Fractions may be added, subtracted, multiplied, and divided. Also provided are several related computations such as finding the greatest common divisor and least common multiple of two integers, reducing a fraction to its lowest terms, approximating the value of a decimal number with fractions, and converting a fraction into a decimal number.

This program demonstrates one method of using the special function keys on your IBM Personal Computer. The function keys work well for setting up a "menu" of selections, as the program demonstrates. Program lines 350 and 540 define and activate the special function keys. When you press a function key, the appropriate subroutine is run just as soon as the program gets to the end of the currently executing program line. Take a close look at program lines 560 to 580. The program sits and spins its wheels by looping through these lines over and over, while it waits for you to press a special function key. And as soon as any activated subroutine is finished (at the return statement) the program immediately branches back to these three lines. Your computer goes through a number of "hurry up and waits" while you make each menu selection. The WHILE—WEND loop terminates when you press F10. Look at the subroutine labeled F10 (line 1920), and see if you can figure out why the program terminates quickly after returning from this subroutine.

After you select a computation from the menu, you will be prompted to enter the appropriate fractions or numbers. The solution will be computed and displayed, and you will be asked to press the space bar to return to the main menu. Several sample calculations are presented for comparison with your results. See Figs. 5-3 through 5-8. Notice that all fractional results are automatically converted to lowest terms. For example, if you add ¼ and ¼ the solution will be ½ instead of 2/4.

The decimal to fraction conversion routine is rather interesting. (Function key F8). In the example presented in Fig. 5-6, we compute increasingly accurate fractions as approximations to the value of pi. Notice that the fraction 355/113 is a very good approximation. If you were to design two gears, one with 355 teeth and one with 113 teeth, the gear ratio would be very close to pi to 1.

```
10 ' *********************
20 ' **      FRACTION     **
30 ' *********************
40 '
50 CLEAR
60 SCREEN 0,0,0,0
70 CLS
80 KEY OFF
90 DEFDBL A-Z
100 LOCATE 1,28
110 PRINT "* * *  FRACTIONS  * * *
120 LOCATE 3,1
130 PRINT "Functions for two fractions ...
140 PRINT
150 PRINT TAB(22)"F1.    Fraction 1    +    Fraction 2
160 PRINT TAB(22)"F2.    Fraction 1    -    Fraction 2
170 PRINT TAB(22)"F3.    Fraction 1    *    Fraction 2
180 PRINT TAB(22)"F4.    Fraction 1    /    Fraction 2
190 PRINT
200 PRINT "Functions of two numbers ...
```

```
210 PRINT
220 PRINT TAB(22)"F5.    Greatest common divisor
230 PRINT TAB(22)"F6.    Least common multiple
240 PRINT TAB(22)"F7.    Reduction to lowest terms
250 PRINT
260 PRINT "Function of one number ...
270 PRINT
280 PRINT TAB(22)"F8.    Decimal to fraction approximation
290 PRINT TAB(22)"F9.    Fraction to decimal conversion
300 PRINT
310 PRINT
320 PRINT TAB(22)"F10.   Quit
330 LOCATE 25,22
340 PRINT "PRESS ANY SPECIAL FUNCTION KEY";
350 ON KEY(1)  GOSUB 620
360 ON KEY(2)  GOSUB 730
370 ON KEY(3)  GOSUB 840
380 ON KEY(4)  GOSUB 950
390 ON KEY(5)  GOSUB 1060
400 ON KEY(6)  GOSUB 1180
410 ON KEY(7)  GOSUB 1300
420 ON KEY(8)  GOSUB 1420
430 ON KEY(9)  GOSUB 1790
440 ON KEY(10) GOSUB 1920
450 KEY(1) ON
460 KEY(2) ON
470 KEY(3) ON
480 KEY(4) ON
490 KEY(5) ON
500 KEY(6) ON
510 KEY(7) ON
520 KEY(8) ON
530 KEY(9) ON
540 KEY(10) ON
550 '
560 WHILE QUIT = NOT.YET
570 KEY.BUFFER.CLEAR$ = INKEY$
580 WEND
590 CLS
600 END
610 '
620 ' F1 Subroutine
630 FUN$ = "+"
640 SCREEN 0,0,1,1
650 GOSUB 1970
660 N = N1 * D2 + N2 * D1
670 D = D1 * D2
```

```
680 GOSUB 2400
690 GOSUB 2510
700 SCREEN 0,0,0,0
710 RETURN
720 '
730 ' F2 Subroutine
740 FUN$ = "-"
750 SCREEN 0,0,1,1
760 GOSUB 1970
770 N = N1 * D2 - N2 * D1
780 D = D1 * D2
790 GOSUB 2400
800 GOSUB 2510
810 SCREEN 0,0,0,0
820 RETURN
830 '
840 ' F3 Subroutine
850 FUN$ = "*"
860 SCREEN 0,0,1,1
870 GOSUB 1970
880 N = N1 * N2
890 D = D1 * D2
900 GOSUB 2400
910 GOSUB 2510
920 SCREEN 0,0,0,0
930 RETURN
940 '
950 ' F4 Subroutine
960 FUN$ = "/"
970 SCREEN 0,0,1,1
980 GOSUB 1970
990 N = N1 * D2
1000 D = D1 * N2
1010 GOSUB 2400
1020 GOSUB 2510
1030 SCREEN 0,0,0,0
1040 RETURN
1050 '
1060 ' F5 Subroutine
1070 SCREEN 0,0,1,1
1080 CLS
1090 LOCATE 7,14
1100 INPUT "Greatest common divisor.  Enter 'A,B' ";A,B
1110 GOSUB 2740
1120 LOCATE 14,14
1130 PRINT "Greatest common divisor is ";GCD
1140 GOSUB 2670
```

```
1150 SCREEN 0,0,0,0
1160 RETURN
1170 '
1180 ' F6 Subroutine
1190 SCREEN 0,0,1,1
1200 CLS
1210 LOCATE 7,14
1220 INPUT "Least common multiple.  Enter 'A,B' ";A,B
1230 GOSUB 2820
1240 LOCATE 14,14
1250 PRINT "Least common multiple is ";LCM
1260 GOSUB 2670
1270 SCREEN 0,0,0,0
1280 RETURN
1290 '
1300 ' F7 Subroutine
1310 SCREEN 0,0,1,1
1320 CLS
1330 LOCATE 7,14
1340 INPUT "Reduce to lowest terms.  Enter 'A,B' ";N,D
1350 GOSUB 2400
1360 LOCATE 14,14
1370 PRINT "Reduced to lowest terms =    ";N;"   ";D
1380 GOSUB 2670
1390 SCREEN 0,0,0,0
1400 RETURN
1410 '
1420 ' F8 Subroutine
1430 SCREEN 0,0,1,1
1440 CLS
1450 LOCATE 7,9
1460 INPUT "Decimal to fraction conversion.  Enter X ";X
1470 PRINT
1480 PRINT TAB(14)"Fraction"TAB(47)"Error from X"
1490 PRINT TAB(13)"--------------"TAB(44)"------------------"
1500 T1 = 1
1510 T2 = 1
1520 T3 = 1
1530 T4 = INT(X)
1540 T5 = X - T4
1550 T7 = 0
1560 T8 = 0
1570 DIF = 1
1580    WHILE ABS(DIF) > 1E-15
1590    NUM = T3 * T4 + T7
1600    DEN = T4 * T8 + T2
1610    DIF = NUM / DEN - X
```

```
1620    IF T5 = 0 THEN 1710
1630    T4 = INT(T1/T5)
1640    T6 = T5
1650    T5 = T1 - T4 * T5
1660    T1 = T6
1670    T7 = T3
1680    T3 = NUM
1690    T2 = T8
1700    T8 = DEN
1710    PRINT TAB(14)NUM;" / ";DEN;
1720    PRINT TAB(49);
1730    PRINT USING "+#.#^^^^";DIF
1740    WEND
1750 GOSUB 2670
1760 SCREEN 0,0,0,0
1770 RETURN
1780 '
1790 ' F9 Subroutine
1800 SCREEN 0,0,1,1
1810 CLS
1820 LOCATE 7,1
1830 PRINT "Enter a fraction,
1840 LINE INPUT "'numerator/denominator' ...";FR$
1850 GOSUB 2230
1860 LOCATE 12,30
1870 PRINT "= ";NF/DF
1880 GOSUB 2670
1890 SCREEN 0,0,0,0
1900 RETURN
1910 '
1920 ' F10 Subroutine
1930 QUIT = 1
1940 RETURN
1950 '
1960 ' Subroutine, input two fractions
1970 CLS
1980 LOCATE 7,1
1990 PRINT "Enter first fraction,
2000 LINE INPUT "'numerator/denominator' ...";FR$
2110 PRINT "Enter second fraction,
2120 LINE INPUT "'numerator/denominator' ...";FR$
2130 IF INSTR(FR$,".") = 0 THEN 2170
2140 BEEP
2150 PRINT TAB(40)"No decimal points please"
2160 GOTO 2120
2170 GOSUB 2230
2180 N2 = NF
```

```
2190 D2 = DF
2200 RETURN
2210 '
2220 ' Subroutine, FR$ to NF and DF
2230 IP = INSTR(FR$,",")
2240 IF IP = Ø THEN 2270
2250 MID$(FR$,IP,1) = "/"
2260 GOTO 2230
2270 IP = INSTR(FR$,"/")
2280 IF IP THEN 2310
2290 FR$ = FR$ + "/1"
2300 GOTO 2270
2310 NF = VAL(LEFT$(FR$,IP))
2320 DF = VAL(MID$(FR$,IP+1))
2330 IF INSTR(FR$,"N") THEN NF = N
2334 IF INSTR(FR$,"n") THEN NF = N
2350 IF INSTR(FR$,"D") THEN DF = D
2360 IF INSTR(FR$,"d") THEN DF = D
2370 RETURN
2380 '
2390 ' Subroutine, reduction of N and D to lowest terms
2400 A = N
2410 B = D
2420 GOSUB 2740
2430 N = N / GCD
2440 D = D / GCD
2450 IF SGN(D) > -1 THEN 2480
2460 N = -N
2470 D = -D
2480 RETURN
2490 '
2500 ' Subroutine, output of two fraction problem results
2510 CLS
2520 LOCATE 7,27
2530 PRINT N1;"/";D1;"   ";FUN$;"   ";N2;"/";D2
2540 LOCATE 10,30
2550 IF D <> 1 THEN 2580
2560 PRINT "=   ";N
2570 GOTO 2630
2580 PRINT "=   ";N;"/";D
2590 IF ABS(N) < D THEN 2630
2600 LOCATE 12,30
2610 NUM = VAL(LEFT$(STR$(N/D),INSTR(STR$(N/D),".")))
2620 PRINT "=   ";NUM;" and ";N - NUM * D;"/";D
2630 GOSUB 2670
2640 RETURN
2650 '
```

```
2660 ' Subroutine, wait until user wants to proceed
2670 LOCATE 25,25
2680 PRINT "PRESS SPACE BAR TO CONTINUE";
2690 K$ = INKEY$
2700 IF K$ <> " " THEN 2690
2710 RETURN
2720 '
2730 ' Subroutine, greatest common divisor of A and B
2740 TEMP = A - B * INT(A/B)
2750 A = B
2760 B = TEMP
2770 IF TEMP THEN 2740
2780 GCD = A
2790 RETURN
2800 '
2810 ' Subroutine, least common multiple of A and B
2820 A2 = A
2830 B2 = B
2840 GOSUB 2740
2850 LCM = ABS(A2 * B2 / GCD)
2860 RETURN
```

```
                        * * *   FRACTIONS   * * *
Functions for two fractions ...


                F1.    Fraction 1    +    Fraction 2
                F2.    Fraction 1    -    Fraction 2
                F3.    Fraction 1    *    Fraction 2
                F4.    Fraction 1    /    Fraction 2


Functions of two numbers ...


                F5.    Greatest common divisor
                F6.    Least common multiple
                F7.    Reduction to lowest terms


Function of one number ...


                F8.    Decimal to fraction approximation
                F9.    Fraction to decimal conversion



                F10.   Quit



                PRESS ANY SPECIAL FUNCTION KEY
```

Fig. 5-3. The options you may use in the *Fractions* program.

```
Enter first fraction,
'numerator/denominator' ...63/21


               +


Enter second fraction,
'numerator/denominator' ...42/12
```

Fig. 5-4. Sample problem being entered into the *Fractions* program.

Fig. 5-5. Sample results of the *Fractions* program.

```
      63 / 21    +    42 / 12


      =    13 / 2

      =    6   and   1 / 2


   PRESS SPACE BAR TO CONTINUE
```

```
Decimal to fraction conversion.   Enter X ? 3.14159265359

     Fraction                        Error from X
   ----------------                  ----------------
      3  /  1                           -1.4D-01
     22  /  7                           +1.3D-03
     333  /  106                        -8.3D-05
     355  /  113                        +2.7D-07
     103993  /  33102                   -5.8D-10
     104348  /  33215                   +3.3D-10
     208341  /  66317                   -1.2D-10
     312689  /  99532                   +2.9D-11
     833719  /  265381                  -8.9D-12
     1146408  /  364913                 +1.4D-12
     5419351  /  1725033                -1.8D-13
     6565759  /  2089946                +9.3D-14
     11985110  /  3814979               -3.3D-14
     18550869  /  5904925               +1.2D-14
     30535979  /  9719904               -5.8D-15
     49086848  /  15624829              +8.3D-16

              PRESS SPACE BAR TO CONTINUE
```

Fig. 5-6. Sample results of the *Fractions* program.

```
Enter a fraction,
'numerator/denominator' ...355/113




                              =   3.141592920353982


                         PRESS SPACE BAR TO CONTINUE
```

Fig. 5-7. Sample results of the *Fractions* program.

FUNCTION ANALYSIS

This program helps you analyze functions of the form Y = f (X). See Fig. 5-8. Starting at line 9000 is the function to be analyzed. The function Y = SIN(X)/X has been programmed to demonstrate the program. Later on, you should alter lines 9000 through the end of the program for your own functions.

Seven analysis options are displayed in the main menu. The first five choices find solutions within an interval. You are asked for the left (X1) and right (X2) endpoints that define the interval of concern. In this interval you can find a minimum point, a maximum point, a zero crossing point, and the area under the curve (integration by Simpson's rule). To help you visualize the function, the fifth choice will sketch the function for the designated interval.

The last two selections find values at a single point of the function. You are asked for the value of X that defines the point; then the function value or the slope of the function (first derivative) at the indicated point is computed and displayed.

```
10 ' ***********************
20 ' **      FUNCTION      **
30 ' ***********************
40 '
50 CLEAR
60 SCREEN 0,0,0,0
70 WIDTH 80
80 KEY OFF
90 '
100 WHILE NOT FINISHED
110 CLS
120 PRINT TAB(18)"* * *   FUNCTION ANALYSIS   * * *
130 LOCATE 4
140 PRINT TAB(21)"Analysis in an interval
150 PRINT
160 PRINT TAB(26)"<1>   Minimum point
170 PRINT TAB(26)"<2>   Maximum point
180 PRINT TAB(26)"<3>   Zero point
190 PRINT TAB(26)"<4>   Area by integration
200 PRINT TAB(26)"<5>   Sketch
```

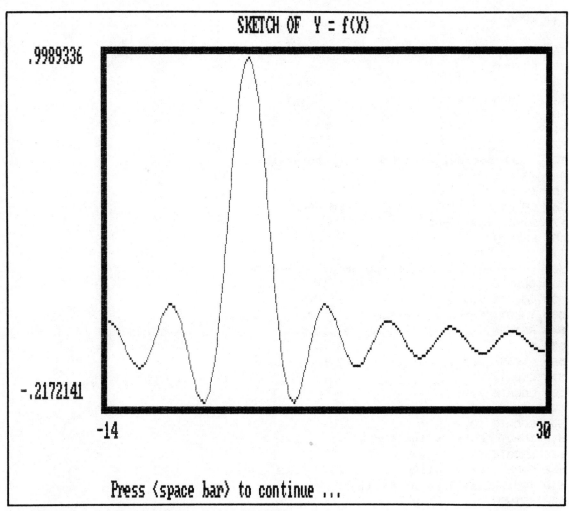

Fig. 5-8. Display produced by the *Function Analysis* program.

```
210 PRINT
220 PRINT TAB(21)"Analysis at a point
230 PRINT
240 PRINT TAB(26)"<6>    Value of f(X)
250 PRINT TAB(26)"<7>    First derivative
260 PRINT
270 PRINT TAB(26)"<8>    End
280 PRINT
290 PRINT
300 PRINT
310 PRINT TAB(21)"....   SELECT ONE  ....";
320 GOSUB 440
330 ON SELECTION GOSUB 870,1120,1370,1800,2030,2430,2510,390,370
```

```
340 WEND
350 '
360 ' Subroutine, immediate return for choice "9"
370 RETURN
380 '
390 ' Terminate program
400 CLS
410 END
420 '
430 ' Subroutine, wait for digit selection
440 K$ = INKEY$
450 IF K$ = "" THEN 440
460 IF K$ < "1" OR K$ > "9" THEN 440
470 SELECTION = VAL(K$)
480 RETURN
490 '
500 ' Subroutine, get X for point of concern
510 CLS
520 LOCATE 9,9
530 INPUT "Enter value for X ...   ",X
540 RETURN
550 '
560 ' Subroutine, get X1 and X2 for interval
570 CLS
580 LOCATE 7,9
590 PRINT "Interval will be from X1 to X2 ...
600 LOCATE 10,9
610 INPUT "Enter value for X1 ...   ",X1
620 LOCATE 11,9
630 INPUT "Enter value for X2 ...   ",X2
640 IF X2 < X1 THEN SWAP X1, X2
650 RETURN
660 '
670 ' Subroutine, wait for user before proceeding
680 PRINT
690 PRINT
700 PRINT
710 PRINT "Press <space bar> to continue ...";
720 K$ = INKEY$
730 IF K$ <> " " THEN 720
740 RETURN
750 '
760 ' Subroutine, slope of function given a delta
770 XT = X
780 X = XT - DELTA / 2
790 GOSUB 9000
800 Y1 = Y
```

```
810 X = XT + DELTA / 2
820 GOSUB 9000
830 SLOPE = (Y - Y1) / DELTA
840 X = XT
850 RETURN
860 '
870 ' Minimum
880 GOSUB 570
890 CLS
900 PRINT "Finding a minimum point ...
910 PRINT
920 WHILE X1 <> X2
930 PRINT ,,X1,X2
940 FOR DX = 0 TO 10
950 X = X1 + DX * (X2 - X1) / 10
960 GOSUB 9000
970 IF DX > 0 AND Y > MIN THEN 1000
980 MIN = Y
990 X3 = DX
1000 NEXT DX
1010 X4 = X1
1020 X5 = X2
1030 IF X3 < 6 THEN X2 = X1 + 6 * (X2 - X1) / 10
1040 IF X3 > 5 THEN X1 = X1 + 5 * (X2 - X1) / 10
1050 IF X1 = X4 AND X2 = X5 THEN X1 = X2
1060 WEND
1070 PRINT
1080 PRINT "Minimum point at X = ";X1;" is Y = ";Y
1090 GOSUB 680
1100 RETURN
1110 '
1120 ' Maximum
1130 GOSUB 570
1140 CLS
1150 PRINT "Finding a maximum point ...
1160 PRINT
1170 WHILE X1 <> X2
1180 PRINT ,,X1,X2
1190 FOR DX = 0 TO 10
1200 X = X1 + DX * (X2 - X1) / 10
1210 GOSUB 9000
1220 IF DX > 0 AND Y < MAX THEN 1250
1230 MAX = Y
1240 X3 = DX
1250 NEXT DX
1260 X4 = X1
1270 X5 = X2
```

```
1280 IF X3 < 6 THEN X2 = X1 + 6 * (X2 - X1) / 10
1290 IF X3 > 5 THEN X1 = X1 + 5 * (X2 - X1) / 10
1300 IF X1 = X4 AND X2 = X5 THEN X1 = X2
1310 WEND
1320 PRINT
1330 PRINT "Maximum point at  X = ";X1;" is Y = ";Y
1340 GOSUB 680
1350 RETURN
1360 '
1370 ' Zero
1380 GOSUB 570
1390 CLS
1400 PRINT "Looking for zero crossing between X1 = ";X1;" and  X2 = ";X2
1410 X = X1
1420 GOSUB 9000
1430 Y1 = Y
1440 X = X2
1450 GOSUB 9000
1460 Y2 = Y
1470 IF SGN(Y1) <> SGN(Y2) THEN 1600
1480 FOR I = 1 TO 27
1490 X = X1 + I * (X2 - X1) / 28
1500 GOSUB 9000
1510 IF SGN(Y) = SGN(Y1) THEN 1540
1520 X2 = X
1530 Y2 = Y
1540 NEXT I
1550 IF SGN(Y1) * SGN(Y2) = -1 THEN 1600
1560 PRINT
1570 PRINT "There doesn't appear to be a zero crossing point
1580 PRINT "in the given interval.
1590 GOTO 1770
1600 PRINT
1610 WHILE X1 <> X2
1620 PRINT ,,X1,X2
1630 X = (X1 + X2) / 2
1640 GOSUB 9000
1650 X3 = X1
1660 X4 = X2
1670 IF SGN(Y) = SGN(Y1) THEN 1710
1680 X2 = X
1690 Y2 = Y
1700 GOTO 1730
1710 X1 = X
1720 Y1 = Y
1730 IF X1 = X3 AND X2 = X4 THEN X1 = X2
1740 WEND
```

```
1750 PRINT
1760 PRINT "Zero crossing is very near X = ";X
1770 GOSUB 680
1780 RETURN
1790 '
1800 ' Subroutine, integration
1810 GOSUB 570
1820 CLS
1830 PRINT "Integration by Simpson's rule ...
1840 LOCATE 5,1
1850 PRINT "Area under curve from X1 = ";X1;" to X2 = ";X2
1860 PRINT
1870 FOR I = 2 TO 7
1880 AREA = Ø
1890 INC = 2 ^ I
1900 H = (X2 - X1) / INC
1910 FLG = 1
1920 FOR J = Ø TO INC
1930 FLG = -(FLG = Ø)
1940 X = X1 + J * H
1950 GOSUB 9000
1960 AREA = AREA + Y + Y + 2 * Y * FLG + Y * ((J=Ø)+(J=INC))
1970 NEXT J
1980 PRINT "Area found with"INC"steps = "TAB(29) AREA * H / 3
1990 NEXT I
2000 GOSUB 680
2010 RETURN
2020 '
2030 ' Graph
2040 GOSUB 570
2050 CLS
2060 LOCATE 12,22
2070 PRINT "Finding sketch boundaries ...
2080 X = X1
2090 GOSUB 9000
2100 YMIN = Y
2110 YMAX = Y
2120 FOR I = Ø TO 100
2130 X = X1 + I * (X2 - X1) / 100
2140 GOSUB 9000
2150 IF Y < YMIN THEN YMIN = Y
2160 IF Y > YMAX THEN YMAX = Y
2170 NEXT I
2180 SCREEN 2
2190 LOCATE 3,1
2200 PRINT YMAX
```

```
2210 LOCATE 20,1
2220 PRINT YMIN
2230 LOCATE 22,12
2240 PRINT X1;TAB(77-LEN(STR$(X2)))X2
2250 LOCATE 1,35
2260 PRINT "SKETCH OF  Y = f(X)
2270 LINE (92,164)-(608,16),,B
2280 LINE (98,162)-(602,18),,B
2290 PAINT (95,161)
2300 FOR I = 0 TO 500 STEP 5
2310 X = X1 + I * (X2 - X1) / 500
2320 GOSUB 9000
2330 IF I THEN 2360
2340 PSET (100 + I, 160 - 140 * (Y - YMIN) / (YMAX - YMIN))
2350 GOTO 2370
2360 LINE -(100 + I, 160 - 140 * (Y - YMIN) / (YMAX - YMIN))
2370 NEXT I
2380 LOCATE 25,14
2390 GOSUB 710
2400 SCREEN 0,0,0,0
2410 RETURN
2420 '
2430 ' Value of f(X)
2440 GOSUB 510
2450 GOSUB 9000
2460 PRINT
2470 PRINT "Value of f(X) at X = ";X;" is Y = ";Y
2480 GOSUB 680
2490 RETURN
2500 '
2510 ' First derivative
2520 GOSUB 510
2530 CLS
2540 PRINT ," DELTA"," SLOPE      ...   at X = ";X
2550 PRINT
2560 FOR I = 0 TO 4
2570 DELTA = VAL("1E-"+STR$(I))
2580 GOSUB 770
2590 PRINT ,DELTA,SLOPE
2600 NEXT. I
2610 GOSUB 680
2620 RETURN
2630 '
2640 ' Subroutine, user defined Y = f(X)
9000 IF X = 0 THEN Y = 1 ELSE Y = SIN(X)/X
9010 RETURN
```

PLOT-3D

This program generates three-dimensional plots for functions of the type $Z = f(X,Y)$. Before running this program, you should edit the subroutine lines beginning with line 9000. This is where you define the function you wish to plot. X and Y are variables passed to this subroutine. Your subroutine should compute a value of Z as a function of X and Y. Be sure to conclude the subroutine lines with a return statement.

Several questions are asked by the program before the actual plotting begins as shown in Fig. 5-9. These questions allow you to define the range of each variable, the number of lines to plot, and whether or

```
                        ┌─────────────────────┐
                        │      PLOT-3D         │
                        └─────────────────────┘


Just a reminder ...
            Your function Z=f(X,Y) should be defined at line 9000

Enter X range ... Minimum, Maximum? -17,17

Enter Y range ... Minimum, Maximum? -17,17

Enter Z range ... Minimum, Maximum? -1,2

Tilt angle (degrees)? 17

Rotation angle (degrees)? 17

Number of X lines to plot? 17

Number of Y lines to plot? 0

Want hidden line removal (y/n) ? y
```

Fig. 5-9. The initial display produced by the *Plot-3D* program.

159

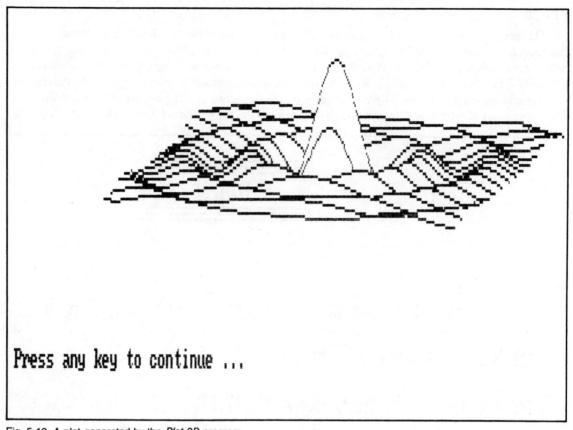

Fig. 5-10. A plot generated by the *Plot-3D* program.

not you want to remove the hidden lines at the back of the plot. By experimenting with different answers to these questions, you can generate a wide variety of plots for a given function. Two sample plots are given in Figs. 5-10 through 5-13 to demonstrate the variety of plots possible. Both of these plots are for the same function.

```
10 '*******************
20 '**    PLOT-3D    **
30 '*******************
40 '
50 CLEAR
60 SCREEN 2
70 KEY OFF
80 CLS
90 DIM HIGH%(640),LOW%(640)
100 DEF FNDTR(X) = X/57.29578
110 LINE (240,5)-(390,17),,B
120 LINE (236,3)-(394,19),,B
130 LINE (232,1)-(398,21),,B
```

```
140 LOCATE 2,37
150 PRINT "PLOT-3D"
160 PRINT
170 '
180 '*******************************************
190 '**  Ask the user for the plot parameters  **
200 '*******************************************
210 LOCATE 7,1
220 PRINT "Just a reminder ..."
230 LOCATE 8,12
240 PRINT "Your function Z=f(X,Y) should be defined at line 9000"
250 PRINT
260 INPUT "Enter X range ... Minimum, Maximum";XMIN,XMAX
270 PRINT
280 INPUT "Enter Y range ... Minimum, Maximum";YMIN,YMAX
290 PRINT
300 INPUT "Enter Z range ... Minimum, Maximum";ZMIN,ZMAX
310 PRINT
320 INPUT "Tilt angle (degrees)";TILT
330 PRINT
340 INPUT "Rotation angle (degrees)";ROTA
350 PRINT
360 INPUT "Number of X lines to plot";XLINES
370 PRINT
```

```
            Your last plot had these parameters ...

            The X values went from -17 to   17
            The Y values went from -17 to   17
            The Z axis went from -1 to  2
            The view was tilted  17 degrees
            The view was rotated  17 degrees
             17 lines were plotted in the X direction
              0 lines were plotted in the Y direction
            The hidden line option was selected

            Your defined function ...

            9000 Z=SQR(X*X+Y*Y)
            9010 IF Z<>0 THEN Z=SIN(Z)/Z ELSE Z=1
            9020 RETURN
            Ok
```

Fig. 5-11. Display produced by the *Plot-3D* program.

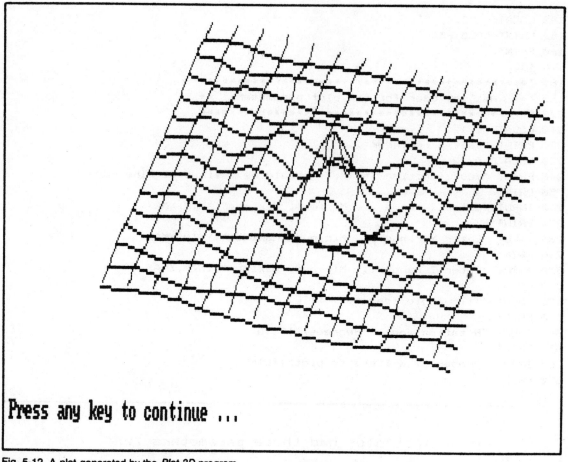

Press any key to continue ...

Fig. 5-12. A plot generated by the *Plot-3D* program.

```
380 INPUT "Number of Y lines to plot";YLINES
390 PRINT
400 INPUT "Want hidden line removal (y/n) ";Q$
410 HIDE = 0
420 IF Q$ = "y" OR Q$ = "Y" THEN HIDE = 1
430 '
440 '***********************************************************************
450 '**   Much of the math is done only once ... speeding things up later **
460 '***********************************************************************
470 CTILT = COS(FNDTR(TILT))
480 STILT = SIN(FNDTR(TILT))
490 CROTA = COS(FNDTR(ROTA))
500 SROTA = SIN(FNDTR(ROTA))
510 XMEAN = (XMAX+XMIN)/2
520 XDIFF = XMAX-XMIN
530 YMEAN = (YMAX+YMIN)/2
```

162

```
540 YDIFF = YMAX-YMIN
550 ZMEAN = (ZMAX+ZMIN)/2
560 ZDIFF = ZMAX-ZMIN
570 '
580 '*********************************
590 '**   Plot the X lines ... if any  **
600 '*********************************
610 CLS
620 LOCATE 9,23
630 IF XLINES < 2 THEN 810
640 IF HIDE = 0 THEN 680
650 PRINT "Initialization is taking place ..."
660 GOSUB 1260
670 CLS
680 FOR Y = YMAX TO YMIN STEP YDIFF/(1-XLINES)
690 FOR X = XMIN TO XMAX STEP XDIFF/50
700 XLAST = XPLOT
710 YLAST = YPLOT
720 GOSUB 1360
730 IF X = XMIN THEN 760
```

```
      Your last plot had these parameters ...

      The X values went from -17 to   17
      The Y values went from -17 to   17
      The Z axis went from -1 to  2
      The view was tilted  57 degrees
      The view was rotated  17 degrees
       15 lines were plotted in the X direction
       15 lines were plotted in the Y direction
      The hidden line option was not selected


      Your defined function ...

      9000  Z=SQR(X*X+Y*Y)
      9010  IF  Z<>0 THEN Z=SIN(Z)/Z ELSE Z=1
      9020  RETURN
      Ok
```

Fig. 5-13. Display produced by the *Plot-3D* program.

```
740 IF HIDE = Ø THEN LINE (XLAST,YLAST)-(XPLOT,YPLOT)
750 IF HIDE = 1 THEN GOSUB 1490
760 NEXT X,Y
770 '
780 '*******************************
790 '**   Plot the Y lines ... if any  **
800 '*******************************
810 IF YLINES < 2 THEN 960
820 IF HIDE THEN GOSUB 1260
830 FOR X = XMIN TO XMAX STEP XDIFF/(YLINES-1)
840 FOR Y = YMIN TO YMAX STEP YDIFF/50
850 XLAST = XPLOT
860 YLAST = YPLOT
870 GOSUB 1360
880 IF Y = YMIN THEN 910
890 IF HIDE = Ø THEN LINE (XLAST,YLAST)-(XPLOT,YPLOT)
900 IF HIDE = 1 THEN GOSUB 1490
910 NEXT Y,X
920 '
930 '***************************************************
940 '**   Review of plot parameters before quitting  **
950 '***************************************************
960 GOSUB 1180
970 CLS
980 PRINT "Your last plot had these parameters ..."
990 PRINT
1000 PRINT "The X values went from ";XMIN;"to ";XMAX
1010 PRINT "The Y values went from ";YMIN;"to ";YMAX
1020 PRINT "The Z axis went from ";ZMIN;"to ";ZMAX
1030 PRINT "The view was tilted ";TILT;"degrees"
1040 PRINT "The view was rotated ";ROTA;"degrees"
1050 PRINT XLINES;"lines were plotted in the X direction"
1060 PRINT YLINES;"lines were plotted in the Y direction"
1070 PRINT "The hidden line option was ";
1080 IF HIDE=Ø THEN PRINT "not ";
1090 PRINT "selected"
1100 PRINT
1110 PRINT "Your defined function ..."
1120 PRINT
1130 LIST 9000-
1140 '
1150 '***********************************************************
1160 '**   Subroutine to wait until user is ready to proceed   **
1170 '***********************************************************
1180 LOCATE 24,1
1190 PRINT"Press any key to continue ...";
1200 K$ = INKEY$
```

```
1210 IF K$ = "" THEN 1200 ELSE RETURN
1220 '
1230 '*****************************************************************
1240 '**   Subroutine to initialize arrays for hidden line algorithm   **
1250 '*****************************************************************
1260 FOR I = 0 TO 640
1270 LOW%(I) = 200
1280 HIGH%(I) = 0
1290 NEXT I
1300 RETURN
1310 '
1320 '*****************************************************************
1330 '**   Subroutine to project space points onto a plane taking   **
1340 '**    into account the tilt and rotation for the viewpoint     **
1350 '*****************************************************************
1360 GOSUB 9000
1370 X2 = (X-XMEAN) / XDIFF
1380 Y2 = (Y-YMEAN) / YDIFF
1390 Z2 = (Z-ZMEAN) / ZDIFF
1400 X3 = X2 * CROTA - Y2 * SROTA
1410 Y3 = Z2 * CTILT - (X2 * SROTA + Y2 * CROTA) * STILT
1420 XPLOT = 320 + 370 * X3
1430 YPLOT = 100 - 116 * Y3
1440 RETURN
1450 '
1460 '*********************************************************
1470 '**   Subroutine for plotting with hidden line check   **
1480 '*********************************************************
1490 FOR XTST% = XLAST TO XPLOT STEP SGN(XPLOT-XLAST)
1500 PFLG = 0
1510 YTST% = YLAST + (XTST%-XLAST) * (YPLOT-YLAST) / (XPLOT-XLAST)
1520 IF LOW%(XTST%) <= YTST% THEN 1550
1530 LOW%(XTST%) = YTST%
1540 PFLG = 1
1550 IF HIGH%(XTST%) >= YTST% THEN 1580
1560 HIGH%(XTST%) = YTST%
1570 PFLG = 1
1580 IF PFLG = 1 THEN PSET(XTST%,YTST%)
1590 NEXT XTST%
1600 RETURN
1610 '
8970 '*********************************************************
8980 '**   User function starts at line 9000 ... Z = f(X,Y)   **
8990 '*********************************************************
9000 Z = SQR(X*X+Y*Y)
9010 IF Z <> 0 THEN Z = SIN(Z)/Z ELSE Z=1
9020 RETURN
```

PRIME NUMBERS

People have been interested in the generation of prime numbers for hundreds of years. This program will calculate all of the prime numbers less than 32767.

A number is prime if it can be divided evenly by 1 and its own value only. Many shortcuts can be incorporated into the calculations necessary to determine if a number is prime. These techniques are the basis of this program.

The first consideration is the range of values the prime number can have. A prime number is a positive integer, but if the integer is even and greater than 2, it is not prime. This immediately cuts the number of integers that can possibly be prime in half.

For the remaining numbers, once you have a likely value in mind, the only thing left to do is to test it. Testing usually involves dividing the number in question by the odd numbers less than itself and seeing if they divide into it evenly. This works well for values of 100 or less, but for a large number, the computational time will be excessive. The time can be cut because only the numbers less than the square root of the value need to be tested. So, for the number 101, it is only necessary to try the numbers 3, 5, 7, and 9. If any of these numbers will divide 101 evenly, it is not prime. You do not have to try to divide by the numbers 11 and above, because any value greater than the square root of the number in question will give a value below the square root of the number, and that value should have already been checked. For example, if the value is 143 and you test it with 13, which is greater than its square root, you end up with 11 which has already been checked.

The final thing that can be done to speed up the search is to check only the prime numbers less than the square root of the value. For our example of 101, once you have checked it with 3, it is not necessary to check it with 9. Any value that can be divided evenly by nine can also be divided by three. To do this, it is necessary to keep a list of all previous prime numbers. This is what the array in the program is for.

Using these basic procedures, it becomes possible to search many numbers for prime values in a short time. This program found the first 63 prime numbers in only 10 seconds!

```
100 '*********************************************************
110 '**              PRIME NUMBER GENERATOR              **
120 '**   VERSION 1.1                  12 DECEMBER 1982  **
130 '*********************************************************
140 '
150 CLS
160 DEFINT A-Z
170 DIM A(10000)
180 A(1) = 3
190 A(2) = 5
200 LATESTELEMENT = 2
210 POINTER = 7
220 TEST = 0
230 IF A(TESTELEMENT)<SQR(POINTER) THEN TESTELEMENT=TESTELEMENT + 1 :
    GOTO 230
240 FOR X = 1 TO TESTELEMENT
250 IF POINTER MOD A(X) = 0 THEN TEST = 1
260 NEXT
270 IF TEST = 1 THEN 310
280 LATESTELEMENT = LATESTELEMENT + 1
```

```
290 A(LATESTELEMENT) = POINTER
300 PRINT POINTER;
310 POINTER = POINTER + 2
320 GOTO 220
```

SIMULTANEOUS EQUATIONS

The *Simultaneous Equations* program solves systems of simultaneous linear equations with a unique twist. The equations are typed in just as they appear on paper. For example, if an equation in a book looks like this ... " 3 Apples + 4 Oranges = 7 ", you could enter it in exactly the same way. The variable names and their coefficients are deduced by the program. All letters are converted to uppercase, spaces are removed, multiplication symbols are inserted where implied, and a few other intricacies are performed for the program to understand the equations. Just in case, the equations are rewritten to the screen in a more formal style for you to check over before the solutions are found. The program will handle a wide variety of

```
        * * *   Simultaneous Equations   * * *


Type in the equations ...

3x + 4y -2z = 2
5 * z - 3 * y + 2 * x    =   19
X - Z + 5Y =-7


Equations entered ...

    3 X   +4 Y   -2 Z   =    2
    2 X   -3 Y   +5 Z   =   19
    1 X   +5 Y   -1 Z   =   -7


Press any key to continue


Working on equation   1
Working on equation   2
Working on equation   3


Results ...

X              4
Y             -2
Z              1

Press any key to continue
```

Fig. 5-14. Sample displays produced by the *Simultaneous Equations* program.

possible input formats, but there's always a way to beat the system. Check the displayed equations carefully to make sure your computer understands you.

After your last equation is entered, press the enter key. The equations will be displayed, and then the analysis will proceed. Any reasonable number of unknowns may be solved for. If the set of equations you've entered won't yield a unique answer, watch for a message to that effect. After all the unknowns are solved for, the solutions are displayed. Figure 5-14 illustrates the entire procedure.

```
10 ' *************************************
20 ' **      SIMULTANEOUS EQUATIONS      **
30 ' *************************************
40 '
50 CLEAR
60 SCREEN 0,0,0
70 KEY OFF
80 CLS
90 OPTION BASE 1
100 SIZE = 25
110 DIM MAT(SIZE,SIZE+1),VAR$(SIZE)
120 LOCATE 1,22
130 PRINT "* * *  Simultaneous Equations  * * *"
140 LOCATE 4,1
150 PRINT "Type in the equations ..."
160 PRINT
170 LINE INPUT A$
180 IF A$ = "" THEN 580
190 GOSUB 1180
200 GOSUB 1290
210 EQ = EQ + 1
220 FOR I = 1 TO LEN(A$)
230 B$ = MID$(A$,I,1)
240 C$ = MID$(A$,I+1,1)
250 D$ = D$ + B$
260 IF B$ >= "A" AND B$ <= "Z" AND (C$ < "A" OR C$ > "Z") THEN GOSUB 300
270 NEXT I
280 GOSUB 300
290 GOTO 170
300 NV = VAL(D$)
310 IF NV <> VAL(D$+"9") THEN RETURN
320 IF LEFT$(D$,1) <> "=" THEN 350
330 MAT(EQ,SIZE+1) = VAL(MID$(D$,2))
340 GOTO 540
350 IF NV THEN 410
360 IF INSTR(D$,"0") THEN 410
370 IF LEFT$(D$,1) = "-" THEN D$ = "-1"+MID$(D$,2)
380 IF LEFT$(D$,1) = "+" THEN D$ = "+1"+MID$(D$,2)
390 IF LEFT$(D$,1) <> "-" AND LEFT$(D$,1) <> "+" THEN D$ = "+1"+D$
400 GOTO 300
```

```
410 J = Ø
420 J = J + 1
430 J$ = MID$(D$,J,1)
440 IF J$ < "A" OR J$ > "Z" THEN D$ = LEFT$(D$,J-1) + MID$(D$,J+1) :
    GOTO 410
450 IF J < LEN(D$) THEN 420
460 PTR = Ø
470 FOR J = 1 TO SIZE
480 IF PTR THEN 51Ø
490 IF VAR$(J) = D$ THEN PTR = J
500 IF VAR$(J) = "" THEN PTR = J
510 NEXT J
520 VAR$(PTR) = D$
530 MAT(EQ,PTR) = NV
540 D$ = ""
550 RETURN
560 '
570 ' output equations
580 CLS
590 PRINT "Equations entered ..."
600 PRINT
610 FOR I = 1 TO EQ
620 IF I MOD 17 = Ø THEN GOSUB 1370
630 FOR J = 1 TO EQ
640 P$ = STR$(MAT(I,J))+" "+VAR$(J)
650 IF MAT(I,J) >= Ø AND J > 1 THEN MID$(P$,1,1) = "+"
660 PRINT "  ";P$;
670 NEXT J
680 PRINT "  = ";MAT(I,SIZE+1)
690 NEXT I
700 GOSUB 1370
710 CLS
720 LOCATE 5,1
730 EQ = Ø
740 FOR I = 1 TO SIZE
750 IF VAR$(I) <> "" THEN EQ = EQ + 1
760 NEXT I
770 FOR I = 1 TO EQ
780 MAT(I,EQ+1) = MAT(I,SIZE+1)
790 NEXT I
800 FOR A = 1 TO EQ
810 PRINT TAB(22) "Working on equation ";A
820 PTR = Ø
830 FOR C = A TO EQ
840 IF MAT(C,A) THEN PTR = C
850 NEXT C
860 IF PTR THEN 91Ø
870 PRINT
```

```
880 PRINT "An infinite number of solutions exist"
890 BEEP
900 GOTO 1140
910 FOR D = 1 TO EQ + 1
920 SWAP MAT(PTR,D),MAT(A,D)
930 NEXT D
940 DENOM = MAT(A,A)
950 FOR C = 1 TO EQ + 1
960 MAT(A,C) = MAT(A,C)/DENOM
970 NEXT C
980 FOR C = 1 TO EQ
990 IF C = A THEN 1040
1000 TEMP = MAT(C,A)
1010 FOR D = 1 TO EQ + 1
1020 MAT(C,D) = MAT(C,D)-MAT(A,D)*TEMP
1030 NEXT D
1040 NEXT C,A
1050 '
1060 ' output results
1070 CLS
1080 PRINT "Results ..."
1090 PRINT
1100 FOR I = 1 TO EQ
1110 PRINT VAR$(I),MAT(I,EQ+1)
1120 IF I MOD 17 = 0 THEN GOSUB 1370
1130 NEXT I
1140 GOSUB 1370
1150 RUN
1160 '
1170 ' sub to eliminate spaces and asterisks
1180 SP = INSTR(A$," ")
1190 IF SP = 0 THEN 1220
1200 A$ = LEFT$(A$,SP-1) + MID$(A$,SP+1)
1210 GOTO 1180
1220 SP = INSTR(A$,"*")
1230 IF SP = 0 THEN 1260
1240 A$ = LEFT$(A$,SP-1) + MID$(A$,SP+1)
1250 GOTO 1220
1260 RETURN
1270 '
1280 ' sub to capitalize A$
1290 FOR CHAR = 1 TO LEN(A$)
1300 IF MID$(A$,CHAR,1) < "a" THEN 1330
1310 IF MID$(A$,CHAR,1) > "z" THEN 1330
1320 MID$(A$,CHAR,1) = CHR$(ASC(MID$(A$,CHAR,1))-32)
1330 NEXT CHAR
1340 RETURN
```

```
1350 '
1360 ' sub to wait before continuing
1370 LOCATE 25,30
1380 POKE 106,0
1390 PRINT "Press any key to continue";
1400 K$ = INKEY$
1410 IF K$ = "" THEN 1400
1420 CLS
1430 LOCATE 3,1
1440 RETURN
```

DOUBLE PRECISION SINE AND COSINE ROUTINES

These routines allow you to generate sine and cosine values with a precision of up to 16 places! These routines come in two forms:

1. As a subroutine that can be called from any program
2. As a defined function which can be called from anywhere inside a basic program.

By using the power expansion formulas for SIN and COS and using double precision throughout, you can obtain a very high degree of precision from these procedures.

You should note that because the trig functions are periodic in nature, you may find that you will acquire greater accuracy if you stay between 0 and 90 degrees on all of the angles to be computed. If you can convert to these angles before you generate the values you will find that you will get a greater degree of accuracy. For example, your results will be more accurate if you use 1 degree instead of 179 degrees, although the absolute value of the result is the same.

```
1000 '**********************************************************************
1010 '**                 DOUBLE PRECISION SIN(X) GENERATOR                **
1020 '**********************************************************************
1030 '** GENERATES DOUBLE PRECISION VALUES FOR SIN IN RADIANS            **
1040 '** FROM THE POWER FORMULA -                                        **
1050 '**                                                                 **
1060 '** SIN X = X - (X**3/3!) + (X**5/5!) - (X**7/7!) +                 **
1070 '** (X**9/9!) - ...                                                 **
1080 '**********************************************************************
1090 '** TWO METHODS ARE GIVEN ....                                      **
1100 '** 1. BY USE OF THE                                                **
1110 '**    DEF FNDS#(VARIABLE#) STATEMENT                               **
1120 '**    THIS REQUIRES THE VALUE PASSED BE IN RADIANS IN THE RANGE    **
1130 '**    0 THRU PI/2   (0 THRU 90 DEGREES) PI = 3.14159265358979323846 **
1140 '**    SIN 90 DEGREES EVALUATES OUT TO 1.0000000066278              **
1150 '** 2. BY A SERIES OF EQUATIONS TO GENERATE A VERY ACCURATE         **
1160 '**    FORM OF THE EQUATION.                                        **
1170 '**    SIN 90 DEGREES EVALUATES OUT TO 1.0000000000000000           **
1180 '**    SIN 360 DEGREES EVALUATES OUT TO 0.0000031126862 APPROX      **
1190 '**    STILL VERY ACCURATE FOR MOST SITUATIONS                      **
```

```
1200 '***************************************************************************
1210 '
1220 '
1230 '***************************************************************************
1240 '**                          FORM #1                                     **
1250 '***************************************************************************
1260 '
1270 DEF FNDS#(X#) =  X#-X#*X#*X#/6+X#*X#*X#*X#*X#/120#-X#*X#*X#*X#*X#*X#*X#*X#
     /5040 +X#*X#*X#*X#*X#*X#*X#*X#*X#/362880#-X#*X#*X#*X#*X#*X#*X#*X#*X#*X#*X#
     *X#/ 39916800#+X#*X#*X#*X#*X#*X#*X#*X#*X#*X#*X#*X#*X#/6227020800#
1280 DEGREES# = 90
1290 VALUE# = 3.141592653589793#/180*DEGREES#
1300 A# = FNDS#(VALUE#)
1310 PRINT A#
1320 '
1330 '
1340 '***************************************************************************
1350 '**                          FORM #2                                     **
1360 '***************************************************************************
1370 '
1380 X# = 3.141592653589793#/180*DEGREES#
1390 A1# = X#
1400 A2# = A1#*X#*X#/6                        '1*2*3
1410 A3# = A2#*X#*X#/20                       '4*5
1420 A4# = A3#*X#*X#/42                       '6*7
1430 A5# = A4#*X#*X#/72  .                    '9*8
1440 A6# = A5#*X#*X#/110                      '10*11
1450 A7# = A6#*X#*X#/156                      '12*13
1460 A8# = A7#*X#*X#/210                      '14*15
1470 A9# = A8#*X#*X#/272                      '16*17
1480 A10# = A9#*X#*X#/342                     '18*19
1490 A11# = A10#*X#*X#/420                    '20*21
1500 A12# = A11#*X#*X#/506                    '22*23
1510 A13# = A12#*X#*X#/600                    '24*25
1520 A14# = A1#-A2#+A3#-A4#+A5#-A6#+A7#-A8#+A9#-A10#+A11#-A12#+A13#
1530 PRINT A14#


1000 '***************************************************************************
1010 '**              DOUBLE PRECISION COS(X) GENERATOR                        **
1020 '***************************************************************************
1030 '** GENERATES DOUBLE PRECISION VALUES FOR COS IN RADIANS                  **
1040 '** FROM THE POWER FORMULA -                                              **
1050 '**                                                                       **
1060 '** COS X = 1 - (X**2/2!) + (X**4/4!) - (X**6/6!) +                       **
1070 '** (X**8/8!) - ...                                                       **
1080 '***************************************************************************
1090 '** TWO METHODS ARE GIVEN ....                                            **
```

```
1100 '** 1. BY USE OF THE                                            **
1110 '**    DEF FNDC#(VARIABLE#) STATEMENT                            **
1120 '**    THIS REQUIRES THE VALUE PASSED BE IN RADIANS IN THE RANGE **
1130 '**    Ø THRU PI/2  (Ø THRU 9Ø DEGREES) PI = 3.14159265358979323846 **
1140 '**    COS 9Ø DEGREES EVALUATES OUT TO 6.321469455459696D-Ø9     **
1150 '** 2. BY A SERIES OF EQUATIONS TO GENERATE A VERY ACCURATE      **
1160 '**    FORM OF THE EQUATION.                                     **
1170 '**    COS 9Ø DEGREES EVALUATES OUT TO 1.247Ø516Ø315211D-16      **
1180 '**    COS 36Ø DEGREES EVALUATES OUT TO 1.ØØØØØ133293157         **
1190 '**    STILL VERY ACCURATE FOR MOST SITUATIONS                   **
1200 '****************************************************************
1210 '
1220 '
1230 '****************************************************************
1240 '**                        FORM #1                              **
1250 '****************************************************************
1260 '
1270 DEF FNDC#(X#) = 1# - X#*X#/2 + X#*X#*X#*X#/24# - X#*X#*X#*X#*X#*X#/72Ø
     #+ X#*X#*X#*X#*X#*X#*X#*X#/4Ø32Ø# - X#*X#*X#*X#*X#*X#*X#*X#*X#*X#
     /3628800#+ X#*X#*X#*X#*X#*X#*X#*X#*X#*X#*X#*X#/479ØØ16ØØ#
1280 DEGREES# = 9Ø#
1290 VALUE# = 3.141592653589793#/18Ø*DEGREES#
1300 A# = FNDC#(VALUE#)
1310 PRINT A#
1320 '
1330 '
1340 '****************************************************************
1350 '**                        FORM #2                              **
1360 '****************************************************************
1370 '
1380 X# = 3.141592653589793#/18Ø*DEGREES#
1390 A1# = 1#
1400 A2# = A1#*X#*X#/2#                        '1*2
1410 A3# = A2#*X#*X#/12#                       '3*4
1420 A4# = A3#*X#*X#/3Ø#                       '5*6
1430 A5# = A4#*X#*X#/56#                       '7*8
1440 A6# = A5#*X#*X#/9Ø#                       '9*1Ø
1450 A7# = A6#*X#*X#/132#                      '11*12
1460 A8# = A7#*X#*X#/182#                      '13*14
1470 A9# = A8#*X#*X#/24Ø#                      '15*16
1480 A1Ø# = A9#*X#*X#/3Ø6#                     '17*18
1490 A11# = A1Ø#*X#*X#/38Ø#                    '19*2Ø
1500 A12# = A11#*X#*X#/462#                    '21*22
1510 A13# = A12#*X#*X#/552#                    '23*24
1520 A14# = A1#-A2#+A3#-A4#+A5#-A6#+A7#-A8#+A9#-A1Ø#+A11#-A12#+A13#
1530 PRINT A14#
```

```
                           VECTOR ANALYSIS

A. Input vector V1 from keyboard.        L. Scalar multiplication of V1.
B. Input vector V2 from keyboard.        M. Cartesian to spherical conversion.
C. Input vector V3 from keyboard.        N. Spherical to cartesian conversion.
D. Input vector V1 from result VR.       O. Cartesian to cylindrical conversion.
E. Input vector V2 from result VR.       P. Cylindrical to cartesian conversion.
F. Input vector V3 from result VR.       Q. V1 + V2.
G. Swap values for vectors V1 and V2.    R. V1 - V2.
H. Swap values for vectors V2 and V3.    S. Cross product of V1 and V2.
I. Magnitude of V1.                      T. Dot product of V1 and V2.
J. Unit vector in direction of V1.       U. Angle between V1 and V2 (degrees).
K. Scalar triple product (V1*V2xV3).     V. Erase screen and redraw the menu.
==============================================================================

V1 =   Ø   Ø   Ø
V2 =   Ø   Ø   Ø
V3 =   Ø   Ø   Ø

VR =   Ø   Ø   Ø
SELECT FUNCTION BY LETTER
```

Fig. 5-15. Options available in the *Vectors* program.

VECTORS

This program performs all the major analytical functions for vector analysis. The vectors are three-dimensional, but by entering zero for the third value, two-dimensional vectors may be analyzed. The menu has twenty-two selections, labeled "A" through "V". The INKEY$ function is used to scan the keyboard, so as soon as you press a letter the associated function is activated.

At the bottom of the menu, all intermediate results are displayed. The three vectors V1, V2, and V3 are always displayed, along with the "result vector" VR. See Fig. 5-15. Single vector functions, such as choices "I" or "J", always operate on vector V1. Functions of two vectors, such as "Q" and "R", always operate on vectors V1 and V2. Three vector functions, such as choice "K", operate on V1, V2, and V3. If the solution to a given operation is a vector, the result is displayed in vector VR. To use this resultant vector in further computations move VR to one of the other three vectors. See menu selections D, E, and F. Scalar results are displayed near the bottom of the screen.

```
10 '**********************
20 '**   VECTOR ANALYSIS   **
30 '**********************
40 '
50 CLEAR
60 SCREEN Ø,Ø,Ø
70 WIDTH 80
80 KEY OFF
90 CLS
100 '
110 DEF FNRTD(RADIANS)=180*RADIANS/3.141593   '  Converts radians to degrees
120 DEF FNDTR(DEGREES)=3.141593*DEGREES/180   '  Converts degrees to radians
130 '
```

174

```
140 '************************
150 '**   Menu generation  **
160 '************************
170 PRINT TAB(32)"VECTOR ANALYSIS"
180 PRINT
190 PRINT "A. Input vector V1 from keyboard.";
200 PRINT TAB(40)"L. Scalar multiplication of V1."
210 PRINT "B. Input vector V2 from keyboard.";
220 PRINT TAB(40)"M. Cartesian to spherical conversion."
230 PRINT "C. Input vector V3 from keyboard.";
240 PRINT TAB(40)"N. Spherical to cartesian conversion."
250 PRINT "D. Input vector V1 from result VR.";
260 PRINT TAB(40)"O. Cartesian to cylindrical conversion."
270 PRINT "E. Input vector V2 from result VR.";
280 PRINT TAB(40)"P. Cylindrical to cartesian conversion."
290 PRINT "F. Input vector V3 from result VR.";
300 PRINT TAB(40)"Q. V1 + V2."
310 PRINT "G. Swap values for vectors V1 and V2.";
320 PRINT TAB(40)"R. V1 - V2."
330 PRINT "H. Swap values for vectors V2 and V3.";
340 PRINT TAB(40)"S. Cross product of V1 and V2."
350 PRINT "I. Magnitude of V1.";
360 PRINT TAB(40)"T. Dot product of V1 and V2."
370 PRINT "J. Unit vector in direction of V1.";
380 PRINT TAB(40)"U. Angle between V1 and V2 (degrees)."
390 PRINT "K. Scalar triple product (V1*V2xV3).";
400 PRINT TAB(40)"V. Erase screen and redraw the menu."
410 PRINT STRING$(80,240);
420 PRINT
430 '
440 '*********************************************
450 '**  Numerical data and prompt to screen  **
460 '*********************************************
470 LOCATE 16,1
480 PRINT "V1 = ";I1 J1 K1 TAB(80)
490 PRINT "V2 = " I2 J2 K2 TAB(80)
500 PRINT "V3 = " I3 J3 K3 TAB(80)
510 LOCATE 20,1
520 PRINT "VR = " IR JR KR TAB(80)
530 GOSUB 2010
540 LOCATE 23,1
550 IF MAG THEN PRINT "Magnitude of V1 = ";MAG : MAG=0
560 IF STPF THEN PRINT "Scalar triple product = ";STP : STPF=0
570 IF DOTF THEN PRINT "Dot product = ";DOT : DOTF=0
580 IF ANF THEN PRINT "Angle V1 to V2 = ";ANG;CHR$(248) : ANF=0
590 IF CSF THEN PRINT "VR is in spherical notation (Rho, Theta, Phi) ";
600 IF CSF THEN PRINT "with the angles in degrees." : CSF=0
```

```
610 IF SCF THEN PRINT "VR is in cartesian notation (X,Y,Z) "; : SCF=0
620 IF CYF THEN PRINT "VR is in cylindrical notation (Rho, Theta, Z) ";
630 IF CYF THEN PRINT "with Theta in degrees." : CYF=0
640 IF YCF THEN PRINT "VR is in cartesian notation (X,Y,Z) "; : YCF=0
650 LOCATE 21,1
660 PRINT "SELECT FUNCTION BY LETTER ";
670 COLOR 23,0
680 PRINT CHR$(219);
690 COLOR 7,0
700 '
710 '***********************************************
720 '** Menu selection and functions performed  **
730 '***********************************************
740 K$=INKEY$
750 IF K$ = "" THEN 740
760 IF K$ >= "a" AND K$ <= "z" THEN K$=CHR$(ASC(K$)-32) '     Capitalize K$
770 '
780 IF K$ <> "A" THEN 820
790 GOSUB 2010
800 INPUT "Enter values for V1 (i,j,k) ";I1,J1,K1
810 '
820 IF K$ <> "B" THEN 860
830 GOSUB 2010
840 INPUT "Enter values for V2 (i,j,k) ";I2,J2,K2
850 '
860 IF K$ <> "C" THEN 900
870 GOSUB 2010
880 INPUT "Enter values for V3 (i,j,k) ";I3,J3,K3
890 '
900 IF K$ <> "D" THEN 930
910 I1=IR : J1=JR : K1=KR
920 '
930 IF K$ <> "E" THEN 960
940 I2=IR : J2=JR : K2=KR
950 '
960 IF K$ <> "F" THEN 990
970 I3=IR : J3=JR : K3=KR
980 '
990 IF K$ <> "G" THEN 1060
1000 I1=I1 : J1=J1 : K1=K1
1010 I2=I2 : J2=J2 : K2=K2
1020 SWAP I1,I2
1030 SWAP J1,J2
1040 SWAP K1,K2
1050 '
1060 IF K$ <> "H" THEN 1130
1070 I2=I2 : J2=J2 : K2=K2
```

176

```
1080 I3=I3 : J3=J3 : K3=K3
1090 SWAP I2,I3
1100 SWAP J2,J3
1110 SWAP K2,K3
1120 '
1130 IF K$ <> "I" THEN 1160
1140 MAG=SQR(I1*I1+J1*J1+K1*K1)
1150 '
1160 IF K$ <> "J" THEN 1220
1170 MAGN=SQR(I1*I1+J1*J1+K1*K1)
1180 IR=I1/MAGN
1190 JR=J1/MAGN
1200 KR=K1/MAGN
1210 '
1220 IF K$ <> "K" THEN 1260
1230 STP=I1*J2*K3+J1*K2*I3+K1*I2*J3-K1*J2*I3-J1*I2*K3-I1*K2*J3
1240 STPF = 1
1250 '
1260 IF K$ <> "L" THEN 1320
1270 GOSUB 2010 : INPUT "Scalar value for multiplication ";SCA
1280 IR=I1*SCA
1290 JR=J1*SCA
1300 KR=K1*SCA
1310 '
1320 IF K$ <> "M" THEN 1410
1330 IR=SQR(I1*I1+J1*J1+K1*K1)
1340 IF I1 THEN JR=ATN(J1/I1) ELSE JR=1.570796*SGN(J1)
1350 IF I1 < 0 THEN JR=JR+((J1<0)-(J1>=0))*3.141593
1360 KR=K1/SQR(I1*I1+J1*J1+K1*K1) : CSF=1
1370 IF KR*KR < 1 THEN KR=1.570796-ATN(KR/SQR(1-KR*KR)) ELSE KR=1.570796
1380 JR=FNRTD(JR)
1390 KR=FNRTD(KR)
1400 '
1410 IF K$ <> "N" THEN 1470
1420 IR=I1*COS(FNDTR(J1))*SIN(FNDTR(K1))
1430 JR=I1*SIN(FNDTR(J1))*SIN(FNDTR(K1))
1440 KR=I1*COS(FNDTR(K1))
1450 SCF = 1
1460 '
1470 IF K$ <> "O" THEN 1550
1480 IR=SQR(I1*I1+J1*J1)
1490 IF I1 THEN JR=ATN(J1/I1) ELSE JR=1.570796*SGN(J1)
1500 IF I1 < 0 THEN JR=JR+((J1<0)-(J1>=0))*3.141593
1510 JR=FNRTD(JR)
1520 KR=K1
1530 CYF=1
1540 '
```

```
1550 IF K$ <> "P" THEN 1610
1560 IR=I1*COS(FNDTR(J1))
1570 JR=I1*SIN(FNDTR(J1))
1580 KR=K1
1590 YCF = 1
1600 '
1610 IF K$ <> "Q" THEN 1660
1620 IR=I1+I2
1630 JR=J1+J2
1640 KR=K1+K2
1650 '
1660 IF K$ <> "R" THEN 1710
1670 IR=I1-I2
1680 JR=J1-J2
1690 KR=K1-K2
1700 '
1710 IF K$ <> "S" THEN 1760
1720 IR=J1*K2-K1*J2
1730 JR=K1*I2-I1*K2
1740 KR=I1*J2-J1*I2
1750 '
1760 IF K$ <> "T" THEN 1800
1770 DOT=I1*I2+J1*J2+K1*K2
1780 DOTF=1
1790 '
1800 IF K$ <> "U" THEN 1920
1810 NUMER1=I1*I2+J1*J2+K1*K2
1820 DENOM1=SQR(I1*I1+J1*J1+K1*K1)
1830 IF DENOM1 = 0 THEN 1920
1840 DENOM2=SQR(I2*I2+J2*J2+K2*K2)
1850 IF DENOM2 = 0 THEN 1920
1860 TERM=NUMER1/DENOM1/DENOM2
1870 IF TERM*TERM >= 1 THEN 1920
1880 RAD=1.570796-ATN(TERM/SQR(1-TERM*TERM))
1890 ANG=RAD*180/3.141593
1900 ANF = 1
1910 '
1920 IF K$ <> "V" THEN 1960
1930 CLS
1940 GOTO 140
1950 '
1960 GOTO 470                 ' End of the menu function selection
1970 '
1980 '*****************************************
1990 '**   Subroutine to clear the message line   **
2000 '*****************************************
2010 LOCATE 21,1
```

```
2020 PRINT SPACE$(239);
2030 LOCATE 21,1
2040 RETURN
```

Chapter 6

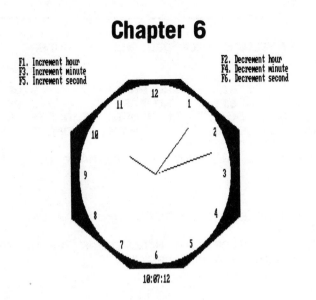

F1. Increment hour
F3. Increment minute
F5. Increment second

F2. Decrement hour
F4. Decrement minute
F6. Decrement second

10:07:12

Modem Communications

The three programs in this chapter will enable you not only to use your RS-232 to transmit data via a modem, but also to set up two remote IBM Personal Computers to exchange data files at midnight when telephone rates are lowest—without human intervention!

ASYNCHRONOUS COMMUNICATIONS ADAPTER DRIVER

This program will allow anyone with an asynchronous (RS-232) communications adapter to use their computer as a dumb terminal. Since the program uses pokes to send data directly to the card, it will work equally well with a cassette or diskette system with 16K of memory or more.

The program allows you to initialize the modem in one of four ways as shown in Fig. 6-1.

1. For 300 baud / 7 bit / no parity / 1 stop bit which is the mode used by many time sharing systems.
2. For 300 baud / 8 bit / no parity / 1 stop bit which is useful in communications which require that all 256 (8 bit) combinations of the byte be used.
3. For a customized setup in which you may select the mode of transmission for the device. In this mode you may select :
    (A) Baud rate from 50 to 9600 baud
    (B) Word length from 5 to 8 bits
    (C) The number of stop bits required (1,1 ½, or 2)
    (D) Parity (Yes or No) and type (Even, Odd, or Stick)
4. For a personalized setup in which you have changed lines 2050 thru 2080 to reflect values that were computed by the program during a prior usage of the customized setup procedure. This option is useful if you use a specific transmission mode frequently. It requires that you run the customized procedure and modify the program listing to the new values that are displayed. Finally you must resave the

```
SELECT THE COMMUNICATIONS MODE DESIRED BY NUMBER
THEN PRESS ENTER

1 =      300 BAUD     7 BIT     NO PARITY     1 STOP BIT
2 =      300 BAUD     8 BIT     NO PARITY     1 STOP BIT
3 =      CUSTOMIZED   SETUP     NEW MODE OF OPERATIONS
4 =      PERSONALIZED SETUP     OLD MODE OF OPERATIONS

NOTE : SELECTION #1 IS THE MODE USED BY MANY TIME-SHARING SYSTEMS

? 1

WOULD YOU LIKE A SIMPLE DRIVER FOR COMMUNICATIONS ?

IF YOU SELECT YES, THIS SEGMENT WILL CLEAR THE SCREEN AND
HOOK YOU TO THE MODEM OR OTHER DEVICE.

 1 =           YES
 2 =           NO

?
```

Fig. 6-1. Options available in the *Asynchronous Communications Driver* program.

program so the new values are permanent. This will allow easy access to a specific mode of communications without having to program it in every time.

Finally, the program will allow you the choice of using a patch which allows characters input via the keyboard to be transmitted through the communications adapter and the incoming data to be displayed on the screen.

Theory of Operation

The different modes on the Asynchronous Communications Adapter are selected by reading from and writing to a series of data ports on the card. These ports are located at addresses &H3F8 thru &H3FE for card number 1 (1016 thru 1022 decimal) and &H2F8 thru &H2FE (760 thru 766 decimal) for card number 2.

The steps involved in the programming of the card are:

1. Transmitting a value of H&80 (128) to address &H3FB (1019). This tells the card to set addresses &H3F8 and &H3F9 (1016 + 1017) for access to the divisor latches of the baud rate generator which determines the rate at which the card will read and write data.
2. Sending a value to &H3F8 and &H3F9 (1016 & 1017) which equals 115,200 divided by the desired baud rate.
3. Sending a value to &H3FB (1019) of less than &H80 (128) which turns &H3F8 and &H3F9 (1016 & 1017) back into the transmit/receive buffer and the interrupt register respectively. This value also tells the card the word length, parity, and number of stop bits desired.

The specific bits in the value sent to &H3FB will program the line control register in the following fashion : (Bit 7 is the most significant bit of the byte, Eg. 76543210)

BIT #	FUNCTION
7	DIVISOR LATCH ACCESS BIT
6	SET BREAK (TRANSMIT A CONTINUOUS SPACE)
5	STICK PARITY
4	EVEN PARITY SELECT
3	PARITY ENABLE
2	THE NUMBER OF STOP BITS
1	WORD LENGTH SELECT BIT #1
0	WORD LENGTH SELECT BIT #0

Specifically, the different functions are programmed as shown in Table 6-1. To illustrate this with a specific example, consider a standard modem that is used in a system which requires a signal of 300 baud, 7 bits, 1 stop bit, and no parity. It is easy to initialize the card by first sending the command **OUT &H3FB,&H80** to the card from BASIC. This tells the card to expect a value that will define the baud rate to be used. From the formula given above it is easy to see that the value of 384 or &H0180 in hex will give us the 300 baud required.

$$\text{VALUE} = 115{,}200 \,/\, \text{BAUD RATE} \qquad (\text{BAUD RATE} = 300)$$
$$= 384 \text{ DECIMAL OR \&H180 HEX}$$

The value of &H180 or &H0180 (equivalent) must be sent to &H3F8 and &H3F9 with the most significant part (the &H01) sent to &H3F9 and the least significant part (the &H80) sent to &H3F8.

Eg. OUT &H3F8,&H80
  OUT &H3F9,&H01

This sets the baud rate. The rest of the parameters will be set with the final byte of data. This byte is output to &H3FB as follows:

  bit 7 set to 0 for normal operation
  bit 6 set to 0 for normal operation
  bits 5, 4, and 3 set to 000 for no parity
  bit 2 set to 0 for 1 stop bit
  bits 1 and 0 set to 10 for 7 bits

This results in a bit pattern of 0000 0010, which, if it is expressed in HEX format, will equal &H02. This value is sent to port &H3FB. A complete program to perform this feat is . . .

```
10   OUT &H3FB,&H80
20   OUT &H3F8,&H80
30   OUT &H3F9,&H1
40   OUT &H3FB,&H2
```

THAT'S IT !!!

Finally, the keyboard driver, which comprises lines 4000 through 4070, simply clears the screen and then :

1. Determines whether or not there is any data from the communications line and if there is, it prints it.
2. Determines whether or not a key has been pressed on the keyboard. If no, it goes back to step one, and if yes, it waits until the device is ready to accept data and then transmits the data. It then goes back to step one.

For more information concerning the asynchronous adapter please refer to your technical reference manual, specifically pages 2-123 through 2-148.

Table 6-1. How the Functions Are Programmed in Preparation for Using the Asynchronous Communications Adapter.

```
7 6 5 4 3 2 1 Ø   (X = NOT CONCERNED WITH IN THIS EXAMPLE)


X X X X X X Ø Ø   5 BIT WORD LENGTH (Bits Ø and 1 work

X X X X X X Ø 1   6 BIT WORD LENGTH  together to program the

X X X X X X 1 Ø   7 BIT WORD LENGTH  length of the bytes as

X X X X X X 1 1   8 BIT WORD LENGTH  they will be transmitted

                                     and received)


X X X X X Ø X X   1 stop bit is generated for each byte

X X X X X 1 X X   1 1/2 stop bits generated if 5 bit word

                        length was selected (or)

                  2 stop bits generated if 6, 7, or 8 bit

                        word length was selected

X X X X Ø X X X   no parity is transmitted or received

X X X X 1 X X X   parity is transmitted & checked on receive

                  (this works in conjunction with bits 4 & 5

                     to determine the type of parity )

X X Ø Ø 1 X X X   even parity is selected

X X Ø 1 1 X X X   odd parity is selected

X X 1 Ø 1 X X X   the parity bit will be transmitted and

                  received as a mark (or ON) always

X X 1 1 1 X X X   the parity bit will be transmitted and

                  received as a space (or OFF) always
```

```
X Ø X X X X X   normal operation

X 1 X X X X X   sets the output to a spacing state and

                locks it there until the bit is changed


Ø X X X X X X   normal operation



1 X X X X X X   allows data output to &H3F8 & &H3F9 to set

                the baud rate for the system
```

Note: If you are using the Hayes Smart Modem or if you have trouble getting the program to function, you might wish to check the configuration switches. For the Hayes Smart Modem, set the configuration switches as follows:

1 — DOWN   This program does not support the DTR lead so you must tell the modem to ignore the state of pin 20 and assume it is true.
2 — UP   This tells the modem to respond with English response codes.
3 — DOWN   This informs the modem you want the response codes sent to the computer.
4 — DOWN   Do not echo characters.
5 — DOWN   Do not answer the phone if it rings. There can be a lot of confusion if someone calls and the modem answers.
6 — DOWN   Tells the terminal to accept information from the modem at all times.
7 — UP   For single phone installations.

```
100 '*******************************************************************
110 '**            ASYNCHRONOUS COMMUNICATIONS ADAPTER DRIVER       **
120 '**                                                             **
130 '**        VERSION 1.1                        4 JULY, 1982      **
140 '*******************************************************************
150 '
160 SCREEN Ø : WIDTH 80 : KEY OFF : CLS
170 PRINT "SELECT THE COMMUNICATIONS MODE DESIRED BY NUMBER
180 PRINT "THEN PRESS ENTER
190 PRINT
200 PRINT "1 =     300 BAUD    7 BIT    NO PARITY    1 STOP BIT
210 PRINT "2 =     300 BAUD    8 BIT    NO PARITY    1 STOP BIT
220 PRINT "3 =     CUSTOMIZED  SETUP    NEW MODE OF OPERATIONS
230 PRINT "4 =     PERSONALIZED SETUP   OLD MODE OF OPERATIONS
```

```
240 PRINT
250 PRINT "NOTE : SELECTION #1 IS THE MODE USED BY MANY TIME-SHARING
    SYSTEMS
260 PRINT
270 INPUT SELECT
280 ON SELECT GOTO 300,400,500,2000
290 INPUT "INCORRECT SELECTION - TRY AGAIN - ":GOTO 270
300 '
310 '*******************************************************************
320 '**                     SELECTION #1                            **
330 '*******************************************************************
340 CLEAR : POKE 106,0              ' CLEAR THE KEYBOARD BUFFER
350 OUT &H3FB,&H80                  ' ACCESS THE DIVISOR LATCHES
360 OUT &H3F8,&H80                  ' LSB OF BAUD RATE DIVISOR
370 OUT &H3F9,&H1                   ' MSB FOR -300 BAUD-
380 OUT &H3FB,&H2                   ' ACCESS TX AND RX - 7 BIT - NO PARITY
390 GOTO 3000
400 '
410 '*******************************************************************
420 '**                     SELECTION #2                            **
430 '*******************************************************************
440 CLEAR : POKE 106,0              ' CLEAR THE KEYBOARD BUFFER
450 OUT &H3FB,&H80                  ' ACCESS THE DIVISOR LATCHES
460 OUT &H3F8,&H80                  ' LSB OF BAUD RATE DIVISOR
470 OUT &H3F9,&H1                   ' MSB FOR -300 BAUD-
480 OUT &H3FB,&H3                   ' ACCESS TX AND RX - 8 BIT - NO PARITY
490 GOTO 3000
500 '
510 '*******************************************************************
520 '**                     SELECTION #3                            **
530 '*******************************************************************
540 CLS
550 PRINT "CUSTOMIZED SETUP PROCEDURES
560 PRINT
570 PRINT "SELECT THE BAUD RATE DESIRED -
580 PRINT
590 PRINT " 1 =       50    BAUD
600 PRINT " 2 =       75    BAUD
610 PRINT " 3 =      110    BAUD
620 PRINT " 4 =      134.5 BAUD
630 PRINT " 5 =      150    BAUD
640 PRINT " 6 =      300    BAUD
650 PRINT " 7 =      600    BAUD
660 PRINT " 8 =     1200    BAUD
670 PRINT " 9 =     1800    BAUD
680 PRINT "10 =     2000    BAUD
```

```
690 PRINT "11 =        2400     BAUD
700 PRINT "12 =        3600     BAUD
710 PRINT "13 =        4800     BAUD
720 PRINT "14 =        7200     BAUD
730 PRINT "15 =        9600     BAUD
740 PRINT
750 INPUT RATE
760 ON RATE GOTO 780,790,800,810,820,830,840,850,860,870,880,890,900,910,920
770 PRINT "ERROR ON BAUD RATE - SELECT AGAIN - ";:GOTO 740
780 CLS : MSB = &H9 : LSB = &H0  : BAUD =    50   : GOTO 930
790 CLS : MSB = &H6 : LSB = &H0  : BAUD =    75   : GOTO 930
800 CLS : MSB = &H4 : LSB = &H17 : BAUD =   110   : GOTO 930
810 CLS : MSB = &H3 : LSB = &H59 : BAUD =   134.5 : GOTO 930
820 CLS : MSB = &H3 : LSB = &H0  : BAUD =   150   : GOTO 930
830 CLS : MSB = &H1 : LSB = &H80 : BAUD =   300   : GOTO 930
840 CLS : MSB = &H0 : LSB = &HC0 : BAUD =   600   : GOTO 930
850 CLS : MSB = &H0 : LSB = &H60 : BAUD =  1200   : GOTO 930
860 CLS : MSB = &H0 : LSB = &H40 : BAUD =  1800   : GOTO 930
870 CLS : MSB = &H0 : LSB = &H3A : BAUD =  2000   : GOTO 930
880 CLS : MSB = &H0 : LSB = &H30 : BAUD =  2400   : GOTO 930
890 CLS : MSB = &H0 : LSB = &H20 : BAUD =  3600   : GOTO 930
900 CLS : MSB = &H0 : LSB = &H18 : BAUD =  4800   : GOTO 930
910 CLS : MSB = &H0 : LSB = &H10 : BAUD =  7200   : GOTO 930
920 CLS : MSB = &H0 : LSB = &HC  : BAUD =  9600   : GOTO 930
930 '
940 PRINT "SELECT THE WORD LENGTH DESIRED -
950 PRINT
960 PRINT " 1 =        5 BITS
970 PRINT " 2 =        6 BITS
980 PRINT " 3 =        7 BITS
990 PRINT " 4 =        8 BITS
1000 PRINT
1010 INPUT WORDLENGTH
1020 ON WORDLENGTH GOTO 1040,1050,1060,1070
1030 PRINT "ERROR ON WORD LENGTH - SELECT AGAIN - ";:GOTO 1010
1040 CLS : BITS10 = 0 : GOTO 1080
1050 CLS : BITS10 = 1 : GOTO 1080
1060 CLS : BITS10 = 2 : GOTO 1080
1070 CLS : BITS10 = 3 : GOTO 1080
1080 '
1090 PRINT "SELECT THE NUMBER OF STOP BITS YOU DESIRE -
1100 PRINT
1110 PRINT " 1 =        1 STOP BIT FOR ALL WORD LENGTHS SELECTED
1120 PRINT
1130 PRINT " 2 =        1 1/2 STOP BITS IF 5   BIT WORD SELECTED OR
1140 PRINT "            2     STOP BITS IF 6-8 BIT WORD SELECTED
```

```
1150 PRINT
1160 INPUT STOPBITS
1170 ON STOPBITS GOTO 1190,1200
1180 PRINT "ERROR ON SELECTION - PLEASE SELECT AGAIN - ";:GOTO 1160
1190 CLS : BIT2 = Ø : GOTO 1210
1200 CLS : BIT2 = 4 : GOTO 1210
1210 '
1220 PRINT "DO YOU WANT A PARITY BIT ?
1230 PRINT
1240 PRINT " 1 =        NO
1250 PRINT " 2 =        YES
1260 PRINT
1270 INPUT PARITY
1280 ON PARITY GOTO 1300,1310
1290 PRINT "ERROR ON SELECTION - PLEASE SELECT AGAIN - ";:GOTO 1270
1300 CLS : BITS543 = Ø : GOTO 1540
1310 PRINT
1320 PRINT "DO YOU WANT ODD,   EVEN,   OR STICK PARITY ?
1330 PRINT
1340 PRINT " 1 =        ODD
1350 PRINT " 2 =        EVEN
1360 PRINT " 3 =        STICK   (ALWAYS ON OR OFF)
1370 PRINT
1380 INPUT PARITY
1390 ON PARITY GOTO 1410,1420,1430
1400 PRINT "ERROR ON SELECTION - PLEASE SELECT AGAIN - ";:GOTO 1380
1410 CLS : BITS543 =  8 : GOTO 1540
1420 CLS : BITS543 = 24 : GOTO 1540
1430 PRINT
1440 PRINT "DO YOU WANT THE PARITY ALWAYS SET TO A 1 OR Ø ?
1450 PRINT
1460 PRINT " 1 =        Ø  (ALWAYS)
1470 PRINT " 2 =        1  (ALWAYS)
1480 PRINT
1490 INPUT PARITY
1500 ON PARITY GOTO 1520,1530
1510 PRINT "ERROR ON SELECTION - PLEASE SELECT AGAIN - ";:GOTO 1490
1520 CLS : BITS543 = 56 : GOTO 1540
1530 CLS : BITS543 = 40 : GOTO 1540
1540 '
1550 PRINT "IF THIS IS THE MODE YOU WANT FOR YOUR PERSONALIZED SETUP -
1560 PRINT
1570 PRINT "REPLACE THE VALUES IN THE LISTING FOR 2060-2080 WITH THESE -
1580 PRINT "2060 OUT &H3F8,LSB   (REPLACE LSB) WITH ";LSB
1590 PRINT "2070 OUT &H3F9,MSB   (REPLACE MSB) WITH ";MSB
1600 PRINT "2080 OUT &H3FB,LCR   (REPLACE LCR) WITH ";BITS10+BIT2+BITS543
1610 PRINT
```

```
1620 PRINT "AND RESAVE A COPY OF THIS PROGRAM OR JUST LINES 2000 TO 2080"
1630 POKE 106,0
1640 OUT &H3FB,&H80
1650 OUT &H3F8,LSB
1660 OUT &H3F9,MSB
1670 OUT &H3FB,BITS10+BIT2+BITS543
1680 GOTO 3000
2000 '*********************************************************************
2010 '**               PERSONALIZED DRIVER ROUTINE                      **
2020 '*********************************************************************
2030 '
2040 CLEAR : POKE 106,0
2050 OUT &H3FB,&H80
2060 OUT &H3F8,LSB
2070 OUT &H3F9,MSB
2080 OUT &H3FB,LCR
3000 '
3010 PRINT
3020 PRINT "WOULD YOU LIKE A SIMPLE DRIVER FOR COMMUNICATIONS ?
3030 PRINT
3040 PRINT "IF YOU SELECT YES, THIS SEGMENT WILL CLEAR THE SCREEN AND
3050 PRINT "HOOK YOU TO THE MODEM OR OTHER DEVICE.
3060 PRINT
3070 PRINT " 1 =             YES
3080 PRINT " 2 =             NO
3090 PRINT
3100 INPUT DRIVER
3110 ON DRIVER GOTO 3130,3140
3120 PRINT "ERROR ON SELECTION - PLEASE SELECT AGAIN ";:GOTO 3100
3130 CLS : GOTO 4000
3140 PRINT "BYE ";:END
4000 '*********************************************************************
4010 '**              KEYBOARD DRIVER FOR COMMUNICATION                 **
4020 '*********************************************************************
4030 '
4040 CLEAR : POKE 106,0 : DEFINT A-Z
4050 IF (INP(1021) AND 1) <> 0 THEN D = INP(1016) : PRINT CHR$(D);
4060 A$ = INKEY$ : IF A$ = "" THEN 4050
4070 IF (INP(1021) AND 32) = 0 THEN 4070 ELSE OUT 1016,ASC(A$):PRINT A$;
     :GOTO 4
050
```

COMMUNICATIONS TRANSFER PROGRAMS: TRANSMIT AND RECEIVE

Communication and data transmission between computer systems is finally becoming a reality even on the personal level. Modern computers have built-in software powerful enough to allow these' capabilities to be implemented easily and inexpensively.

These two programs allow for unattended data or program exchange between personal computers. When this program is used in conjunction with the very powerful Hayes Smart Modem, the two computer systems do not have to be in the same room or even in the same state.

The purpose behind these programs was simple. In designing the programs and writing the text for the book, the authors had to keep each other informed of the progress of their work. When a large amount of data and program material needed to be transmitted, the options available were:

1. creating a disk with the necessary files on it and mailing it across the country, or
2. using the phone and transmitting the information while the systems are manned on both ends.

The first option has the disadvantage of requiring up to a week for the information to travel across the country, and the second option has the disadvantage that either prime phone rates are paid or both parties must man the systems at night to take advantage of the lower rates. To overcome these difficulties, we created these programs, which enable the computers to automatically wait until midnight when the rates are lowest, and then dial and exchange data or programs with each other. Finally, the systems hang up at the end of the exchange.

Theory of Operation

For two computer systems to communicate, several conditions must be met. One of these conditions is that there must be a hardware connection between the two systems. Many times this is a cable or set of wires between the systems. Because of the differences between systems and the many possible ways the systems could be connected, some form of standardization was necessary. For many systems, including most of the microcomputers requiring duplex or two way communications, one system was selected as the standard. RS-232C was the standard chosen. Now, any system could communicate with any other system as long as they both generated signals in accordance with the standard. In the IBM Personal Computer, the Asynchronous Communications Adapter Card converts the information on the data and address lines to standard RS-232C format.

Now that there is a standard, it is just a matter of correctly connecting the output of the adapter to the adapter or RS-232C output of the second device. This setup works well for systems located near each other, but if communication is desired over long distances, another device must be used.

A *modem* is a device that takes the data and serially converts it into a series of tones which can be transmitted around the world if necessary, and at the same time, it can receive tones from another modem and convert them back into the data that they represented to the other system.

This brings us back to the IBM Personal Computer. By using the Asynchronous Communications Adapter Card, which plugs into one of the system expansion slots, and a modem that has been connected to the telephone system, data can be transmitted and received almost anywhere in the world.

As a bonus, the new breed of modems has been equipped with microprocessors, which have given them many additional capabilities. One of these modems, and the one this program was designed around, is the Hayes Smartmodem. Besides normal functions, this device will dial phone numbers and report on the status of the connection. Besides functioning in the normal mode, the Smartmodem will also operate in the autoanswer mode. This means that the modem will wait for another system to call it and then will automatically answer the call.

Program Operation

The two programs operate in strict relation to one another. Once the two modems are in communication, both systems will go through a specific series of events that culminate in the storage on a disk of a file that was transmitted from the other end.

At the beginning of each program is a list of remarks stating the positions the programming switches inside the Smart Modem must be in for the program to work. Depending on what you normally use your system for, these switches may or may not be in these positions, and this is a simple reminder to check them.

The sequence of operation for the two programs is as follows:

(T) = Transmit Program   (R) = Receive Program

(T) The correct time is verified or entered. The time is used to start the dialing sequence at midnight. The filename for the ASCII formatted file is entered.

This file can be a program listing if desired and will be the file that is to be transmitted.

The filename where the received data will be stored is entered.

The phone number to call at midnight is entered.

The program then enters a waiting loop until midnight.

(R) The filename for the file that will be transmitted to the other end is entered.

The filename where the received file will be stored is entered.

The modem is placed into the autoanswer mode to await a call from the distant end. Once a connection has been made with the other end, this program waits for the file that the other end will send.

(T) At midnight, this program exits from a waiting loop in the program and sends the string of characters that represent the phone number to be called to the modem. The modem dials the number and waits for a connection with the other end. Once a connection has been made and the modems are locked together, this program transmits the ASCII file to the receive version of the program. To signal an end to the file, the program sends the string "65000" to the distant computer. At this time a message is displayed on the screen verifying the complete transmission of the file, and this program waits for a file to be transmitted from the distant computer.

(R) As soon as the modems signal they are connected, this program sets itself up to store the ASCII string in an array. As the strings are received, they are checked for a value of greater than 64000. If the value is not above 64000, the program waits for another string. As soon as a string with a value above 64000 is received, the program knows that the other end is finished transmitting data and it stores the data on a disk or cassette. Once the data is stored, the program starts sending the data in its file to be transmitted. At the end of the transmission, this program sends the string "65000" to tell the other end that the transmission is complete. The files are closed; the modem is shut off; and the program terminates.

(T) As the data is received, it is tested for a value of 65000. If the strings do not have that high a value, they are stored into an array. Once a value over 64000 is found, the program takes the strings from the array and stores them onto the disk or cassette. When finished the program ends, closing all files and breaking the connection on the modem.

Since the programs follow a strict procedure, it was possible to have them test for unusual events and terminate themselves automatically. This way, if anything happened to the connection, the two ends would hang up and save you from getting a large phone bill.

```
1000 SCREEN 2 : CLS : KEY OFF : DIM DATAIO$(999)
1010 PRINT "**************************************************"
1020 PRINT "**   COMMUNICATIONS TRANSFER PROGRAM - TRANSMIT   **"
1030 PRINT "**   SEPT 19,1982                    VERSION 1.1   **"
1040 PRINT "**************************************************"
```

```
1050 PRINT "**   REQUIRES THE SMART MODEM SWITCHES TO BE SET   **"
1060 PRINT "**   AS :                                          **"
1070 PRINT "**   1 = UP        COMPUTER SUPPORT OF DTR LEAD     **"
1080 PRINT "**   2 = DOWN      NON-VERBOSE RESULT CODES         **"
1090 PRINT "**   3 = DOWN      RESULT CODES SENT TO SCREEN      **"
1100 PRINT "**   4 = DOWN      NO ECHO OF CHARACTERS            **"
1110 PRINT "**   5 = DOWN      NO AUTO ANSWER OF PHONE          **"
1120 PRINT "**   6 = DOWN      COMPUTER FORCED TO ACCEPT DATA   **"
1130 PRINT "**   7 = UP        SINGLE LINE PHONE                **"
1140 PRINT "******************************************************"
1150 '
1160 '**************************************************************
1170 '**   routine to enter the current correct time         **
1180 '**************************************************************
1190 LOCATE 17,1
1200 PRINT "THE CURRENT TIME IS - "; TIME$
1210 PRINT "IS THIS CORRECT  (YES = 1      NO = Ø)  - ";
1220 A$ = INKEY$ : IF A$ = "" THEN 1220
1230 IF (A$ = "1") OR (A$ = CHR$(13)) THEN PRINT : GOTO 1400
1240 '
1250 ON ERROR GOTO 1330
1260 LOCATE 20,1
1270 PRINT "ENTER CORRECT TIME AS HH:MM:SS   - ";
1280 INPUT A$
1290 IF A$ <> "" THEN TIME$ = A$
1300 GOTO 1400
1310 '
1320 '**************************************************************
1330 '**   error handling routine for time input             **
1340 '**************************************************************
1350 CLS : LOCATE 15,1
1360 PRINT "ERROR IN INPUT - PLEASE TRY AGAIN "
1370 RESUME 1270
1380 '
1390 '**************************************************************
1400 '**   transmit file name entry section                  **
1410 '**************************************************************
1420 ON ERROR GOTO 1530
1430 CLS
1440 PRINT "ENTER COMPLETE FILENAME INCLUDING EXTENSION OF THE FILE"
     TO BE
1450 PRINT "TRANSMITTED - NOTE : FILE MUST BE IN ASCII FORMAT FOR "
     PROGRAM
1460 PRINT "TO WORK. "
1470 PRINT
1480 INPUT "FILENAME = " ; TRANSMIT$
1490 OPEN TRANSMIT$ FOR INPUT AS #1
```

```
1500 GOTO 1630
1510 '
1520 '**********************************************************
1530 '**   error handling routine for name entry section      **
1540 '**********************************************************
1550 FOR X = 1 TO 1000 : NEXT : CLS : FOR X = 1 TO 1000 : NEXT
1560 IF ERR = 53 THEN PRINT "FILE NOT FOUND "
1570 IF ERR = 64 THEN PRINT "BAD FILE NAME "
1580 IF (ERR <> 53) AND (ERR <> 64) THEN PRINT "ERROR IN FILE NAME INPUT "
1590 LOCATE 5,1
1600 RESUME 1440
1610 '
1620 '**********************************************************
1630 '**   receive file name entry section                    **
1640 '**********************************************************
1650 ON ERROR GOTO 1750
1660 CLS
1670 PRINT "ENTER COMPLETE FILENAME INCLUDING EXTENSION WHERE THE "
1680 PRINT "FILE TO BE RECEIVED WILL BE STORED."
1690 PRINT
1700 INPUT "FILENAME = " ; RECIEVE$
1710 OPEN RECIEVE$ FOR OUTPUT AS #2
1720 GOTO 1850
1730 '
1740 '**********************************************************
1750 '**   error handling routine for name input section      **
1760 '**********************************************************
1770 FOR X = 1 TO 1000 : NEXT : CLS : FOR X = 1 TO 1000 : NEXT
1780 IF ERR = 53 THEN PRINT "FILE NOT FOUND "
1790 IF ERR = 64 THEN PRINT "BAD FILE NAME "
1800 IF (ERR <> 53) AND (ERR <> 64) THEN PRINT "ERROR IN FILE NAME INPUT "
1810 LOCATE 5,1
1820 RESUME 1670
1830 '
1840 '**********************************************************
1850 '**   routine to enter phone number for call             **
1860 '**********************************************************
1870 CLS
1880 INPUT "ENTER TELEPHONE NUMBER TO BE CALLED - ";TELE$
1890 LOCATE 4,1
1900 PRINT "THE PHONE NUMBER TO BE DIALED IS - ";TELE$
1910 PRINT "IS THIS CORRECT ? (YES = 1      NO = 0) "
1920 B$ = INKEY$ : IF B$ = "" THEN 1920
1930 IF (B$ = "1") OR (B$ = "Y") OR (B$ = "y") THEN 1970 ELSE 1940
1940 FOR X = 1 TO 1000  : NEXT  : CLS : FOR X = 1 TO 1000 : NEXT : GOTO 1850
1950 '
1960 '**********************************************************
```

```
1970 '**  routine to wait until 12:00 midnight to phone      **
1980 '*****************************************************************
1990 CLS
2000 B$ = LEFT$(TIME$,2)
2010 LOCATE 1,1
2020 PRINT TIME$,DATE$
2030 IF B$ = "24" THEN 2040 ELSE 2000
2040 PRINT "INITIATING CALL - MIDNIGHT"
2050 '
2060 '*****************************************************************
2070 '**   routine to initiate communications              **
2080 '*****************************************************************
2090 ON ERROR GOTO 0
2100 OPEN "com1:" AS #3
2110 IF (INP(&H3FD) AND &H20) = 0 THEN 2110 'TRANS HOLD REGISTER EMPTY?
2120 PRINT #3, "AT Z"
2130 GOSUB 2200
2140 SEC = 3 : GOSUB 2290
2150 PRINT #3, "AT DP " + TELE$
2160 GOSUB 2200
2170 END                ' IF HERE THEN ERROR - CLOSE AND STOP
2180 '
2190 '*****************************************************************
2200 '**   routine to input a line from modem               **
2210 '*****************************************************************
2220 LINE INPUT #3, RECEIVEDATA$
2230 PRINT
2240 IF RECEIVEDATA$ = "0" THEN PRINT "RESPONSE = OK" : RETURN
2250 IF RECEIVEDATA$ = "1" THEN PRINT "RESPONSE = CONNECT" : RETURN 2370
2260 IF RECEIVEDATA$ = "2" THEN PRINT "RESPONSE = RING" : END
2270 IF RECEIVEDATA$ = "3" THEN PRINT "RESPONSE = NO CARRIER" : END
2280 IF RECEIVEDATA$ = "4" THEN PRINT "RESPONSE = ERROR" : END
2290 '
2300 '*****************************************************************
2310 '**   time delay for SEC seconds                       **
2320 '*****************************************************************
2330 FOR DELAY = 1 TO 700*SEC : NEXT DELAY
2340 RETURN
2350 '
2360 '*****************************************************************
2370 '**   routine to transmit data to distant end          **
2380 '*****************************************************************
2390 ON COM(1) GOSUB 2660
2400 COM(1) ON
2410 ON ERROR GOTO 2880         ' TERMINATE
2420 SEC = 3 : GOSUB 2310
2430 WHILE NOT EOF(1)
```

```
2440 LINE INPUT #1 , SENDDATA$
2450 PRINT #3, SENDDATA$
2460 WEND
2470 PRINT #3, "65000 ' "
2480 PRINT : PRINT "FILE - ";TRANSMIT$;" TRANSMITTED OK"
2490 '
2500 '************************************************************
2510 '**   routine to receive data and store it               **
2520 '************************************************************
2530 ON COM(1) GOSUB 2780
2540 IF VAL(RECEIVEDATA$) < 64000! THEN 2540
2550 COM(1) OFF
2560 '
2570 FOR I = 1 TO POINTER
2580 PRINT #2 , DATAIO$(I)
2590 NEXT I
2600 '
2610 CLOSE
2620 PRINT : PRINT "FILE - ";RECEIVE$;" RECEIVED AND STORED"
2630 GOTO 2880
2640 '
2650 '************************************************************
2660 '**   routine to tell if data sent from distant end      **
2670 '************************************************************
2680 LINE INPUT #3 , RECEIVEDATA$
2690 PRINT "DATA RECEIVED DURING FILE TRANSMISSION " ; RECEIVEDATA$
2700 IF RECEIVEDATA$ = "0" THEN PRINT "RESPONSE = OK"
2710 IF RECEIVEDATA$ = "1" THEN PRINT "RESPONSE = CONNECT"
2720 IF RECEIVEDATA$ = "2" THEN PRINT "RESPONSE = RING"
2730 IF RECEIVEDATA$ = "3" THEN PRINT "RESPONSE = NO CARRIER"
2740 IF RECEIVEDATA$ = "4" THEN PRINT "RESPONSE = ERROR"
2750 RETURN 2880 'TREAT ANY TRANSMISSION AS AN ERROR AND TERMINATE
2760 '
2770 '************************************************************
2780 '**   store each line in array DATAIO$ via interrupt     **
2790 '************************************************************
2800 LINE INPUT #3, RECEIVEDATA$
2810 POINTER = POINTER + 1
2820 DATAIO$(POINTER) = RECEIVEDATA$
2830 IF (RECEIVEDATA$ = "3") THEN PRINT : PRINT "LOSS OF CARRIER" : END
2840 IF VAL(RECEIVEDATA$) > 64000! THEN COM(1) OFF
2850 RETURN
2860 '
2870 '************************************************************
2880 '**                 TERMINATE PROGRAM                    **
2890 '************************************************************
2900 END
```

```
1000 SCREEN 2 : CLS : KEY OFF : DIM DATAIO$(999)
1010 '******************************************************
1020 '**    COMMUNICATIONS TRANSFER PROGRAM - RECEIVE        **
1030 '**    OCT 3,1982                    VERSION 1.1        **
1040 '******************************************************
1050 '**    REQUIRES THE SMART MODEM SWITCHES TO BE SET      **
1060 '**        AS :                                         **
1070 '**            1 = UP      COMPUTER SUPPORT OF DTR LEAD  **
1080 '**            2 = DOWN    NON-VERBOSE RESULT CODES      **
1090 '**            3 = DOWN    RESULT CODES SENT TO SCREEN   **
1100 '**            4 = DOWN    NO ECHO OF CHARACTERS         **
1110 '**            5 = DOWN    NO AUTO ANSWER OF PHONE       **
1120 '**            6 = DOWN    COMPUTER FORCED TO ACCEPT DATA **
1130 '**            7 = UP      SINGLE LINE PHONE             **
1140 '******************************************************
1150 '
1160 '******************************************************
1170 '**    transmit file name entry section                 **
1180 '******************************************************
1190 ON ERROR GOTO 1300
1200 CLS
1210 PRINT "ENTER COMPLETE FILENAME INCLUDING EXTENSION OF THE FILE "
     TO BE
1220 PRINT "TRANSMITTED - NOTE : FILE MUST BE IN ASCII FORMAT FOR "
     PROGRAM
1230 PRINT "TO WORK. "
1240 PRINT
1250 INPUT "FILENAME = " ; TRANSMIT$
1260 OPEN TRANSMIT$ FOR INPUT AS #1
1270 GOTO 1400
1280 '
1290 '******************************************************
1300 '**    error handling routine for name entry section    **
1310 '******************************************************
1320 FOR X = 1 TO 1000 : NEXT : CLS : FOR X = 1 TO 1000 : NEXT
1330 IF ERR = 53 THEN PRINT "FILE NOT FOUND "
1340 IF ERR = 64 THEN PRINT "BAD FILE NAME "
1350 IF (ERR <> 53) AND (ERR <> 64) THEN PRINT "ERROR IN FILE NAME INPUT "
1360 LOCATE 5,1
1370 RESUME 1210
1380 '
1390 '******************************************************
1400 '**    receive file name entry section                  **
1410 '******************************************************
1420 ON ERROR GOTO 1520
1430 CLS
1440 PRINT "ENTER COMPLETE FILENAME INCLUDING EXTENSION WHERE THE "
1450 PRINT "FILE TO BE RECEIVED WILL BE STORED."
```

```
1460 PRINT
1470 INPUT "FILENAME = " ; RECIEVE$
1480 OPEN RECIEVE$ FOR OUTPUT AS #2
1490 GOTO 1620
1500 '
1510 '**************************************************************
1520 '**    error handling routine for name input section      **
1530 '**************************************************************
1540 FOR X = 1 TO 1000 : NEXT : CLS : FOR X = 1 TO 1000 : NEXT
1550 IF ERR = 53 THEN PRINT "FILE NOT FOUND "
1560 IF ERR = 64 THEN PRINT "BAD FILE NAME "
1570 IF (ERR <> 53) AND (ERR <> 64) THEN PRINT "ERROR IN FILE NAME INPUT "
1580 LOCATE 5,1
1590 RESUME 1440
1600 '
1610 '**************************************************************
1620 '**    routine to initiate communications                **
1630 '**************************************************************
1640 ON ERROR GOTO 0
1650 OPEN "com1:" AS #3
1660 IF (INP(&H3FD) AND &H20) = 0 THEN 1660 'TRANS HOLD REGISTER EMPTY?
1670 PRINT #3, "AT Z"
1680 GOSUB 1780
1690 SEC = 3 : GOSUB 1870
1700 PRINT #3, "AT S0 = 1"
1710 GOSUB 1780
1720 SEC = 3 : GOSUB 1870
1730 GOSUB 1780
1740 GOTO 1730       ' IF ANY NON-CONNECT SIGNAL THEN LOOP (DO NOT CONTINUE)
1750 END            ' IF HERE THEN ERROR - CLOSE AND STOP
1760 '
1770 '**************************************************************
1780 '**    routine to input a line from modem                **
1790 '**************************************************************
1800 LINE INPUT #3, RECEIVEDATA$
1810 PRINT
1820 IF RECEIVEDATA$ = "0" THEN PRINT "RESPONSE = OK" : RETURN
1830 IF RECEIVEDATA$ = "1" THEN PRINT "RESPONSE = CONNECT" : RETURN 1950
1840 IF RECEIVEDATA$ = "2" THEN PRINT "RESPONSE = RING" : RETURN
1850 IF RECEIVEDATA$ = "3" THEN PRINT "RESPONSE = NO CARRIER" : END
1860 IF RECEIVEDATA$ = "4" THEN PRINT "RESPONSE = ERROR" : END
1870 '
1880 '**************************************************************
1890 '**    time delay for SEC seconds                        **
1900 '**************************************************************
1910 FOR DELAY = 1 TO 700*SEC : NEXT DELAY
1920 RETURN
```

```
1930 '
1940 '*****************************************************************
1950 '**    routine to receive data and store it                    **
1960 '*****************************************************************
1970 ON COM(1) GOSUB 2100
1980 COM(1) ON
1990 IF VAL(RECEIVEDATA$) < 64000! THEN 1990
2000 '
2010 FOR I = 1 TO POINTER
2020 PRINT #2 , DATAIO$(I)
2030 NEXT I
2040 '
2050 CLOSE #2
2060 PRINT : PRINT "FILE - ";RECEIVE$;" RECEIVED AND STORED"
2070 GOTO 2200
2080 '
2090 '*****************************************************************
2100 '**    store each line in array DATAIO$ via interrupt         **
2110 '*****************************************************************
2120 LINE INPUT #3, RECEIVEDATA$
2130 POINTER = POINTER + 1
2140 DATAIO$(POINTER) = RECEIVEDATA$
2150 IF (RECEIVEDATA$ = "3") THEN PRINT : PRINT "LOSS OF CARRIER" : END
2160 IF VAL(RECEIVEDATA$) > 64000! THEN COM(1) OFF
2170 RETURN
2180 '
2190 '*****************************************************************
2200 '**    routine to transmit data to distant end                **
2210 '*****************************************************************
2220 COM(1) OFF
2230 ON ERROR GOTO 2330        ' TERMINATE
2240 SEC = 3 : GOSUB 1890
2250 WHILE NOT EOF(1)
2260 LINE INPUT #1 , SENDDATA$
2270 PRINT #3, SENDDATA$
2280 WEND
2290 PRINT #3, "65000 '"
2300 PRINT : PRINT "FILE - ";TRANSMIT$;" TRANSMITTED OK"
2310 '
2320 '*****************************************************************
2330 '**                    TERMINATE PROGRAM                       **
2340 '*****************************************************************
2350 SEC = 20 : GOSUB 1890
2360 PRINT #3,"+++";
2370 SEC = 1 : GOSUB 1890
2380 PRINT #3,"AT Z"
```

```
2390 END
2400 RETURN
65000 '
```

Chapter 7

F1. Increment hour   F2. Decrement hour
F3. Increment minute   F4. Decrement minute
F5. Increment second   F6. Decrement second

10:07:12

Programming Aids, Subroutines, and Utilities

The programs in this chapter range from utilities that allow you to create your own character fonts, alter the message on your DOS, and check out your color monitor to subroutines that you may use in your own programs to make your programming tasks simpler.

PERSONALIZED DOS

This utility allows you to personalize the message that appears whenever you use the disk operating system or DOS. The standard disk drive that comes with the IBM Personal Computer is a single sided, double-density drive, although there is a trend toward using double sided drives, and they may become the standard shortly. The drives allow you to store 163,840 bytes of information on a 5 ¼ inch disk. The data is stored on any of 40 concentric tracks each of which contains 4,096 bytes. Each track is further divided into 8 sectors giving you 512 bytes per sector.

Normally, it is impossible to access the specific information in a particular sector, but thanks to an excellent utility included on the disk you received with the DOS, it becomes relatively simple.

Debug is a machine-language program written to help the programmers of machine and assembly-language programs examine and correct mistakes in their programs. The side benefit of *Debug* that we will use here is its ability to read and write to specific tracks on the diskette.

Whenever a disk is formatted with the FORMAT A:/S command, several things happen automatically:

1. The disk is formatted. That means that specific patterns are written onto the disk to prepare it for new information. Using these patterns, the entire disk is checked for bad spots on its surface where it would be impossible to write to. These bad spots are "locked out" so they cannot be used. A directory to be used for the identification of the files that will be stored on the disk later is created.

2. Three files are copied onto the disk. Two of these files are hidden and cannot be listed with the DIR command from DOS or the files command from BASIC. These are IBMBIOS.COM and IBMDOS.COM which are the heart of the system. The third file called COMMAND.COM is then stored on the disk. This file completes the DOS and allows you to enter commands to the system.

These files contain the programs that operate when the computer powers up (along with the ROM). Also included in these programs are the messages that the system displays. When the system first powers up, it performs a check of all functions and then asks for the time and date. After you have entered the time and date, the computer displays a message identifying the DOS. This is the message we will modify.

To start, format a new disk using the FORMAT A:/S command. You should never make modifications to a DOS except on a backup copy, because if you make a mistake on your master copy you will destroy your operating system.

Consider what you would like the message to read. For the example, I will add the following line to the message:

Created Especially For John Q. Public

Using the following table:
space = 20   double quotes = 22

		@ = 40	P = 50	` = 60	p = 70
! = 21	1 = 31	A = 41	Q = 51	a = 61	q = 71
	2 = 32	B = 42	R = 52	b = 62	r = 72
# = 23	3 = 33	C = 43	S = 53	c = 63	s = 73
$ = 24	4 = 34	D = 44	T = 54	d = 64	t = 74
% = 25	5 = 35	E = 45	U = 55	e = 65	u = 75
& = 26	6 = 36	F = 46	V = 56	f = 66	v = 76
' = 27	7 = 37	G = 47	W = 57	g = 67	w = 77
(= 28	8 = 38	H = 48	X = 58	h = 68	x = 78
) = 29	9 = 39	I = 49	Y = 59	i = 69	y = 79
* = 2A	: = 3A	J = 4A	Z = 5A	j = 6A	z = 7A
+ = 2B	; = 3B	K = 4B	[= 5B	k = 6B	{ = 7B
, = 2C	< = 3C	L = 4C	\ = 5C	l = 6C	¦ = 7C
− = 2D	= = 3D	M = 4D	] = 5D	m = 6D	} = 7D
. = 2E	> = 3E	N = 4E	^ = 5E	n = 6E	~ = 7E
/ = 2F	? = 3F	O = 4F	_ = 5F	o = 6F	

Note: 0 = 30

Compute the values that have to be entered for the characters you selected. For the example use

```
C r e a t e d     E s p e c i a l l y
43 72 65 61 74 65 64 20 45 73 70 65 63 69 61 6C 6C 79 20
  F o r     J o h n     Q .     P u b l i c
46 6F 72 20 4A 6F 68 6E 20 51 2E 20 50 75 62 6C 69 63
```

Load the *Debug* program and insert the newly formatted disk. Enter the line **L 0000:8000 0,19,2** This command loads the sectors that should contain the information we are looking for off the disk. If your version of DOS is different than mine, you will have to search around for the correct sectors on the disk.

Next enter the line **D 0000:8000 8400** This displays a memory dump of the data we just loaded from the disk sectors into memory. The left side of the screen lists the starting memory address of the information that is displayed on that line. 16 groups of characters that tell the value of the next 16 memory locations, follow the starting address, and then there is a short segment that displays the printable characters.

At about 0000:8200 on the dump, you should start seeing the DOS message. Press the break key to stop the display and examine the listing. On my version of DOS I find the dollar sign at the memory location 0000:8205. This is the character that tells DOS to stop printing. At this point we will use the examine command to change the actual values at these memory locations. The entries I used are displayed in the table below. To conserve paper they are listed in two columns but they were entered as one column.

E 0000:8205 43	E 0000:8217 20
E 0000:8206 72	E 0000:8218 46
E 0000:8207 65	E 0000:8219 6F
E 0000:8208 61	E 0000:821A 72
E 0000:8209 74	E 0000:821B 20
E 0000:820A 65	E 0000:821C 4A
E 0000:820B 64	E 0000:821D 6F
E 0000:820C 20	E 0000:821E 68
E 0000:820D 45	E 0000:821F 6E
E 0000:820E 73	E 0000:8220 20
E 0000:820F 70	E 0000:8221 51
E 0000:8210 65	E 0000:8222 2E
E 0000:8211 63	E 0000:8223 20
E 0000:8212 69	E 0000:8224 50
E 0000:8213 61	E 0000:8225 75
E 0000:8214 6C	E 0000:8226 62

```
E 0000:8215 6C        E 0000:8227 6C

E 0000:8216 79        E 0000:8228 69

                      E 0000:8229 63
```

Then in the next three locations enter

```
E 0000:822A 0D

E 0000:822B 0A

E 0000:822C 24
```

These values correspond to carriage return, line feed, and stop print.

Performing another memory dump should show whether or not the memory change was performed correctly. If everything is as you want it, all that needs to be done is to write the block of memory back to the disk. This is done using the same information you supplied on the load command:

W 0000:8000 0,19,2

This will rewrite the data back to the same disk location that it was originally taken from. At this point, all that you must do is to see if the disk was modified correctly. Simply perform a system reset and see if the new message appears.

LETTER WRITER

This program is designed to help you easily and quickly send a letter on a diskette to any of your friends who also have IBM Personal Computers. When you type **RUN** the program first displays the current contents of the Envelope file as shown in Fig. 7-1. The Envelope file may contain any reasonable number of text lines. After each screen full of lines is displayed, the program will pause and wait for you to press any key before continuing.

After reading the current letter you are given the options of quitting or of writing a new letter. If you quit, the Envelope file is left undisturbed. If you write a new letter the contents of the Envelope file will be replaced with the new lines of text you type in.

With a couple of minor changes, this program allows you to read and write letters on a cassette tape. The file name in line 60 should be changed to **CAS1:ENVELOPE** in order for the program to access a cassette file. Also, program line 150 should be turned into a remark line (or deleted) if the current tape doesn't have an Envelope file recorded on it. Line 150 (GOSUB 250) will cause a device timeout error if the tape doesn't have a letter to be read on it. In addition, remember to rewind the tape and to press the play and record buttons at the correct times.

```
10 ' ******************
20 ' **     LETTER     **
30 ' ******************
40 '
50 CLEAR
60 FILESPEC$ = "ENVELOPE"
70 SCREEN 0,0,0,0
80 CLS
90 KEY OFF
```

```
100 WIDTH 80
110 PRINT TAB(27)CHR$(201);STRING$(24,205);CHR$(187)
120 PRINT TAB(27)CHR$(186)TAB(37)"LETTER"TAB(52)CHR$(186)
130 PRINT TAB(27)CHR$(200);STRING$(24,205);CHR$(188)
140 PRINT
150 GOSUB 250
160 LOCATE 25,14
170 PRINT " - - - - - <W>rite new letter, or <Q>uit ? - - - - -";
180 K$ = INKEY$
190 IF K$ = "w" OR K$ = "W" THEN 420
200 IF K$ <> "q" AND K$ <> "Q" THEN 180
210 CLS
220 END
230 '
240 ' Read the letter in the envelope
250 ON ERROR GOTO 610
260 OPEN FILESPEC$ FOR INPUT AS #1
270 WHILE NOT EOF(1)
280 LINE INPUT #1,A$
290 IF A$ <> "###" THEN PRINT A$
300 IF CSRLIN > 22 THEN GOSUB 360
310 WEND
320 CLOSE #1
330 RETURN
340 '
350 ' Subroutine, wait before continuing
360 LOCATE 24,25:PRINT "Press any key to continue ...";
370 K$=INKEY$
380 IF K$ = "" THEN 370
390 CLS
400 RETURN
410 '
420 ' Write a letter and put it into envelope
430 CLS
440 PRINT "Type in your letter ..."
450 PRINT "Edit only on the current line.  ";
460 PRINT "Once you press <enter> a line is filed away.
470 PRINT "After the last line type in these three characters ... ";
480 PRINT CHR$(34);"###";CHR$(34)
490 LOCATE 9
500 OPEN FILESPEC$ FOR OUTPUT AS #1
510 WHILE TEXT$ <> "###"
520 LINE INPUT TEXT$
530 PRINT #1,TEXT$
540 WEND
550 CLS
560 LOCATE 12,25
```

```
570 PRINT "The envelope has been stuffed."
580 END
590 '
600 ' Error trapping, probably no FILESPEC$ file
610 IF ERR <> 53 THEN ON ERROR GOTO 0
620 OPEN FILESPEC$ FOR OUTPUT AS #1
630 PRINT #1,"###"
640 CLOSE #1
650 RESUME
```

```
              IMMMMMMMMMMMMMMMMMMMMMMM;
              :           LETTER           :
              HMMMMMMMMMMMMMMMMMMMMMMM<

Dear Don:

      Congratulations on your recent purchase of a new IBM Personal
Computer!  You made a good choice.  I've been very satisfied with the
powerful features and quality construction of mine.

      Sorry I haven't written more often.  Now that we both have
our P.C.'s let's try writing letters to each other with this LETTER
program.  It's easy to use and the postage for mailing a diskette
is surprisingly little.

      Say hi to your family for me.  I'm looking forward to hearing
from you.

                                    Best regards,
                                    John




      - - - - - <W>rite new letter, or <Q>uit ? - - - - -
```

Fig. 7-1. Sample display produced by the *Letter* program.

CIRCLES

If you have a system that uses Cassette BASIC and you are still just dreaming of installing your first disk drive, you have found that a few of the commands will work only with the more advanced disk BASICs. The circle command is one of these. Luckily, this is a simple command that will simulate the circle command.

If you use a piece of graph paper, a circle with a radius of 100 units is easy, if tedious, to graph. With the center at zero for this exercise, the relationship for the points around the circle is $X*X + Y*Y = R*R$. So to graph the circle just rearrange the formula to the form:

Yval = square root of (radius * radius − Xval * Xval)

    Or

        $Y = SQR(100 \uparrow 2 - X \uparrow 2)$

    As it would be written from BASIC.

Next we start by letting the value of x change from 0 to the value of the radius, or 100, and compute the value of y according to the formula. Or, we write a short program to do this for us.

```
10 '*************************************************
20 '**        THE GREAT CIRCLE CALCULATOR PROGRAM         **
30 '*************************************************
40 '
50 FOR X = Ø TO 100
60 Y = SQR ( 10000 - X*X )
70 PRINT "X = ";X,"Y = ";Y
80 NEXT X
```

Now we plot all of these points on the graph. When we finally finish we have a picture of—just ¼ of a circle. But hold on just a minute. Hidden back in the original equation is the rest of the circle! It seems that when you have an equation like 25 = ? * ?, it is obvious that the value of 5 will solve the equation, but the value of −5 will work just as well! So, from our original equation of x∧2+y∧2 =r∧2, we will find that both x and y can be positive or negative and the result will still be correct. So now you can plot the points with (+X, +Y), (+X, −Y), (−X, +Y) and (−X, −Y).

    This formula works well on graph paper, but if you use it and the PSET command to draw on the screen, a new problem arises: you draw elipses on screen 2. This contortion occurs because there are 640 dots horizontally and only 200 dots vertically on the screen. This is compensated for a bit by the fact that the screen is slightly wider than it is high, but it leaves us with a tall and skinny circle. This is easily compensated for by dividing all Y values by 2.

    The last problem arises from the fact that between the points where x = 100 and x = 99, y changes from 0 to 14.1. This leaves us with a large hole in the circle. To get around this problem, just redraw the circle changing the Y values and calculating the X values. Don't forget to multiply the x values by 2 to scale them for the screen. To speed up the programs that draw more than one circle, just plot ½ of each quadrant for the circles that are closely spaced, instead of plotting full quadrants.

```
10 '**********************************************
20 '**                  CIRCLE                  **
30 '**                                          **
40 '**   DRAWS A CIRCLE FROM CASSETTE BASIC     **
50 '**********************************************
60 '
70 CLS : KEY OFF : SCREEN 2
80 FOR X = -100 TO 100
90 Y = (10000 - X*X)^.5 * .5
```

```
100 PSET (X+319,Y+100)
110 PSET (X+319,100-Y)
120 NEXT
130 FOR Y = -50 TO 50
140 X = (2500 - Y*Y)^.5 * 2
150 PSET (319+X,100+Y)
160 PSET (319-X,100+Y)
170 NEXT


100 '*****************************************
110 '**           CONCENTRIC CIRCLES          **
120 '**                                       **
130 '**   DRAWS CIRCLES FROM CASSETTE BASIC  **
140 '*****************************************
150 '
160 CLS : SCREEN 2 : KEY OFF
170 FOR A = 0 TO 178 STEP 4
180 '
190 FOR X = -A TO A
200 Y = (A*A-X*X)^.5 *.5
210 PSET (319+X,100+Y)
220 PSET (319+X,100-Y)
230 NEXT X
240 '
250 FOR Y = -A\2 TO A\2
260 X = (A*A\4-Y*Y)^.5 * 2
270 PSET (319+X,100+Y)
280 PSET (319-X,100+Y)
290 NEXT Y
300 '
310 NEXT A
320 '
330 A$ = INKEY$ : IF A$ = "" THEN 330


10 '*****************************************
20 '**             ROTATING CIRCLE            **
30 '**                                        **
40 '**   DRAWS A CIRCLE FROM CASSETTE BASIC  **
50 '*****************************************
60 '
100 CLS : KEY OFF : SCREEN 2
110 FOR X = -150 TO 150
120 Y = (22500 - X*X)^.5 *.5
130 PSET (319+X,100+Y)
140 PSET (319+X,100-Y)
150 NEXT
160 FOR Y = -75 TO 75
```

```
170 X = (5625 - Y*Y)^.5 * 2
180 PSET (319+X,100+Y)
190 PSET (319-X,100+Y)
200 NEXT
210 PERCENT = 3.14159 * 2 / 100
220 FOR B = 0 TO 95 STEP 5
230 X = COS(PERCENT * B) * 150
240 Y = SIN(PERCENT * B) * 75
250 LINE (319,100)-(319+X,100-Y),0
260 FOR Z = 1 TO 10 : NEXT Z
270 LINE (319,100)-(319+X,100-Y)
280 NEXT B
290 GOTO 220
```

TIMED DELAYS

Here are two very useful routines for use in Disk BASIC. Time delays are sometimes very useful to the operation of a program, especially if you need to display something on the screen for a second or two. Normally, time delays are generated with a for-next loop. This has the disadvantage that as a program grows in size during development, the time it takes BASIC to scan through the active variables to increment the counter increases. What started out as a small time delay for a small program, can suddenly become a large delay later. That is why it is better to use the built-in clock. Simply **INPUT TIMES$** and store the string. Then as long as you get a match between the stored string and TIMES$, you are still on the same second. The same principle works for days using DATE$.

```
100 '**********************************************
110 '**   SUBROUTINE TO PROVIDE ACCURATE TIME DELAYS **
120 '**        (+- 1 SEC) FROM DISK BASIC            **
130 '**********************************************
140 '
150 CLS
160 SEC = 15
170 PRINT "START !"
180 '**********************************************
190 FOR X = 1 TO SEC
200 A$ = TIME$
210 WHILE A$ = TIME$
220 WEND
230 NEXT X
240 '**********************************************
250 PRINT "FINISH - 15 SEC"

100 '**********************************************
110 '**   SUBROUTINE IN CASE YOU WANT SOMETHING TO   **
120 '** HAPPEN JUST AT MIDNIGHT (TIME$ MUST BE SET) **
130 '**********************************************
140 '
150 CLS
```

```
160 PRINT "START !"
170 '**********************************************
180 A$ = DATE$
190 WHILE A$ = DATE$
200 WEND
210 '**********************************************
220 PRINT "MIDNIGHT !"
```

BARE-BONES TEXT CREATION USING DATA STATEMENTS

Sometimes it is convenient to be able to create and modify text files without having to resort to a text editor. This may be the case when you want to leave yourself a memo on a disk or on a tape for future reference, or when you want to print a simple memo and would like to view it first on the screen. Routines to accomplish these tasks are very simple to write, and three examples are shown here. For the three programs, the data statements are simply added onto the end of the programs.

The first example, *Bare-Bones #1*, allows you to select the device you want to send the output to. The program is currently set up to select between the screen or the printer, but other devices could be added very simply. Having these two options allows you to check the final form of the text before you print it. The text is sent exactly as it is displayed on the screen, which saves paper on continuous forms.

The second program, *Bare-Bone #2*, is a program that was intended to be used for the creation of text files on a disk or tape from BASIC. But, shortly after I started using it, I found that if I named my file **SCRN:** or **LPT1:** or **COM1**; etc, I could easily direct the data to the device of my choosing. In this program, a linefeed is inserted after every line to put it into a form suitable for reports. Also, the text is output in 60 line "pages." This allows you to center the printing neatly on a printed page and use the perforations on continuous forms.

The final example, *Bare-Bones #3*, is a modification of the second program. In this program, the text is output exactly as entered except for the fact that the data is padded with blanks to make the lines all 80 characters long. This is useful if you want to modify the saved text later using a regular text editor. For example, this program works well with the text editor listed later in this book. The text is single spaced and formated at 60 lines per page. After all of the text has been output, an **OUT OF DATA** message is displayed and that page is padded to line number 60 with 80 character blank lines.

A possible use for the text generated by these programs would be to save it in an ASCII file which can be read with the **TYPE PROGRAM-NAME** command from DOS. This command could be entered as a part of an **AUTOEXEC.BAT** file which would start up automatically whenever the system is powered up. Messages and reminders could be stored here for future reference.

```
10 '**********************************************
15 '**                 BARE-BONES #1              **
20 '**   NOV 15,1982              VERS 1.1   **
25 '**                                            **
30 '**   PRINTS DATA STATEMENTS TO SCREEN OR PRINTER   **
35 '**********************************************
40 '
45 PRINT "DO YOU WANT THE OUTPUT TO GO TO THE SCREEN OR THE PRINTER - "
50 PRINT "(1 = SCREEN)     (2 = PRINTER)
55 INPUT A : ON A GOTO 65,70
60 CLS : GOTO 45
```

```
65 OPEN "SCRN:" FOR OUTPUT AS #1 : GOTO 75
70 OPEN "LPT1:" FOR OUTPUT AS #1
75 ON ERROR GOTO 95
80 CLS
85 READ A$ : PRINT #1 , A$
90 GOTO 85
95 END
100 DATA "FILL IN WITH YOUR OWN DATA STATEMENTS


10 '******************************************************
12 '**                  BARE-BONES #2                  **
14 '**  NOV 15,1982                      VERS 1.1  **
16 '**                                                 **
18 '**   PRINTS DATA STATEMENTS TO DISK WITH LINEFEED  **
20 '******************************************************
22 '
24 PRINT "enter the filename please -;
26 INPUT A$
28 ON ERROR GOTO 44
30 OPEN A$ FOR OUTPUT AS #1
32 FOR X = 1 TO 30
34 READ B$ : PRINT #1,B$
36 B$ = " " : PRINT #1,B$
38 NEXT X
40 CLOSE
42 GOTO 24
44 PRINT "out of data"
46 FOR Y = X TO 30
48 B$ = " " : PRINT #1,B$
50 B$ = " " : PRINT #1,B$
52 NEXT Y
54 CLOSE
56 END


10 '************************************************************
15 '**                  BARE-BONES #3                        **
20 '**  VERSION 1.1                      DEC 15, 1982  **
25 '************************************************************
30 '**   Driver To Create ASCII File Out Of DATA Statements   **
35 '************************************************************
40 PRINT "enter the filename please -;
45 INPUT A$
50 ON ERROR GOTO 90
55 OPEN A$ FOR OUTPUT AS #1
60 FOR X = 1 TO 60
65 READ B$ : FOR A = LEN(B$) TO 80 : B$ = B$ + " " : NEXT A
70 PRINT #1,B$
```

```
75 NEXT X
80 CLOSE
85 GOTO 40
90 PRINT "out of data"
95 FOR Y = X TO 60
100 B$ = STRING$(80,32) : PRINT #1,B$
105 NEXT Y
110 CLOSE
115 END
120 '
```

AUTOMATIC STARTUP PROCEDURE

AUTOEXEC.BAT is a very useful procedure hidden within the DOS and BASIC manuals. This procedure allows you to start up the Personal Computer in a configuration that is best suited to the application you are working on at the present time. You may also use this procedure to enable a person who is not proficient in the use of the computer to go from turning on the computer directly to running a program.

Although there are many options, I will only describe the setup I use and let you expand upon it to suit your own needs. On powering up the computer, the system goes through the normal checkout procedure. Next, as usual, it asks for the data and time. From this point on, things are different. For about one second the computer displays the cryptic message — A>BASICA AUTOBOOT.BAS Very quickly the screen clears, even the 25th line, a list of all files on the disk is displayed, and the computer stops with the word — OK.

To autostart the system, all that is needed is two short programs. Running the first program . . .

```
10 OPEN "AUTOEXEC.BAT" FOR OUTPUT AS #1

20 PRINT #1, "DATE"

30 PRINT #1, "TIME"

40 PRINT #1, "BASICA AUTOBOOT.BAS"

50 CLOSE
```

. . . performs two functions. From power on, the system checks itself out and then loads in the disk operating system. At this point the DOS checks if there is a file called AUTOEXEC. BAT. If not, it procedes to ask for the data and time etc., but if there is such a file, it follows the instructions in the file as if they had been typed in. So, the program above creates a file called AUTOEXEC.BAT and tells the system to . . .

(1) set the date and time
(2) load BASICA and from BASICA to load and run a program called AUTOBOOT.BAS

This, the second program, is saved as file AUTOBOOT.BAS

```
10 'Initialization Procedure For the I.B.M.  P.C.

20 '

30 CLS : KEY OFF : SCREEN 0 : WIDTH 80
```

212

```
40 KEY 5, "FILES"+CHR$(13)

50 KEY 6, "KILL"+CHR$(34)

60 KEY 7, "LINE ("

70 KEY 8, ")-("

80 KEY 9, "RENUM "

90 KEY 10, "NAME"+CHR$(34)

100 FILES

110 NEW
```

This program, which is automatically loaded and run by the first program, in turn performs several functions.

(1) It presets the screen to the 80 column text screen and
(2) clears the screen including the 25th line.
(3) It resets the function keys 5 thru 10. The functions that are preset with BASIC are not always the best for a particular situation and this is a convenient place to reset them to suit your preferences. The CHR$(13) is the character entered when you hit return, and CHR$(34) is the ASCII character code for a quote mark.
(4) It displays all the files on the disk in the default drive on the screen, and then
(5) it clears itself out of memory with -NEW-.

Now, when I turn on the system, I set the date and time, and the system automatically sets the screen and function keys, displays all files on the disk, and stands by ready to work.

One last thing: after I run the first program which creates the **AUTOEXEC.BAT** file, I save the program itself to disk so that later if I decide to change the **BAT** file to include commands such as CHKDSK and PAUSE to enable me to check for remaining disk space, I will not have to retype the entire program.

```
10 ' **************
20 ' **   BOOT   **
30 ' **************
40 '
50 OPEN "AUTOEXEC.BAT" FOR OUTPUT AS #1
60 PRINT #1,"date"
70 PRINT #1,"time"
80 PRINT #1,"basica mainmenu"
90 CLOSE #1
100 END


10 ' ****************
20 ' **   MAINMENU   **
30 ' ****************
40 '
50 '   This program appears magically as system wakes up !
```

```
60 '   Set up a main menu or have this program do any processing
70 '   you wish, all automatically after BASICA is loaded.
80 '
90 '   For example ...
100 '
110 SCREEN 0,0,0
120 WIDTH 80
130 CLS
140 KEY OFF
150 FILES
160 PRINT
170 INPUT "Program name to RUN ";PROGRAM$
180 LOAD PROGRAM$,R
```

COLOR MONITOR ALIGNMENT

Color monitors and televisions work well with regular video broadcasts, but when you try to use them with high-resolution graphics or with 80-character lines on the screen, any misalignment can cause you trouble. This program will allow you to observe any irregularities in the way your set is aligned.

The first test is for registration. In a color set, there are three pictures being generated on the screen. These three pictures, one red, one blue, and one green, combine to form the picture you see. If the three pictures do not lie directly on top of one another, you will see words that are hard to read, and a single white line will appear to be three lines. To test for registration, a series of white lines are drawn vertically and horizontally on the screen as shown in Fig. 7-2. The lines should be reasonably white, especially in the center. If there are any areas where the lines split badly into two or three colors, it may mean the set should be serviced.

The second test is for purity. This test is performed by turning on only one color at a time and seeing if the color is pure across the entire screen. This test is repeated for the red, blue, and green screens.

The final test displays a test pattern consisting of colored bars. With this test you can adjust tint, brightness, and contrast on the set, if your set has these controls. Some sets, in particular, the RGB monitors, may only have a brightness control.

After you go through the three tests once, and have adjusted the various user controls, go back over the tests from the beginning. Some controls, like tint, may affect purity, and while it may appear that you have problems the first time through, a simple adjustment may clear everything up.

And finally . . .

If it looks good . . . don't touch it!

```
100 '**************************************************
110 '**   TELEVISION OR MONITOR ALIGNMENT PROGRAM   **
120 '**************************************************
130 '
140 '** PART #1        REGISTRATION
150 SCREEN 2,0 : KEY OFF : CLS
160 OUT 980,2 : OUT 981,43
170 LINE (0,0)-(639,0)
180 FOR X = 63 TO 639 STEP 64
190 LINE (X,0)-(X,199)
```

```
200 NEXT
210 LINE (0,0)-(0,199)
220 FOR Y = 19 TO 199 STEP 20
230 LINE (0,Y)-(639,Y)
240 NEXT
250 LOCATE 24,18
260 PRINT "THE LINES SHOULD BE WHITE AND EVENLY SPACED";
270 '
280 '** PART #2    PURITY
290 A$ = INKEY$ : IF A$ = "" THEN 290
300 SCREEN 0,1 : WIDTH 40
```

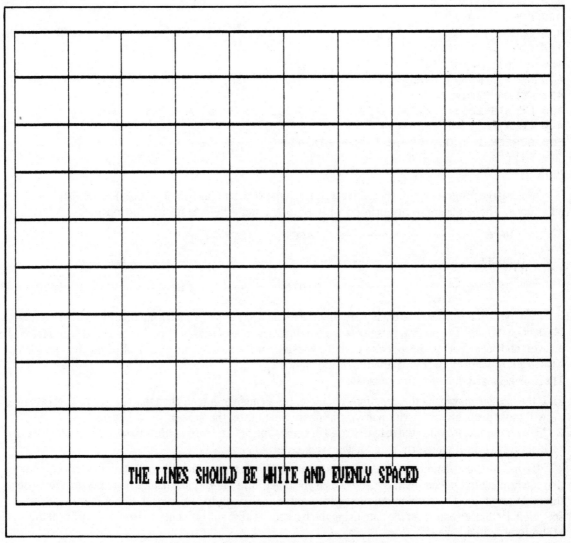

Fig. 7-2. Display for testing your monitor produced by the *Monitor Alignment* program.

```
305 OUT 980,2 : OUT 981,43
310 COLOR 4,4,4 : CLS : COLOR 7,0 : LOCATE 10,9 : PRINT "RED      ";
320 INPUT A$
330 COLOR 2,2,2 : CLS : COLOR 7,0 : LOCATE 10,9 : PRINT "GREEN    ";
340 INPUT A$
350 COLOR 1,1,1 : CLS : COLOR 7,0 : LOCATE 10,9 : PRINT "BLUE     ";
360 INPUT A$
370 '
380 '**  PART #3     COLOR BARS
390 SCREEN 0,1
400 COLOR 0,0,0 : CLS
410 FOR X = 1 TO 24
420 FOR Y = 0 TO 7
430 COLOR Y
440 FOR Z = 1 TO 5
450 PRINT CHR$(219);
460 NEXT : NEXT  : NEXT
470 COLOR 7,0,0
480 LOCATE 25,1 : PRINT "BLA  BLU  GR   CY    RED  MAG  BR   WH";
490 LOCATE 1,1 : INPUT A$
500 SCREEN 2 : OUT 980,2 : OUT 981,43
```

DATA-IN

Many large programs print an entire screen of questions, such as **NAME, AGE, PRESENT HEALTH** all at once. These questions are printed with a prompt and a field to fill in. For example:

```
NAME -------------------- AGE --- SEX (M/F) -

ADDRESS -----------------------------------------------

CITY ------------------- STATE --------- ZIP -----
```

The person at the keyboard answers the questions and the program automatically jumps to the next block of questions. The program also sets the maximum number of characters that can be entered for each answer and makes sure the person cannot type an answer longer than that allowed for and cannot backspace to before the first character of the answer.

These checks are done for two reasons:

1. If the person answering the questions should enter an answer longer than that allowed for, the answer will most probably overwrite part of the next question on the screen.
2. Many programs in which the data is stored in some type of fixed format file will eventually show data or printing errors if an overly long answer was entered.

To handle these conditions, *Data-in* was created. This is a short (less than 25 active lines) subroutine that can be placed at the end of most programs if you make sure the variable names do not duplicate those of the main program. The subroutine allows free entry of data up to the maximum number of characters specified, facilitates editing of the data using the backspace key, and presents a visual indication of the size of the total field allowed.

Once you have the layout of the screen established, the subroutine becomes very easy to use. Simply state the row and column on the screen where you would like the data to be entered. Then give the maximum number of characters allowed in the input. On the same line you may enter the routine with **GOSUB 30330.**

100 ROW = 10 : COLUMN = 15 : LENGTH = 20 : GOSUB 30330

At this time the routine will locate 10,15 on the screen and print 20 minus signs. So with a prompt of **LAST ADDRESS** we have . . .

LAST ADDRESS --------------------

As the data is entered it will overlay the characters, for example,

LAST ADDRESS KANSAS CITY, MISSO--

Editing can be accomplished by using the backspace key which will delete the last character and insert a minus sign in its place.

LAST ADDRESS KANSAS CITY, MISS---

More characters can now be deleted or added up to the limit set by the length you indicated in the main program, until you have the data in the form you desire.

LAST ADDRESS KANSAS CITY, MO. ----

Now, simply hit the enter key and

>>>KANSAS CITY, MO.<<<

free of minus signs will be returned to your main program as a string of characters in the variable B$.

You may change the character printed initially, the minus signs, by changing lines 30350, 30510, and 30520 to reflect the character you desire. For use on the graphics screens, I found the minus sign to work well, and on the text screen I found CHR$(254) which is displayed as a small square centered in the space allowed for the individual character to work best. CHR$(254) may be added to the text of the program easily by centering the cursor over the character to be replaced and then holding down the ALT key while you enter 254 from the numeric keypad keys located on the right hand side of the keyboard. When you release the ALT key, the minus sign will be replaced with the new character.

```
30000 ROW = 20 : COLUMN = 20 : LENGTH = 20
30010 CLS
30020 GOSUB 30330
30030 PRINT B$
30040 STOP
30050 '*************************************************************
30060 '** INPUT SUBROUTINE          VERS 1.1          JUNE 20, 1982  **
30070 '**                                                            **
30080 '**FOR THIS SUBROUTINE,  GIVE THE ROW AND COLUMN WHERE YOU WOULD **
30090 '**LIKE THE INPUT TO APPEAR ON THE SCREEN,  AND THE MAXIMUM LENGTH **
30100 '**OF THE INPUT STRING. THEN GOSUB 30330 (OR WHAT YOU RENUM IT TO) **
30110 '**                                                            **
30120 '**THIS PROGRAM WILL PRINT -LENGTH- # OF SMALL SQUARES AT THE  **
30130 '**GIVEN LOCATION IN THIS FORM    ~~~~~~~~~~~  ,  AND THEN START **
30140 '**ACCEPTING INPUT FROM THE KEYBOARD.  AS YOU TYPE IN THE DATA, **
30150 '**IT WILL OVERLAY THE SMALL SQUARES IN THIS FASHION -         **
```

```
30160 '**                                                          **
30170 '**SMITH~~~~~~                                               **
30180 '**                                                          **
30190 '**AT ANY TIME YOU MAY -                                     **
30200 '**(1) TYPE MORE LETTERS UP TO THE LIMIT SET BY 'LENGTH'     **
30210 '**(2) BACKSPACE BY USE OF THE BACK-ARROW KEY (TO CORRECT ERRORS) **
30220 '**(3) FINISH BY HITING THE 'RETURN' KEY                     **
30230 '**                                                          **
30240 '**THE PROGRAM WILL NOT LET YOU CREATE AN INPUT LONGER THAN  **
30250 '**LENGTH OR BACKSPACE TO BEFORE THE FIRST CHARACTER         **
30260 '**                                                          **
30270 '**IF YOU ENTERED AN ANSWER TO THE POINT ILLUSTRATED ABOVE,  **
30280 '**AND THEN HIT 'RETURN',  THE SUBROUTINE WILL RETURN TO THE MAIN **
30290 '**WITH THE INPUT IN B$,  EG. B$ = "SMITH"  NOT "SMITH~~~~~~" **
30300 '**                                                          **
30310 '************************************************************************
30320 '
30330 B$ = " "
30340 FOR X = 1 TO LENGTH
30350 B$ = B$ + CHR$(254)
30360 NEXT X
30370 LOCATE ROW,COLUMN
30380 PRINT B$;
30390 '
30400 '
30410 '
30420 POINTER = 1 : A$ = " "
30430 WHILE (ASC(A$) <> 13)
30440 A$ = INPUT$(1)
30450 IF (POINTER > LENGTH) AND (ASC(A$) = 13) THEN 30570
30460 IF (POINTER > LENGTH) AND (ASC(A$) = 8) THEN 30520
30470 IF (POINTER > LENGTH) THEN 30570
30480 IF (ASC(A$) >= 32) THEN MID$(B$,POINTER,1) = A$ : POINTER =
      POINTER + 1 : GOTO 30550
30490 IF (POINTER = 1) AND (ASC(A$) = 8) GOTO 30550
30500 IF (ASC(A$) <> 8) THEN 30540
30510    MID$(B$,POINTER,1) = CHR$(254)
30520    MID$(B$,POINTER-1,1) = CHR$(254)
30530    POINTER = POINTER -1
30540 IF (ASC(A$) = 13) THEN B$ = MID$(B$,1,POINTER-1) : POINTER =
      LENGTH + 1
30550 LOCATE ROW,COLUMN
30560 PRINT B$
30570 WEND
30580 RETURN
```

MEMORY DUMP ROUTINE

The IBM Personal Computer contains a large amount of memory. Between the 16K of video RAM, the 40K of ROM containing the BASIC and BIOS routines, and the 16 to 64K of user memory, there is a lot going on in there. This program allows you to read the contents of memory, 16 bytes at a time, and have it displayed in both HEX and ASCII.

The program allows you to enter a segment address so you can address any area in the 1 million bytes of possible memory. Then the program asks for a starting address which is an offset from the segment address. From this point on, the program displays the current segment and offset address as ssss:oooo in hex notation. Then 16 bytes of memory are displayed as hex values, and finally, the 16 bytes are displayed as ASCII characters if they are within the range of normally printed characters, or as periods if they are not. Then the program drops to the next line and starts over with the next 16 characters. A sample screen display is shown in Fig. 7-3. The program runs very fast, and gives a clear indication of the contents of the memory.

```
Enter segment pointer address - &HB800
Enter first memory address      - 0


B800:0000   45 07 6E 07 74 07 65 07 - 72 07 20 07 73 07 65 07   E.n.t.e.r. .s.e.
B800:0010   67 07 6D 07 65 07 6E 07 - 74 07 20 07 70 07 6F 07   g.m.e.n.t. .p.o.
B800:0020   69 07 6E 07 74 07 65 07 - 72 07 20 07 61 07 64 07   i.n.t.e.r. .a.d.
B800:0030   64 07 72 07 65 07 73 07 - 73 07 20 07 2D 07 20 07   d.r.e.s.s. .-. .
B800:0040   26 07 48 07 42 07 38 07 - 30 07 30 07 20 07 20 07   &.H.B.8.0.0. . .
B800:0050   20 07 20 07 20 07 20 07 - 20 07 20 07 20 07 20 07   . . . . . . . .
B800:0060   20 07 20 07 20 07 20 07 - 20 07 20 07 20 07 20 07   . . . . . . . .
B800:0070   20 07 20 07 20 07 20 07 - 20 07 20 07 20 07 20 07   . . . . . . . .
B800:0080   20 07 20 07 20 07 20 07 - 20 07 20 07 20 07 20 07   . . . . . . . .
B800:0090   20 07 20 07 20 07 20 07 - 20 07 20 07 20 07 20 07   . . . . . . . .
B800:00A0   45 07 6E 07 74 07 65 07 - 72 07 20 07 66 07 69 07   E.n.t.e.r. .f.i.
B800:00B0   72 07 73 07 74 07 20 07 - 6D 07 65 07 6D 07 6F 07   r.s.t. .m.e.m.o.
B800:00C0   72 07 79 07 20 07 61 07 - 64 07 64 07 72 07 65 07   r.y. .a.d.d.r.e.
B800:00D0   73 07 73 07 20 07 20 07 - 20 07 20 07 2D 07 20 07   s.s. . . .-. .
B800:00E0   30 07 20 07 20 07 20 07 - 20 07 20 07 20 07 20 07   0. . . . . . . .
B800:00F0   20 07 20 07 20 07 20 07 - 20 07 20 07 20 07 20 07   . . . . . . . .


B800:0100   20 07 20 07 20 07 20 07 - 20 07 20 07 20 07 20 07   . . . . . . . .
B800:0110   20 07 20 07 20 07 20 07 - 20 07 20 07 20 07 20 07   . . . . . . . .
```

Fig. 7-3. Sample display produced by the *Memory Dump* routine.

```
100 '***************************************************
110 '**   Memory Dump Routine for the I.B.M.  P.C.  **
120 '**                                              **
130 '**   Version 1.1              27 November 1982  **
140 '***************************************************
150 '
160 CLEAR : DEFINT A-Z
170 SCREEN 0 : WIDTH 80 : CLS : KEY OFF
180 INPUT "Enter segment pointer address - " , A
190 INPUT "Enter first memory address      - " , B
```

```
200 LINECOUNT = Ø
210 DEF SEG = A
220 LOCATE 24,1
230 ON LEN(HEX$(A)) GOTO 240,250,260,270
240 PRINT "ØØØ";HEX$(A);:GOTO 280
250 PRINT "ØØ";HEX$(A);:GOTO 280
260 PRINT "Ø";HEX$(A);:GOTO 280
270 PRINT HEX$(A);:GOTO 280
280 PRINT CHR$(58);
290 ON LEN(HEX$(B)) GOTO 300,310,320,330
300 PRINT "ØØØ";HEX$(B);:GOTO 340
310 PRINT "ØØ";HEX$(B);:GOTO 340
320 PRINT "Ø";HEX$(B);:GOTO 340
330 PRINT HEX$(B);
340 LOCATE 24,12
350 FOR X = B TO B+7
360 IF(PEEK(X)<16)THEN PRINT"Ø";HEX$(PEEK(X));" ";ELSE PRINT HEX$
    (PEEK(X));" ";
370 NEXT
380 PRINT "- ";
390 FOR X = B+8 TO B+15
400 IF(PEEK(X)<16)THEN PRINT"Ø";HEX$(PEEK(X));" ";ELSE PRINT HEX$
    (PEEK(X));" ";
410 NEXT
420 LOCATE 24,64
430 FOR X = B TO B+15
440 IF (PEEK(X)>31) AND (PEEK(X)<128) THEN PRINT CHR$(PEEK(X));
    ELSE PRINT ".";
450 NEXT
460 PRINT
470 Z$ =INKEY$ : IF Z$ <> "" THEN 180
480 LINECOUNT = LINECOUNT + 1 : IF LINECOUNT = 16 THEN PRINT : LINECOUNT = Ø
500 B=B+&H1Ø :IF (B<16) AND (B>-1) THEN A = A + &H1ØØØ : GOTO 210
510 GOTO 220
```

FILESORT

The *Filesort* program is an enhanced version of the files statement. The filenames are first read from the diskette directory and displayed on the screen. See Fig. 7-4. (The program uses the files command to accomplish this.) At this point the filenames are copied character by character into a string array. An alphabetical sort is performed on the array of filenames, and the results are displayed, as shown in Fig. 7-5.

This program demonstrates a couple of techniques that you may find useful in other programs. Reading the filenames from the screen after doing a files statement appears to be the only way to get the diskette filenames from the directory into string variables for further processing. This is a tricky way of accomplishing what appears at first glance to be an impossible task.

A very short and reasonably efficient method of sorting data is used to alphabetize the file names. Unless your arrays are very large or your data to be sorted resides in a large diskette file this short sort works well.

```
AMORT    .BAS CAROLS   .BAS CHOMPER .BAS COMM     .BAS COS#(X#).BAS CRYPTO   .BAS
DATA-IN .BAS DEMO      .BAS DENVER  .BAS DONKEY   .BAS DRIVER   .BAS FIGHTER .BAS
FLY      .BAS FONT_80 .BAS GRAPH    .BAS HI-RES   .BAS JUMBLE   .BAS LUNAR    .BAS
MESSAGE .BAS MUSIC     .BAS NEW_FONT.BAS ANNIES   .BAS PLOT-3D .BAS SIN#(X#).BAS
SORT     .BAS SPHERE   .BAS STAR     .BAS WAND     .BAS WRITEJF .BAS TRAK      .BAS
TREE     .BAS VECTORS .BAS ZAG       .BAS ZIG      .BAS TRANSMIT.BAS RECEIVE  .BAS
AMAZE    .BAS SIMULTAN.BAS LEM       .BAS GEOSYNCH.BAS ZIGZAG   .BAS COMPLEX  .BAS
FRACTION.BAS DESIGN2  .BAS DESIGN3  .BAS SCROLL   .BAS PRINTOUT.BAS CLOCK     .BAS
SIDEREAL.BAS CALENDAR.BAS PIC#4     .BAS BOOT      .BAS LETTER   .BAS PIC3D4   .BAS
MAIL     .BAS BIORYTHM.BAS FROMJ         FROMJEFF.BAS ZAPP      .BAS KALEIDOS.BAS
MAILDATA     PICDMP   .BAS FUNCTION.BAS FILESORT.BAS XREF      .BAS SPRINT    .BAS
CALLJEFF.BAS MAINMENU.BAS WWV       .BAS SORT$    .BAS SPELL    .BAS PRTR      .BAS
PAINTING.BAS


Reading from the screen ...
```

Fig. 7-4. Sample of the initial display produced by the *Filesort* program.

```
AMAZE    .BAS CRYPTO   .BAS FROMJ         MAINMENU.BAS SIDEREAL.BAS WAND     .BAS
AMORT    .BAS DATA-IN .BAS FROMJEFF.BAS MESSAGE .BAS SIMULTAN.BAS WRITEJF .BAS
ANNIES   .BAS DEMO     .BAS FUNCTION.BAS MUSIC    .BAS SIN#(X#).BAS WWV      .BAS
BIORYTHM.BAS DENVER   .BAS GEOSYNCH.BAS NEW_FONT.BAS SORT     .BAS XREF     .BAS
BOOT     .BAS DESIGN2 .BAS GRAPH    .BAS PAINTING.BAS SORT$    .BAS ZAG      .BAS
CALENDAR.BAS DESIGN3 .BAS HI-RES   .BAS PIC#4     .BAS SPELL    .BAS ZAPP     .BAS
CALLJEFF.BAS DONKEY   .BAS JUMBLE   .BAS PIC3D4   .BAS SPHERE   .BAS ZIG      .BAS
CAROLS   .BAS DRIVER   .BAS KALEIDOS.BAS PICDMP   .BAS SPRINT   .BAS ZIGZAG  .BAS
CHOMPER .BAS FIGHTER .BAS LEM       .BAS PLOT-3D .BAS STAR      .BAS
CLOCK    .BAS FILESORT.BAS LETTER   .BAS PRINTOUT.BAS TRAK      .BAS
COMM     .BAS FLY      .BAS LUNAR    .BAS PRTR     .BAS TRANSMIT.BAS
COMPLEX .BAS FONT_80 .BAS MAIL      .BAS RECEIVE .BAS TREE      .BAS
COS#(X#).BAS FRACTION.BAS MAILDATA      SCROLL   .BAS VECTORS .BAS
Ok
```

Fig. 7-5. Example of the final display produced by the *Filesort* program.

```
10 ' *********************
20 ' **      FILESORT      **
30 ' *********************
40 '
50 CLEAR
60 SCREEN Ø,Ø,Ø,Ø
70 CLS
80 KEY OFF
90 FILES
100 DIM A$(114)
```

```
110 SP$ = SPACE$(13)
120 PRINT
130 PRINT
140 '
150 PRINT "Reading from the screen ...
160    FOR ROW = 1 TO 19
170    IF A$(POINTER) = SP$ THEN 240
180       FOR COLUMN = 1 TO 78
190       LOCATE ROW,COLUMN,1,0,6
200       IF A$(POINTER) = SP$ THEN 230
210       IF COLUMN MOD 13 = 1 THEN POINTER = POINTER + 1
220       A$(POINTER) = A$(POINTER) + CHR$(SCREEN(ROW,COLUMN))
230       NEXT COLUMN
240    NEXT ROW
250 '
260 LOCATE CSRLIN + 3,1,0,7,7
270 COUNT = POINTER - 1
280 '
290 PRINT "Sorting alphabetically  ...
300 PRINT
310    FOR I = 1 TO COUNT - 1
320    LOCATE CSRLIN,1
330    PRINT A$(I);
340       FOR J = I + 1 TO COUNT
350       IF A$(I) > A$(J) THEN SWAP A$(I),A$(J)
360       NEXT J
370    NEXT I
380 '
390 ' Print the sorted file names
400 CLS
410 K = INT((COUNT-1)/6+1)
420    FOR I = 1 TO K
430       FOR J = 0 TO 5
440       PRINT A$(I+J*K);
450       NEXT J
460    PRINT
470    NEXT I
480 LOCATE CSRLIN,1,1
```

FONT-80

This program will generate the TRS-80 graphic set. One of the disadvantages of most new computers is in the way they are different from the systems that came before them. My first system was a TRS-80, and during the 2 years I owned it, I collected quite a few games and other programs that used TRS-80 graphics. So naturally, one of my first programs for the P.C. concerned itself with generating the pattern of rectangles that formed the TRS-80 graphics.

The graphics were formed in a rectangle that was divided up into 6 smaller rectangles like this ......

The meaning of the numbers will be explained shortly.

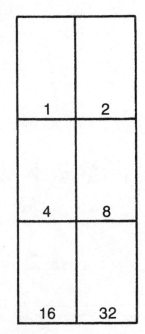

Characters with a value of less than 128, which includes all of the alphabet, the numbers, and punctuation, are formed from patterns stored on a ROM chip (a type of permanent memory). The rest of the values (128 thru 255) are handled by a special section of circuitry. This circuit looks at the 6 least significant bits in the ASCII value of the character. Just as our decimal system uses powers of ten to assign place values, the binary system uses powers of two to assign values to the bits. These values are 128, 64, 32, 16, 8, 4, 2, 1 for each of the 8 bits respectively.

So for a value of 173, which has a binary pattern of 10101101, there are

```
1 GROUP  OF 128  = 128.
0 GROUPS OF  64  =   0
1 GROUP  OF  32  =  32
0 GROUPS OF  16  =   0
1 GROUP  OF   8  =   8
1 GROUP  OF   4  =   4
0 GROUPS OF   2  =   0
1 GROUP  OF   1  =   1 for a total of 173.
```

Using only the last 6 bits, which can have a value of 0 (all bits = 0) thru 63 (all bits = 1), the circuit would look at the value, and turn on the segments whose sum equaled the value in question.

Luckily, in the graphics mode, the P.C. uses a pointer that tells the system where to look in order to find the patterns for the characters with an ASCII value of 128 thru 255. That pointer is at the absolute address &H7D. If that address is changed by a poke into memory, the system will look at the new location for the character patterns.

This program starts by creating a 1K buffer to store the information at the end of memory (48K as written).

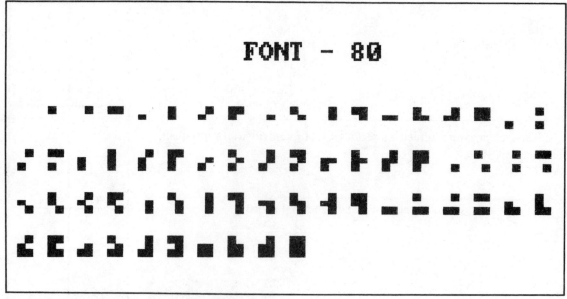

Fig. 7-6. Graphics produced by the *Font 80* program.

If you have a   16K system use &H3C AND &H3C00
              32K system use &H7C AND &H7C00
              48K system use &HBC AND &HBC00
              64K system use &HEC AND &HEC00

and change all lines that refer to these values.

The program then goes through the characters from 128 which is all segments off through 191 which is all segments on and proceeds to create the patterns. It then pokes the patterns into the table at the end of the memory. From this point on, any reference to a character whose value is greater than 127 will print out as a TRS-80 graphics character. See Fig. 7-6.

```
10 SCREEN 1 : KEY OFF : CLS
11 CLEAR ,20000,1000
12 DEF SEG = 0 : POKE &H7D,&HBC              ' BUFFER STARTS AT 47K
13 POINTER = &HBC00
14 '
15 '
16 '*****************************************************************
17 '**      TRS-80 FONT       **  IN SCREEN 1 OR 2 - THIS PROGRAM    **
18 '**                        **  WILL CREATE THE GRAPHICS OF THE    **
19 '**      VERSION 1.1       **  TRS-80.  CHR$(128) TO CHR$(191)    **
20 '**                        **  IT THEN POINTS THE FONT DATA       **
21 '**      JUNE 14,1982      **  POINTER AT THE START OF THE TABLE  **
22 '*****************************************************************
23 '
24 '
```

```
100 FOR X = 0 TO 63
110 CHARACTER = X
120 LINE3 = 0 : LINE2 = 0 : LINE1 = 0
130 IF (CHARACTER > 31) THEN LINE3 = LINE3 + 15   :CHARACTER = CHARACTER - 32
140 IF (CHARACTER > 15) THEN LINE3 = LINE3 + 240  :CHARACTER = CHARACTER - 16
150 IF (CHARACTER > 7) THEN LINE2 = LINE2 + 15    :CHARACTER = CHARACTER - 8
160 IF (CHARACTER > 3) THEN LINE2 = LINE2 + 240   :CHARACTER = CHARACTER - 4
170 IF (CHARACTER > 1) THEN LINE1 = LINE1 + 15    :CHARACTER = CHARACTER - 2
180 IF (CHARACTER = 1) THEN LINE1 = LINE1 + 240
190 POKE POINTER+0,LINE1
200 POKE POINTER+1,LINE1
210 POKE POINTER+2,LINE1
220 POKE POINTER+3,LINE2
230 POKE POINTER+4,LINE2
240 POKE POINTER+5,LINE3
250 POKE POINTER+6,LINE3
260 POKE POINTER+7,LINE3
270 POINTER = POINTER + 8
280 NEXT X
290 FOR X = 128 TO 191
300 PRINT CHR$(X);" ";
310 IF POS(0) > 35 THEN PRINT CHR$(13)
320 NEXT
```

MESSAGE CENTER

This program examines the BIOS routines at the end of ROM, scanning the table at &HFFA6E, and prints out the message you typed into the computer in 8 × 8 character blocks. This style of type is reminiscent of the headings used on the printouts on large mainframes. The message will print out 29 characters with 10 characters in the first and second rows and 9 characters in the last row as shown in Fig. 7-7.

The theory behind the program's operation is very simple. The program asks for a message to be printed and makes sure it is not longer than 29 characters. Then a scan of memory is performed to find the binary patterns that match the first character of the message. Starting in the top left-hand corner of the screen, the program prints the characters in a series of squares 8 lines high by 8 character spaces wide. On each line, a character will be printed in a character space only if the corresponding bit in the byte is a 1 or "marking" state. A space will be printed for every bit that is in the 0 state. This process will produce a character that is 8 lines high and 8 character spaces wide. The program then moves over to the next block of 8 spaces on the screen and proceeds to create a character pattern corresponding to the next character in the message to be printed.

The finished message may be dumped to a printer with the PrtSc key or used as a title for a program as seen in the *Trak* program. Since the entire standard ASCII character set is supported, this program may be used to create the prompts in an educational program for young children, in arithmetic or spelling for example.

```
10 '***************************************************
20 '**              MESSAGE CENTER              **
30 '**                                          **
```

```
40 '**   VERSION 1.1              JUNE 5, 1982  **
50 '*********************************************
60 SCREEN Ø : WIDTH 80 : KEY OFF : CLS
70 LOCATE 25,1 : INPUT "ENTER MESSAGE HERE - ";A$ : CLS
80 IF LEN(A$) < 30 THEN 120
90 B$ = ""
100 FOR S = 1 TO 29 : B$ = B$ + MID$(A$,S,1) : NEXT
110 A$ = B$
120 FOR S = LEN(A$) + 1 TO 29
130 A$ = A$ + " "
140 NEXT
150 DEF SEG = &HF000      ' LAST 64K OF MEMORY MAP
160 TABLE = &HFA6E        ' LOCATION OF FIRST CHARACTER
170 X = 1 : Y = 1 : LOCATE X,Y
180 FOR CHARACTER = 1 TO 29          ' FOR EACH CHARACTER
190 A = ASC(MID$(A$,CHARACTER,1))    ' GET THE ASCII VALUE
200 CODE = TABLE + A * 8             ' POINT INTO THE TABLE
210 FOR BYTE = Ø TO 7                ' FOR EACH BYTE
220 PATTERN = PEEK (CODE + BYTE)
230 LOCATE X,Y
240 IF PATTERN < 128 THEN PRINT " ";:GOTO 270
250 PRINT CHR$(A);
260 PATTERN = PATTERN - 128
270 IF PATTERN < 64 THEN PRINT " ";:GOTO 300
280 PRINT CHR$(A);
290 PATTERN = PATTERN - 64
300 IF PATTERN < 32 THEN PRINT " ";:GOTO 330
310 PRINT CHR$(A);
320 PATTERN = PATTERN - 32
330 IF PATTERN < 16 THEN PRINT " ";:GOTO 360
340 PRINT CHR$(A);
350 PATTERN = PATTERN - 16
360 IF PATTERN < 8 THEN PRINT " ";:GOTO 390
370 PRINT CHR$(A);
380 PATTERN = PATTERN - 8
390 IF PATTERN < 4 THEN PRINT " ";:GOTO 420
400 PRINT CHR$(A);
410 PATTERN = PATTERN - 4
420 IF PATTERN < 2 THEN PRINT " ";:GOTO 450
430 PRINT CHR$(A);
440 PATTERN = PATTERN - 2
450 IF PATTERN < 1 THEN PRINT " ";:GOTO 470
460 PRINT CHR$(A);
470 PATTERN = PATTERN - 1
480 X = X + 1
490 NEXT BYTE
500 X = X - 8 : Y = Y + 8 : IF Y > 75 THEN X = X + 8 : Y = 1
```

```
510 NEXT CHARACTER
520 GOTO 70
```

```
   IIII    BBBBBB  MM    MM   ''
    II      BB  BB  MMM MMM   ''
    II      BB  BB  MMMMMMM  ''          sssss
    II      BBBBB   MMMMMMM          ss
    II      BB  BB  MM M MM          ssss
    II      BB  BB  MM    MM               ss
   IIII     BBBBBB  MM    MM          sssss

 PPPPP                                                    111
   PP  PP                                                  11
   PP  PP   eeee   rr rrr   sssss   oooo   nnnnn   aaaa    11
   PPPPP    ee ee  rrr rr ss        oo oo  nn  nn    aa    11
   PP       eeeeee  rr  rr ssss     oo oo  nn  nn  aaaaa   11
   PP       ee      rr         ss   oo oo  nn  nn  aa aa   11
   PPPP     eeee   rrrr    sssss    oooo   nn  nn  aaa aa  1111

    CCCC                                   t                      !!
   CC  CC                                  tt                    !!!!
   CC         oooo   mm    mm  pp ppp  uu  uu  ttttt   eeee   rr rrr  !!!!
   CC         oo  oo mmmmmmm   pp  pp  uu  uu    tt    ee  ee  rrr rr  !!
   CC         oo  oo mmmmmmm   pp  pp  uu  uu    tt    eeeeee  rr  rr  !!
   CC  CC oo  oo  mm m mm  ppppp   uu  uu  tt t  ee        rr
    CCCC  oooo   mm    mm  pp      uuu uu   tt    eeee   rrrr         !!
                            pppp
 ENTER MESSAGE HERE - ? IBM's     Personal    Computer!
```

Fig. 7-7. Display produced by the *Message Center* program.

NEW-FONT

This program is a useful tool both in that it creates a new font or type style and in that it teaches the methods required to create a large variety of specialized graphic symbols. These symbols could be used for a variety of purposes such as a game board by printing a set of shapes around the screen or displaying charts and graphs using special characters and shapes that you have defined. The characters created by the program as it is written are shown in Fig. 7-8.

The interrupt vectors at &H7C thru &H7F define a pointer. This pointer refers to the address of a 1K block of data in memory where the patterns for the characters whose codes are 128 thru 255 will reside. Fortunately, this area is in read/write memory (sometimes referred to as RAM) and its contents can be changed to any value.

After the pointer and reserved memory have been changed using the clear command so BASIC will not write over it, it becomes a simple matter to poke the table with data to create any character or graphic set you desire. The only additional information needed at this point concerns how the table is organized so the data may be entered into it correctly.

All characters displayed on the different screens are generated within a block of 64 dots arranged in an 8 by 8 rectangle. If we were to enlarge one of the characters, the F character for example, we would find that it looks something like this . . . .

```
        7 6 5 4 3 2 1 0

1  * * * * * * * -      &HFE  OR  254

2  * * - - - - * -      &HC2  OR  194

3  * * - - * - - -      &HC8  OR  200

4  * * * * - - - -      &HF8  OR  248

5  * * - - * - - -      &HC8  OR  200

6  * * - - - - - -      &HC0  OR  192

7  * * - - - - - -      &HC0  OR  192

8  - - - - - - - -      &H00  OR    0
```

where the * means the screen at this point is on, and the - means the screen is off.

The values at the end of the horizontal rows are the values that are required to create the row of dots; they are simply the binary value of the dots.

The table is organized so that the software will look at the first 8 bytes of data and assign them to CHR$(128) to define its pattern. The program will then use the second 8 bytes of the table to define the pattern for CHR$(129), and so on.

This is in essence what this program does. A 1K buffer is created in memory, and in the relative positions of the table, a version of a standard ASCII character set is created by reading in data and then poking the values into the table. With the pointers correctly assigned, any future reference to an ASCII character in the range of 128 through 255 will print out in the new font.

By keeping the relative positions of the new characters the same as the old ones, it is easy to get the new corresponding characters by simply adding 128 to the ASCII value of the old character.

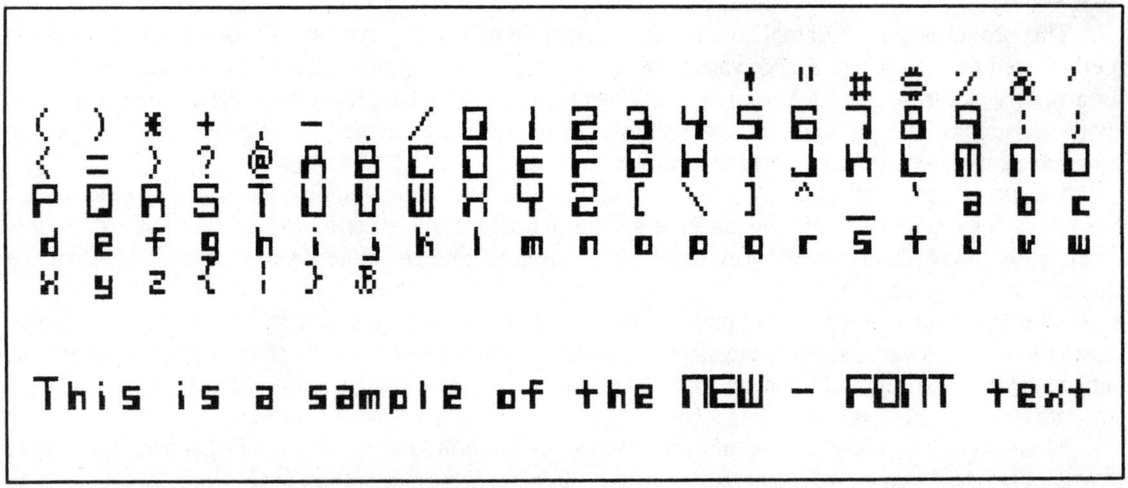

Fig. 7-8. Sample character set produced by the *New-Font* program.

Note: the first 32 characters in the new font were left undefined (they will print as spaces) so you can design your own characters for these. For the regular ASCII set, characters 0 thru 31 are control functions as you can see in the table at the end of the *IBM BASIC Manual*. This leaves you with 32 normally unused character locations to be creative with. Have fun!

```
10 SCREEN 1 : KEY OFF : CLS
11 CLEAR ,20000,1000
12 DEF SEG = 0 : POKE &H7D,&HBC          .' BUFFER STARTS AT 47K
13 FOR X = &HBC00 TO &HBFFF               ' 47K TO 48K (1K OF DATA)
14 READ A : POKE X,A
15 NEXT
16 '*******************************************************************
17 '**        NEW FONT        **  LOADS A MODERNISTIC FONT INTO       ** ·
18 '**                        **  THE LAST 1024 BYTES OF MEMORY       **
19 '**      VERSION 1.1       **  (IN THIS CASE - 48K)               **
20 '**                        **  IT THEN POINTS THE FONT DATA        **
21 '**      JUNE 6,1982       **  POINTER AT THE START OF THE TABLE   **
22 '*******************************************************************
23 '
24 '
100 DATA &H000, &H000, &H000, &H000, &H000, &H000, &H000, &H000 :' 00 NULL
101 DATA &H000, &H000, &H000, &H000, &H000, &H000, &H000, &H000 :' 01
102 DATA &H000, &H000, &H000, &H000, &H000, &H000, &H000, &H000 :' 02
103 DATA &H000, &H000, &H000, &H000, &H000, &H000, &H000, &H000 :' 03
104 DATA &H000, &H000, &H000, &H000, &H000, &H000, &H000, &H000 :' 04
105 DATA &H000, &H000, &H000, &H000, &H000, &H000, &H000, &H000 :' 05
106 DATA &H000, &H000, &H000, &H000, &H000, &H000, &H000, &H000 :' 06
107 DATA &H000, &H000, &H000, &H000, &H000, &H000, &H000, &H000 :' 07 BEEP
108 DATA &H000, &H000, &H000, &H000, &H000, &H000, &H000, &H000 :' 08 BACKSP
109 DATA &H000, &H000, &H000, &H000, &H000, &H000, &H000, &H000 :' 09 TAB
110 DATA &H000, &H000, &H000, &H000, &H000, &H000, &H000, &H000 :' 10 LINEFEED
111 DATA &H000, &H000, &H000, &H000, &H000, &H000, &H000, &H000 :' 11 HOME
112 DATA &H000, &H000, &H000, &H000, &H000, &H000, &H000, &H000 :' 12 FORMFEED
113 DATA &H000, &H000, &H000, &H000, &H000, &H000, &H000, &H000 :' 13 CR
114 DATA &H000, &H000, &H000, &H000, &H000, &H000, &H000, &H000 :' 14
115 DATA &H000, &H000, &H000, &H000, &H000, &H000, &H000, &H000 :' 15
116 DATA &H000, &H000, &H000, &H000, &H000, &H000, &H000, &H000 :' 16
117 DATA &H000, &H000, &H000, &H000, &H000, &H000, &H000, &H000 :' 17
118 DATA &H000, &H000, &H000, &H000, &H000, &H000, &H000, &H000 :' 18
119 DATA &H000, &H000, &H000, &H000, &H000, &H000, &H000, &H000 :' 19
120 DATA &H000, &H000, &H000, &H000, &H000, &H000, &H000, &H000 :' 20
121 DATA &H000, &H000, &H000, &H000, &H000, &H000, &H000, &H000 :' 21
122 DATA &H000, &H000, &H000, &H000, &H000, &H000, &H000, &H000 :' 22
123 DATA &H000, &H000, &H000, &H000, &H000, &H000, &H000, &H000 :' 23
124 DATA &H000, &H000, &H000, &H000, &H000, &H000, &H000, &H000 :' 24
```

```
125 DATA &H000, &H000, &H000, &H000, &H000, &H000, &H000, &H000 :' 25
126 DATA &H000, &H000, &H000, &H000, &H000, &H000, &H000, &H000 :' 26
127 DATA &H000, &H000, &H000, &H000, &H000, &H000, &H000, &H000 :' 27
128 DATA &H000, &H000, &H000, &H000, &H000, &H000, &H000, &H000 :' 28
129 DATA &H000, &H000, &H000, &H000, &H000, &H000, &H000, &H000 :' 29
130 DATA &H000, &H000, &H000, &H000, &H000, &H000, &H000, &H000 :' 30
131 DATA &H000, &H000, &H000, &H000, &H000, &H000, &H000, &H000 :' 31
132 DATA &H000, &H000, &H000, &H000, &H000, &H000, &H000, &H000 :' 32 SPACE
133 DATA &H010, &H038, &H038, &H010, &H010, &H000, &H010, &H000 :' 33 !
134 DATA &H024, &H024, &H024, &H000, &H000, &H000, &H000, &H000 :' 34 "
135 DATA &H000, &H024, &H07E, &H024, &H024, &H07E, &H024, &H000 :' 35 #
136 DATA &H028, &H07C, &H080, &H07C, &H002, &H0FC, &H028, &H000 :' 36 $
137 DATA &H000, &H084, &H008, &H010, &H020, &H040, &H084, &H000 :' 37 %
138 DATA &H038, &H044, &H038, &H072, &H08C, &H08C, &H072, &H000 :' 38 &
139 DATA &H020, &H020, &H040, &H000, &H000, &H000, &H000, &H000 :' 39 '
140 DATA &H010, &H020, &H040, &H040, &H040, &H020, &H010, &H000 :' 40 (
141 DATA &H020, &H010, &H008, &H008, &H008, &H010, &H020, &H000 :' 41 )
142 DATA &H000, &H054, &H038, &H07C, &H038, &H054, &H000, &H000 :' 42 *
143 DATA &H000, &H010, &H010, &H07C, &H010, &H010, &H000, &H000 :' 43 +
144 DATA &H000, &H000, &H000, &H000, &H000, &H010, &H010, &H020 :' 44 ,
145 DATA &H000, &H000, &H000, &H0FC, &H000, &H000, &H000, &H000 :' 45 -
146 DATA &H000, &H000, &H000, &H000, &H000, &H000, &H010, &H000 :' 46 .
147 DATA &H002, &H004, &H008, &H010, &H020, &H040, &H080, &H000 :' 47 /
148 DATA &H0FE, &H082, &H082, &H086, &H086, &H086, &H0FE, &H000 :' 48 0
149 DATA &H008, &H008, &H008, &H018, &H018, &H018, &H018, &H000 :' 49 1
150 DATA &H0FE, &H082, &H002, &H0FE, &H0C0, &H0C2, &H0FE, &H000 :' 50 2
151 DATA &H0FC, &H084, &H004, &H03E, &H006, &H086, &H0FE, &H000 :' 51 3
152 DATA &H084, &H084, &H084, &H0FE, &H00C, &H00C, &H00C, &H000 :' 52 4
153 DATA &H0FE, &H080, &H080, &H0FE, &H006, &H006, &H0FE, &H000 :' 53 5
154 DATA &H0FE, &H082, &H080, &H0FE, &H0C2, &H0C2, &H0FE, &H000 :' 54 6
155 DATA &H0FE, &H002, &H002, &H002, &H006, &H006, &H006, &H000 :' 55 7
156 DATA &H07C, &H044, &H044, &H0FE, &H086, &H086, &H0FE, &H000 :' 56 8
157 DATA &H0FE, &H082, &H082, &H0FE, &H006, &H006, &H006, &H000 :' 57 9
158 DATA &H000, &H010, &H010, &H000, &H010, &H010, &H000, &H000 :' 58 :
159 DATA &H000, &H010, &H010, &H000, &H010, &H010, &H020, &H000 :' 59 ;
160 DATA &H008, &H010, &H020, &H040, &H020, &H010, &H008, &H000 :' 60 <
161 DATA &H000, &H000, &H0FC, &H000, &H000, &H0FC, &H000, &H000 :' 61 =
162 DATA &H020, &H010, &H008, &H004, &H008, &H010, &H020, &H000 :' 62 >
163 DATA &H038, &H044, &H004, &H008, &H010, &H000, &H010, &H000 :' 63 ?
164 DATA &H03C, &H042, &H0BA, &H0AA, &H0BC, &H040, &H03C, &H000 :' 64 @
165 DATA &H07C, &H044, &H044, &H0FE, &H0C2, &H0C2, &H0C2, &H000 :' 65 A
166 DATA &H0FC, &H084, &H084, &H0FE, &H0C2, &H0C2, &H0FE, &H000 :' 66 B
167 DATA &H0FE, &H082, &H080, &H0C0, &H0C0, &H0C2, &H0FE, &H000 :' 67 C
168 DATA &H0FE, &H082, &H082, &H0C2, &H0C2, &H0C2, &H0FE, &H000 :' 68 D
169 DATA &H0FE, &H080, &H080, &H0FE, &H0C0, &H0C0, &H0FE, &H000 :' 69 E
170 DATA &H0FE, &H080, &H080, &H0FE, &H0C0, &H0C0, &H0C0, &H000 :' 70 F
171 DATA &H0FE, &H082, &H080, &H0CE, &H0C2, &H0C2, &H0FE, &H000 :' 71 G
```

```
172 DATA &H082, &H082, &H082, &H0FE, &H0C2, &H0C2, &H0C2, &H000 :' 72 H
173 DATA &H010, &H010, &H010, &H018, &H018, &H018, &H018, &H000 :' 73 I
174 DATA &H004, &H004, &H004, &H006, &H006, &H086, &H0FE, &H000 :' 74 J
175 DATA &H084, &H084, &H084, &H0FE, &H0C2, &H0C2, &H0C2, &H000 :' 75 K
176 DATA &H080, &H080, &H080, &H0C0, &H0C0, &H0C0, &H0FE, &H000 :' 76 L
177 DATA &H0FE, &H092, &H092, &H0D2, &H0D2, &H0D2, &H0D2, &H000 :' 77 M
178 DATA &H0FE, &H082, &H082, &H0C2, &H0C2, &H0C2, &H0C2, &H000 :' 78 N
179 DATA &H0FE, &H082, &H082, &H0C2, &H0C2, &H0C2, &H0FE, &H000 :' 79 O
180 DATA &H0FE, &H082, &H082, &H0FE, &H0C0, &H0C0, &H0C0, &H000 :' 80 P
181 DATA &H0FE, &H082, &H082, &H082, &H082, &H09E, &H0FE, &H000 :' 81 Q
182 DATA &H0FC, &H084, &H084, &H0FE, &H0C2, &H0C2, &H0C2, &H000 :' 82 R
183 DATA &H0FE, &H082, &H080, &H0FE, &H002, &H082, &H0FE, &H000 :' 83 S
184 DATA &H0FE, &H010, &H010, &H018, &H018, &H018, &H018, &H000 :' 84 T
185 DATA &H082, &H082, &H082, &H0C2, &H0C2, &H0C2, &H0FE, &H000 :' 85 U
186 DATA &H0C2, &H0C2, &H0C2, &H0C6, &H044, &H044, &H07C, &H000 :' 86 V
187 DATA &H092, &H092, &H092, &H0D2, &H0D2, &H0D2, &H0FE, &H000 :' 87 W
188 DATA &H082, &H082, &H082, &H07C, &H0C2, &H0C2, &H0C2, &H000 :' 88 X
189 DATA &H082, &H082, &H082, &H0FE, &H018, &H018, &H018, &H000 :' 89 Y
190 DATA &H0FE, &H082, &H002, &H07C, &H0C0, &H0C2, &H0FE, &H000 :' 90 Z
191 DATA &H038, &H020, &H020, &H020, &H020, &H020, &H038, &H000 :' 91 [
192 DATA &H080, &H040, &H020, &H010, &H008, &H004, &H002, &H000 :' 92 \
193 DATA &H038, &H008, &H008, &H008, &H008, &H008, &H038, &H000 :' 93 ]
194 DATA &H010, &H028, &H044, &H000, &H000, &H000, &H000, &H000 :' 94 ^
195 DATA &H000, &H000, &H000, &H000, &H000, &H000, &H000, &H0FF :' 95 _
196 DATA &H010, &H010, &H008, &H000, &H000, &H000, &H000, &H000 :' 96 '
197 DATA &H000, &H000, &H03E, &H002, &H03E, &H032, &H03E, &H000 :' 97 a
198 DATA &H000, &H020, &H020, &H03E, &H032, &H032, &H03E, &H000 :' 98 b
199 DATA &H000, &H000, &H000, &H03E, &H030, &H030, &H03E, &H000 :' 99 c
200 DATA &H000, &H002, &H002, &H03E, &H032, &H032, &H03E, &H000 :'100 d
201 DATA &H000, &H000, &H03E, &H022, &H03E, &H030, &H03E, &H000 :'101 e
202 DATA &H000, &H01E, &H010, &H07E, &H018, &H018, &H018, &H000 :'102 f
203 DATA &H000, &H000, &H03E, &H032, &H032, &H03E, &H002, &H03E :'103 g
204 DATA &H000, &H020, &H020, &H03E, &H032, &H032, &H032, &H000 :'104 h
205 DATA &H000, &H010, &H000, &H010, &H018, &H018, &H018, &H000 :'105 i
206 DATA &H000, &H004, &H000, &H004, &H006, &H006, &H002, &H03E :'106 j
207 DATA &H000, &H020, &H024, &H038, &H036, &H032, &H032, &H000 :'107 k
208 DATA &H000, &H010, &H010, &H018, &H018, &H018, &H018, &H000 :'108 l
209 DATA &H000, &H000, &H000, &H07E, &H06A, &H06A, &H06A, &H000 :'109 m
210 DATA &H000, &H000, &H000, &H03E, &H032, &H032, &H032, &H000 :'110 n
211 DATA &H000, &H000, &H000, &H03E, &H032, &H032, &H03E, &H000 :'111 o
212 DATA &H000, &H000, &H000, &H03E, &H032, &H032, &H03E, &H020 :'112 p
213 DATA &H000, &H000, &H000, &H03E, &H032, &H032, &H03E, &H002 :'113 q
214 DATA &H000, &H000, &H000, &H03E, &H030, &H030, &H030, &H000 :'114 r
215 DATA &H000, &H000, &H03E, &H020, &H03E, &H006, &H03E, &H000 :'115 s
216 DATA &H000, &H010, &H010, &H07E, &H018, &H018, &H018, &H000 :'116 t
217 DATA &H000, &H000, &H000, &H032, &H032, &H032, &H03E, &H000 :'117 u
218 DATA &H000, &H000, &H000, &H032, &H036, &H034, &H03C, &H000 :'118 v
```

```
219 DATA &H000, &H000, &H000, &H06A, &H06A, &H06A, &H07E, &H000 :'119 w
220 DATA &H000, &H000, &H022, &H022, &H01C, &H032, &H032, &H000 :'120 x
221 DATA &H000, &H000, &H000, &H032, &H032, &H03E, &H002, &H03E :'121 y
222 DATA &H000, &H000, &H03E, &H002, &H01C, &H020, &H03E, &H000 :'122 z
223 DATA &H00C, &H010, &H010, &H060, &H010, &H010, &H00C, &H000 :'123 {
224 DATA &H008, &H008, &H008, &H000, &H008, &H008, &H008, &H000 :'124 |
225 DATA &H060, &H010, &H010, &H00C, &H010, &H010, &H060, &H000 :'125 }
226 DATA &H000, &H078, &H024, &H038, &H0A4, &H0A4, &H058, &H000 :'126 ~
227 DATA &H000, &H078, &H024, &H038, &H0A4, &H0A4, &H058, &H000 :'127
950 PRINT :PRINT :PRINT :PRINT
1000 FOR X = 128 TO 255 : PRINT CHR$(X);" ";:NEXT
1010 INPUT A$:CLS:WIDTH 80
```

PRINTOUT

The *Printout* program is a handy utility for printing out copies of your graphics screens. You must have an IBM Personal Computer printer (or its equivalent) with the graphics ROM installed, and a graphics board in your computer. Most of the illustrations in this book were produced using this program.

The first step in producing a printed picture is to copy the screen image to a disk file. Fortunately, there's an easy way to dump the entire screen full of graphics data bytes into a file. Use the following subroutine by patching it into the program that creates the desired graphics.

```
60000 DEF SEG = &HB800
60010 BSAVE "FILENAME",0,&H4000
60020 RETURN
```

At the appropriate point in your program, insert a **GOSUB 60000** statement. Change the filename in line 60010 for each image file you create. This subroutine creates a binary data file of all the bytes comprising the graphics you see on your screen.

Now for the fun part. Load your *Printout* program and run it. A list of the current disk files is displayed for your reference, then you're asked for the name of the graphics image file to be printed. Go ahead and enter the filename. Now you have to decide whether you want black on white, or white on black output. For most graphics the first choice is preferable, because your printer won't wear itself out as fast and the printed image will look right. So, press key "1" to start the action.

The file is loaded back into the screen memory. The original image appears on your screen before the printing begins. A large number of bytes are manipulated during the printing, which means you'll have to wait roughly five minutes for the finished product. This sounds slow, but is far faster than any other BASIC screen dump programs we have. There are faster machine language versions around, but you'll have to dig into the old billfold for them.

An interesting thing happens if you use the short subroutine mentioned above to dump medium-resolution color graphics to a file. The *Printout* program later loads the file using high-resolution (screen 2). Suddenly your colorful graphics appear in black and white! This enables you to preview the printed image, an advantage because some color combinations work better than others. With high-resolution graphics, what you see is what you get.

```
10 ' *********************
20 ' **    PRINTOUT    **
30 ' *********************
```

```
40  '
50  CLEAR
60  SCREEN 2
70  KEY OFF
80  CLS
90  DEFINT A-Z
100 PRINT "************************************************************"
110 PRINT "**                      PRINTER DRIVER                    **"
120 PRINT "**        PRINTS A COPY OF THE SCREEN IN BLACK ON WHITE    **"
130 PRINT "**                   OR WHITE ON BLACK                    **"
140 PRINT "************************************************************"
150 PRINT
160 FILES
170 PRINT
180 PRINT "Enter the name of the memory image file to be printed - ";
190 INPUT FILENAME$
200 PRINT
210 PRINT "(1) = Black on white        (2) = Reversed, white on black
220 K$ = INKEY$
230 IF K$ = "1" THEN WOB = 0 ELSE IF K$ = "2" THEN WOB = 255 ELSE 220
240 DEF SEG = &HB800
250 BLOAD FILENAME$
260 E$ = CHR$(27)
270 WIDTH "LPT1:",255
280 LPRINT E$ + "1"
290 LPRINT E$ + "W" + CHR$(1)
300    FOR ROW = 0 TO 79
310    LPRINT E$ + "K" + MKI$(400) ;
320       FOR COL = 99 TO 0 STEP -1
330       LOCA = COL * 80 + ROW
340       BYTE = PEEK(LOCA + &H2000) XOR WOB
350       LPRINT CHR$(BYTE) ; CHR$(BYTE) ;
360       BYTE = PEEK(LOCA) XOR WOB
370       LPRINT CHR$(BYTE) ; CHR$(BYTE) ;
380       NEXT COL
390    LPRINT
400    NEXT ROW
410 LPRINT CHR$(12);
420 END
```

ROTATE-A-FONT

Here is a program that will give you a different outlook on things. This program functions in much the same way as *New-Font* and *Font-80* do in creating a new character set for the computer. What this program does is to take the patterns for the characters stored in ROM at FFA6E - FFE6D (20 bit address) and rotate all of the sets of binary patterns by 90 degrees giving you a character set that appears to be resting on its back. The resulting letters can be very useful in printing out graphs because you can have the label for the Y axis running vertically up the page.

In text mode screen 0 with a width 40 or 80, the computer uses information stored in a character generator clip to create the ASCII characters that appear on the screen. The 16K of memory is divided up into either four 80-character wide screens where each screen requires 4K of memory or eight 40-character wide screens where each screen requires 2K of video memory. The 80-character wide screen has 80 characters per row and 25 rows on the screen, which means there are 2,000 characters on the screen at once. Each character requires 2 bytes. The first byte determines which character the character generator clip will produce, and the second byte determines what the foreground and background colors will be. A total of 4,000 bytes of screen memory are consumed. Likewise, the 40-character wide screen requires 2,000 bytes of memory. Because only 2,000 bytes are used for each screen, you have the option of using any one of 8 different screens which you may display and write to individually.

But in graphics mode, all of the characters are generated using patterns in the ROM of the BIOS routines. The IBM BASIC software supplied with the Personal Computer uses this data to print characters on the screen. Each printable character is displayed in an 8 × 8 *pixel* box on the screen. A pixel is the smallest object the computer can display. In screen 1 the pixel is 1 dot high by 2 dots wide and in screen 2 the pixel is 1 dot by 1 dot! With 640 dots per row, screen 1 will give you 40 characters per row, and screen 2 will give you 80 characters per row.

When you print the character A, for example, in graphics mode, the computer looks at the corresponding 8 bytes in the BIOS routines which define the pattern for that letter. These 8 bytes are then moved to video memory where every bit that was in a one state lights a dot on the screen. All 8 bytes, if placed correctly, produce the character A as you recognize it on the screen.

So, to print a letter that is rotated on the screen, all that is required is to look at the appropriate 8 bytes in ROM, mathematically rotate the pattern of dots, and assign them to 8 new memory locations which are in a table that has been especially set up for this purpose. Then redirect the pointer at address &H7C (absolute) to the start of this table. Now for every character you want to display in the rotated format, simply add 128 to the ASCII value of the character, and print it on the screen. For example, to display your rotated A, find the ASCII value of the letter (the ASC function works well for this), add 128 to that value (65 in this case), and use the total, 193, in your BASIC statement. **PRINT CHR$(193)**. That is all there is to it!

The *Rotate* program counts to 127 as it creates each of the rotated versions of the characters. Because of the job required to split up the pattern and rebuild it in the rotated format, the program requires about 2 minutes to run.

After the table has been generated, the program asks if you would like a driver for the characters. This driver allows you to type any message on the screen in a most unusual way. After you have played around with the driver for a while, simply press the break key and type **BSAVE "FONT-1.BAS"**. You now have a permanent copy for any program you develop.

If you are feeling adventurous and need multiple sets of fonts and character patterns for a program, you will find it very easy to create these tables in the highest memory available for your system. Simply allow 1K of memory for each table required and have the programs poke the patterns into these tables. Using the BSAVE command, save the tables after you create them. After you have all of the different tables created and saved, BLOAD them back in memory and save the entire bock of tables at once. Now, when you need a particular font, just redirect the pointer to the appropriate table in memory, and print that pattern. This saves time because instead of having to create each font before you use it, you can just load it in from cassette or disk.

As an example, a program you have created requires the use of the characters created by *New-Font*, *Font-80*, and *Rotate*, and a set you created by running *Rotate* against itself to create a character set that prints upside down. In a 64K system, your memory runs from 0000 through FFFF hex, or 0 through 65535 decimal; so you could set up your tables in this fashion:

16K	32K	48K	64K	
---	---	---	---	
2FFF	6FFF	AFFF	EFFF	START OF TABLE FOR NEW-FONT
33FF	73FF	B3FF	F3FF	START OF TABLE FOR FONT-80
37FF	77FF	B7FF	F7FF	START OF TABLE FOR ROTATE
3BFF	7BFF	BBFF	FBFF	START OF TABLE FOR ROTATE-2

For each of the fonts, reset the pointer at &H7C through &H7F to these values.
The program in BASIC for a 48K system might look like this:

```
1 CLEAR ,????    SET MEMORY AREA ASIDE FOR TABLES
2 DEF SEG = 0   POINT TO ABSOLUTE ADDRESSES
```

CREATE THE TABLE OF DATA . . . .

```
1000 BSAVE "FONT-1.BAS" ,&HAFFF,&400
```

Repeat the process for the rest of the tables using the appropriate table locations and saving them invidually. Finally, with the tables stored on cassette or disk, write a small program such as

```
1 CLEAR ,????

2 DEF SEG = Ø

3 BLOAD "FONT-1.BAS"

4 BLOAD "FONT-2.BAS"

5 BLOAD "FONT-3.BAS"

6 BLOAD "FONT-4.BAS"

7 INPUT A$

8 BSAVE "FONT-5.BAS" ,&HAFFF,&H1ØØØ
```

The program that will use these fonts should include a line such as

100   BLOAD "FONT-5.BAS"

Now whenever you need the second character set, use the lines

110   DEF SEG = 0
120   POKE &H7D,&HB3   (FIRST 2 CHAR OF TABLE ADDRESS)
130   POKE &H7C,&HFF   (LAST 2 CHAR OF TABLE ADDRESS)

and use CHR$(128) through CHR$ (255).

```
100 '*************************************************************
110 '**         ROTATE FONT     **  ROTATES AND STORES IN CHR$(128)    **
120 '**                         **  THRU CHR$(255) THE PATTERNS OF THE **
130 '**         VERSION 1.1     **  CHARACTERS FOR CHR$(0) THRU        **
140 '**                         **  CHR$(127).  TO USE - ADD 128 TO    **
150 '**         JUNE 6,1982     **  THE VALUE OF THE ASCII CHARACTER    **
160 '*************************************************************
170 '
180 SCREEN 2 : KEY OFF : CLS
190 CLEAR ,20000,1000
200 DEF SEG = &HB800
210 '
220 '*****************************************************************
230 '**   THIS ROUTINE STORES A ROTATED VERSION OF CHR$ (0 THRU 127)   **
240 '**   IN CHR$ (128 THRU 255)                                      **
250 '*****************************************************************
260 '
270 FOR X = 0 TO 127
280 PRINT X;
290 DEF SEG = &HFF00              'POINT TO CHARACTER PATTERN IN ROM AT &HFFA6E
300 POINTER = &HA6E + X*8         'POINT TO START OF INDIVIDUAL PATTERN
310 FOR Y = 0 TO 7                'FOR 8 BYTES
320 A(Y+1) = PEEK(POINTER+Y)      'GET PATTERN
330 NEXT Y                        'AND STORE IN A(Y+1)'
340 '
350 GOSUB 510                     'ROTATE PATTERN 90 DEGREES
360 '
370 DEF SEG = 0
380 POKE &H7D,&HBC
390 '
400 FOR Y = 0 TO 7
410 POKE &HBC00+X*8+Y,B(Y+1)
420 NEXT Y
430 '
440 NEXT X
450 '
```

```
460 DEF SEG = 0
470 POKE &H7D,&HBC
480 CLS : FOR X = 0 TO 255 : PRINT CHR$(X);" "; : NEXT
490 PRINT
500 INPUT " PRESS ENTER FOR A DRIVER FOR THE GRAPHICS ";A$ : GOTO 720
510 '
520 '*****************************************************************
530 '**   THIS SUBROUTINE TAKES AN 8 BYTE PATTERN AND ROTATES IT 90 DEG  **
540 '**   INPUT IN A(1) TO A(8)                OUTPUT IN B(1) THRU B(8)  **
550 '*****************************************************************
560 '
570 FOR C = 1 TO 8 : B(C) = 0 : NEXT C
580 '
590 FOR C = 1 TO 8
600 A = A(C)
610 '
620 FOR D = 8 TO 1 STEP -1
630 A = A + A
640 B(D) = B(D) * 2
650 IF A > 255 THEN B(D) = B(D) + 1
660 A = A MOD 256
670 NEXT D
680 '
690 NEXT C
700 '
710 RETURN
720 '
730 '*****************************************************************
740 '**   THIS ROUTINE IS A SIMPLE DRIVER SO YOU CAN PRINT OUT MESSAGES   **
750 '**   WITH THIS PROGRAM WITH THE LINES GOING UP THE PAGE             **
760 '*****************************************************************
770 '
780 CLS : SCREEN 1 : X = 24 : Y = 1
790 LOCATE X,Y : PRINT CHR$(128+45) ;
800 A$ = INKEY$ : IF A$ = "" THEN 800
810 B = ASC(A$) + 128
820 LOCATE X,Y : PRINT CHR$(B);
830 X = X-1 : IF X = 0 THEN X = 24 : Y = Y + 2
840 IF Y > 40 THEN GOTO 840
850 GOTO 790
```

ROTATE-A-LETTER

This program is an addition for the *Rotate-A-Font* program. Replace lines 720 through 850 in the *Rotate-A-Font* program with lines 650 through 1570 in the listing for this program as explained in the listing, and you will have a new way to send a letter or message to someone else.

Enter your message between the quotation marks, and when the program is run, you will have a message that prints out in lines going up the screen. The program gives room for seven pages of text, but this amount can be changed easily to meet your needs.

```
100 '****************************************************************
110 '**                     ROTATE-A-LETTER                       **
120 '**                                                           **
130 '**   VERS 1.1                              SEPT 11,1982      **
140 '**                                                           **
150 '**   WHEN USED WITH 'ROTATE-FONT' THIS PROGRAM WILL PRINT A  **
160 '**   7 PAGE MESSAGE THAT WILL PRINT UP THE PAGE WITH ALL     **
170 '**   CHARACTERS ON THEIR SIDE                                **
180 '**   TO USE EXCHANGE THESE LINES (650 THRU THE END OF THE LISTING) **
190 '**   WITH THE LAST LINES IN ROTATE-FONT (LINES 720 ON)       **
200 '****************************************************************
210 '
650 '****************************************************************
660 '**   THIS ROUTINE IS A SIMPLE DRIVER SO YOU CAN PRINT OUT MESSAGES **
670 '**   WITH THIS PROGRAM WITH THE LINES GOING UP THE PAGE      **
680 '****************************************************************
690 ON ERROR GOTO 800
700 CLS : SCREEN 1 : X = 24 : Y = 1
710 READ Z$ : FOR M = 1 TO 24
720 Q$ = MID$(Z$,M,1)
730 B = ASC(Q$) + 128
740 LOCATE X,Y : PRINT CHR$(B);
750 X = X-1 : IF X = 0 THEN X = 24 : Y = Y + 2
760 IF Y > 40 THEN GOTO 790
770 NEXT M
780 GOTO 710
790 C$ = INKEY$ : IF C$ = "" THEN 790 ELSE 700
800 GOTO 800
810 '**************************   TOP OF PAGE #1
820 DATA "1                        ","2                        "
830 DATA "3                        ","4                        "
840 DATA "5                        ","6                        "
850 DATA "7                        ","8                        "
860 DATA "9                        ","10                       "
870 DATA "11                       ","12                       "
880 DATA "13                       ","14                       "
890 DATA "15                       ","16                       "
900 DATA "17                       ","18                       "
910 DATA "19                       ","PRESS ENTER TO CONTINUE  "
920 '**************************   TOP OF PAGE #2
930 DATA "                         ","                         "
940 DATA "                         ","                         "
950 DATA "                         ","                         "
960 DATA "                         ","                         "
```

238

```
970 DATA "                              "," "                                    "
980 DATA "                              "," "                                    "
990 DATA "                              "," "                                    "
1000 DATA "                             "," "                                    "
1010 DATA "                             "," "                                    "
1020 DATA "                             ","PRESS ENTER TO CONTINUE "
1030 '***************************  TOP OF PAGE #3
1040 DATA "                             "," "                                    "
1050 DATA "                             "," "                                    "
1060 DATA "                             "," "                                    "
1070 DATA "                             "," "                                    "
1080 DATA "                             "," "                                    "
1090 DATA "                             "," "                                    "
1100 DATA "                             "," "                                    "
1110 DATA "                             "," "                                    "
1120 DATA "                             "," "                                    "
1130 DATA "                             ","PRESS ENTER TO CONTINUE "
1140 '***************************  TOP OF PAGE #4
1150 DATA "                             "," "                                    "
1160 DATA "                             "," "                                    "
1170 DATA "                             "," "                                    "
1180 DATA "                             "," "                                    "
1190 DATA "                             "," "                                    "
1200 DATA "                             "," "                                    "
1210 DATA "                             "," "                                    "
1220 DATA "                             "," "                                    "
1230 DATA "                             "," "                                    "
1240 DATA "                             ","PRESS ENTER TO CONTINUE "
1250 '***************************  TOP OF PAGE #5
1260 DATA "                             "," "                                    "
1270 DATA "                             "," "                                    "
1280 DATA "                             "," "                                    "
1290 DATA "                             "," "                                    "
1300 DATA "                             "," "                                    "
1310 DATA "                             "," "                                    "
1320 DATA "                             "," "                                    "
1330 DATA "                             "," "                                    "
1340 DATA "                             "," "                                    "
1350 DATA "                             ","PRESS ENTER TO CONTINUE "
1360 '***************************  TOP OF PAGE #6
1370 DATA "                             "," "                                    "
1380 DATA "                             "," "                                    "
1390 DATA "                             "," "                                    "
1400 DATA "                             "," "                                    "
1410 DATA "                             "," "                                    "
1420 DATA "                             "," "                                    "
1430 DATA "                             "," "                                    "
```

```
1440 DATA "                              "," "                              "
1450 DATA "                              "," "                              "
1460 DATA "                              ","PRESS ENTER TO CONTINUE "
1470 '************************    TOP OF PAGE #7
1480 DATA "                              "," "                              "
1490 DATA "                              "," "                              "
1500 DATA "                              "," "                              "
1510 DATA "                              "," "                              "
1520 DATA "                              "," "                              "
1530 DATA "                              "," "                              "
1540 DATA "                              "," "                              "
1550 DATA "                              "," "                              "
1560 DATA "                              "," "                              "
1570 DATA "                              ","PRESS ENTER TO CONTINUE "
```

SUBROUTINES AND FUNCTIONS

The subroutines and functions in this list are of two types, those that we used repeatedly in our programming, and those that are useful but never found their way into any of the programs in this book. A short explanation describing the operation and the variables involved immediately precedes each subroutine.

The lines are numbered starting with 50000. In most cases the subroutines can be patched into an existing program without overlapping line numbers. There are several methods of patching programs together. Here is one idea. Let's assume you have a program and wish to include a subroutine from this listing. First save your program to a diskette file in ASCII format by using the ",A" option at the end of your save command. Now load this subroutine file, and delete all the lines except for those you want to include in your program. The next step is to merge your program file, which will add your program lines to the subroutine lines currently in memory. Make sure all your GOSUB statements are aimed at the new subroutine(s), do a RENUM if you wish, and save the program to a diskette file.

```
50000 ' ******************************************
50010 ' **      SUBROUTINES AND FUNCTIONS      **
50020 ' ******************************************
50030 '
50040 '
50050 ' Function, scale a value to screen in medium resolution.
50060 ' Screen 1 is scaled from XMIN to XMAX, left to right.
50070 ' Value X is converted to screen position.
50080 DEF FNSCRN1X(X) = INT(319*(X-XMIN)/(XMAX-XMIN))
50090 '
50100 '
50110 ' Function, scale a value to screen in high resolution.
50120 ' Screen 2 is scaled from XMIN to XMAX, left to right.
50130 ' Value X is converted to screen position.
50140 DEF FNSCRN2X(X) = INT(639*(X-XMIN)/(XMAX-XMIN))
50150 '
50160 '
```

```
50170 ' Function, scale a value to screen.
50180 ' Screen is scaled from YMIN to YMAX, bottom to top.
50190 ' Value Y is converted to screen position.
50200 DEF FNSCRNY(Y) = INT(199*(YMAX-Y)/(YMAX-YMIN))
50210 '
50220 '
50230 ' Function, generate random real number in range REALA to REALB.
50240 DEF FNRNDREAL(REALA,REALB) = REALA + RND * (REALB - REALA)
50250 '
50260 '
50270 ' Function, generate random integer in range INTA to INTB.
50280 DEF FNRNDINT(INTA,INTB) = INT(INTA + RND * (INTB - INTA + 1))
50290 '
50300 '
50310 ' Function, convert degrees to radians.
50320 DEF FNDTR(DEGREES) = DEGREES / 57.29578
50330 '
50340 '
50350 ' Function, convert radians to degrees.
50360 DEF FNRTD(RADIANS) = RADIANS * 57.29578
50370 '
50380 '
50390 ' Function, ATN correct for any X,Y point in the plane.
50400 DEF FNATN2(Y,X) = -ATN(Y/(X-(X=0)))*(X<>0)-1.570796*SGN(Y)
                        *(X=0)+3.141593*(X<0)*((Y>=0)-(Y<0))
50410 '
50420 '
50430 ' Function, double precision SIN.
50440 ' (See SIN program for other alternatives)
50450 DEF FNDS#(X#) = X#-X#*X#*X#/6 + X#*X#*X#*X#*X#/120# - X#*X#*X#*X#*
      X#*X#*X#/5040 + X#*X#*X#*X#*X#*X#*X#*X#*X#/362880#-X#*X#*X#*X#*X#
      #*X#*X#*X#*X#*X#*X#/ 39916800#+X#*X#*X#*X#*X#*X#*X#*X#*X#*X#*X#
      *X#*X#/6227020800#
50460 '
50470 '
50480 ' Function, double precision COS.
50490 ' (See COS program for other alternatives)
50500 DEF FNDC#(X#) = 1# - X#*X#/2 + X#*X#*X#*X#/24# - X#*X#*X#*X#*X#*X#
      #/720# + X#*X#*X#*X#*X#*X#*X#*X#/40320# - X#*X#*X#*X#*X#*X#*X#*X#
      #*X#*X#/3628800#  + X#*X#*X#*X#*X#*X#*X#*X#*X#*X#*X#*X#/4790016
      00#
50510 DEF FNDT#(X#) = FNS#(X#) / FNC#(X#)
50520 '
50530 '
50540 ' Subroutine, convert WORK$ to upper case.
50550 FOR CHAR = 1 TO LEN(WORK$)
50560 IF MID$(WORK$,CHAR,1) < "a" THEN 50590
```

```
50570 IF MID$(WORK$,CHAR,1) > "z" THEN 50590
50580 MID$(WORK$,CHAR,1) = CHR$(ASC(MID$(WORK$,CHAR,1))-32)
50590 NEXT CHAR
50600 RETURN
50610 '
50620 '
50630 ' Subroutine, remove all spaces from WORK$
50640 SP = INSTR(WORK$," ")
50650 IF SP = 0 THEN 50680
50660 WORK$ = LEFT$(WORK$,SP-1) + MID$(WORK$,SP+1)
50670 GOTO 50640
50680 RETURN
50690 '
50700 '
50710 ' Subroutine, rectangular to polar ... X,Y to MAG,ANG
50720 MAG = SQR(X*X + Y*Y)
50730 NINETY = 2 * ATN(1)
50740 IF X THEN ANG = ATN(Y/X) ELSE ANG = NINETY * ((Y<0) - (Y>0))
50750 IF X < 0 THEN ANG = ANG + 2 * NINETY * ((ANG>0) - (ANG<=0))
50760 RETURN
50770 '
50780 '
50790 ' Subroutine, polar to rectangular ... MAG,ANG to X,Y
50800 X = MAG * COS(ANG)
50810 Y = MAG * SIN(ANG)
50820 RETURN
50830 '
50840 '
50850 ' Subroutine, clear the key buffer
50860 IF LEN(INKEY$) THEN 50860
50870 RETURN
50880 '
50890 '
50900 ' Subroutine, clear key buffer, then get next key into K$
50910 IF LEN(INKEY$) THEN 50910
50920 K$ = INKEY$
50930 IF K$ = "" THEN 50920
50940 RETURN
50950 '
50960 '
50970 ' Subroutine, adjustable delay
50980 FOR INCREMENT = 1 TO DELAY
50990 NEXT INCREMENT
51000 RETURN
51010 '
51020 '
51030 ' Subroutine, delay whole number of SECONDS
```

```
51040 WHILE SECONDS > 0
51050 TIME2$ = TIME$
51060 WHILE TIME2$ = TIME$
51070 WEND
51080 SECONDS = SECONDS - 1
51090 WEND
51100 RETURN
51110 '
51120 '
51130 ' Subroutine, wait for EXACT.TIME$ of day
51140 WHILE TIME$ <> EXACT.TIME$
51150 WEND
51160 RETURN
51170 '
51180 '
51190 ' Subroutine, wait'til user presses any key
51200 LOCATE 25,25
51210 PRINT "Press any key to continue ...";
51220 IF LEN(INKEY$) = 0 THEN 51220
51230 RETURN
51240 '
51250 '
51260 ' Subroutine, wait'til user presses space bar
51270 LOCATE 25,23
51280 PRINT "Press <space bar> to continue ...";
51290 IF INKEY$ <> " " THEN 51290
51300 RETURN
51310 '
51320 '
51330 ' Subroutine, wait for yes or no answer
51340 ' Returned value of ANSWER indicates yes or no (1 or 0).
51350 K$ = INKEY$
51360 ANSWER = 9
51370 IF K$ = "y" OR K$ = "Y" THEN ANSWER = 1
51380 IF K$ = "n" OR K$ = "N" THEN ANSWER = 0
51390 IF ANSWER = 9 THEN 51350
51400 RETURN
51410 '
51420 '
51430 ' Subroutine, randomizing the random numbers.
51440 ' New seed for each second of an hour.
51450 RANDOMIZE VAL(MID$(TIME$,4,2) + RIGHT$(TIME$,2))
51460 '
51470 '
51480 ' Subroutine, thoroughly randomize random numbers.
51490 ' Start with new seed for each second of an hour.
51500 ' Then randomize an unpredictable number of times.
```

```
51510 TM$ = TIME$
51520 RANDOMIZE VAL(MID$(TM$,4,2) + RIGHT$(TM$,2))
51530 WHILE TM$ = TIME$
51540 RANDOMIZE 64000! * RND - 32000
51550 WEND
51560 RETURN
51570 '
51580 '
51590 ' Subroutine, randomizing while waiting for user
51600 K$ = INKEY$
51610 RANDOMIZE 64000! * RND - 32000
51620 IF K$ = "" THEN 51600
51630 RETURN
51640 '
51650 '
51660 ' Subroutine, convert TIME$ to HOUR, MINUTE, SECOND
51670 HOUR = VAL(TIME$)
51680 MINUTE = VAL(MID$(TIME$,4))
51690 SECOND = VAL(RIGHT$(TIME$,2))
51700 RETURN
51710 '
51720 '
51730 ' Subroutine, convert HOUR, MINUTE, SECOND to TIME$
51740 TIME$ = CHR$(48+HOUR\10) + CHR$(48+HOUR MOD 10) + ":" +
             CHR$(48+MINUTE\10) + CHR$(48+MINUTE MOD 10) + ":" +
             CHR$(48+SECOND\10) + CHR$(48+SECOND MOD 10)
51750 RETURN
51760 '
51770 '
51780 ' Subroutine, convert DATE$ to MONTH, DAY, YEAR
51790 MONTH = VAL(DATE$)
51800 DAY = VAL(MID$(DATE$,4))
51810 YEAR = VAL(RIGHT$(DATE$,4))
51820 RETURN
51830 '
51840 '
51850 ' Subroutine, convert MONTH, DAY, YEAR to DATE$
51860 DATE$ = CHR$(48+MONTH\10) + CHR$(48+MONTH MOD 10) + "/" +
             CHR$(48+DAY\10) + CHR$(48+DAY MOD 10) + "/" +
             MID$(STR$(YEAR),2)
51870 RETURN
51880 '
51890 '
51900 ' Subroutine, numerical array sort.
51910 ' Array A() is sorted into ascending order.
51920 ' To reverse order, change test from ">" to "<".
51930 FOR I = 1 TO SIZE - 1
```

```
51940 FOR J = I + 1 TO SIZE
51950 IF A(I) > A(J) THEN SWAP A(I), A(J)
51960 NEXT J,I
51970 RETURN
51980 '
51990 '
52000 ' Subroutine, string array sort.
52010 ' Array A$() is sorted into ascending order.
52020 ' To reverse order, change test from ">" to "<".
52030 FOR I = 1 TO SIZE - 1
52040 FOR J = I + 1 TO SIZE
52050 IF A$(I) > A$(J) THEN SWAP A$(I), A$(J)
52060 NEXT J,I
52070 RETURN
52080 '
52090 '
52100 ' Subroutine, dump screen to printer (40 wide).
52110 ' This simulates pressing the <shift> <PrtSc> keys,
52120 ' but it can be done under program control.
52130 WIDTH "lpt1:",40
52140 FOR ROW = 1 TO 25
52150 FOR COL = 1 TO 40
52160 CHAR = SCREEN(ROW,COL)
52170 IF CHAR = 0 THEN CHAR = 32
52180 LPRINT CHR$(CHAR);
52190 NEXT COL,ROW
52200 RETURN
52210 '
52220 '
52230 ' Subroutine, dump screen to printer (80 wide).
52240 ' This simulates pressing the <shift> <PrtSc> keys,
52250 ' but it can be done under program control.
52260 WIDTH "lpt1:",80
52270 FOR ROW = 1 TO 25
52280 FOR COL = 1 TO 80
52290 CHAR = SCREEN(ROW,COL)
52300 IF CHAR = 0 THEN CHAR = 32
52310 LPRINT CHR$(CHAR);
52320 NEXT COL,ROW
52330 RETURN
52340 '
52350 '
52360 ' Subroutine, dump graphics to FILENAME$
52370 DEF SEG = &HB800
52380 BSAVE FILENAME$,0,&H4000
52390 RETURN
52400 '
```

```
52410 '
52420 ' Subroutine, load graphics from FILENAME$
52430 DEF SEG = &HB800
52440 BLOAD FILENAME$
52450 RETURN
52460 '
52470 '
52480 'Subroutine, form statistical summation registers.
52490 ' Delete those summation registers you don't need.
52500 ' Add similar registers for further capabilities.
52510 ' Note that linear regression analysis is performed
52520 ' by this subroutine.   (Y = LIN.REG.A * X + LIN.REG.B).
52530 SUM.X = SUM.X + X
52540 SUM.Y = SUM.Y + Y
52550 SUM.XX = SUM.XX + X * X
52560 SUM.YY = SUM.YY + Y * Y
52570 SUM.XY = SUM.XY + X * Y
52580 SUM.X2Y = SUM.X2Y + X * X * Y
52590 SUM.X3Y = SUM.X3Y + X ^ 3 * Y
52600 SUM.X4Y = SUM.X4Y + X ^ 4 * Y
52610 SUM.X5Y = SUM.X5Y + X ^ 5 * Y
52620 SUM.N = SUM.N + 1
52630 IF SUM.N < 2 THEN 52760
52640 LIN.REG.B = (SUM.N*SUM.XY-SUM.X*SUM.Y)/(SUM.N*SUM.XX-SUM.X^2)
52650 LIN.REG.A = (SUM.Y-LIN.REG.B*SUM.X)/SUM.N
52660 CORR.R = (SUM.N*SUM.XY-SUM.X*SUM.Y)
             /SQR((SUM.N*SUM.XX-SUM.X^2)*(SUM.N*SUM.YY-SUM.Y^2))
52670 CORR.R2 = CORR.R*CORR.R
52680 MEAN.X = SUM.X/SUM.N
52690 MEAN.Y = SUM.Y/SUM.N
52700 COVARIANCE = (SUM.XY-SUM.N*MEAN.X*MEAN.Y)/(SUM.N-1)
52710 POP.COVARIANCE = (SUM.XY-SUM.N*MEAN.X*MEAN.Y)/SUM.N
52720 STANDEV.X = SQR((SUM.XX-SUM.X^2/SUM.N)/(SUM.N-1))
52730 STANDEV.Y = SQR((SUM.YY-SUM.Y^2/SUM.N)/(SUM.N-1))
52740 POP.STANDEV.X = STANDEV.X*SQR((SUM.N-1)/SUM.N)
52750 POP.STANDEV.Y = STANDEV.Y*SQR((SUM.N-1)/SUM.N)
52760 RETURN
52770 '
52780 '
52790 ' Subroutine, convert MONTH, DAY, YEAR to JULIAN, WEEKDAY.
52800 ' JULIAN is astronomical Julian day number.
52810 ' WEEKDAY is 1 for Sunday, 2 for Monday ... 7 for Saturday.
52820 JULIAN = INT(365.2422# * YEAR + 30.44 * (MONTH-1) + DAY + 1)
52830 T1 = MONTH - 2 - 12 * (MONTH < 3)
52840 T2 = YEAR + (MONTH < 3)
52850 T3 = INT(T2 / 100)
52860 T2 = T2 - 100 * T3
```

```
52870 WEEKDAY = INT(2.61 * T1 - .2) + DAY + T2 + INT(T2 / 4)
52880 WEEKDAY = (WEEKDAY + INT(T3 / 4) - T3 - T3 + 77) MOD 7 + 1
52890 T4 = JULIAN - 7 * INT(JULIAN / 7)
52900 JULIAN = JULIAN - T4 + WEEKDAY + 7 * (T4 < WEEKDAY - 1) + 1721060#
52910 RETURN
52920 '
52930 ' Subroutine, convertJULIAN to MONTH, DAY, YEAR, and WEEKDAY.
52940 ' JULIAN is astronomical Julian day number.
52950 ' WEEKDAY is 1 for Sunday, 2 for Monday ... 7 for Saturday.
52960 T5 = JULIAN
52970 YEAR = INT((JULIAN - 1721061!) / 365.25 + 1)
52980 MONTH = 1
52990 DAY = 1
53000 GOSUB 52820
53010 IF JULIAN <= T5 THEN 53040
53020 YEAR = YEAR - 1
53030 GOTO 53000
53040 MONTH = INT((T5 - JULIAN) / 29 + 1)
53050 GOSUB 52820
53060 IF JULIAN <= T5 THEN 53090
53070 MONTH = MONTH - 1
53080 GOTO 53050
53090 DAY = T5 - JULIAN + 1
53100 GOSUB 52820
53110 RETURN
53120 '
```

XREF (CROSS REFERENCE)

This program is a handy utility for polishing up long program listings. It will locate all lines that contain any given string of characters, and if you wish replace all occurrences with a replacement string. For example, the replacement option would be useful if you wanted to change the variable X1 to VOLTS everywhere that it occurs in a long program. Attempting this kind of editing by hand is a real headache. If you miss even one occurrence of X1, your program will probably "crash" the next time it is run. With the *Xref* program, this kind of editing is simple to perform. Several of the programs in this book were originally written using short variable names, (such as X1, Y, and Z. They occurred so often that considerable typing could be saved by using short names. Later, to increase the readability, these short variables were changed to longer, more self-documenting variable names. One of the outstanding features of the BASIC in your IBM Personal Computer is its ability to use these longer variable names, a feature that aids program readability tremendously.

Before processing a program using *Xref* you must save the program in ASCII format. For example, if your program is named **TAXES.BAS** you would create the proper ASCII file by executing **SAVE "TAXES",A**. The ",A" option causes the program to be be recorded on disk in the ASCII format.

The first request that *Xref* makes after you type run is for the filename of the program to be edited. For our example, you would answer **TAXES.BAS**. If the file you specify is not in ASCII format a message will appear to that effect. If the file loads properly, the main menu of *Xref* will appear.

The first two menu selections allow you to locate or locate and replace any given string of characters.

Lines that have multiple occurrences of the string to be replaced will have each occurrence replaced properly. The program won't let you make a replacement that would result in an infinite loop. For example, if you try to replace all ocurrences of "V" with "VOLTS", the program recognizes that there would be a never ending number of "V" characters to be replaced. You'll get a message warning of the problem. (As a way around this problem, consider changing "V" to "XXX" and then later changing "XXX" to "VOLTS").

There is another potential problem when you use certain replacement strings. For example, if you replace all occurrences of "I" with "AMPS" then every print statement will end up as "PRAMPSNT". There are ways around this type of problem. You could change all "PRINT" characters to "XXX"; change all "I"'s to "AMPS"; then change all "XXX"'s back to "PRINT". Before you make any replacements, you should do a search for all occurrences of the string to be replaced. This gives you a chance to notice any unwanted replacements that would occur before it's too late.

At any point in your editing you can use the save option in the menu to save the current state of the edited program lines. An extension of ".XRF" is tacked onto the file name, so your original file is left undisturbed. When your editing session with *Xref* is over you can load the new file (**TAXES.XRF** in our example) and give it a try. If anything went wrong you still have the original file **TAXES.BAS**).

The fourth menu selection allows you to back up a step and load the most recent copy of the edited file. This gives you an escape route if you try a replacement that creates a mess. (Be sure to save the file every once in awhile.)

```
10 ' ******************
20 ' **     XREF     **
30 ' ******************
40 '
50 CLEAR
60 SCREEN Ø,Ø
70 WIDTH 80
80 KEY OFF
90 CLS
100 OPTION BASE 1
110 DIM PROGRAM$(999)
120 LOCATE 2,30
130 PRINT "* * *   XREF   * * *
140 LOCATE 7,1
150 INPUT "Program name (with extension) ";FILE$
160 OPEN FILE$ FOR INPUT AS # 1
170     WHILE NOT EOF(1)
180     COUNT=COUNT+1
190     LINE INPUT #1,PROGRAM$(COUNT)
200     TEST$=LEFT$(PROGRAM$(COUNT),1)
210     IF TEST$ >= "1" AND TEST$ <= "9" THEN 270
220     BEEP
230     PRINT
240     PRINT "File isn't an ascii program file ...
250     PRINT
260     END
270     WEND
280 CLOSE #1
```

```
290 FILE$=LEFT$(FILE$,INSTR(FILE$,"."))+"XRF"
300 RESTORE
310 SELECTIONS = 5
320    FOR I = 1 TO SELECTIONS
330    READ FL$(I)
340    NEXT I
350 DATA Search for all occurences of a string
360 DATA Replace all occurences of a string
370 DATA "SAVE "
380 DATA "LOAD "
390 DATA Quit
400 FL$(3) = FL$(3)+CHR$(34)+FILE$+CHR$(34)
410 FL$(4) = FL$(4)+CHR$(34)+FILE$+CHR$(34)
420 GOSUB 1060
430 ON CHOICE GOTO 460,630,920,1010
440 CLS
450 END
460 CLS
470 LOCATE 7,1
480 INPUT "String to search for ";SEARCH$
490 PRINT
500 LINES=0
510    FOR I = 1 TO COUNT
520    IF INSTR(PROGRAM$(I),SEARCH$) = 0 THEN 580
530    PRINT PROGRAM$(I)
540    LINES=LINES+1
550    IF LINES < 21 THEN 580
560    GOSUB 1200
570    LINES = 0
580    NEXT I
590 PRINT
600 PRINT "... end of search ..."
610 GOSUB 1200
620 GOTO 300
630 CLS
640 LOCATE 7,1
650 INPUT "String to search for ";SEARCH$
660 PRINT "String to replace each occurence of ";
670 PRINT CHR$(34);SEARCH$;CHR$(34);
680 INPUT RP$
690 IF INSTR(RP$,SEARCH$) = 0 THEN 750
700 BEEP
710 PRINT
720 PRINT "This replacement would result in an infinite loop !"
730 GOSUB 1200
740 GOTO 300
750 PRINT
```

```
760 LINES=0
770    FOR I = 1 TO COUNT
780    PTR=INSTR(PROGRAM$(I),SEARCH$)
790    IF PTR = 0 THEN 870
800    PROGRAM$(I) = LEFT$(PROGRAM$(I),PTR-1) + RP$ +
                     MID$(PROGRAM$(I),PTR+LEN(SEARCH$))
810    PRINT PROGRAM$(I)
820    LINES=LINES+1
830    IF LINES < 21 THEN 860
840    GOSUB 1200
850    LINES = 0
860    GOTO 780
870    NEXT I
880 PRINT
890 PRINT "... end of replace ..."
900 GOSUB 1200
910 GOTO 300
920 CLS
930 LOCATE 7,1
940 PRINT "Writing ";FILE$;" out to the disk ..."
950 OPEN FILE$ FOR OUTPUT AS #1
960    FOR I = 1 TO COUNT
970    PRINT #1,PROGRAM$(I)
980    NEXT I
990 CLOSE #1
1000 GOTO 300
1010 COUNT = 0
1020 CLS
1030 LOCATE 7,1
1040 PRINT "Re-LOADing ";FILE$
1050 GOTO 160
1060 CLS
1070 LOCATE 12-SELECTIONS/2,1
1080    FOR FLI = 1 TO SELECTIONS
1090    COLOR 23
1100    PRINT CHR$(64+FLI);
1110    COLOR 7
1120    PRINT "   ";FL$(FLI)
1130    NEXT FLI
1140 GOSUB 1270
1150 IF K$ >= "a" AND K$ <= "z" THEN K$=CHR$(ASC(K$)-32)
1160 CHOICE=ASC(K$)-64
1170 IF CHOICE < 1 OR CHOICE > SELECTIONS THEN 1140
1180 CLS
1190 RETURN
1200 ROW=CSRLIN
1210 COL=POS(0)
```

```
1220 LOCATE 25,25
1230 COLOR 23
1240 PRINT "Press any key to continue ..."
1250 LOCATE ROW,COL
1260 COLOR 7
1270 K$=INKEY$
1280 IF K$ = "" THEN 1270
1290 RETURN
```

Chapter 8

F1. Increment hour   F2. Decrement hour
F3. Increment minute   F4. Decrement minute
F5. Increment second   F6. Decrement second

12
11   1
10   2
9   3
8   4
7   5
6

10:07:12

Programs for a Small Business

The programs in this chapter meet many needs. The average individual as well as the business person will find the checkbook balancing program very useful. Anyone who wants a simple way to write and print reports or letters will appreciate the text editor. The IBM Personal Computer is also transformed into a graph generator and a mail list handler by the powerful programs in this chapter.

CHECKBOOK BALANCER

This program is dedicated to everyone who has as much trouble balancing a checkbook as I have. The program grew out of a need for accurate records and some way of analyzing expenditures over a period of time. Some of the highlights of the system are;

1. The program is menu driven. From one section of the program, you have access to all of the different sections of the program. After you have completed a section, the program returns you to the menu where you can select a different section.
2. Besides keeping a correct balance on the checking, the program keeps a record of the total expenditures in different categories.
3. Files are read and saved using the month they were entered as their filename. This allows you to keep a full years transactions on one disk. This is useful for keeping historical records.

Program Operation

The first major action of the program is to initialize the variables for the program and define array space for 100 active entries and the 50 different categories. From here, the program goes to the menu. The menu section prints a screen of information and sets up the function keys to allow the selection of one of the major routines of the program. As shown in Fig. 8-1, the selections are:

```
*******************************************************************
*   *************************************************************   *
*   *   *****************************************************   *   *
*   *   **        CHECKBOOK MASTER BY JEFFRY L. BRETZ        **   *   *
*   *   **            OF OMAHA, NEBRASKA                     **   *   *
*   *   *****************************************************   *   *
*   *************************************************************   *
*******************************************************************

USING THE SOFT KEYS (F1,F2,F3,F4,F5 AND F10)
SELECT THE FUNCTION DESIRED ->>>>>   ?

F1  = MENU       = REPRINT THIS MENU PAGE

F2  = READ       = READ THE OLD MASTER FILE FROM DISK OR CASSETTE

F3  = SAVE       = SAVE THE NEW MASTER FILE TO DISK OR CASSETTE

F4  = UPDATE     = UPDATE OR ENTER NEW CHECKS TO THE FILE

F5  = REVIEW     = PRINTS A LISTING OF THE CATAGORY CODES

F10 = TERMINATE  = END PROGRAM

F1 = MENU    F2 = READ    F3 = SAVE    F4 = UPDATE    F5 = REVIEW    F10 = TERMINATE
```

Fig. 8-1. Options available in the *Checkbook Balancer* program.

(1) MENU — reprint the menu
(2) READ — read in the old master file from disk
(3) SAVE — save the new updated file to disk
(4) UPDATE — delete and enter checks, deposits, and withdrawals
(5) REVIEW — print a listing of the categories on the screen
(6) TERMINATE — exit from the program

The read and save sections of the program are almost exact copies of one another. Their function is to create and read the files from the disk. Using this section is easy. All you must do is enter a number that corresponds to the month of the file in question.

The review section simply prints a listing of the different categories that the checks and deposits, or withdrawals may be entered under. This way you may keep track of "food," "car" and other categories of expenditures so you can see where your finances are going. The titles for the different categories are simply strings as listed in the program and may easily be changed to suit your own needs.

The terminate section contains a check to see if you remembered to save the file to disk. If you remembered, the program terminates so you can continue with other work. If not, the program jumps to the save section so you may save an updated copy of the information entered. The final section of the program, update, contains all of the logic needed to enter and delete the entries.

The section starts with deletions. This way, if you have a very active account with many outstanding

254

entries, you will not exceed the limit of 100 entries except under extreme conditions. If you anticipate that it is possible for you to exceed the limit of 100 active entries at one time, you should change the DIM statements in the initialization section of the program.

First, the program will delete the check entries. Once you receive the returned check, there is no longer any reason to keep accessing it, and it should be deleted from the list. Enter the check number and the program will print the date and amount of the check. If this information is correct, the program will delete the check from the listing.

Second, the program deletes the deposits and withdrawals. The program will display them one at a time and ask if they should be deleted. If you respond positively, they are deleted from the listing.

After you are through with the deletions, the program scans through the listing of entries and packs the list to remove spaces in the array left by the deletions. This gives you the maximum amount of space for entries and keeps the list in order because all new entries will be added onto the end of the list.

From here we move to the entry section. Enter the check number or the letter D for deposit or W for withdrawal. Then enter the date, description, category code, and amount. The program will display the information for approval. If the entry is correct, the entry is added onto the end of the listing.

After the entries have been completed, the program checks to see if you would like a printout or a screen listing of the updated list. If you select either choice, the program outputs the entire listing of checks, deposits, and withdrawals to the indicated device and then prints out an updated listing of all of the categories with totals printed.

Finally, pressing the enter key will return you to the menu.

```
100 SCREEN 0 :WIDTH 80 :CLS :KEY OFF
110 IF INITIALIZE = 0 THEN GOSUB 1000 : INITIALIZE = 1
120 '
130 PRINT "*************************************************************
140 PRINT "* ********************************************************** *
150 PRINT "* * ******************************************************* * *
160 PRINT "* * **       CHECKBOOK MASTER BY JEFFRY L. BRETZ       ** * *
170 PRINT "* * **             OF OMAHA,  NEBRASKA                 ** * *
180 PRINT "* * ******************************************************* * *
190 PRINT "* ********************************************************** *
200 PRINT "*************************************************************
210 '
220 FOR X = 1 TO 10                        ' INITIALIZE THE SOFT KEYS
230 KEY X,""
240 NEXT X
250 KEY 1, "MENU     "+CHR$(13)
260 KEY 2, "READ     "+CHR$(13)
270 KEY 3, "SAVE     "+CHR$(13)
280 KEY 4, "UPDATE   "+CHR$(13)
290 KEY 5, "REVIEW   "+CHR$(13)
300 KEY 10,"TERMINATE"+CHR$(13)
310 '
320 LOCATE 25,1  : PRINT "F1 = MENU";      ' REPRINT LINE 25
330 LOCATE 25,13 : PRINT "F2 = READ";
340 LOCATE 25,25 : PRINT "F3 = SAVE";
350 LOCATE 25,37 : PRINT "F4 = UPDATE";
```

```
360 LOCATE 25,51 : PRINT "F5 = REVIEW";
370 LOCATE 25,65 : PRINT "F10 = TERMINATE";
380 '
390 LOCATE 10,1                              ' SET UP MENU SELECTION
400 PRINT "USING THE SOFT KEYS (F1,F2,F3,F4,F5 AND F10)
410 PRINT "SELECT THE FUNCTION DESIRED -
420 PRINT
430 PRINT "F1  = MENU     = REPRINT THIS MENU PAGE
440 PRINT
450 PRINT "F2  = READ     = READ THE OLD MASTER FILE FROM DISK OR CASSETTE
460 PRINT
470 PRINT "F3  = SAVE     = SAVE THE NEW MASTER FILE TO DISK OR CASSETTE
480 PRINT
490 PRINT "F4  = UPDATE   = UPDATE OR ENTER NEW CHECKS TO THE FILE
500 PRINT
510 PRINT "F5  = REVIEW   = PRINTS A LISTING OF THE CATEGORY CODES
520 PRINT
530 PRINT "F10 = TERMINATE = END PROGRAM
540 LOCATE 11,30 :INPUT ">>>>>   ";A$
550 FOR X = 1 TO 1000 : NEXT
560 IF A$ = "MENU"    THEN GOTO 100
570 IF A$ = "READ"    THEN GOTO 2000
580 IF A$ = "SAVE"    THEN GOTO 3000
590 IF A$ = "UPDATE"  THEN GOTO 6000
600 IF A$ = "REVIEW"  THEN GOTO 4000
610 IF A$ = "TERMINATE" THEN GOTO 5000
620 CLS
630 PRINT "INVALID REQUEST -
640 PRINT "PLEASE USE ONLY THE SOFT KEYS (F1,F2,F3,F4,F5, AND F10)
650 PRINT "LOCATED ON THE LEFT HAND SIDE OF THE KEYBOARD
660 PRINT
670 PRINT "PRESS ANY KEY TO RETURN TO MENU -
680 A$ = INKEY$ : IF A$ = "" THEN 680 ELSE 100
1000 '
1010 ' **************************************************************
1020 ' * ********************************************************** *
1030 ' * * ****************************************************** * *
1040 ' * * **             INITIALIZATION                ** * *
1050 ' * * ****************************************************** * *
1060 ' * ********************************************************** *
1070 ' **************************************************************
1080 '
1090 '
1100 ' THE INITIALIZATION PROCESS SETS THE CATEGORY CODES FOR USE
1110 ' IN THE MAIN PROGRAM.
1120 '
1130 ' THESE CODES ARE LOCATED IN LINES 1230 THRU 1720 OF THE LISTING.
```

```
1140 '
1150 ' IF THIS SELECTION OF CATEGORY CODES DOES NOT MEET YOUR NEEDS, YOU
1160 ' MAY CHANGE THEM TO FIT ANY SYSTEM YOU HAVE.
1170 '
1180 ' PLEASE DO NOT CHANGE THE LENGTHS OF THE QUOTE MARKS AS THIS MAY
1190 ' MESS UP THE DISPLAY OF THE REVIEW PORTION OF THE PROGRAM.
1200 '
1210 OPTION BASE 1
1220 DEFINT A-Z : DIM A$(50),CATEGORY#(50)
1230 DIM CHECK%(100)
1240 DIM DATES$(100)
1250 DIM AMOUNT#(100)
1260 DIM CODE%(100)
1270 DIM DESCRIPT$(100)
1280 '
1290 FOR X = 1 TO 100
1300 CHECK%(X) = Ø : DATES$(X) = SPACE$(5) : AMOUNT#(X) = Ø
1310 CODE%(X) = Ø : DESCRIPT$(X) = SPACE$(20)
1320 NEXT X
1330 '
1340 ' ******************************************************************
1350 ' * * **                CATEGORY  INITIALIZATION            ** * *
1360 ' ******************************************************************
1370 '
1380 A$( 1) = "Ø1 = DEPOSIT          "
1390 A$( 2) = "Ø2 = W/D FOR CASH     "
1400 A$( 3) = "Ø3 = HOUSE/RENT       "
1410 A$( 4) = "Ø4 = CAR #1           "
1420 A$( 5) = "Ø5 = CAR #2           "
1430 A$( 6) = "Ø6 = TELEPHONE        "
1440 A$( 7) = "Ø7 = GAS/HOME         "
1450 A$( 8) = "Ø8 = WATER/HOME       "
1460 A$( 9) = "Ø9 = SEWER/HOME       "
1470 A$(10) = "10 = ELECTRICITY      "
1480 A$(11) = "11 = MISC-UTILITIES   "
1490 A$(12) = "12 = GROCERIES        "
1500 A$(13) = "13 = INSURANCE/HOME   "
1510 A$(14) = "14 = INSURANCE/CAR    "
1520 A$(15) = "15 = INSURANCE/LIFE   "
1530 A$(16) = "16 = INSURANCE/MEDIC  "
1540 A$(17) = "17 = INSURANCE/DENTL  "
1550 A$(18) = "18 = INSURANCE/BUS    "
1560 A$(19) = "19 = VISA             "
1570 A$(20) = "20 = MASTER-CARD      "
1580 A$(21) = "21 = AMER-EXPRESS     "
1590 A$(22) = "22 = ENTERTAINMENT    "
1600 A$(23) = "23 = RESTAURANT       "
```

```
1610 A$(24) = "24 = TUITION           "
1620 A$(25) = "25 = BOOKS             "
1630 A$(26) = "26 = COMPUTER EQUIP    "
1640 A$(27) = "27 = SUBSCRIPTIONS     "
1650 A$(28) = "28 = GAS FOR CAR       "
1660 A$(29) = "29 = AUTO SERVICE      "
1670 A$(30) = "30 = TRAVEL EXPENSES"
1680 A$(31) = "31 = MEDICINES         "
1690 A$(32) = "32 = GIFTS             "
1700 A$(33) = "33 = TAXES/FEDERAL     "
1710 A$(34) = "34 = TAXES/STATE       "
1720 A$(35) = "35 = CLOTHES           "
1730 A$(36) = "36 = FURNITURE         "
1740 A$(37) = "37 =                   "
1750 A$(38) = "38 =                   "
1760 A$(39) = "39 =                   "
1770 A$(40) = "40 =                   "
1780 A$(41) = "41 =                   "
1790 A$(42) = "42 =                   "
1800 A$(43) = "43 = INVESTMENTS       "
1810 A$(44) = "44 = -NOW- INTEREST    "
1820 A$(45) = "45 = BALANCE FORWARD"
1830 RETURN
2000 '
2010 CLS : SCREEN Ø : WIDTH 80 : LASTENTRY = Ø
2020 '
2030 PRINT "***********************************************************
2040 PRINT "* ******************************************************** *
2050 PRINT "* * ****************************************************** * *
2060 PRINT "* * **           READ INPUT FILE            ** * *
2070 PRINT "* * ****************************************************** * *
2080 PRINT "* ******************************************************** *
2090 PRINT "***********************************************************
2100 '
2110 LOCATE 9,1
2120 PRINT "ENTER THE MONTH OF THE LAST STATEMENT ":PRINT
2130 PRINT "JANUARY      = /  1 ."
2140 PRINT "FEBUARY      = /  2 ."
2150 PRINT "MARCH        = /  3 ."
2160 PRINT "APRIL        = /  4 ."
2170 PRINT "MAY          = /  5 ."
2180 PRINT "JUNE         = /  6 ."
2190 PRINT "JULY         = /  7 ."
2200 PRINT "AUGUST       = /  8 ."
2210 PRINT "SEPTEMBER    = /  9 ."
2220 PRINT "OCTOBER      = / 10 ."
2230 PRINT "NOVEMBER     = / 11 ."
```

```
2240 PRINT "DECEMBER    = / 12 ." : LOCATE 9,40 : PRINT ">>>>   ";
2250 '
2260 INPUT MONTH:IF (MONTH > 12) OR (MONTH < 1) THEN CLS : GOTO 2000
2270 LOCATE 10,40 : CLOSE
2280 ON MONTH GOTO 2300,2310,2320,2330,2340,2350,2360,2370,2380,2390,2400,2410
2290 '
2300 OPEN "JANUARY " FOR INPUT AS #1 : PRINT "READING JANUARY   "::GOTO 2420
2310 OPEN "FEBUARY " FOR INPUT AS #1 : PRINT "READING FEBUARY   "::GOTO 2420
2320 OPEN "MARCH   " FOR INPUT AS #1 : PRINT "READING MARCH     "::GOTO 2420
2330 OPEN "APRIL   " FOR INPUT AS #1 : PRINT "READING APRIL     "::GOTO 2420
2340 OPEN "MAY     " FOR INPUT AS #1 : PRINT "READING MAY       "::GOTO 2420
2350 OPEN "JUNE    " FOR INPUT AS #1 : PRINT "READING JUNE      "::GOTO 2420
2360 OPEN "JULY    " FOR INPUT AS #1 : PRINT "READING JULY      "::GOTO 2420
2370 OPEN "AUGUST  " FOR INPUT AS #1 : PRINT "READING AUGUST    "::GOTO 2420
2380 OPEN "SEPTEMBE" FOR INPUT AS #1 : PRINT "READING SEPTEMBER "::GOTO 2420
2390 OPEN "OCTOBER " FOR INPUT AS #1 : PRINT "READING OCTOBER   "::GOTO 2420
2400 OPEN "NOVEMBER" FOR INPUT AS #1 : PRINT "READING NOVEMBER  "::GOTO 2420
2410 OPEN "DECEMBER" FOR INPUT AS #1 : PRINT "READING DECEMBER  "::GOTO 2420
2420 'colection point for BASIC / CASE . STATEMENT
2430 FOR X = 1 TO 100
2440 CHECK%(X) = 0 : DATES$(X) = SPACE$(5) : AMOUNT#(X) = 0
2450 CODE%(X) = 0 : DESCRIPT$(X) = SPACE$(20)
2460 NEXT X
2470 INPUT #1,LASTENTRY
2480 X = 1
2490 WHILE X < LASTENTRY + 1
2500 INPUT #1,CHECK%(X),DATES$(X),AMOUNT#(X)
2510 X = X + 1
2520 WEND
2530 X = 1
2540 WHILE X < 51
2550 INPUT #1,CATEGORY#(X)
2560 X = X + 1
2570 WEND
2580 '
2590 CLOSE #1
2600 '
2610 LOCATE 24,1
2620 PRINT "FILE READ COMPLETED - PRESS ANY KEY TO RETURN TO MENU -";
2630 A$ = INKEY$ : IF A$ = "" THEN 2630
2640 CLS : GOTO 100
3000 '
3010 CLS : SCREEN 0 : WIDTH 80
3020 CATEGORY#(45) = BALANCE#
3030 PRINT "*******************************************************
3040 PRINT "* ***************************************************** *
3050 PRINT "* * *************************************************** * *
```

```
3060 PRINT "* * **              SAVE OUTPUT FILE              ** * *
3070 PRINT "* * ************************************************** * *
3080 PRINT "* ***************************************************** *
3090 PRINT "******************************************************
3100 '
3110 LOCATE 9,1
3120 PRINT "ENTER THE MONTH OF THIS STATEMENT ":PRINT
3130 PRINT "JANUARY       = /   1 ."
3140 PRINT "FEBUARY       = /   2 ."
3150 PRINT "MARCH         = /   3 ."
3160 PRINT "APRIL         = /   4 ."
3170 PRINT "MAY           = /   5 ."
3180 PRINT "JUNE          = /   6 ."
3190 PRINT "JULY          = /   7 ."
3200 PRINT "AUGUST        = /   8 ."
3210 PRINT "SEPTEMBER     = /   9 ."
3220 PRINT "OCTOBER       = /  10 ."
3230 PRINT "NOVEMBER      = /  11 ."
3240 PRINT "DECEMBER      = /  12 ." : LOCATE 9,40 : PRINT ">>>>   ";
3250 '
3260 INPUT MONTH:IF (MONTH > 12) OR (MONTH < 1) THEN CLS : GOTO 3000
3270 LOCATE 10,40 : CLOSE
3280 ON MONTH GOTO 3300,3310,3320,3330,3340,3350,3360,3370,3380,3390,3400,3410
3290 '
3300 OPEN "JANUARY " FOR OUTPUT AS #1 : PRINT "WRITING JANUARY   ":GOTO 3420
3310 OPEN "FEBUARY " FOR OUTPUT AS #1 : PRINT "WRITING FEBUARY   ":GOTO 3420
3320 OPEN "MARCH   " FOR OUTPUT AS #1 : PRINT "WRITING MARCH     ":GOTO 3420
3330 OPEN "APRIL   " FOR OUTPUT AS #1 : PRINT "WRITING APRIL     ":GOTO 3420
3340 OPEN "MAY     " FOR OUTPUT AS #1 : PRINT "WRITING MAY       ":GOTO 3420
3350 OPEN "JUNE    " FOR OUTPUT AS #1 : PRINT "WRITING JUNE      ":GOTO 3420
3360 OPEN "JULY    " FOR OUTPUT AS #1 : PRINT "WRITING JULY      ":GOTO 3420
3370 OPEN "AUGUST  " FOR OUTPUT AS #1 : PRINT "WRIRING AUGUST    ":GOTO 3420
3380 OPEN "SEPTEMBE" FOR OUTPUT AS #1 : PRINT "WRITING SEPTEMBER ":GOTO 3420
3390 OPEN "OCTOBER " FOR OUTPUT AS #1 : PRINT "WRITING OCTOBER   ":GOTO 3420
3400 OPEN "NOVEMBER" FOR OUTPUT AS #1 : PRINT "WRITING NOVEMBER  ":GOTO 3420
3410 OPEN "DECEMBER" FOR OUTPUT AS #1 : PRINT "WRITING DECEMBER  ":GOTO 3420
3420 'colection point for BASIC / CASE . STATEMENT
3430 WRITE #1,LASTENTRY
3440 X = 1
3450 WHILE X < LASTENTRY +1
3460 WRITE #1,CHECK%(X),DATES$(X),AMOUNT#(X)
3470 X = X + 1
3480 WEND
3490 X = 1
3500 WHILE X < 51
3510 PRINT #1,CATEGORY#(X)
3520 X = X + 1
```

```
3530 WEND
3540 '
3550 CLOSE #1
3560 '
3570 LOCATE 24,1
3580 PRINT "FILE WRITE COMPLETED - PRESS ANY KEY TO RETURN TO MENU -";
3590 A$ = INKEY$ : IF A$ = "" THEN 3590
3600 RUN
4000 '
4010 CLS : SCREEN 0 : WIDTH 80
4020 '
4030 PRINT "*****************************************************************
4040 PRINT "* ************************************************************* *
4050 PRINT "* * ********************************************************* * *
4060 PRINT "* * **          EXPENSE CATEGORY REVIEW            ** * *
4070 PRINT "* * ********************************************************* * *
4080 PRINT "* ************************************************************* *
4090 PRINT "*****************************************************************
4100 '
4110 LOCATE 9,1
4120 FOR X = 1 TO 45 : PRINT A$(X) ,: NEXT
4130 LOCATE 25,1
4140 PRINT "PRESS ANY KEY TO CONTINUE -";
4150 A$ = INKEY$ : IF A$ = "" THEN 4150
4160 CLS : GOTO 100
5000 '
5010 CLS : SCREEN 0 : WIDTH 80
5020 '
5030 PRINT "*****************************************************************
5040 PRINT "* ************************************************************* *
5050 PRINT "* * ********************************************************* * *
5060 PRINT "* * **            PROGRAM TERMINATION             ** * *
5070 PRINT "* * ********************************************************* * *
5080 PRINT "* ************************************************************* *
5090 PRINT "*****************************************************************
5100 '
5110 LOCATE 9,1
5120 PRINT "HAVE YOU SAVED THE UPDATED FILE ONTO TAPE ? (Y) OR (N) ..."
5130 A$ = INKEY$ : IF A$ = "" THEN 5130
5140 IF A$ = "N" THEN 3000
5150 PRINT FRE(X)
5160 LOCATE 20,1:KEY ON:CLEAR
6000 '
6010 CLS : SCREEN 0 : WIDTH 80 : CLOSE
6020 '
6030 PRINT "*****************************************************************
6040 PRINT "* ************************************************************* *
```

```
6050 PRINT "* * *********************************************************** * *
6060 PRINT "* * **                    FILE UPDATE                       ** * *
6070 PRINT "* * *********************************************************** * *
6080 PRINT "* ************************************************************** *
6090 PRINT "****************************************************************
6100 '
6110 '******************** FIND OUT IF THERE ARE ENTRIES TO DELETE
6120 PRINT "DO YOU HAVE ANY CANCELLED CHECKS OR DEP-W/D RECEIPTS TO BE
6130 INPUT "DELETED FROM THE LISTING ? (1=YES 2=NO) ";A
6140 IF A = 1 THEN 6170
6150 IF A = 2 THEN 6980
6160 GOTO 6000
6170 '******************** DELETE THE APPROPIATE ENTRIES
6180 CLS
6190 PRINT "DELETION BEGINS WITH CHECKS
6200 PRINT "PLEASE ENTER THE CHECK NUMBERS - (1 TO 32700 ONLY)"
6210 PRINT "AND IF (C)ORRECT OR (I)NCORRECT
6220 LOCATE 25,1
6230 A% = 0
6240 POINTER = 1
6250 PRINT "ENTER A NEGATIVE NUMBER TO TERMINATE ";
6260 LOCATE 5,1
6270 WHILE A% >= 0
6280 PRINT
6290 INPUT; A%
6300 IF (A%<=0) OR (A%>32700) THEN PRINT : GOTO 6270
6310 GOSUB 6350
6320 WEND
6330 GOSUB 6850
6340 GOTO 6520
6350 '******************** SUBROUTINE TO FIND AND DELETE CHECKS
6360 X% = .1
6370 IF X% > LASTENTRY THEN PRINT : PRINT "UNABLE TO FIND ENTRY "; : RETURN
6380 IF CHECK%(X%) <> A% THEN X% = X% + 1 : GOTO 6370
6390 LOCATE ,10
6400 PRINT DATES$(X%);                           ' PRINT THE DATE
6410 LOCATE ,20
6420 PRINT USING "$$#######,.##" ; AMOUNT#(X%); ' AMOUNT
6430 LOCATE ,40
6440 INPUT; "(C)ORRECT OR (I)NCORRECT - ";A$
6450 IF MID$(A$,1,1) = "C" THEN 6490
6460 IF MID$(A$,1,1) = "c" THEN 6490
6470 PRINT : PRINT "ENTRY NOT DELETED : PLEASE ENTER NEXT CHECK NUMBER ";
6480 RETURN
6490 CHECK%(X%) = 0 : DATES$(X%) = "        " : AMOUNT#(X%) = 0
6500 CODE%(X%) = 0 : DESCRIPT$(X%) = SPACE$(20)
6510 RETURN
```

262

```
6520 '******************* DELETE THE DEPOSITS AND WITHDRAWALS
6530 GOSUB 7460 ' 2 sec delay
6540 MARKER = 0
6550 FOR X% = 1 TO LASTENTRY
6560 IF CHECK%(X%) > 32700 THEN MARKER = 1
6570 NEXT X%
6580 IF MARKER = 0 THEN GOTO 6980 ' if no dep-w/d goto insert section
6590 CLS
6600 PRINT "DELETION CONTINUES WITH WITHDRAWALS AND DEPOSITS
6610 PRINT "PLEASE CHECK THE LISTING AND DECIDE IF YOU WANT TO"
6620 PRINT "(D)ELETE IT OR (L)EAVE IT ALONE
6630 LOCATE 5,1
6640 FOR X% = 1 TO LASTENTRY
6650 IF CHECK%(X%) > 32700 THEN GOSUB 6690
6660 NEXT X%
6670 GOSUB 6850
6680 GOTO 6980
6690 '************** SUBROUTINE TO DELETE THE DEPOSIT OR WITHDRAWAL
6700 IF CHECK%(X%) = 32750 THEN PRINT "WITHDRAWAL      ";
6710 IF CHECK%(X%) = 32760 THEN PRINT "DEPOSIT         ";
6720 LOCATE ,15
6730 PRINT DATES$(X%);
6740 LOCATE ,25
6750 PRINT USING "$$########,.##" ; AMOUNT#(X%); ' AMOUNT
6760 LOCATE ,45
6770 INPUT "(D)ELETE  OR (L)EAVE ALONE ";A$
6780 IF MID$(A$,1,1) = "D" THEN 6820
6790 IF MID$(A$,1,1) = "d" THEN 6820
6800 PRINT : PRINT "ENTRY NOT DELETED "
6810 RETURN
6820 CHECK%(X%) = 0 : DATES$(X%) = "        " : AMOUNT#(X%) = 0
6830 CODE%(X%) = 0 : DESCRIPT$(X%) = SPACE$(20)
6840 RETURN
6850 '****************** ROUTINE TO PACK ALL DELETED ENTRIES IN ARRAY
6860 X% = 1
6870 IF X% > LASTENTRY THEN RETURN
6880 IF CHECK%(X%) <> 0 THEN X% = X% + 1 : GOTO 6870
6890 FOR Y% = X% TO LASTENTRY - 1
6900 CHECK%(Y%) = CHECK%(Y%+1)
6910 DATES$(Y%) = DATES$(Y%+1)
6920 AMOUNT#(Y%) = AMOUNT#(Y%+1)
6930 CODE%(Y%) = CODE%(Y%+1)
6940 DESCRIPT$(Y%) = DESCRIPT$(Y%+1)
6950 NEXT Y
6960 LASTENTRY = LASTENTRY - 1
6970 GOTO 6870
6980 '****************** ROUTINE TO ENTER NEW CHECKS OR DEP's OR W/D's
```

```
6990 CLS : PRINT "NEW ENTRIES SECTION " : PRINT
7000 PRINT "ENTER  1. CHECK NUMBER (1 THRU 32700) OR
7010 PRINT "           (D) FOR DEPOSIT OR
7020 PRINT "           (W) FOR WITHDRAWAL
7030 PRINT "        2. THE DATE AS MM/DD
7040 PRINT "        3. THE AMOUNT
7050 PRINT "        4. THE CATEGORY CODE
7060 PRINT "        5. THE DESCRIPTION
7070 LOCATE 25,1
7080 PRINT "ENTER A NEGATIVE CHECK NUMBER TO RETURN TO THE MENU ";
7090 LOCATE 10,1
7100 INPUT "CHECK NUMBER OR (D)EPOSIT OR (W)ITHDRAWAL - ";C$
7110 C% = VAL(C$)
7120 IF C% > 32765 THEN 6990 'out of range - try again
7130 IF C% > Ø THEN A1% = C% : GOTO 7200
7140 IF C% < Ø THEN 7830 ' neg means to exit
7150 IF ASC(C$)=68  THEN A1% = 32760 : GOTO 7200
7160 IF ASC(C$)=100 THEN A1% = 32760 : GOTO 7200
7170 IF ASC(C$)=87  THEN A1% = 32750 : GOTO 7200
7180 IF ASC(C$)=119 THEN A1% = 32750 : GOTO 7200
7190 GOTO 6990 ' invalid input
7200 LOCATE 12,1
7210 INPUT "THE DATE AS MM/DD                      - ";D$
7220 IF LEN(D$) = 5 THEN GOTO 7240
7230 A$ = STRING$(79,32) : LOCATE 12,1 : PRINT A$ : GOTO 7200
7240 A2$ = D$
7250 LOCATE 14,1
7260 INPUT "THE AMOUNT FROM $.00 TO $9,999,999.99 - ";E$
7270 IF VAL(E$) < 10000000# THEN GOTO 7290
7280 A$ = STRING$(79,32) : LOCATE 14,1 : PRINT A$ : GOTO 7250
7290 A3# = VAL(E$)
7300 LOCATE 16,1
7310 INPUT "THE CATEGORY CODE                      - ";F$
7320 IF (VAL(F$)>Ø) AND (VAL(F$)<46) THEN 7340
7330 A$ = STRING$(79,32) : LOCATE 16,1 : PRINT A$ : GOTO 7300
7340 A4% = VAL(F$)
7350 LOCATE 18,1
7360 PRINT "DESCRIPTION USING UP TO 20 CHARACTERS   - "
7370 PRINT "DO NOT ENTER DESCRIPTION PAST THE MARKER   "
7380 PRINT "                  <<<<<<<<<<<<<<<<<<<<< "
7390 INPUT G$
7400 IF LEN(G$) < 21 THEN GOTO 7420
7410 A$ = STRING$(79,32) : LOCATE 21,1 : PRINT A$ : GOTO 7350
7420 A5$ = G$
7430 GOSUB 7450
7440 GOTO 7530
7450 '******************** WAIT 2 SECONDS BEFORE CLEARING THE SCREEN
```

```
7460 FOR X = 1 TO 2
7470 Z$ = TIME$
7480 WHILE Z$ = TIME$
7490 WEND
7500 NEXT X
7510 CLS
7520 RETURN
7530 '****************** DISPLAY CHECK FOR APPROVAL
7540 LOCATE 5,1
7550 IF A1% = 32760 THEN PRINT "DEPOSIT   " : GOTO 7580
7560 IF A1% = 32750 THEN PRINT "WITHDRAWAL" : GOTO 7580
7570 PRINT A1%
7580 LOCATE 5,11
7590 PRINT A2$                              ' DATE
7600 LOCATE 5,17
7610 PRINT A5$                              ' DESCRIPTION
7620 LOCATE 5,38
7630 PRINT USING "$$#######,.##";A3#        ' AMOUNT
7640 LOCATE 5,53
7650 PRINT "CATEGORY CODE = ";A4%
7660 LOCATE 10,1
7670 PRINT "IS THIS CORRECT (Y)ES OR (N)O  - ";
7680 INPUT A$
7690 IF (A$ = "Y") OR (A$ = "y") THEN GOTO 7730
7700 CLS : PRINT ">>>>> CHECK NOT ENTERED <<<<< "
7710 GOSUB 7450                             ' delay
7720 GOTO 7000                              ' insert section / no cls
7730 '****************** ENTER CORRECT CHECK INTO FILE
7740 CATEGORY#(A4%) = CATEGORY#(A4%) + A3#
7750 LASTENTRY = LASTENTRY + 1
7760 CHECK%(LASTENTRY)      = A1%
7770 DATES$(LASTENTRY)      = A2$
7780 AMOUNT#(LASTENTRY)     = A3#
7790 CODE%(LASTENTRY)       = A4%
7800 DESCRIPT$(LASTENTRY) = A5$
7810 GOSUB 7450                             ' delay
7820 GOTO 6980                              ' top of insert section
7830 '****************** ROUTINE TO PRINT OUT ALL CHECKS
7840 CLS : PRINTOUT = 0 : SCREENOUT = 0 : BALANCE# = CATEGORY#(45)
7850 PRINT "WOULD YOU LIKE A PRINTOUT OF THE UPDATED FILE ?"
7860 INPUT "(Y)ES OR (N)O - ",A$
7870 IF MID$(A$,1,1) = "Y" THEN OPEN "LPT1:" FOR OUTPUT AS #1 : PRINTOUT = 1
7880 IF MID$(A$,1,1) = "y" THEN OPEN "LPT1:" FOR OUTPUT AS #1 : PRINTOUT = 1
7890 LOCATE 4,1
7900 PRINT "WOULD YOU LIKE A SCREEN LISTING OF THE UPDATED FILE ?"
7910 INPUT "(Y)ES OR (N)O - ",A$
7920 IF MID$(A$,1,1) = "Y" THEN OPEN "SCRN:" FOR OUTPUT AS #2 : SCREENOUT = 1
```

```
7930 IF MID$(A$,1,1) = "y" THEN OPEN "SCRN:" FOR OUTPUT AS #2 :
     SCREENOUT = 1
7940 GOSUB 7450                                          ' delay
7950 MARKER = 0
7960 FOR X = 1 TO LASTENTRY
7970 B% = CODE%(X)
7980 IF B% = 0 THEN 8020                                     '
     if printing old listing -
7990 IF MARKER = 1 THEN 8020                                 '
     if bal-fwd already printed
8000 PRINT : PRINT "BALANCE FORWARD FROM LAST UPDATE = ";CATEGORY#(45): PRINT
8010 PRINT : MARKER = 1
8020 '******************** ROUTINE TO PRINT STRING
8030 A1% = CHECK%(X)
8040 A2$ = DATES$(X)
8050 A3# = AMOUNT#(X)
8060 A4% = CODE%(X)
8070 A5$ = DESCRIPT$(X)
8080 '******************** PRINT CHECK NUMBER / DEP / W/D
8090 IF PRINTOUT <> 1 THEN 8140
8100 IF A1% < 32700 THEN PRINT #1,USING "######";A1%;
8110 IF A1% = 32760 THEN PRINT #1,"DEP    ";
8120 IF A1% = 32750 THEN PRINT #1,"W/D    ";
8130 PRINT #1," ";
8140 IF SCREENOUT <> 1 THEN 8190
8150 IF A1% < 32700 THEN PRINT #2,USING "######";A1%;
8160 IF A1% = 32760 THEN PRINT #2,"DEP    ";
8170 IF A1% = 32750 THEN PRINT #2,"W/D    ";
8180 PRINT #2," ";
8190 '******************** PRINT DATE
8200 IF PRINTOUT <> 1 THEN 8220
8210 PRINT #1,A2$;" ";
8220 IF SCREENOUT <> 1 THEN 8240
8230 PRINT #2,A2$;" ";
8240 '******************** PRINT DESCRIPTION
8250 C$ = SPACE$(20) : LSET C$ = A5$
8260 IF PRINTOUT <> 1 THEN 8280
8270 PRINT #1,C$;" ";
8280 IF SCREENOUT <> 1 THEN 8300
8290 PRINT #2,C$;" ";
8300 GOTO 8370
8310 '******************** PRINT SPACES IF NO DESCRIPTION
8320 C$ = SPACE$(20)
8330 IF PRINTOUT <> 1 THEN 8350
8340 PRINT #1,C$;" ";
8350 IF SCREENOUT <> 1 THEN 8370
8360 PRINT #2,C$;" ";
```

```
8370 '***************** PRINT CATEGORY CODE
8380 IF PRINTOUT <> 1 THEN 8410
8390 PRINT #1,USING "##";A4%;
8400 PRINT #1," ";
8410 IF SCREENOUT <> 1 THEN 8440
8420 PRINT #2,USING "##";A4%;
8430 PRINT #2," ";
8440 GOTO 8500
8450 '***************** PRINT SPACES IF NO CATEGORY CODE
8460 IF PRINTOUT <> 1 THEN 8480
8470 PRINT #1,"   "; ' 3 SPACES
8480 IF SCREENOUT <> 1 THEN 8500
8490 PRINT #2,"   "; ' 3 SPACES
8500 '***************** PRINT AMOUNT
8510 IF PRINTOUT <> 1 THEN 8530
8520 PRINT #1,USING "$$########.## ";A3#;
8530 IF SCREENOUT <> 1 THEN 8550
8540 PRINT #2,USING "$$########.## ";A3#;
8550 '***************** PRINT BALANCE
8560 IF A4% = 0 THEN 8630
8570 IF A1% = 32760 THEN BALANCE# = BALANCE# + A3# : GOTO 8590
8580 BALANCE# = BALANCE# - A3#
8590 IF PRINTOUT <> 1 THEN 8610
8600 PRINT #1,USING "$$#########.##- ";BALANCE#;
8610 IF SCREENOUT <> 1 THEN 8630
8620 PRINT #2,USING "$$#########.##- ";BALANCE#;
8630 '***************** PRINT CARRIAGE RETURN AND END LOOP
8640 IF PRINTOUT <> 1 THEN 8660
8650 PRINT #1," "
8660 IF SCREENOUT <> 1 THEN 8680
8670 PRINT #2," "
8680 NEXT X
8690 '
8700 '***************** PRINT FINAL BALANCE
8710 PRINT
8720 IF PRINTOUT <> 1 THEN 8740
8730 PRINT #1,"FINAL BALANCE = ";BALANCE#
8740 IF SCREENOUT <> 1 THEN 8760
8750 PRINT #2,"FINAL BALANCE = ";BALANCE#
8760 '
8770 PRINT : PRINT
8780 PRINT "PRESS ENTER TO CONTINUE - "
8790 PRINT : PRINT : PRINT
8800 POKE 106,0
8810 A$ = INKEY$ : IF A$ = "" THEN 8810
8820 '
8830 IF PRINTOUT <> 1 THEN 8870
```

```
8840 FOR X = 1 TO 45
8850 PRINT #1,A$(X),CATEGORY#(X)
8860 NEXT X
8870 IF SCREENOUT <> 1 THEN 8930
8880 FOR X = 1 TO 45
8890 PRINT #2,A$(X),CATEGORY#(X)
8900 NEXT X
8910 '
8920 PRINT : PRINT
8930 PRINT "PRESS ENTER TO RETURN TO MENU - "
8940 A$ = INKEY$ : IF A$ = "" THEN 8940
8950 GOTO 100
```

GRAPH MASTER

This program is a complete system for the creation, storage, and retrieval of computer generated graphs. In the creation section, you can generate graphs of four major types: a line graph, a bar graph, a horizontal bar graph, and a circle graph as shown in Figs. 8-2 through 8-5. Creation consists of entering the title of the graph (2 lines), labels for the two axis, and labels and values for the data to be plotted.

After this information has been entered, the program allows you to generate the graphs. At this point, you may select any of the four graph types, and if it is required, the system will ask for maximum and minimum values to scale the graph with. The program will then generate the graph with the information given. At this time, you have several options.

First, you might wish to see what the graph would look like in a different format. After the graph has been completed, press the enter key to return to the menu, and enter the number for the new graph type. The new graph will be generated without your having to reenter all of the information.

Second, you might wish to rescale the graph to enhance some detail of interest. To accomplish this, press the enter key to return to the menu, and then select the same graph type as before. When the program asks for the maximum and minimum values for the graph, enter the new values. For instance, if the graph was a chart of grades on a test and all scores were in the 90 to 100 range, simply enter 90 for the new minimum and 100 for the new maximum. This rescaling will create a graph that is easy to read, and the differences will be easier to determine.

Third, you might wish to change a label or a data value on the graph. Simply press the enter key to return to the menu for the graph generator section, and then enter 1 to return to the main *Graph Master* menu. From the main menu, change whatever you wish and regenerate the graph.

Fourth, you might want to save the graph. To accomplish this, return to the main menu and select 3. The data that makes up the graph will be written out to cassette or disk so you can recreate the graph at any time. If you have a cassette-based system, you might change the sections of the program that read and write cassette data to accept data under only one filename. Lines such as:

OPEN "PLOTDATA " FOR OUTPUT AS #1

and

OPEN "PLOTDATA " FOR INPUT AS #1

for the input and output sections of the program will allow you to create and save graphs to a cassette and then read them in without having to reenter a filename each time. If you make these changes, remove the lines that ask for a filename input.

After you have created and saved a number of graphs, you can view them again at any time. Simply run the program and enter 2 to input data from cassette or diskette into the program. After you enter the

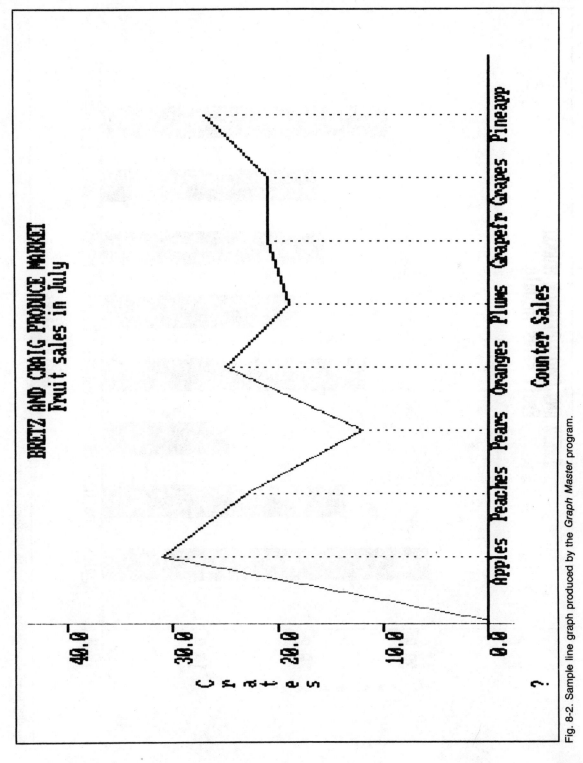

Fig. 8-2. Sample line graph produced by the *Graph Master* program.

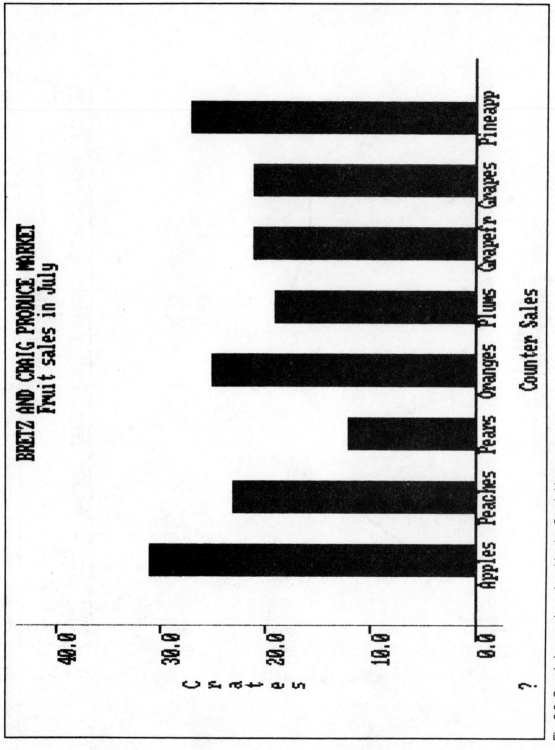

Fig. 8-3. Sample bar graph produced by the *Graph Master* program.

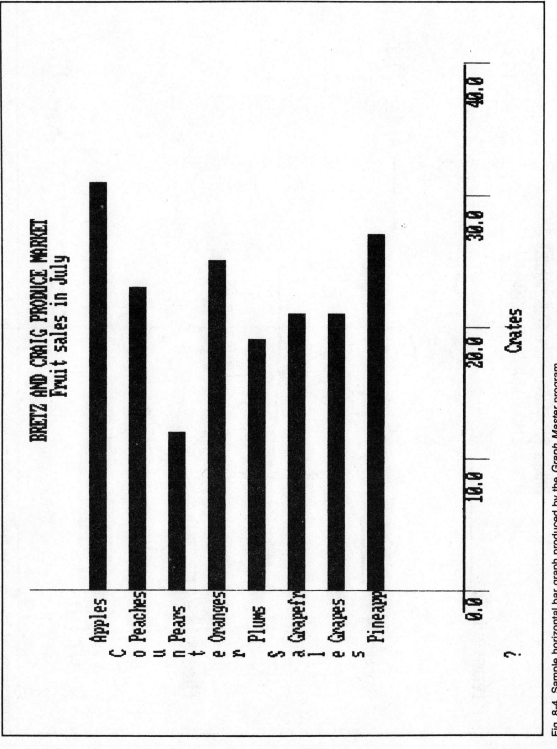

Fig. 8-4. Sample horizontal bar graph produced by the *Graph Master* program.

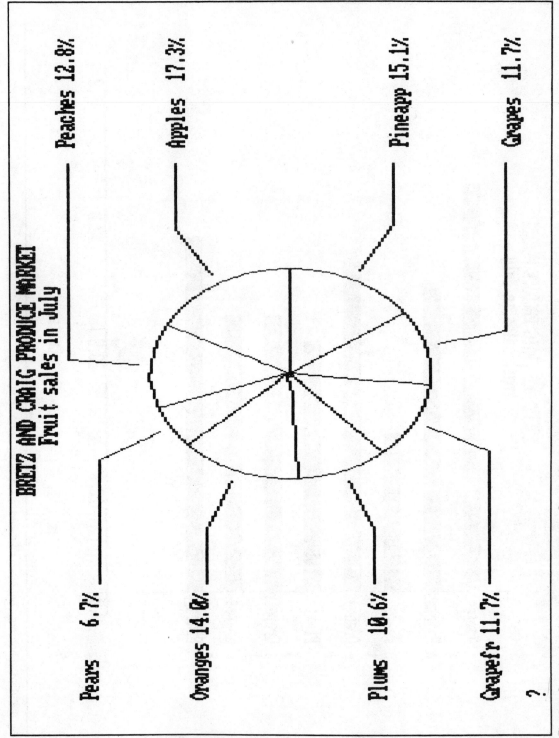

BRETZ AND CRAIG PRODUCE MARKET
Fruit sales in July

Peaches 12.8%

Apples 17.3%

Pineapp 15.1%

Grapes 11.7%

Pears 6.7%

Oranges 14.0%

Plums 10.6%

Grapefr 11.7%

?

Fig. 8-5. Sample circle graph produced by the *Graph Master* program.

filename for the graph you want, the program will immediately load and generate the graph. When you are ready to continue, simply press the enter key, and the program will ask if you want a different graph or if you want to return to the menu.

Program Operation

Graph Master is a menu driven, modular program. Graphs can be created with or without labels or titles. If labels or data are being reentered, you may keep selected values and labels by simply pressing the enter key instead of reentering the information.

When you are entering the data and labels, the program will limit you to a certain number of characters for your input so that the information can be displayed clearly on the screen. Thus, if you are labelling data points, you are limited to 35 entries (using labels of one character and one separating space), but if you are not using labels, you can have up to 200 data points. The labels can be from 1 to seven characters in length, depending on the numbers of data points. The program will compute the number to keep the display neat.

Finally, standard programming techniques were used so that if a problem developed in the program, it would be easy to trace it to the section in error and correct it.

Although the program was not set up to produce graphs of functions, they are easy to implement outside of the program.

1. Load the program and type RUN
2. Press the break key
3. Enter this . . . . (for example the sine function)

FOR B = 1 TO 200 : DATAVAL (B) = SIN(B/50) : NEXT B : GOTO 240

(Enter the above as one line.)

From the menu select 4 to enter data values and labels. Set up for . . .

1. No Labels
2. 200 Data Points

and answer the prompt for data with END in capital letters. Then proceed to create a line or bar graph.

Because of the complexity of the program, you will require 48K of memory with a cassette-based system and 64K of memory with a disk-based system. The listing itself requires about 24K.

```
100 '***********************************************************************
110 '**                      GRAPH MASTER                               **
120 '**              CREATES GRAPHS FOR DISPLAY                         **
130 '**                                                                 **
140 '**          VERSION 1.1                    JULY 14, 1982           **
150 '**                                                                 **
160 '***********************************************************************
170 '
180 SCREEN 2 : KEY OFF : OPTION BASE 1 : GOSUB 500
190 '
200 '***********************************************************************
210 '**   THIS SECTION PRINTS THE MENU FOR THE SELECTIONS               **
220 '***********************************************************************
230 '
240 SCREEN 0 : WIDTH 80 : CLS
```

```
250 LOCATE 2,24 : PRINT "****************"
260 LOCATE 3,24 : PRINT "* GRAPH MASTER *"
270 LOCATE 4,24 : PRINT "****************"
280 LOCATE 7,20 : PRINT "1 = Labels For Graph
290 LOCATE 8,20 : PRINT "2 = Input Data From Cassette Or Disk
300 LOCATE 9,20 : PRINT "3 = Output Data To Cassette Or Disk
310 LOCATE 10,20 : PRINT "4 = Enter Data Values And Labels
320 LOCATE 11,20 : PRINT "5 = Generate Graphs
330 LOCATE 17,1 : PRINT "ENTER SELECTION AT DASH   (1 THRU 5 ONLY)
340 LOCATE 18,1 : PRINT "USE THE ";CHR$(27);" (BACKSPACE) KEY TO BACKSPACE
350 ROW = 18 : COLUMN = 50 : LENGTH = 1
360 GOSUB 30000
370 IF (B$>CHR$(48)) AND (B$<CHR$(54)) THEN B = ASC(B$) - 48 : GOTO 420
380 COLOR 23 : LOCATE 14,1 : PRINT "ERROR IN INPUT - PLEASE SELECT AGAIN
390 FOR X = 1 TO 2000 : NEXT
400 COLOR 7 : LOCATE 14,1 : PRINT "                                        "
410 GOTO 350
420 ON B GOTO 1000,2000,3000,4000,6000
500 '
510 '*****************************************************************************
520 '**   THIS SECTION INITIALIZES THE VARIABLES IN A SUBROUTINE         **
530 '*****************************************************************************
540 '
550 DEFSTR A : DIM A(100),DATAVAL(200),DATALABEL$(36)
560 MAXCOUNT = 20 : PRINTLABELS = 1 : DATAPOINTS = 12
570 ATITLE1 = "" : ATITLE2 = "" : ATITLE3 = "" : ATITLE4 = ""
580 RETURN
1000 '
1010 '*****************************************************************************
1020 '**   This Section Allows You To Enter The Labels For The Graph       **
1030 '*****************************************************************************
1040 '
1050 CLS
1060 PRINT "This Section Sets Up The Labels For The Graph
1070 PRINT "------------------------------------------------
1080 LOCATE 4,1
1090 PRINT "If You Would Like To Keep The Present Label, Simply Press <Return>
1100 PRINT "Else,  Enter The New Label On The Dashes     --------
1110 '
1120 LOCATE 7,1
1130 PRINT "The First Line Of The Title Is -          ";
1140 PRINT ATITLE1
1150 ROW = 9 : COLUMN = 1 : LENGTH = 40 : GOSUB 30010
1160 IF B$ = "" THEN 1180
1170 ATITLE1 = B$
1180 '
1190 LOCATE 11,1
```

```
1200 PRINT "The Second Line Of The Title Is -         ";
1210 PRINT ATITLE2
1220 ROW = 13 : COLUMN = 1 : LENGTH = 40 : GOSUB 30010
1230 IF B$ = "" THEN 1250
1240 ATITLE2 = B$
1250 '
1260 LOCATE 16,1
1270 PRINT "The Label For The Data Catagories Is -  ";
1280 PRINT ATITLE3
1290 ROW = 18 : COLUMN = 1 : LENGTH = 40 : GOSUB 30010
1300 IF B$ = "" THEN 1320
1310 ATITLE3 = B$
1320 '
1330 LOCATE 21,1
1340 PRINT "The Label For The Data Values Is -       ";
1350 PRINT ATITLE4
1360 ROW = 23 : COLUMN = 1 : LENGTH = 40 : GOSUB 30010
1370 IF B$ = "" THEN 1390
1380 ATITLE4 = B$
1390 '
1400 GOTO 240          ' RETURN TO MENU
2000 '
2010 '****************************************************************************
2020 '**   This Section Reads Data Input From Cassette Or Disk              **
2030 '****************************************************************************
2040 '
2050 CLS : SCREEN 2
2060 INPUT "ENTER FILENAME INCLUDING EXTENSIONS " ; FILEDATA$ : CLS
2070 OPEN FILEDATA$ FOR INPUT AS #1
2080 INPUT#1,ATITLE1,ATITLE2
2090 INPUT#1,ATITLE3,ATITLE4
2100 INPUT#1,DATAPOINTS,GRAPHTYPE,PRINTLABELS,MAXVAL,MINVAL,LABELLENGTH
2110 FOR X = 1 TO DATAPOINTS
2120 INPUT#1,DATAVAL(X)
2130 IF PRINTLABELS = 1 THEN 2140 ELSE 2150
2140 INPUT#1,DATALABEL$(X)
2150 NEXT X : CLOSE
2160 '
2170 ON GRAPHTYPE GOSUB 8070,9070,10070,12070
2180 '
2190 CLS
2200 PRINT "PRESS 1 FOR MENU"
2210 PRINT "PRESS 2 FOR NEXT GRAPH"
2220 A$ = INKEY$ : IF A$ = "" THEN 2220
2230 IF VAL(A$) = 1 THEN GOTO 240
2240 IF VAL(A$) = 2 THEN GOTO 2050
2250 GOTO 2180
```

```
3000 '
3010 '***********************************************************************
3020 '**    This Section Writes Data Out To Cassette Or Disk              **
3030 '***********************************************************************
3040 '
3050 CLS : SCREEN 2
3060 INPUT "ENTER FILENAME INCLUDING EXTENSIONS " ; FILEDATA$
3070 OPEN FILEDATA$ FOR OUTPUT AS #1
3080 PRINT#1,CHR$(34);ATITLE1;CHR$(34);CHR$(34);ATITLE2;CHR$(34)
3090 PRINT#1,CHR$(34);ATITLE3;CHR$(34);CHR$(34);ATITLE4;CHR$(34)
3100 PRINT#1,DATAPOINTS;GRAPHTYPE;PRINTLABELS,MAXVAL,MINVAL,LABELLENGTH
3110 FOR X = 1 TO DATAPOINTS
3120 PRINT#1,DATAVAL(X)
3130 IF PRINTLABELS = 1 THEN 3140 ELSE 3150
3140 PRINT#1,CHR$(34);DATALABEL$(X);CHR$(34)
3150 NEXT X
3160 '
3170 LOCATE 25,1 : INPUT "PRESS ENTER TO RETURN TO MENU -";A$
3180 CLOSE : GOTO 240
4000 '
4010 '***********************************************************************
4020 '**    This Section Gets The Data For The Graph                      **
4030 '***********************************************************************
4040 '
4050 CLS
4060 LOCATE 1,25 : PRINT "Data Entry
4070 LOCATE 2,25 : PRINT "---- -----
4080 LOCATE 5,1
4090 PRINT "Here We Will Enter The Data And Their Corresponding Labels
4100 PRINT
4110 PRINT "If You Would Like To Keep The Present Values, Simply Press
      <Return>
4120 PRINT "Else,  Enter The New Values On The Dashes    ---------
4130 LOCATE 10,1
4140 PRINT "Would You Like To Have Labels For The Data Entries ?
4150 PRINT "For Example - (1981 or Hogs) etc.
4160 PRINT "Presently You Are Set Up For ";
4170 IF PRINTLABELS = 1 THEN PRINT "USING Labels" ELSE PRINT
      "NOT USING Labels
4180 LOCATE 14,1 : PRINT "Yes = 1
4190 LOCATE 15,1 : PRINT "No  = 2
4200 ROW = 15 : COLUMN = 10 : LENGTH = 1 : GOSUB 30010
4210 IF B$ = "" THEN 4230
4220 IF (ASC(B$)-48) = 1 THEN PRINTLABELS = 1 ELSE PRINTLABELS = 2
4230 LOCATE 17,1
4240 PRINT "Please Enter The Number Of Data Points To Be Graphed
4250 PRINT "This Number May Be From 1-35 If You Are Using Labels Or
```

```
4260 PRINT "                    From 1-200 If You Are Not.
4270 PRINT "Presently You Are Set Up For ";DATAPOINTS;" Data Points.
4280 PRINT ">>>>>>>"
4290 ROW = 21 : COLUMN = 10 : LENGTH = 3 : GOSUB 30010
4300 IF B$ = "" THEN 4410
4310 B = VAL(B$) : IF B < 1 THEN B = 500
4320 IF (PRINTLABELS = 1) AND (B > 35) THEN 4330 ELSE 4360
4330 LOCATE 23,1 : PRINT "FROM 1 TO 35 WHEN USING LABELS (ONLY) "
4340 FOR X = 1 TO 1000 : NEXT X
4350 LOCATE 23,1 : PRINT "                                        ":GOTO 4230
4360 IF (PRINTLABELS = 2) AND (B > 200) THEN 4370 ELSE 4400
4370 LOCATE 23,1 : PRINT "FROM 1 TO 200 WITHOUT LABELS (ONLY) "
4380 FOR X = 1 TO 1000 : NEXT X
4390 LOCATE 23,1 : PRINT "                                        ":GOTO 4230
4400 DATAPOINTS = B : GOTO 4420
4410 IF (PRINTLABELS = 1) AND (DATAPOINTS > 35) THEN 4330
4420 LOCATE 25,1
4430 PRINT "Press Enter To Continue ";:INPUT A$
4440 '
4450 CLS
4460 PRINT "Enter The Value Of The Data - <Or>
4470 PRINT
4480 PRINT "Enter The Word <END> If This Is The Last Data
4490 PRINT "        And You Would Like To Return To The Menu - <Or>
4500 PRINT
4510 PRINT "Enter The Word <EDIT> If You Would Like To Change
4520 PRINT "        Some Data Values (Allows You To Skip Around) - <Or>
4530 PRINT
4540 PRINT "If You Would Like To Keep The Present Values, Simply Press
     <Return>
4550 LOCATE 17,1
4560 PRINT "Next -
4570 PRINT
4580 PRINT "Enter The Label For This Data Element - <Or>
4590 PRINT
4600 PRINT "If You Would Like To Keep The Present Labels, Simply Press
     <Return>
4610 PRINT
4620 LOCATE 25,1 : PRINT "PRESS ENTER TO CONTINUE - ";:INPUT A$
4630 '
4640 CLS
4650 LOCATE 25,1 : PRINT "Number    Data ";
4660 LOCATE 25,21 : IF PRINTLABELS = 1 THEN PRINT "Label ";
4670 LOCATE 25,40 : PRINT "<END> or <EDIT> on data entry";
4680 '
4690 COUNT = 1
4700 LABELLENGTH = FIX(65/DATAPOINTS )-1
```

```
4710 IF LABELLENGTH > 7 THEN LABELLENGTH = 7
4720 IF (LABELLENGTH < 1) AND (DATAPOINTS < 35) THEN LABELLENGTH = 1
4730 LOCATE 22,1 : PRINT USING "###";COUNT
4740 '
4750 ROW = 22 : COLUMN = 11 : LENGTH = 4 : GOSUB 30000
4760 IF B$ = "END" THEN 240
4770 IF B$ = "EDIT" THEN 4810
4780 IF B$ = "" THEN 4880
4790 GOTO 4850
4800 '
4810 LOCATE 22,1 : PRINT "                              ";
4820 LOCATE 22,1 : INPUT "Edit Which Number - "; COUNT
4825 LOCATE 22,1 : PRINT "                              ";
4830 GOTO 4730
4840 '
4850 B = VAL(B$) : IF B < 0 THEN B = 0
4860 DATAVAL(COUNT) = B
4870 '
4880 LOCATE 22,11 : PRINT USING "####.##";DATAVAL(COUNT);
4890 '
4900 IF PRINTLABELS = 2 THEN 4980
4905 IF LABELLENGTH < 1 THEN 4980
4910 ROW = 22 : COLUMN = 21 : LENGTH = LABELLENGTH : GOSUB 30000
4920 IF B$ = "" THEN 4950
4930 DATALABEL$(COUNT) = B$
4940 '
4950 LOCATE 22,21 : PRINT "          ";
4960 LOCATE 22,21 : PRINT DATALABEL$(COUNT);
4970 '
4980 PRINT : PRINT : PRINT
4990 IF COUNT < DATAPOINTS THEN COUNT = COUNT + 1 : GOTO 4730
5000 '
5010 LOCATE 25,1 : PRINT "                                              ";
5015 LOCATE 25,40 : PRINT "                          ";
5020 LOCATE 25,1 : INPUT "Press Enter To Continue ";A$ : GOTO 240
6000 '
6010 '******************************************************************
6020 '**    This Section Generates The Graphs                        **
6030 '******************************************************************
6040 '
6050 SCREEN 2 : WIDTH 80 : CLS
6060 LOCATE 2,24 : PRINT "********************"
6070 LOCATE 3,24 : PRINT "* GRAPH GENERATOR *"
6080 LOCATE 4,24 : PRINT "********************"
6090 LOCATE 7,20 : PRINT "1 = Return To Main Menu (Save,Change,etc) Graphs
6100 LOCATE 8,20 : PRINT
6110 LOCATE 9,20 : PRINT "2 = Line Graph
```

```
6120 LOCATE 10,20 : PRINT "3 = Bar Graph
6130 LOCATE 11,20 : PRINT "4 = Horizontal Bar Graph (Max 20 Data Points)
6140 LOCATE 12,20 : PRINT "5 = Circle Graph
6150 LOCATE 17,1 : PRINT "ENTER SELECTION AT DASH  (1 THRU 5 ONLY)
6160 LOCATE 18,1 : PRINT "USE THE ";CHR$(27);" (BACKSPACE) KEY TO BACKSPACE
6170 ROW = 18 : COLUMN = 50 : LENGTH = 1
6180 GOSUB 30000
6190 IF (B$>CHR$(48)) AND (B$<CHR$(54)) THEN B = ASC(B$) - 48 : GOTO 6240
6200 LOCATE 14,1 : PRINT "ERROR IN INPUT - PLEASE SELECT AGAIN
6210 FOR X = 1 TO 2000 : NEXT
6220 LOCATE 14,1 : PRINT "                                          "
6230 GOTO 6170
6240 IF B = 1 GOTO 240
6250 ON B GOSUB 240,8000,9000,10000,12000
6260 GOTO 6000
7000 '
7010 '****************************************************************************
7020 '**   This Section Gets Minimum And Maximum Values For The Scales     **
7030 '****************************************************************************
7040 '
7050 KEY OFF : SCREEN 2 : CLS
7060 '
7070 '** GET MAX AND MIN VALUES OF INPUT ************************************
7080 MAXVAL = DATAVAL(1) : MINVAL = DATAVAL(1)
7090 FOR X = 1 TO DATAPOINTS
7100 IF (DATAVAL(X) > MAXVAL) THEN MAXVAL = DATAVAL(X)
7110 IF (DATAVAL(X) < MINVAL) THEN MINVAL = DATAVAL(X)
7120 NEXT X
7130 '
7140 '** CALCULATE A MAX VALUE FOR THE GRAPH LABEL : SET MIN = 0 ***********
7150 '
7160 IF MAXVAL < 10000 THEN MAX =  10000
7170 IF MAXVAL <  8000 THEN MAX =   8000
7180 IF MAXVAL <  6000 THEN MAX =   6000
7190 IF MAXVAL <  4000 THEN MAX =   4000
7200 IF MAXVAL <  2000 THEN MAX =   2000
7210 IF MAXVAL <  1000 THEN MAX =   1000
7220 IF MAXVAL <   800 THEN MAX =    800
7230 IF MAXVAL <   600 THEN MAX =    600
7240 IF MAXVAL <   400 THEN MAX =    400
7250 IF MAXVAL <   200 THEN MAX =    200
7260 IF MAXVAL <   100 THEN MAX =    100
7270 IF MAXVAL <    80 THEN MAX =     80
7280 IF MAXVAL <    60 THEN MAX =     60
7290 IF MAXVAL <    40 THEN MAX =     40
7300 IF MAXVAL <    20 THEN MAX =     20
7310 IF MAXVAL <    10 THEN MAX =     10
```

```
7320 IF MAXVAL <      8 THEN MAX =       8
7330 IF MAXVAL <      6 THEN MAX =       6
7340 IF MAXVAL <      4 THEN MAX =       4
7350 IF MAXVAL <      2 THEN MAX =       2
7360 IF MAXVAL <      1 THEN MAX =       1
7370 MIN = Ø
7380 '
7390 '** GET MAX AND MIN VALUES FOR GRAPH LABEL ****************************
7400 '
7410 PRINT "The Largest Entered Data Value Was -   ";MAXVAL
7420 PRINT "The Smallest Entered Data Value Was - ";MINVAL
7430 PRINT
7440 PRINT "The Calculated Values For The Maximum And Minimum Graph Scales
7450 PRINT "To Give The Finished Graph A Balanced Look Is -
7460 PRINT
7470 PRINT "Maximum Graph Value = ";MAX
7480 PRINT "Minimum Graph Value = ";MIN
7490 PRINT
7500 PRINT "Enter The Maximum Value For The Graph Scales <Or>
7510 PRINT "Press Enter For The Computed Value >>>";
7520 ROW = 11 : COLUMN = 40 : LENGTH = 5 : GOSUB 30000
7530 IF B$ = "" THEN MAXVAL = MAX : GOTO 7560
7540 B = VAL(B$) : IF B > MAXVAL THEN MAXVAL = B
7550 '
7560 LOCATE 11,40 : PRINT "             "
7570 LOCATE 11,40 : PRINT USING "#####";MAXVAL
7580 '
7590 LOCATE 15,1
7600 PRINT "Enter The Minimum Value For The Graph Scales <Or>
7610 PRINT "Press Enter For The Computed Value >>>"
7620 ROW = 16 : COLUMN = 40 : LENGTH = 5 : GOSUB 30000
7630 IF B$ = "" THEN MINVAL = MIN : GOTO 7660
7640 B = VAL(B$) : IF B < MINVAL THEN MINVAL = B
7650 IF MINVAL < Ø THEN MINVAL = Ø
7660 LOCATE 16,40 : PRINT "             "
7670 LOCATE 16,40 : PRINT USING "#####";MINVAL
7680 '
7690 LOCATE 25,1 : PRINT "Press Enter To Continue -";
7700 INPUT A$ : CLS :RETURN
7710 '
8000 '
8010 '**************************************************************************
8020 '**   This Section Draws A Line Graph                              **
8030 '**************************************************************************
8040 '
8050 KEY OFF : SCREEN 2 : CLS : GRAPHTYPE = 1
8060 GOSUB 7000
```

```
8070 GOSUB 15000
8080 '
8090 LINE (63,175)-(63,175)
8100 SCALEFACTOR = (MAXVAL-MINVAL)/160
8110 OLDX = 67 : OLDY = 175
8120 '
8130 LABELDISTANCE = LABELLENGTH + 1
8140 PLOTDISTANCE = LABELDISTANCE * 8
8150 IF DATAPOINTS > 35 THEN PLOTDISTANCE = 575 \ DATAPOINTS
8160 FOR PLOTPOINTS = 1 TO DATAPOINTS
8170 NEWX = OLDX + PLOTDISTANCE
8180 NEWY = 175 - (DATAVAL(PLOTPOINTS)-MINVAL)/SCALEFACTOR
8190 LINE (OLDX,OLDY)-(NEWX,NEWY)
8200 FOR Y = NEWY TO 175 STEP 3 : PSET (NEWX,Y) : NEXT Y
8210 OLDX = NEWX : OLDY = NEWY
8220 IF PRINTLABELS = 2 THEN 8260
8230 LABELPOSITION = 9+(LABELDISTANCE*PLOTPOINTS)-LEN(DATALABEL$
     (PLOTPOINTS))/2
8240 LOCATE 23,LABELPOSITION
8250 PRINT DATALABEL$(PLOTPOINTS);
8260 NEXT PLOTPOINTS
8270 LOCATE 25,1 : INPUT A$ : RETURN
9000 '
9010 '****************************************************************
9020 '**   This Section Draws A Bar Graph                          **
9030 '****************************************************************
9040 '
9050 KEY OFF : SCREEN 2 : CLS : GRAPHTYPE = 2
9060 GOSUB 7000
9070 GOSUB 15000
9080 '
9090 SCALEFACTOR = (MAXVAL-MINVAL)/160
9100 OLDX = 67 : OLDY = 175
9110 '
9120 LABELDISTANCE = LABELLENGTH + 1
9130 PLOTDISTANCE = LABELDISTANCE * 8
9140 IF DATAPOINTS > 35 THEN PLOTDISTANCE = 575 \ DATAPOINTS
9150 FOR PLOTPOINTS = 1 TO DATAPOINTS
9160 NEWX = OLDX + PLOTDISTANCE
9170 NEWY = 175 - (DATAVAL(PLOTPOINTS)-MINVAL)/SCALEFACTOR
9180 FOR X = -(PLOTDISTANCE/4) TO (PLOTDISTANCE/4)
9190 LINE (NEWX-X,NEWY)-(NEWX-X,175)
9200 NEXT X
9210 OLDX = NEWX : OLDY = NEWY
9220 IF PRINTLABELS = 2 THEN 9260
9230 LABELPOSITION = 9+(LABELDISTANCE*PLOTPOINTS)-LEN(DATALABEL$
     (PLOTPOINTS))/2
```

```
9240 LOCATE 23,LABELPOSITION
9250 PRINT DATALABEL$(PLOTPOINTS);
9260 NEXT PLOTPOINTS
9270 LOCATE 25,1 : INPUT A$ : RETURN
10000 '
10010 '****************************************************************************
10020 '**    This Section Draws A Horizontal Bar Graph (20 Bars Maximun)      **
10030 '****************************************************************************
10040 '
10050 KEY OFF : SCREEN 2 : CLS : GRAPHTYPE = 3
10060 GOSUB 7000
10070 '
10080 '
10090 LINE (72,0)-(72,185) : LINE (48,175)-(636,175)
10100 LOCATE 1,25+(40-LEN(ATITLE1))/2 : PRINT ATITLE1;
10110 LOCATE 2,25+(40-LEN(ATITLE2))/2 : PRINT ATITLE2;
10120 LOCATE 25,25+(40-LEN(ATITLE4))/2 : PRINT ATITLE4;
10130 '
10140 '** FOR THE VERTICAL AXIS, CENTER THE LABEL WITHIN 18 CHAR OF BLANKS
10150 A$ = "" : L = LEN(ATITLE3) : L1 = (18-L)/2
10160 FOR X = 1 TO L1 : A$ = A$ + " " : NEXT X
10170 A$ = A$ + ATITLE3
10180 FOR X = LEN(A$) TO 18 : A$ = A$ + " " : NEXT X
10190 '
10200 '** NOW PRINT THE LABEL ON THE LEFT OF THE SCREEN
10210 FOR X = 3 TO 20
10220 LOCATE X,1 : PRINT MID$(A$,X-2,1);
10230 NEXT X
10240 '
10250 SCALEFACTOR = (MAXVAL - MINVAL) / 564
10260 '
10270 '**   DRAW OUT THE BARS (SPACED PROPERLY OF COURSE)
10280 GOSUB 10770
10290 '
10300 LINE (213,175)-(213,185) : LINE (354,175)-(354,185)
10310 LINE (495,175)-(495,185) : LINE (638,175)-(638,185)
10320 '
10330 '** CALCULATE OUT HOW TO PRINT THE VERTICAL SCALE AND PRINT IT
10340 '**
10350 '** IF MAXVAL >= 10000 THEN PRINT AS XXXXX
10360 '** IF 1000 >= MAXVAL > 10000 THEN PRINT AS XXXX
10370 '** IF  100 >= MAXVAL >  1000 THEN PRINT AS  XXX.X
10380 '** IF   10 >= MAXVAL >   100 THEN PRINT AS   XX.XX
10390 '** IF    1 >= MAXVAL >    10 THEN PRINT AS    X.XXX
10400 '** IF    0 >= MAXVAL >     1 THEN PRINT AS    0.XXX
10410 '**
10420 MAX = 2 + LOG(MAXVAL)/LOG(10) ' LOG BASE 10 = LN(X)/LN(10)
```

282

```
10430 IF MAX < 1 THEN MAX = 1
10440 IF MAX > 6 THEN MAX = 6
10450 ON MAX GOTO 10460,10460,10530,10600,10670,10670
10460 '
10470 '** VALUES FROM 0.001 TO 9.999
10480 LOCATE 23,74 : PRINT USING "#.###";MAXVAL;
10490 LOCATE 23,56 : PRINT USING "#.###";(MAXVAL - (MAXVAL - MINVAL) * .25);
10500 LOCATE 23,39 : PRINT USING "#.###";(MAXVAL - (MAXVAL - MINVAL) * .5);
10510 LOCATE 23,21 : PRINT USING "#.###";(MAXVAL - (MAXVAL - MINVAL) * .75);
10520 LOCATE 23,4  : PRINT USING "#.###";MINVAL; : GOTO 10740
10530 '
10540 '** VALUES FROM 10.00 TO 99.99
10550 LOCATE 23,74 : PRINT USING "##.##";MAXVAL;
10560 LOCATE 23,56 : PRINT USING "##.##";(MAXVAL - (MAXVAL - MINVAL) * .25);
10570 LOCATE 23,39 : PRINT USING "##.##";(MAXVAL - (MAXVAL - MINVAL) * .5);
10580 LOCATE 23,21 : PRINT USING "##.##";(MAXVAL - (MAXVAL - MINVAL) * .75);
10590 LOCATE 23,4  : PRINT USING "##.##";MINVAL; : GOTO 10740
10600 '
10610 '** VALUES FROM 100.0 TO 999.9
10620 LOCATE 23,74 : PRINT USING "###.#";MAXVAL;
10630 LOCATE 23,56 : PRINT USING "###.#";(MAXVAL - (MAXVAL - MINVAL) * .25);
10640 LOCATE 23,39 : PRINT USING "###.#";(MAXVAL - (MAXVAL - MINVAL) * .5);
10650 LOCATE 23,21 : PRINT USING "###.#";(MAXVAL - (MAXVAL - MINVAL) * .75);
10660 LOCATE 23,4  : PRINT USING "###.#";MINVAL; : GOTO 10740
10670 '
10680 '** VALUES FROM 1000 TO 99999
10690 LOCATE 23,74 : PRINT USING "#####";MAXVAL;
10700 LOCATE 23,56 : PRINT USING "#####";(MAXVAL - (MAXVAL - MINVAL) * .25);
10710 LOCATE 23,39 : PRINT USING "#####";(MAXVAL - (MAXVAL - MINVAL) * .5);
10720 LOCATE 23,21 : PRINT USING "#####";(MAXVAL - (MAXVAL - MINVAL) * .75);
10730 LOCATE 23,4  : PRINT USING "#####";MINVAL; : GOTO 10740
10740 '
10750 LOCATE 25,1 : INPUT A$ : RETURN
10760 '
10770 '** DRAW THE HORIZONTAL BARS
10780 '
10790 BAR = DATAPOINTS
10800 IF BAR > 20 THEN BAR = 20
10810 ON BAR GOTO 10840,10840,10840,10970,11110,11240,11240,11370,11370,11370
10820 '** IF HERE THEN 11 > BAR > 21
10830 GOTO 11500
10840 '
10850 '**   DRAWS BARS FOR 1 TO 3 ELEMENTS
10860 '
10870 SCALEFACTOR = (MAXVAL - MINVAL) / 564
10880 FOR X = 1 TO BAR
10890 LOCATE 2+X*6,3 : PRINT USING "\      \";DATALABEL$(X);
```

```
10900 BAR = (DATAVAL(X)-MINVAL)/SCALEFACTOR
10910 IF BAR < Ø THEN BAR = Ø
10920 FOR Y = (8 + X*48) TO (14 + X*48)
10930 LINE (72,Y)-(72+BAR,Y)
10940 NEXT Y
10950 NEXT X
10960 RETURN
10970 '
10980 '**  DRAWS BARS FOR 4 ELEMENTS
10990 '
11000 SCALEFACTOR = (MAXVAL - MINVAL) / 564
11010 FOR X = 1 TO BAR
11020 LOCATE 1+X*5,3 : PRINT USING "\      \";DATALABEL$(X);
11030 BAR = (DATAVAL(X)-MINVAL)/SCALEFACTOR
11040 IF BAR < Ø THEN BAR = Ø
11050 FOR Y = (X*40) TO (6 + X*40)
11060 LINE (72,Y)-(72+BAR,Y)
11070 BAR = (DATAVAL(X)-MINVAL)/SCALEFACTOR
11080 NEXT Y
11090 NEXT X
11100 RETURN
11110 '
11120 '**  DRAWS BARS FOR 5 ELEMENTS
11130 '
11140 SCALEFACTOR = (MAXVAL - MINVAL) / 564
11150 FOR X = 1 TO BAR
11160 LOCATE 5+X*3,3 : PRINT USING "\      \";DATALABEL$(X);
11170 BAR = (DATAVAL(X)-MINVAL)/SCALEFACTOR
11180 IF BAR < Ø THEN BAR = Ø
11190 FOR Y = (32 + X*24) TO (38 + X*24)
11200 LINE (72,Y)-(72+BAR,Y)
11210 NEXT Y
11220 NEXT X
11230 RETURN
11240 '
11250 '**  DRAWS BARS FOR 6 THRU 7 ELEMENTS
11260 '
11270 SCALEFACTOR = (MAXVAL - MINVAL) / 564
11280 FOR X = 1 TO BAR
11290 LOCATE X*3,3 : PRINT USING "\      \";DATALABEL$(X);
11300 BAR = (DATAVAL(X)-MINVAL)/SCALEFACTOR
11310 IF BAR < Ø THEN BAR = Ø
11320 FOR Y = (-8 + X*24) TO (-2 + X*24)
11330 LINE (72,Y)-(72+BAR,Y)
11340 NEXT Y
11350 NEXT X
11360 RETURN
```

```
11370 '
11380 '**   DRAWS BARS FOR 8 THRU 10 ELEMENTS
11390 '
11400 SCALEFACTOR = (MAXVAL - MINVAL) / 564
11410 FOR X = 1 TO BAR
11420 LOCATE 2+X*2,3 : PRINT USING "\      \";DATALABEL$(X);
11430 BAR = (DATAVAL(X)-MINVAL)/SCALEFACTOR
11440 IF BAR < 0 THEN BAR = 0
11450 FOR Y = (8 + X*16) TO (14 + X*16)
11460 LINE (72,Y)-(72+BAR,Y)
11470 NEXT Y
11480 NEXT X
11490 RETURN
11500 '
11510 '**   DRAWS BARS FOR 11 THRU 20 ELEMENTS
11520 '
11530 SCALEFACTOR = (MAXVAL - MINVAL) / 564
11540 FOR X = 1 TO BAR : W = 20 - DATAPOINTS
11550 LOCATE 2+X+W,3 : PRINT USING "\      \";DATALABEL$(X);
11560 BAR = (DATAVAL(X)-MINVAL)/SCALEFACTOR
11570 IF BAR < 0 THEN BAR = 0
11580 FOR Y = (8 + X*8 + W*8) TO (14 + X*8 + W*8)
11590 LINE (72,Y)-(72+BAR,Y)
11600 NEXT Y
11610 NEXT X
11620 RETURN
12000 '
12010 '****************************************************************
12020 '**    This Section Draws A Circle Graph                      **
12030 '****************************************************************
12040 '
12050 KEY OFF : SCREEN 2 : CLS : GRAPHTYPE = 4
12060 '
12070 '** Draw A Circle
12080 FOR X = -100 TO 100
12090 Y = (10000 - X*X)^.5 * .5
12100 PSET (319+X,100+Y)
12110 PSET (319+X,100-Y)
12120 NEXT X
12130 FOR Y = -37 TO 37
12140 X = (2500 - Y*Y)^.5 * 2
12150 PSET (319+X,100+Y)
12160 PSET (319-X,100+Y)
12170 NEXT
12180 '
12190 '** Find The Sum Of The Input Datapoints
12200 SUM = 0
```

```
12210 LASTPOINT = DATAPOINTS : IF LASTPOINT > 20 THEN LASTPOINT = 20
12220 FOR X = 1 TO LASTPOINT
12230 SUM = SUM + DATAVAL(X)
12240 NEXT X
12250 '
12260 '** Define A Couple Of Values
12270 PERCENT = 3.14159 * 2
12280 SCALEVALUE = PERCENT/SUM
12290 '
12300 '.
12310 '** Draw The Pie Lines
12320 LINEVALUE = 0 : LINE (319,100)-(419,100)
12330 FOR Z = 1 TO DATAPOINTS
12340 LINEVALUE = LINEVALUE + DATAVAL(Z)
12350 X = COS (LINEVALUE * SCALEVALUE) * 100
12360 Y = SIN (LINEVALUE * SCALEVALUE) * 50
12370 LINE (319,100)-(319+X,100-Y)
12380 NEXT Z
12390 '
12400 '** Draw The Marker Lines And Labels
12410 LINEVALUE = 0
12420 FOR Z = 1 TO DATAPOINTS
12430 LINEVALUE = LINEVALUE + DATAVAL(Z)/2
12440 X = COS (LINEVALUE * SCALEVALUE) * 100
12450 Y = SIN (LINEVALUE * SCALEVALUE) * 50
12460 X2 = COS (LINEVALUE * SCALEVALUE) * 110
12470 Y2 = SIN (LINEVALUE * SCALEVALUE) * 55
12480 X1 = COS (LINEVALUE * SCALEVALUE) * 160
12490 Y1 = SIN (LINEVALUE * SCALEVALUE) * 80
12500 LINE (319+X2,100-Y2)-(319+X1,100-Y1)
12510 IF X1 >= 0 THEN 12520 ELSE 12540
12520 LINE (319+X1,100-Y1)-(519,100-Y1)
12530 LOCATE (104-Y1)/8,68 : PRINT USING "\     \";DATALABEL$(Z);:
      PRINT USING "###.#";DATAVAL(Z)/SUM*100;: PRINT "%"; : GOTO 12560
12540 LINE (319+X1,100-Y1)-(119,100-Y1)
12550 LOCATE (104-Y1)/8,2  : PRINT USING "\     \";DATALABEL$(Z);:
      PRINT USING "###.#";DATAVAL(Z)/SUM*100;: PRINT "%"; : GOTO 12560
12560 '
12570 LINEVALUE = LINEVALUE + DATAVAL(Z)/2
12580 NEXT Z
12590 LOCATE 1,20+(40-LEN(ATITLE1))/2 : PRINT ATITLE1;
12600 LOCATE 2,20+(40-LEN(ATITLE2))/2 : PRINT ATITLE2;
12610 LOCATE 25,1 :INPUT A$
12620 RETURN
15000 '
15010 '******************************************************************
15020 '**    This Section Has Common Parts For Different Graph Types    **
```

```
15030 '***************************************************************************
15040 '
15050 LINE (63,0)-(63,185) : LINE (48,175)-(639,175)
15060 LOCATE 1,25+(40-LEN(ATITLE1))/2 : PRINT ATITLE1;
15070 LOCATE 2,25+(40-LEN(ATITLE2))/2 : PRINT ATITLE2;
15080 LOCATE 25,25+(40-LEN(ATITLE3))/2 : PRINT ATITLE3;
15090 '
15100 '** FOR THE VERTICAL AXIS, CENTER THE LABEL WITHIN 18 CHAR OF BLANKS
15110 A$ = "" : L = LEN(ATITLE4) : L1 = (18-L)/2
15120 FOR X = 1 TO L1 : A$ = A$ + " " : NEXT X
15130 A$ = A$ + ATITLE4
15140 FOR X = LEN(A$) TO 18 : A$ = A$ + " " : NEXT X
15150 '
15160 '** NOW PRINT THE LABEL ON THE LEFT OF THE SCREEN
15170 FOR X = 3 TO 20
15180 LOCATE X,1 : PRINT MID$(A$,X-2,1);
15190 NEXT X
15200 '
15210 '** CALCULATE OUT HOW TO PRINT THE VERTICAL SCALE AND PRINT IT
15220 '**
15230 '** IF MAXVAL >= 10000 THEN PRINT AS XXXXX
15240 '** IF 1000 >= MAXVAL > 10000 THEN PRINT AS XXXX
15250 '** IF  100 >= MAXVAL >  1000 THEN PRINT AS  XXX.X
15260 '** IF   10 >= MAXVAL >   100 THEN PRINT AS   XX.XX
15270 '** IF    1 >= MAXVAL >    10 THEN PRINT AS    X.XXX
15280 '** IF    0 >= MAXVAL >     1 THEN PRINT AS    0.XXX
15290 '**
15300 MAX = 2 + LOG(MAXVAL)/LOG(10) ' LOG BASE 10 = LN(X)/LN(10)
15310 IF MAX < 1 THEN MAX = 1
15320 IF MAX > 6 THEN MAX = 6
15330 ON MAX GOTO 15340,15340,15410,15480,15550,15550
15340 '
15350 '** VALUES FROM 0.001 TO 9.999
15360 LOCATE  3,3 : PRINT USING "#.###";MAXVAL;
15370 LOCATE  8,3 : PRINT USING "#.###";(MAXVAL - (MAXVAL - MINVAL) * .25);
15380 LOCATE 13,3 : PRINT USING "#.###";(MAXVAL - (MAXVAL - MINVAL) * .5);
15390 LOCATE 18,3 : PRINT USING "#.###";(MAXVAL - (MAXVAL - MINVAL) * .75);
15400 LOCATE 23,3 : PRINT USING "#.###";MINVAL; : GOTO 15620
15410 '
15420 '** VALUES FROM 10.00 TO 99.99
15430 LOCATE  3,3 : PRINT USING "##.##";MAXVAL;
15440 LOCATE  8,3 : PRINT USING "##.##";(MAXVAL - (MAXVAL - MINVAL) * .25);
15450 LOCATE 13,3 : PRINT USING "##.##";(MAXVAL - (MAXVAL - MINVAL) * .5);
15460 LOCATE 18,3 : PRINT USING "##.##";(MAXVAL - (MAXVAL - MINVAL) * .75);
15470 LOCATE 23,3 : PRINT USING "##.##";MINVAL; : GOTO 15620
15480 '
15490 '** VALUES FROM 100.0 TO 999.9
```

```
15500 LOCATE  3,3 : PRINT USING "###.#";MAXVAL;
15510 LOCATE  8,3 : PRINT USING "###.#";(MAXVAL - (MAXVAL - MINVAL) * .25);
15520 LOCATE 13,3 : PRINT USING "###.#";(MAXVAL - (MAXVAL - MINVAL) * .5);
15530 LOCATE 18,3 : PRINT USING "###.#";(MAXVAL - (MAXVAL - MINVAL) * .75);
15540 LOCATE 23,3 : PRINT USING "###.#";MINVAL; : GOTO 15620
15550 '
15560 '** VALUES FROM 1000 TO 99999
15570 LOCATE  3,3 : PRINT USING "#####";MAXVAL;
15580 LOCATE  8,3 : PRINT USING "#####";(MAXVAL - (MAXVAL - MINVAL) * .25);
15590 LOCATE 13,3 : PRINT USING "#####";(MAXVAL - (MAXVAL - MINVAL) * .5);
15600 LOCATE 18,3 : PRINT USING "#####";(MAXVAL - (MAXVAL - MINVAL) * .75);
15610 LOCATE 23,3 : PRINT USING "#####";MINVAL; : GOTO 15620
15620 '
15630 '** PRINT DASHES ON VERTICAL AXIS
15640 '
15650 LINE (56,15)-(63,15)
15660 LINE (56,55)-(63,55)
15670 LINE (56,95)-(63,95)
15680 LINE (56,135)-(63,135)
15690 '
15700 RETURN
30000 '
30010 '**********************************************************************
30020 '**    Data-In Subroutine                                           **
30030 '**********************************************************************
30040 'ROW = 20 : COLUMN = 20 : LENGTH = 20   **   USE THIS AS AN EXAMPLE  **
30050 'GOSUB 30080                            **   ON HOW TO ACCESS THIS   **
30060 'PRINT B$                              **   SUBROUTINE              **
30070 '**********************************************************************
30080 B$ = ""
30090 FOR X = 1 TO LENGTH
30100 B$ = B$ + "-"
30110 NEXT X
30120 LOCATE ROW,COLUMN
30130 PRINT B$;
30140 '
30150 POINTER = 1 : A$ = " "
30160 WHILE (ASC(A$) <> 13)
30170 A$ = INPUT$(1)
30180 IF (POINTER > LENGTH) AND (ASC(A$) = 13) THEN 30300
30190 IF (POINTER > LENGTH) AND (ASC(A$) = 8) THEN 30250
30200 IF (POINTER > LENGTH) THEN 30300
30210 IF (ASC(A$) >= 32) THEN MID$(B$,POINTER,1) = A$ : POINTER =
      POINTER + 1 : GOTO 30280
30220 IF (POINTER = 1) AND (ASC(A$) = 8) GOTO 30280
30230 IF (ASC(A$) <> 8) THEN 30270
```

```
30240     MID$(B$,POINTER,1) = "-"
30250     MID$(B$,POINTER-1,1) = "-"
30260     POINTER = POINTER -1
30270 IF (ASC(A$) = 13) THEN B$ = MID$(B$,1,POINTER-1) : POINTER = LENGTH + 1
30280 LOCATE ROW,COLUMN
30290 PRINT B$;
30300 WEND
30310 RETURN
```

MAIL

The *Mail* program helps you create and manipulate a file of mailing labels. Functions are provided for entering, deleting, editing, sorting, locating, and printing the labels in the file. The labels are stored as 99 character records in an expandable random access file named **MAILDATA**.

The random file commands in IBM Personal Computer BASIC are powerful. The record size can be chosen at will, and the fields of a record can be defined more than once. Take a look at program lines 100 and 110. The record fields are first defined as six end to end string variables, then as one 99 character field. Some manipulations of the data are accomplished much more efficiently by treating the entire record as a single string. For example, swapping records during sorting is easier when the entire record is swapped. At other times, such as during data entry, the smaller data fields are more useful. This ability to overlay data field definitions is considered to be one of the features of COBOL, PL/1, and other languages.

The function keys are defined for efficient menu selection. See Fig. 8-6. During the execution of a selected menu option, the special function keys are temporarily disabled. Two subroutines near the end of the program are used to activate and deactivate the function keys. These routines prevent simultaneous selection of two menu functions.

Function key FB selects the "print mailing labels" function. Several questions are asked before the actual printing begins. These questions provide the flexibility needed for a variety of possible printer and mailing label configurations. For example, peel-off labels come on printer paper one, two, or four across. Or perhaps you desire to print the labels as close together as possible on regular printer paper.

To begin building your mailing-label data base, select function key F3. You'll be prompted to enter the data for each of the six data fields for the new mailing label record. Don't panic if you make a mistake, just go ahead and finish the rest of the fields and return later to edit your mistake by using function key F4. During the edit function, you can replace the data in any or all of the fields.

When your file gets larger you'll find increasing use for the "find" function of key F6. For example, if you want to locate a label and all you can remember for sure is that the person lives in Seattle, you can search for any occurrence of **SEATTLE**. You can continue the search for further occurrences in case there are several addresses with the word **SEATTLE** in them. Just follow the directions after you press special function key F6.

The sort function shuffles the diskette data into alphabetical order and may take awhile if you have a large number of file entries. The data may be sorted by any one of the six data fields as shown in Fig. 8-7. Press F7 to activate the sort function.

Special function key F9 displays a table of two letter abbreviations of states as shown in Fig. 8-8. This table is printed to page number two of the four available pages in text mode. The first time you press F9 it will take a couple of seconds to print the table on the screen. Afterwards the table will appear instantly as the program simply switches the display pages.

The "comment/code" field is displayed but not printed. This 11 character field can be used for telephone numbers, dates, or other codes that can help you sort your file as desired.

```
          * * *    M A I L    * * *

========================================================

         SANTA CLAUS
         123 CANDY CANE LANE
         NORTH POLE AK 98765

         TOY MARKET


========================================================

     F1.   Get the next address in the file
     F2.   Get the previous address in the file
     F3.   Enter a new address to the file
     F4.   Edit the displayed address
     F5.   Delete the displayed address from the file
     F6.   Find a file entry
     F7.   Sort the file
     F8.   Print mailing labels
     F9.   List state abbreviations
     F10.  Quit
```

Fig. 8-6. Options available in the *Mail* program.

```
     A.   Name
     B.   Street
     C.   Town
     D.   State
     E.   Zip code
     F.   Comment/code


     Z.   Don't sort ... go back to main menu


     Select the field for the sort ...
```

Fig. 8-7. Sort categories available in the *Mail* program.

```
10 ' *******************
20 ' ***    MAIL    ***
30 ' *******************
40 '
50 CLEAR
60 SCREEN 0,0,0,0
70 WIDTH 80
80 KEY OFF
90 OPEN "MAILDATA" AS #1
100 FIELD #1,30 AS N$,30 AS A$,20 AS T$,2 AS S$,5 AS Z$,11 AS C$
```

```
110 FIELD #1,99 AS X$
120 ZERO$ = STRING$(99,0)
130 BLANK$ = SPACE$(99)
140 PTR.LAST = PTR.LAST + 1
150 GET #1,PTR.LAST
160 IF X$ <> ZERO$ THEN 140
170 PTR.LAST = PTR.LAST - 1
180 ON KEY(1) GOSUB 580
190 ON KEY(2) GOSUB 650
200 ON KEY(3) GOSUB 710
210 ON KEY(4) GOSUB 790
220 ON KEY(5) GOSUB 1100
230 ON KEY(6) GOSUB 1240
240 ON KEY(7) GOSUB 1510
250 ON KEY(8) GOSUB 1970
260 ON KEY(9) GOSUB 2400
270 ON KEY(10) GOSUB 2710
280 GOSUB 3080
290 '
300 CLS
310 LOCATE 1,27
320 PRINT "* * *   M A I L   * * *
330 PRINT
340 PRINT STRING$(80,"=");
350 LOCATE 11
360 PRINT STRING$(80,"=");
370 FOR I = 1 TO 10
380 READ MENU$
390 LOCATE 12+I,17
400 PRINT MENU$
410 NEXT I
420 DATA F1.   Get the next address in the file
430 DATA F2.   Get the previous address in the file
440 DATA F3.   Enter a new address to the file
450 DATA F4.   Edit the displayed address
460 DATA F5.   Delete the displayed address from the file
470 DATA F6.   Find a file entry
480 DATA F7.   Sort the file
490 DATA F8.   Print mailing labels
500 DATA F9.   List state abbreviations
510 DATA F10. Quit
520 GOSUB 580
530 '
540 WHILE NOT RAIN OR SNOW
550 KEY.BUFFER.CLEAR$ = INKEY$
560 WEND
570 '
```

```
580 '   Subroutine F1, next address
590 PTR = PTR - (PTR < PTR.LAST)
600 IF PTR = 0 THEN PTR = 1 : PTR.LAST = 1
610 GET #1,PTR
620 GOSUB 2750
630 RETURN
640 '
650 '   Subroutine F2, previous address
660 PTR = PTR + (PTR > 1)
670 GET #1,PTR
680 GOSUB 2750
690 RETURN
700 '
710 ' Subroutine F3, enter new address
720 IF X$ = BLANK$ OR X$ = ZERO$ THEN 760
730 PTR = PTR.LAST  + 1
740 PTR.LAST = PTR
750 LSET X$ = BLANK$
760 GOSUB 790
770 RETURN
780 '
790 ' Subroutine F4, edit displayed address
800 GOSUB 3020
810 SCREEN 0,0,1,0
820 CLS
830 GOSUB 2750
840 SCREEN 0,0,1,1
850 LOCATE 12
860 IF X$ = BLANK$ OR X$ = ZERO$ THEN 880
870 PRINT "Just press <enter> if a data item is not to be changed ...
880 PRINT
890 INPUT "Name           ... ";NAIM$
900 INPUT "Street         ... ";ADDRESS$
910 INPUT "Town           ... ";TOWN$
920 INPUT "State (2 letters)  ";STATE$
930 INPUT "Zip code       ... ";ZIP$
940 INPUT "Comments/codes ... ";CODE$
950 IF NAIM$ <> "" THEN LSET N$ = NAIM$
960 IF ADDRESS$ <> "" THEN LSET A$ = ADDRESS$
970 IF TOWN$ <> "" THEN LSET T$ = TOWN$
980 IF STATE$ <> "" THEN LSET S$ = STATE$
990 IF ZIP$ <> "" THEN LSET Z$ = ZIP$
1000 IF CODE$ <> "" THEN LSET C$ = CODE$
1010 CAP$ = X$
1020 GOSUB 2940
1030 LSET X$ = CAP$
1040 SCREEN 0,0,0,0
```

```
1050 GOSUB 2750
1060 PUT #1,PTR
1070 GOSUB 3080
1080 RETURN
1090 '
1100 ' Subroutine F5, delete displayed address
1110 GOSUB 3020
1120 IF PTR.LAST = PTR THEN 1150
1130 GET #1,PTR.LAST
1140 PUT #1,PTR
1150 LSET X$ = ZERO$
1160 PUT #1,PTR.LAST
1170 PTR.LAST = PTR.LAST + (PTR.LAST > 1)
1180 IF PTR > PTR.LAST THEN PTR = PTR.LAST
1190 GET #1,PTR
1200 GOSUB 2750
1210 GOSUB 3080
1220 RETURN
1230 '
1240 ' Subroutine F6, find an address
1250 GOSUB 3020
1260 SCREEN 0,0,1,1
1270 CLS
1280 LOCATE 7,7
1290 IF FIND$ = "" THEN 1330
1300 PRINT "Current search characters are ";CHR$(34);FIND$;CHR$(34);
1310 PRINT "Just press <enter> to search for next occurence ...";
1320 PRINT
1330 PRINT
1340 LINE INPUT "Enter string of characters to find in file ... ";CAP$
1350 IF CAP$ = "" THEN 1390
1360 GOSUB 2950
1370 FIND$ = CAP$
1380 IF FIND2$ <> "" THEN FIND$ = FIND2$
1390 CNT = 1
1400 PTR = PTR MOD PTR.LAST + 1
1410 CNT = CNT + 1
1420 IF CNT > PTR.LAST THEN BEEP : GOTO 1450
1430 GET #1,PTR
1440 IF INSTR(X$,FIND$) = 0 THEN 1400
1450 GET #1,PTR
1460 SCREEN 0,0,0,0
1470 GOSUB 2750
1480 GOSUB 3080
1490 RETURN
1500 '
1510 ' Subroutine F7, sort the file
```

```
1520 GOSUB 3020
1530 SCREEN 0,0,1,1
1540 CLS
1550 PRINT "A.   Name
1560 PRINT "B.   Street
1570 PRINT "C.   Town
1580 PRINT "D.   State
1590 PRINT "E.   Zip code
1600 PRINT "F.   Comment/code
1610 PRINT
1620 PRINT "Z.   Don't sort ... go back to main menu
1630 PRINT
1640 PRINT "Select the field for the sort ...";
1650 CAP$ = INKEY$
1660 IF CAP$ = "" THEN 1650
1670 GOSUB 2940
1680 IF CAP$ < "A" OR CAP$ > "F" THEN 1900
1690 LOCATE 12,17
1700 PRINT "Sorting by field ";CAP$;" ...";
1710 IF CAP$ = "A" THEN SPTR = 1 : SLEN = 30
1720 IF CAP$ = "B" THEN SPTR = 31 : SLEN = 30
1730 IF CAP$ = "C" THEN SPTR = 61 : SLEN = 20
1740 IF CAP$ = "D" THEN SPTR = 81 : SLEN = 2
1750 IF CAP$ = "E" THEN SPTR = 83 : SLEN = 5
1760 IF CAP$ = "F" THEN SPTR = 88 : SLEN = 11
1770 IZ = 0
1780 IZ = IZ + 1
1790 IS = IZ
1800 IF IS = PTR.LAST THEN 1900
1810 GET #1,IS
1820 X2$ = X$
1830 GET #1,IS + 1
1840 IF MID$(X2$,SPTR,SLEN) <= MID$(X$,SPTR,SLEN) THEN 1780
1850 PUT #1,IS
1860 LSET X$ = X2$
1870 PUT #1,IS + 1
1880 IS = IS + (IS > 1)
1890 GOTO 1810
1900 SCREEN 0,0,0,0
1910 PTR = 1
1920 GET #1,PTR
1930 GOSUB 2760
1940 GOSUB 3080
1950 RETURN
1960 '
1970 ' Subroutine F8, print mailing labels
1980 GOSUB 3020
```

```
1990 SCREEN 0,0,1,1
2000 CLS
2010 LOCATE 12,12
2020 INPUT "How many labels across ";NLA
2030 IF NLA = 1 THEN 2050
2040 INPUT "Number of characters across from label to label ";NALL
2050 INPUT "Number of lines down from label to label ";NDLL
2060 INPUT "First label number to print (if not no. 1) ";START
2070 IF START = 0 THEN START = 1
2080 INPUT "Last label number to print (if not entire file) ";FINISH
2090 IF FINISH = 0 THEN FINISH = PTR.LAST
2100 INPUT "Want to change any of these values (y/n) ";CHNG$
2110 IF CHNG$ = "y" OR CHNG$ = "Y" THEN 2000
2120 LOCATE 20
2130 PRINT "Press any key if you want to stop printing labels ...
2140 STPFLAG = 0
2150 FOR LABEL = START TO FINISH STEP NLA
2160 KY$ = INKEY$
2170 IF KY$ <> "" THEN STPFLAG = 1
2180 IF STPFLAG THEN 2350
2190 PN$ = SPACE$(80)
2200 PA$ = PN$
2210 PT$ = PN$
2220 FOR INC = 1 TO NLA
2230 IF LABEL + INC - 1 > FINISH THEN 2300
2240 GET #1,LABEL + INC - 1
2250 TC = (INC - 1) * NALL + 1
2260 MID$(PN$,TC,30) = N$
2270 MID$(PA$,TC,30) = A$
2280 MID$(PT$,TC,20) = T$
2290 MID$(PT$,TC+INSTR(T$,"  "),8) = S$ + " " + Z$
2300 NEXT INC
2310 LPRINT PN$;PA$;PT$;
2320 FOR CNT = 4 TO NDLL
2330 LPRINT
2340 NEXT CNT
2350 NEXT LABEL
2360 SCREEN 0,0,0,0
2370 GOSUB 3080
2380 RETURN
2390 '
2400 ' Subroutine F9, list state abbreviations
2410 GOSUB 3020
2420 SCREEN 0,0,2,2
2430 IF ST.ABBREV$ <> "" THEN 2650
2440 CLS
2450 FOR I = 1 TO 51
```

```
2460 LOCATE (I - 1) MOD 17 + 4, INT((I - 1) / 17) * 26 + 7
2470 READ ST.ABBREV$
2480 PRINT ST.ABBREV$;
2490 NEXT I
2500 DATA AL Alabama,AK Alaska,AZ Arizona,AR Arkansas,CA California
2510 DATA CO Colorado,CT Connecticut,DE Delaware,DC District of Columbia
2520 DATA FL Florida,GA Georgia,HI Hawaii,ID Idaho,IL Illinois,IN Indiana
2530 DATA IA Iowa,KS Kansas,KY Kentucky,LA Louisiana,ME Maine,MD Maryland
2540 DATA MA Massachusetts,MI Michigan,MN Minnesota,MS Mississippi
2550 DATA MO Missourri,MT Montana,NE Nebraska,NV Nevada,NH New Hampshire
2560 DATA NJ New Jersey,NM New Mexico,NY New York,NC North Carolina
2570 DATA ND North Dakota,OH Ohio,OK Oklahoma,OR Oregon,PA Pennsylvania
2580 DATA RI Rhode Island,SC South Carolina,SD South Dakota,TN Tennessee
2590 DATA TX Texas,UT Utah,VT Vermont,VA Virginia,WA Washington
2600 DATA WV West Virginia,WI Wisconsin,WY Wyoming
2610 LOCATE 1,25
2620 PRINT "TWO-LETTER STATE ABBREVIATIONS";
2630 LOCATE 25,27
2640 PRINT "Press space bar to continue";
2650 KY$ = INKEY$
2660 IF KY$ <> " " THEN 2650
2670 SCREEN 0,0,0,0
2680 GOSUB 3080
2690 RETURN
2700 '
2710 ' Subroutine F10, quit
2720 CLS
2730 END
2740 '
2750 ' Subroutine, put current address on display
2760 LOCATE 2,1
2770 PRINT PTR;"       ";
2780 LOCATE 7,35
2790 PRINT STRING$(17,32);
2800 LOCATE 5,22
2810 PRINT N$;
2820 LOCATE 6,22
2830 PRINT A$;
2840 LOCATE 7,22
2850 PRINT T$;" ";
2860 LOCATE ,POS(0) - 1
2870 IF SCREEN(CSRLIN,POS(0)) = 32 AND POS(0) > 22 THEN 2860
2880 LOCATE ,POS(0) + 2
2890 PRINT S$;" ";Z$;
2900 LOCATE 9,22
2910 PRINT C$;
2920 RETURN
```

```
2930 '
2940 ' Subroutine, capitalize CAP$
2950 FOR CHAR = 1 TO LEN(CAP$)
2960 CHAR$ = MID$(CAP$,CHAR,1)
2970 IF CHAR$ < "a" OR CHAR$ > "z" THEN 2990
2980 MID$(CAP$,CHAR,1) = CHR$(ASC(CHAR$) - 32)
2990 NEXT CHAR
3000 RETURN
3010 '
3020 ' Subroutine, deactivate special function keys
3030 FOR KEYPTR = 1 TO 10
3040 KEY (KEYPTR) OFF
3050 NEXT KEYPTR
3060 RETURN
3070 '
3080 ' Subroutine, activate special function keys
3090 FOR KEYPTR = 1 TO 10
3100 KEY (KEYPTR) ON
3110 NEXT KEYPTR
3120 RETURN
```

```
                    TWO-LETTER STATE ABBREVIATIONS


AL Alabama              KY Kentucky           ND North Dakota
AK Alaska               LA Louisiana          OH Ohio
AZ Arizona              ME Maine              OK Oklahoma
AR Arkansas             MD Maryland           OR Oregon
CA California           MA Massachusetts      PA Pennsylvania
CO Colorado             MI Michigan           RI Rhode Island
CT Connecticut          MN Minnesota          SC South Carolina
DE Delaware             MS Mississippi        SD South Dakota
DC District of Columbia MO Missourri          TN Tennessee
FL Florida              MT Montana            TX Texas
GA Georgia              NE Nebraska           UT Utah
HI Hawaii               NV Nevada             VT Vermont
ID Idaho                NH New Hampshire      VA Virginia
IL Illinois             NJ New Jersey         WA Washington
IN Indiana              NM New Mexico         WV West Virginia
IA Iowa                 NY New York           WI Wisconsin
KS Kansas               NC North Carolina     WY Wyoming




              Press space bar to continue
```

Fig. 8-8. Display of state abbreviations from the *Mail* program.

```
=========1=========2=========3=========4=========5=========6=========7==========
TEXT

        There are several powerful text editors available for
your IBM Personal Computer.  Most of these programs feature
advanced functions that will allow you to do just about any
type of text manipulation you desire.  However, many of these
programs require considerable time and effort to learn.
        This program was designed with a different idea in mind.
The text is edited with the same editing functions that you
use to edit BASIC program listings.  The various key operations
were simulated to match what you already know.  The delete,
----------1----------2----------3----------4----------5----------6----------7----------
    Alt-S Save text    Alt-I Insert line(s)    Alt-T Tab set    Alt-P Print text
    Alt-L Load text    Alt-D Delete line(s)    Alt-C Clr tab    Alt-M Mark line
```

Fig. 8-9. Display showing how text is entered into the *Text* program.

TEXT

There are several powerful text editors available for your IBM Personal Computer. Most of these programs feature advanced functions that will allow you to do just about any type of text manipulation you desire. However, many of these programs require considerable time and effort to learn.

This program was designed with a different idea in mind. The text is edited with the same editing functions that you use to edit BASIC program listings. The various key operations were simulated to match what you already know. The delete, insert, cursor control, and other keys operate in the same manner as they do when you are editing a program listing.

Several "alternate-key" functions have been added. All of these functions are listed at the bottom of the screen for reference as shown in Fig. 8-9. These functions allow you to set or clear tabs, insert or delete lines, save or load a page of text to or from a diskette file, print the current page of text, and mark lines for the insert and delete functions.

You work on one page of text at a time. This page is composed of sixty lines of 80 characters each and is displayed 20 lines at a time. As you type past line 20 (or 40), the next group of 20 lines will appear on the screen. Or, you may jump up and down through the three groups of 20 lines by using the "PgUp" and PgDn" keys.

Lines are edited by moving the cursor around on the screen and making changes as you wish. The cursor is limited to the part of the screen containing the 20 lines of text.

You may set up to 80 tabs. Move the cursor to where you want to set a tab; then press "Alt-T" (press and hold the "Alt" key; then press the "t" key). To clear a tab, press "Alt-C". The cursor will move to the next tabbed column whenever a forward or backward tab is pressed.

To save your page of text on the diskette, press "Alt-S". The screen will temporarily clear, a list of all diskette files will be displayed, and you'll be asked for a name for the text file. If you don't specify an extension (the decimal point and the three letters following it), a default extension of ".TXT" will be automatically tacked on. To load in a previously saved page of text, press "Alt-L". The operation is similar to the "save" described above, but the indicated file will be copied from the diskette file into the computer's memory.

When you press "Alt-M", the line that the cursor is on will be marked (it will change to inverse video, or black on white rather than white on black). Marked lines are moved around or deleted when you use the insert or delete functions. To "unmark" a line, press "Alt-M" again for that line.

The insert function is activated by pressing "Alt-I". If no lines have been marked, a single blank line will be inserted where the cursor is, and all remaining lines will be shifted down a notch. If one or more lines have been marked, they will all be grouped together and inserted starting at the line where the cursor is. The lines are moved (not copied). They disappear from where they were and reappear at the insert point. You can thus shuffle sentences and paragraphs around on the page. Remember that the blank line is inserted only if no lines were marked.

The delete function works in a similar way. Press "Alt-D" with no lines marked, and the line that the cursor is sitting on will be erased. If one or more lines have been marked, only the marked lines will disappear. In both cases, the remaining lines will move up to fill in the gaps.

To send your current page of text to the printer, press 'Alt-P". The 60 lines of text will be printed, followed by a form feed. The 60 lines form one page of text on your IBM Personal Computer printer.

Some of the functions operate a little slowly as text editors go. This is because this program is written entirely in BASIC. For example, press the ctrl-cursor key to jump to the next word in the line. The operation is the same as in other text editors, just not quite as fast. However, most of the functions work fast enough so that you won't notice any difference in operating speed.

This program works well for letter writing and other simple text editing tasks. It's simple, quick, and (most importantly) easy to learn and use. Much of the text in this book was originally produced using this program.

```
10 ' *********************************************************
20 ' **                        TEXT                        **
30 ' **              SINGLE-PAGE TEXT EDITOR                **
40 ' **      VERS 1.1                       OCT, 1982       **
50 ' *********************************************************
60 '
70 CLEAR
80 SCREEN Ø
90 WIDTH 80
100 KEY OFF
110 DEFINT A-Z
120 OPTION BASE 1
130 DEF FNR = 20 * PAGE + ROW - 1
140 DEF FNC(X$)= X$<"Ø" OR (X$>"9" AND X$<"A") OR (X$>"Z" AND X$<"a")
    OR X$>"z"
150 DIM ARRAY$(60),TEMP$(60),MARK(60)
160 TABS$ = SPACE$(80)
170 MID$(TABS$,8,1)  = "T"              ' Default tabs set
180 MID$(TABS$,50,1) = "T"              ' at columns 8 and 50
190 TOP = Ø
```

```
200 MID = 1
210 BOT = 2
220 LST = 3
230 EDGE$ = STRING$(80,205)
240 FOR PLACE = 1 TO 7
250 MID$(EDGE$,10 * PLACE,1) = CHR$(48 + PLACE)
260 NEXT PLACE
270 MIDDLE$ = STRING$(80,176)
280 '
290 FOR PAGE = TOP TO BOT                          ' Initialize the three screens
300 SCREEN 0,0,PAGE,0
310 CLS
320 LOCATE 1,1,1,7,7
330 IF PAGE = TOP THEN PRINT EDGE$ ELSE PRINT MIDDLE$
340 LOCATE 22,1,1,7,7
350 IF PAGE = BOT THEN PRINT EDGE$ ELSE PRINT MIDDLE$
360 LOCATE 24,3
370 PRINT "Alt-S Save text     Alt-I Insert line(s)      ";
380 PRINT "Alt-T Tab set    Alt-P Print text";
390 LOCATE 25,3
400 PRINT "Alt-L Load text     Alt-D Delete line(s)      ";
410 PRINT "Alt-C Clr tab     Alt-M Mark line";
420 NEXT PAGE
430 '
440 FOR I = 1 TO 60
450 ARRAY$(I) = SPACE$(80)
460 NEXT I
470 PAGE = TOP
480 SCREEN 0,0,PAGE,PAGE
490 ROW = 2
500 COL = 1
510 '
520 WHILE PFLAG                                    ' Most functions return to here
530 LOCATE ROW,1
540 PRINT ARRAY$(FNR);
550 COL = INSTR(ARRAY$(FNR)," ")
560 PFLAG = 0
570 WEND
580 IF INSERT = 0 THEN LOCATE ROW,COL + (COL > 80),1,7,7
590 IF INSERT = 1 THEN LOCATE ROW,COL + (COL > 80),1,4,6
600 '
610 K$ = INKEY$                                    ' Scan keyboard over and over
620 IF K$ = "" THEN 610
630 K = ASC(K$)
640 IF K = 0 THEN 1250                             ' Probably an Alt-key
650 '
660 IF K <> 3 THEN 700                             ' Ctrl-Break
```

300

```
670 CLS
680 END
690 '
700 IF K <> 8 THEN 750                          ' Back arrow
710 IF COL = 1 THEN 520
720 COL = COL - 1
730 GOTO 2980
740 '
750 IF K <> 9 THEN 830                          ' Tab
760 INSERT = 0
770 COL = COL - (COL < 80)
780 LOCATE ROW,COL,1,7,7
790 IF COL = 80 THEN 520
800 IF MID$(TABS$,COL,1) = " " THEN 770
810 GOTO 520
820 '
830 IF K <> 13 THEN 900                         ' Enter
840 INSERT = 0
850 COL = 1
860 ROW = ROW + 1
870 IF ROW > 21 THEN K$ = CHR$(0)+CHR$(81) : GOTO 1250
880 GOTO 520
890 '
900 IF K <> 27 THEN 980                         ' Esc
910 INSERT = 0
920 ARRAY$(FNR) = SPACE$(80)
930 COL = 1
940 LOCATE ROW,COL,1,7,7
950 PRINT SPACE$(80);
960 GOTO 520
970 '
980 IF K < 32 OR K > 126 THEN 3780
990 '
1000 IF INSERT = 0 THEN 1050                    ' Character
1010 ARRAY$(FNR) = LEFT$(ARRAY$(FNR),COL-1)+K$+MID$(ARRAY$(FNR),COL,80-COL)
1020 LOCATE ROW,1,0
1030 PRINT ARRAY$(FNR);
1040 GOTO 1200
1050 IF COL < 81 THEN 1180
1060 IF FNR = 60 THEN 1220
1070 SPP = 1
1080 ARRAY$(FNR) = LEFT$(ARRAY$(FNR),80)
1090 WHILE INSTR(SPP,ARRAY$(FNR)," ")
1100 SPP = INSTR(SPP,ARRAY$(FNR)," ") + 1
1110 WEND
1120 ARRAY$(FNR+1)= MID$(ARRAY$(FNR),SPP) + K$ +" "+ LEFT$(ARRAY$(FNR+1),
     SPP-3)
1130 ARRAY$(FNR) = LEFT$(ARRAY$(FNR),SPP-1) + SPACE$(81-SPP)
```

```
1140 LOCATE ROW,1,0
1150 PRINT ARRAY$(FNR);
1160 PFLAG = 1
1170 GOTO 860
1180 PRINT K$;
1190 MID$(ARRAY$(FNR),COL,1) = K$
1200 COL = COL + 1
1210 IF COL = 72 THEN SOUND 999,1
1220 IF COL > 80 THEN SOUND 777,3
1230 GOTO 520
1240 '
1250 K = ASC(RIGHT$(K$,1))                      ' Double byte INKEY$ codes
1260 IF K <> 15 THEN 1340                       ' Back tab
1270 INSERT = 0
1280 COL = COL + (COL > 1)
1290 LOCATE ROW,COL,1,7,7
1300 IF COL = 1 THEN 520
1310 IF MID$(TABS$,COL,1) = " " THEN 1280
1320 GOTO 520
1330 '
1340 IF K <> 20 THEN 1390                       ' Alt-T
1350 INSERT = 0
1360 MID$(TABS$,COL,1) = "T"
1370 GOTO 520
1380 '
1390 IF K <> 23 THEN 1830                       ' Alt-I
1400 INSERT = 0
1410 SCREEN 0,0,LST,LST
1420 CLS
1430 LOCATE 12,22
1440 BFLAG = 1
1450 FOR I = 1 TO 60
1460 IF MARK(I) THEN BFLAG = 0
1470 NEXT I
1480 IF BFLAG THEN 1740
1490 PRINT "Inserting marked lines ..."
1500 FUNROW = FNR
1510 FOR I = 1 TO 60
1520 TEMP$(I) = ARRAY$(I)
1530 NEXT I
1540 I = 0
1550 J = 0
1560 WHILE I < 60
1570 I = I + 1
1580 IF MARK(I) THEN FUNROW = FUNROW + (FUNROW > 1)
1590 IF I <> FUNROW THEN 1650
1600 FOR L = 1 TO 60
```

```
1610 IF MARK(L) = Ø THEN 1640
1620 ARRAY$(I) = TEMP$(L)
1630 I = I + 1
1640 NEXT L
1650 J = J + 1
1660 IF J > 60 THEN 1690
1670 IF MARK(J) THEN 1650
1680 ARRAY$(I) = TEMP$(J)
1690 WEND
1700 FOR I = 1 TO 60
1710 MARK(I) = Ø
1720 NEXT I
1730 GOTO 1790
1740 PRINT "Inserting a blank line ..."
1750 FOR I = 59 TO FNR STEP -1
1760 ARRAY$(I+1) = ARRAY$(I)
1770 NEXT I
1780 ARRAY$(FNR) = SPACE$(80)
1790 GOSUB 3810
1800 SCREEN Ø,Ø,PAGE,PAGE
1810 GOTO 520
1820 '
1830 IF K <> 25 THEN 1930                          ' Alt-P
1840 INSERT = Ø
1850 FOR I = 1 TO 60
1860 LPRINT SPACE$(7);LEFT$(ARRAY$(I),73);
1870 NEXT I
1880 LPRINT CHR$(12);
1890 SCREEN Ø,Ø,PAGE,PAGE
1900 POKE 106,0
1910 GOTO 520
1920 '
1930 IF K <> 32 THEN 2230                          ' Alt-D
1940 INSERT = Ø
1950 SCREEN Ø,Ø,LST,LST
1960 CLS
1970 LOCATE 12,22
1980 BFLAG = Ø
1990 FOR I = 1 TO 60
2000 IF MARK(I) THEN BFLAG = 1
2010 NEXT I
2020 IF BFLAG THEN 2060
2030 MARK(FNR) = 1
2040 PRINT "Deleting line at cursor ..."
2050 GOTO 2070
2060 PRINT "Deleting marked lines ..."
2070 FOR I = 1 TO 60
```

```
2080 WHILE MARK(I)
2090 FOR J = I TO 60
2100 IF J = 60 THEN 2140
2110 ARRAY$(J) = ARRAY$(J+1)
2120 MARK(J) = MARK(J+1)
2130 GOTO 2160
2140 ARRAY$(J) = SPACE$(80)
2150 MARK(J) = 0
2160 NEXT J
2170 WEND
2180 NEXT I
2190 GOSUB 3810
2200 SCREEN 0,0,PAGE,PAGE
2210 GOTO 520
2220 '
2230 IF K <> 46 THEN 2280                    ' Alt-C
2240 INSERT = 0
2250 MID$(TABS$,COL,1) = " "
2260 GOTO 520
2270 '
2280 IF K <> 50 THEN 2400                    ' Alt-M
2290 INSERT = 0
2300 RW = CSRLIN
2310 IF SCREEN(RW,1,1) MOD 17 = 7 THEN COLOR 0,7
2320 FOR CL = 1 TO 80
2330 LOCATE RW,CL
2340 PRINT CHR$(SCREEN(RW,CL));
2350 NEXT CL
2360 MARK(FNR) = (MARK(FNR) = 0)
2370 COLOR 7,0
2380 GOTO 520
2390 '
2400 IF K <> 71 THEN 2440                    ' Home
2410 INSERT = 0
2420 GOTO 490
2430 '
2440 IF K <> 72 THEN 2500                    ' cursor up
2450 INSERT = 0
2460 ROW = ROW - 1
2470 IF ROW < 2 THEN ROW = 2
2480 GOTO 520
2490 '
2500 IF K <> 73 THEN 2580                    ' PgUp
2510 INSERT = 0
2520 IF PAGE = TOP THEN SOUND 300,2
2530 IF PAGE = MID THEN PAGE = TOP
2540 IF PAGE = BOT THEN PAGE = MID
```

```
2550 SCREEN 0,0,PAGE,PAGE
2560 GOTO 490
2570 '
2580 IF K <> 75 THEN 2640                    ' Cursor left
2590 INSERT = 0
2600 COL = COL - 1
2610 IF COL < 1 THEN COL = 1
2620 GOTO 520
2630 '
2640 IF K <> 77 THEN 2700                    ' Cursor right
2650 INSERT = 0
2660 COL = COL + 1
2670 IF COL > 80 THEN COL = 80
2680 GOTO 520
2690 '
2700 IF K <> 79 THEN 2780                    ' End
2710 INSERT = 0
2720 COL = 80
2730 IF SCREEN(ROW,COL) <> 32 THEN 2660
2740 COL = COL - 1
2750 IF COL > 1 THEN 2730
2760 GOTO 520
2770 '
2780 IF K <> 80 THEN 2840                    ' Cursor down
2790 INSERT = 0
2800 ROW = ROW + 1
2810 IF ROW > 21 THEN ROW = 21
2820 GOTO 520
2830 '
2840 IF K <> 81 THEN 2920                    ' PgDn
2850 INSERT = 0
2860 IF PAGE = BOT THEN SOUND 300,2
2870 IF PAGE = MID THEN PAGE = BOT
2880 IF PAGE = TOP THEN PAGE = MID
2890 SCREEN 0,0,PAGE,PAGE
2900 GOTO 490
2910 '
2920 IF K <> 82 THEN 2960                    ' Ins
2930 INSERT = 1
2940 GOTO 520
2950 '
2960 IF K <> 83 THEN 3030                    ' Del
2970 INSERT = 0
2980 ARRAY$(FNR) = LEFT$(ARRAY$(FNR),COL-1)+MID$(ARRAY$(FNR),COL+1)+" "
2990 LOCATE ROW,1,0
3000 PRINT ARRAY$(FNR);
3010 GOTO 520
```

```
3020 '
3030 IF K <> 115 THEN 3170                   ' Ctrl-cursor left
3040 INSERT = 0
3050 TGA = 1
3060 TGB = 0
3070 LOCATE ROW,COL
3080 COL = COL + (COL > 1)
3090 IF COL = 1 THEN 3150
3100 T$ = MID$(ARRAY$(FNR),COL,1)
3110 IF FNC(T$) AND TGA = TGB THEN TGA = TGA + 1
3120 IF FNC(T$) = 0 AND TGA > TGB THEN TGB = TGB + 1
3130 IF TGA < 2 THEN 3070
3140 COL = COL + 1
3150 GOTO 520
3160 '
3170 IF K <> 116 THEN 3300                   ' Ctrl-cursor right
3180 INSERT = 0
3190 TGA = 0
3200 TGB = 0
3210 COL = COL - (COL < 80)
3220 LOCATE ROW,COL
3230 IF COL = 80 THEN 3280
3240 T$ = MID$(ARRAY$(FNR),COL,1)
3250 IF FNC(T$) = 0 AND TGA = TGB THEN TGA = TGA + 1
3260 IF FNC(T$) AND TGA > TGB THEN TGB = TGB + 1
3270 IF TGA < 2 THEN 3210
3280 GOTO 520
3290 '
3300 IF K <> 117 THEN 3360                   ' Ctrl-End
3310 INSERT = 0
3320 PRINT SPACE$(81-COL);
3330 ARRAY$(FNR) = LEFT$(ARRAY$(FNR),COL-1)+SPACE$(81-COL)
3340 GOTO 520
3350 '
3360 IF K <> 119 THEN 3400                   ' Ctrl-Home
3370 INSERT = 0
3380 GOTO 290
3390 '
3400 IF K <> 31 THEN 3560                    ' Alt-S
3410 INSERT = 0
3420 SCREEN 0,0,LST,LST
3430 CLS
3440 FILES
3450 PRINT
3460 INPUT "File name for save ";FILE$
3470 IF FILE$ = "" THEN 3530
3480 OPEN FILE$+".TXT" FOR OUTPUT AS #1
```

```
3490 FOR I = 1 TO 60
3500 PRINT #1,ARRAY$(I)
3510 NEXT I
3520 CLOSE #1
3530 SCREEN 0,0,PAGE,PAGE
3540 GOTO 520
3550 '
3560 IF K <> 38 THEN 3780                        ' Alt-L
3570 INSERT = 0
3580 SCREEN 0,0,LST,LST
3590 CLS
3600 FILES
3610 PRINT
3620 INPUT "File name for load ";FILE$
3630 IF FILE$ = "" THEN 3530
3640 ON ERROR GOTO 3910
3650 OPEN FILE$+".TXT" FOR INPUT AS #1
3660 ON ERROR GOTO 0
3670 FOR I = 1 TO 60
3680 IF NOT EOF(1) THEN LINE INPUT #1,ARRAY$(I) ELSE ARRAY$(I) = ""
3690 IF LEN(ARRAY$(I)) > 80 THEN ARRAY$(I) = LEFT$(ARRAY$(I),80)
3700 WHILE LEN(ARRAY$(I)) < 80
3710 ARRAY$(I) = ARRAY$(I) + SPACE$(80-LEN(ARRAY$(I)))
3720 WEND
3730 NEXT I
3740 CLOSE #1
3750 GOSUB 3810
3760 GOTO 470
3770 '
3780 SOUND 200,3                             ' no match found for k$
3790 GOTO 610
3800 '
3810 TLINE = 0                               ' Subroutine, string array to screen
3820 FOR APAGE = TOP TO BOT
3830 SCREEN 0,0,APAGE,APAGE
3840 FOR AROW = 2 TO 21
3850 TLINE = TLINE + 1
3860 LOCATE AROW,1,1,7,7
3870 PRINT ARRAY$(TLINE);
3880 NEXT AROW,APAGE
3890 RETURN
3900 '
3910 IF ERR <> 53 THEN 3940                    ' Error trap for bad file name
3920 PRINT "File not found, try again"
3930 RESUME 3620
3940 ON ERROR GOTO 0
```

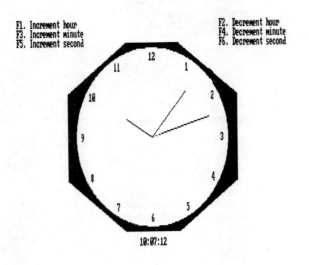

F1. Increment hour   F2. Decrement hour
F3. Increment minute   F4. Decrement minute
F5. Increment second   F6. Decrement second

10:07:12

Index

100 Ready-to-Run Programs and Subroutines for the IBM PC®

If you are intrigued with the possibilities of the programs included in *100 Ready-to-Run Programs and Subroutines for the IBM PC®* (TAB book no. 1540), you should definitely consider having the ready-to-run disk containing the software applications. This software is guaranteed free of manufacturer's defects. (If you have any problems, return the disk within 30 days and we'll send you a new one.) Not only will you save the time and effort of typing the programs, the disk eliminates the possibility of errors that can prevent the programs from functioning. Interested?

Available on disk for the IBM PC, 48K at $29.95 for each disk plus $1.00 each shipping and handling.